THE EMPIRE WITHIN

STUDIES ON THE HISTORY OF QUEBEC / ÉTUDES D'HISTOIRE DU QUÉBEC

Magda Fahrni and Jarrett Rudy
Series Editors / Directeurs de la collection

THE EMPIRE WITHIN

POSTCOLONIAL THOUGHT AND
POLITICAL ACTIVISM IN SIXTIES MONTREAL

■ ■ ■

SEAN MILLS

McGill-Queen's University Press

MONTREAL & KINGSTON • LONDON • ITHACA

© McGill-Queen's University Press 2010
ISBN 978-0-7735-3683-8 (cloth)
ISBN 978-0-7735-3695-1 (paper)

Legal deposit first quarter 2010
Bibliothèque nationale du Québec

Printed in Canada on acid-free paper that is 100% ancient forest free (100% post-consumer recycled), processed chlorine free
Reprinted 2010, 2012

This book has been published with the help of a grant from the Canadian Federation for the Humanities and Social Sciences, through the Aid to Scholarly Publications Programme, using funds provided by the Social Sciences and Humanities Research Council of Canada.

McGill-Queen's University Press acknowledges the support of the Canada Council for the Arts for our publishing program. We also acknowledge the financial support of the Government of Canada through the Book Publishing Industry Development Program (BPIDP) for our publishing activities.

Library and Archives Canada Cataloguing in Publication

Mills, Sean, 1978–
    The empire within : postcolonial thought and political activism in sixties Montreal / Sean Mills.

(Studies on the history of Quebec ; 23)
Includes bibliographical references and index.
ISBN 978-0-7735-3683-8 (bnd)
ISBN 978-0-7735-3695-1 (pbk)

    1. Montréal (Québec) – Intellectual life – 20th century. 2. Radicalism – Québec (Province) – Montréal – History – 20th century. 3. Social movements – Québec (Province) – Montréal – History – 20th century. 4. Political activists – Québec (Province) – Montréal – History – 20th century. 5. Nineteen sixties. 6. Decolonization. I. Title. II. Series: Studies on the history of Quebec 23

FC2947.394.M54   2010   971.4'2804   C2009-906544-4

For Anna

CONTENTS

ACKNOWLEDGMENTS

While I alone am responsible for whatever errors remain in this book, I cannot take sole credit for its accomplishments. This study owes its existence to the vitality of intellectual life in Montreal, a world that I first encountered when I moved to the city over a decade ago. During the years I was writing it, many friends and colleagues pushed me to ask bigger questions than I had originally thought possible. Marc-André Lavigne, Benoit Dubreuil, and Dominique Perrault-Joncas first introduced me to political debate about Quebec, and Matt Rankin, Damien-Claude Bélanger, and Louis-Raphaël Pelletier have discussed many of the ideas in this study. At an early stage, Stéphanie Poirier shared her expertise as well as her files on the Montreal Central Council of the CSN, as did Marc Comby with the FRAP. Philippe Fournier has been an indefatigable friend and colleague and has helped in more ways than I can innumerate.

I was first initiated into the Montreal History Group as an undergraduate, and I found in it a community of scholars committed to engagement and collaboration across the linguistically divided Canadian academy. The Group's members – Denyse Baillargeon, Amélie Bourbeau, Bettina Bradbury, Jean-François Constant, Magda Fahrni, Donald Fyson, Karine Hébert, Daniel Horner, Darcy Ingram, Nicolas Kenny, Maude-Emmanuelle Lambert, Liz Kirkland, Andrée Lévesque, Tamara Myers, Mary Anne Poutanen, Sonya Roy, Jarrett Rudy, Sylvie Tachereau, and Brian Young – have provided material, moral and intellectual support. Brian Young, whom I first met while I was an exchange student at McGill, has remained a mentor and friend. His confidence in my work did much to convince me to go on to graduate school, and his encouragement, advice, and careful reading of an earlier draft helped make this a better book.

These have been good years to study the 1960s, as a resurgence of interest in the period has created new debates and revitalized old questions. Marcel Martel and Cynthia Wright shared both sources and insights, as did Stuart Henderson, Stephanie Jowett, Jodi Burkett, Alexis Lachaîne, Ivan Carel, and Catherine LeGrand. Mathieu Lavigne, Susan Lord, Bryan Palmer, and Paul Jackson read earlier versions of the project and offered useful comments that helped me to rethink it. Jean-Philippe Warren, whose own work has done much to stimulate inquiry into the period, carefully read and commented on an earlier version, and the final product is better for it.

Many years ago Suzanne Morton encouraged me to put myself in unfamiliar situations and try to understand life from the perspective of others. In many ways, this book is a result of that advice, and I thank her for it, and for her help and encouragement along the way. At the Université de Montréal, Denyse Baillargeon taught me a great deal, and has continually supported my work, and Andrée Lévesque has been a model of dynamic commitment to intellectual life. My Belgian colleagues, especially Serge Jaumain, Anne Morelli, and José Gotovitch, who twice hosted me in Brussels, offered important feedback on parts of this project, and Van Gosse's comments and encouragement greatly helped as I set out to complete the book.

I could not have written this book without the support of friends and family. My sisters Al, Sue, and Jillian have set a standard of academic excellence that I have constantly attempted to attain, and my parents, Alan and Pat, have supported me from the very beginning, instilling in me the values of hard work and integrity. Sarina Kumar, even from a distance, has offered sage advice and constant friendship, as have Heather Johnson, Belinda Hewitt, Rob Dennis, Alyssa Tomkins, Gwen Rushton, James Dunlop, Rob Morency, Sayyida Jaffer, Greg Griffin, Stephanie Bolton, Claire Abraham, Adrian McKerracher, Kareen Latour, Annie Gagnon, Sara Finley, James Barrington, Andrea Dawes, Matt McKean, and Megan Webster. Peter Deitz's own efforts to build a more humane world have been an inspiration. In my beloved café Utopik (now L'Escalier), where so much of this project was initially written, I have been able to watch many of the transformations of Quebec society unfold before me, from student strikes to public debate around poverty and social marginalization. Meeting me there and elsewhere have been Nicolas Kenny, Liz Kirkland, and Dave Meren, three friends and colleagues who always helped keep things in perspective. Jarrett Rudy's enthusiasm for history – and for life in general – has continued to remind me of the excitement of writing. Jamie Swift, Bradford Lyttle, Stan Gray, Kari Levitt, Dimitri Roussopoulos, Anne Cools, Robert Comeau, Carmen Miller, Daya Varma, Fernand Foisy, and Jean-Marc Piotte shared their memories and thoughts about the 1960s. Mark Wilson sat down on many occasions with me, and dug up old documents from his student days at McGill. And long meals and conversations with Kari Levitt have clarified my thinking about the Caribbean, politics, and life in general.

This book originated in the dynamic history department at Queen's University, where Jane Errington, Robert Shenton, Sandra den Otter, Adnan Husain, and Barrington Walker offered various forms of encouragement. During my time at Queen's, I had the opportunity of working with some of the best historians anywhere. Karen Dubinsky did much to foster an environment of excitement that should be at the centre of intellectual endeavours. Ian McKay's commitment to meaningful and honest intellectual work place him in a league of his own among historians, and I am privileged to have had the chance to work with him. His friendship has meant a great deal to me.

Financial support from the Social Sciences and Humanities Research Council of Canada, the Queen's History Department, the Montreal History Group, and the Fonds québécois de la recherche sur la société et la culture, made this research possible, and librarians and archivists at the BANQ, McMaster, Concordia, and especially Claude Cantin at UQAM and Yves Lacroix at the CSN helped to track down rare documents and pursue leads. At McGill-Queen's University Press, expert advice from Jonathan Crago, Susan Glickman, and Joan McGilvray helped the manuscript achieve its present state. This book was completed as I was a postdoctoral fellow at the University of Wisconsin-Madison, where Jeremi Suri helped me learn about historical writing. Since moving to New York University, Robert J.C. Young has generously helped me find my way in the world of postcolonial studies.

I owe a particular debt to two colleagues. David Austin's own work on Caribbean politics in Montreal in the 1960s and his generosity with his knowledge and sources have helped me enormously, and Scott Rutherford has, through extended conversations over many years, helped me to sharpen my analysis and focus. Both good friends and stellar scholars, Scott and David read over the entire product, and their feedback and ideas are very much a part of it.

My greatest debt is to Anna Shea. It has been many years since we first began our parallel yet overlapping projects. Over the years, she has debated every idea and challenged my every word. Above all, her own work and belief in the possibilities of building a better future have continually inspired me. It is to her that I dedicate this book.

NOTE ON LANGUAGE

Writing in English about movements operating largely in French poses challenges. I have made the difficult decision to translate all of the French-language text within the main body of the book. When possible, I have quoted published translations of works. For consistency, I have also standardized the capitalization of titles and names.

ABBREVIATIONS

ASIQ   Action socialiste pour l'indépendance du Québec
BANQ   Bibliothèque et Archives nationales du Québec
CCSNM   Conseil central des syndicats nationaux de Montréal
CEQ   Corporation des enseignants du Québec
CSN   Confédération des syndicats nationaux
FFQ   Fédération des femmes du Québec
FLF   Front de libération des femmes
FLN   Front de libération nationale
FLP   Front de libération populaire
FLQ   Front de libération du Québec
FQF   Front du Québec français
FRAP   Front d'action politique
FRI   Front républicain pour l'indépendance
FTQ   Fédération des travailleurs du Québec
LIS   Ligue pour l'intégration scolaire
MIS   Mouvement pour l'intégration scolaire
MLP   Mouvement de libération populaire
MDN   Mouvement pour le désarmement nucléaire
MSA   Mouvement souveraineté-association
MSP   Mouvement syndical et politique
MWLM   Montreal Women's Liberation Movement
NDP   New Democratic Party

SDS	Students for a Democratic Society
SSJB	Société Saint-Jean-Baptiste
PQ	Parti Québécois
PSQ	Parti socialiste du Québec
RSA	Radical Student Alliance
RIN	Rassemblement pour l'indépendance nationale
UGEQ	Union générale des étudiants du Québec
UQAM	Université du Québec à Montréal

ARCHIVAL COLLECTIONS

ACSN	Archives, Confédération des syndicats nationaux
CUA	Concordia University Archives
CWMA	The Canadian Women's Movement Archives
MUA	McGill University Archives
UQAM	Archives, Université du Québec à Montréal
WRDA	William Ready Division of Archives and Research Collections, McMaster University Library

THE EMPIRE WITHIN

INTRODUCTION

In the aftermath of the Second World War, the age of European imperialism appeared to be coming undone. In 1947, India became independent from Britain, and in 1956 Morocco achieved formal sovereignty, as did Ghana (formerly the Gold Coast) and Malaya in 1957, and Guinea in 1958. In 1959 the Cuban revolution shifted the world's attention to Latin America, and in 1962 the Algerian War of Independence drew to a close with Algeria's sovereignty. As a result of the multi-faceted decolonization of Africa and Asia, Frederick Cooper maintains, "the aura of normality attached to empire for millennia" began to give way.[1] By the 1960s, in a context shaped by global decolonization as well as by the polarizing forces of the Cold War, Western intellectuals were forced to recognize what Kristin Ross has called "one of the great gauchiste particularities of the time." Theory itself, she argues, "was being generated not from Europe but from the third world."[2]

No North American city was as profoundly affected by Third World theory as Montreal. Beginning in the late 1950s and early 1960s, dissident writers in Montreal adapted the ideas of Frantz Fanon, Aimé Césaire, Jacques Berque, Albert Memmi, and others, to develop a movement proposing that Quebec join with the nations of the Third World in forming, in Benita Parry's words, "different social imaginaries and alternative rationalities."[3] At first glance, Montreal appears an unlikely site for a mass movement of opposition based on theories of Third World decolonization.

During the 1960s the city was not only the most populous and economically powerful in Canada, but was also a major centre of North American industrialization and capitalist expansion. Yet throughout the 1960s, the vast majority of local activists drew on anti-colonial theory to imagine Quebec as a colony and Montreal as a colonial city.

Despite the city's relative prosperity, it is perhaps not difficult to understand the appeal of the concept of decolonization. Montreal – first occupied by Aboriginals and then controlled by the French, British, and (many in the 1960s argued) American empires – has a complicated and layered history of colonization and conquest and, by the 1960s, this history had scarred the city's landscape with distinct geographies of power. Nearly two thirds of the city's population primarily spoke French, yet in the city's wealthiest neighbourhoods, the commercial establishments of the downtown core, and the halls of the most prestigious financial, cultural, and educational institutions, English prevailed. Montreal's francophone majority, along with its racial and ethnic minorities, were far removed from the centres of power, often living in the poorest parts of town. Their language and culture were devalued in the workplace and in the encounters of everyday urban life.

Many reacted to these injustices by advocating a form of nationalism that sought to redress the flagrant differences between the living standards of francophones and those of anglophones. They hoped to give francophones an equal opportunity to be managers and business executives, technicians and engineers, and to create a modern nation-state based in Quebec City. Studies of the rise of neo-nationalism in Quebec have demonstrated the structural and ideological changes that occurred in the post-war period, and they have shown the role that neo-nationalism played in transforming the nature of Quebec society and its relationship with the rest of Canada. In addition to the neo-nationalist project of modernization, however, there was also another, alternative way of imagining the possibility of overcoming the injustices of daily life.

This alternative political movement fomented in Montreal's working-class neighbourhoods and in its avant-garde cafés, and it took shape in the hallways and meeting-places of its expanding education system. It gained intellectual grounding in journals, conferences, consciousness-raising groups, and in the educational programs of radicalizing labour organizations. It was fed intellectually and politically by a movement that spanned the globe, and it imagined itself as part of this larger global movement. The alternative movement that emerged in the 1960s placed questions of language, culture, and empire alongside those of social class, advocating a broad project of decolonization. In the pages of newly-founded journals and flowing out of the city's political and artistic cafés, young poets and writers began to reinterpret the ideas of anti-colonial thinkers for the needs of their own complex society. At various points in the 1960s, major theorists such as Andre Gunder Frank, Immanuel Wallerstein, and Jacques Berque lived in Montreal. Others, including C.L.R. James, Albert Memmi, Stokely Carmichael, Gustavo Gutiérrez, Walter Rodney, Salvador Allende, and many more, spent time in the city, contributing to the feeling that the local and the global were connected spheres of activity.

■ ■ ■

If the concept of decolonization kindled dreams, it was not without its own inner contradictions, tensions, and ambiguities. Quebec's status as a colony was always contested, continually being challenged both within the province and by potential sympathizers abroad. How could the descendents of European colonizers, many asked, claim to be fighting the same battle as the liberation movements of Algeria and Cuba? By the late 1960s, many began to openly wonder how Aboriginal peoples could fit within the larger conception of Quebec decolonization. Even within francophone radical circles, while nearly everyone agreed that Quebec was thoroughly colonized, there remained many interpretations as to who formed the colonizing power.[4] Throughout the 1960s, conceptions of colonization by English Canada co-existed with those emphasizing domination by the United States. The advocates of these two different ways of understanding Quebec's colonial situation sometimes clashed with one another, their interpretations contributing to the ambiguity of the situation.

For those who had developed their ideas in the context of French settler-colonialism in North Africa, seeing White descendents of French settlers claiming to be "colonized" immediately raised questions. Albert Memmi spoke of being a "bit frightened" by the influence that his book, *The Colonizer and the Colonized*, was having on those who were not "well-defined colonized people," like certain South Americans, Japanese, Black Americans, and French Canadians. And he "looked with astonishment on all this, much as a father, with a mixture of pride and apprehension, watches his son achieve a scandalous and applauded fame."[5] Another well-known theorist who supported the struggle for autonomy and self-determination in Que-

bec, Islamic scholar Jacques Berque, wrote that Quebeckers, as the "colonized among the colonizers," were so entangled in their exceptions that
they were no longer understood by anyone.[6] Jean-Paul Sartre refused
throughout the 1960s to believe that Quebec formed a colony, but changed
his mind during the October Crisis of 1970.[7] And Aimé Césaire, Martini-
quan intellectual, activist, and poet, recalls his confusion and surprise when
he first learned that francophone Quebeckers were employing the insights
of *négritude* to understand their own identity as the "colonized." He would
go on to state, however, that even if he still considered their claim a bit of
an exaggeration, Quebec intellectuals had at least understood the concept.[8]
Because of the ambiguities, challenges, and questions that surrounded
Quebec's historical and political status, interpretations of decolonization
in Quebec were constantly in flux, never settling into a stable interpretation, continuously melting away before they could ossify.

Another problem loomed on the horizon for those who attempted to
portray Quebec as a colonized society. If, for the majority of activists in
Montreal, "decolonization" meant *Quebec* decolonization, this was far from
being the only way to conceive either the present or a possible liberated
future. Montreal was a city where various understandings of "empire" collided with one another, becoming the site for not one, but many different
movements of resistance. Already in 1965, at the public hearings of the
Royal Commission on Bilingualism and Biculturalism, Khan-Tineta Horn
pointed out that, from an Aboriginal perspective, French Canadians were
far from being colonized subjects. Rather, she argued, they should be considered "the first invading race."[9] Horn indirectly articulated a critique of
the idea of Quebec decolonization by turning its language back on itself,
and by claiming that francophone Quebeckers themselves constituted a
colonizing power. And at roughly the same time that Horn was defending
Aboriginal rights in Quebec, a more sustained alternative understanding
of empire, imperialism, and decolonization was being developed by Black
Montrealers of West Indian origin who had come together to form political organizations of their own.

Caribbean and other Black political groups demonstrated the multi-
faceted nature of politics in Montreal. As a shift in immigration policy was
changing the make-up of Canadian society, many newcomers, whether
they came to Canada to study or whether they immigrated permanently,
brought with them new ideas, theories, and understandings of the world.[10]
Their very presence demonstrates that during the 1960s the West was not

only being greatly influenced by the Third World, but that it was also significantly composed of many people who had originated there. Exploring
the nature of Caribbean and Black politics in Montreal challenges simplistic distinctions between First and Third World revolts. Viewed from a
West Indian perspective, Montreal, far from being a colonized city, acted
as an imperial metropole, a place in which the decision-makers of Western
capital decided the economic fate of the Caribbean.[11] And like imperial
metropoles elsewhere, Montreal became a meeting place for different colonized subjects, a site where they could meet each other and imagine a
different future for their countries of origin.[12]

Through a study of anti-colonial and anti-imperialist thought in Montreal, I hope to demonstrate the ways in which both theory and people
travelled across the barriers separating various parts of the world. Political activists and intellectuals in Montreal drew on the examples and theoretical works of Third World decolonization to interpret their own conditions and to imagine their place in the world, constituting something of
what Edward Said has termed "the tangled, many-sided legacy of imperialism."[13] By adopting and adapting decolonization theory, Montreal radicals demonstrated that theory can travel and be reinterpreted in a completely different location than its home of origin.[14]

The idea of decolonization had appeal in Sixties Montreal partly because
of the lived experience of unequal power relations in the city. Not only
were inequitable class and language structures powerfully inscribed onto
Montreal's physical landscape, but merely walking in downtown Montreal
was enough to convince many that the French language, although first in
terms of number of speakers, was second in terms of power and prestige.
By reading their local situation through the broader frame of empire,
activists in Montreal came to interpret the power relations that shaped
their everyday lives as part of a broader pattern of global oppression. For
alternative narratives of the world to order and make sense of material
and cultural oppression, alternative means of communication are required.
According to Marc Raboy, the "stakes of communication are nothing less
than control over the production of social interpretations of reality."[15] In
Montreal, the construction of oppositional ideas and the establishment of
alternative publications went hand-in-hand. Theoretical journals emerged
and folded, new publishing houses were established, and for five years, the
co-operative weekly newspaper *Québec-Presse* reported both world and
local events.

Democracy begins when people can imagine different futures; when these visions relativize the present, inspiring citizens to shape the world in which they live. And these ideas of different possible futures emerge not only through alternative media, but also through activism. Collective social movements, Robin Kelley argues, "are incubators of new knowledge," and new ideas often emerge out of "a concrete intellectual engagement with the problems of aggrieved populations confronting systems of oppression."[16] Not only did ideas of decolonization provide citizens with new ways of understanding material and cultural oppression, but the movements these citizens created also reshaped the ideas that had originally inspired them. Along the way, an increasing number of people came to believe that society, rather than being the natural or inevitable result of history, was an active project of creation. Individuals and groups, in other words, began asserting their claim to be the makers rather than just the inheritors of culture.[17]

By the late 1960s, the vast majority of oppositional groups in the city had come to accept that Quebec was a colonized society, but this does not mean that they were united on all questions. Tensions, rivalries, and ideological conflict divided movements. French- and English-speaking activists generally worked apart from one another, although their worlds overlapped and intersected to a greater degree than is generally acknowledged. Ideological differences were reinforced by conflicting ideas of political praxis, and few questions caused as much controversy as that of the campaign of political violence initiated by the various waves of the Front de libération du Québec (FLQ).

From 1963 to the early 1970s, various groups calling themselves the FLQ, believing themselves to be waging an anti-colonial guerrilla war, set off bombs, robbed banks, and were responsible for the death of nine people. The violence culminated in the "October Crisis" of 1970 when, in response to the FLQ's kidnapping of British diplomat James Cross and Quebec cabinet minister Pierre Laporte (later murdered), the federal government sent the army into Montreal and suspended civil liberties by enacting the War Measures Act. Because of its dramatic actions, the FLQ has become the subject of many documentaries, fictional representations, government reports, and historical studies. It has often been remembered as being at the very centre of oppositional politics during the period.[18] While the political violence of the FLQ, which was both morally and politically destructive, needs to be understood, there is a serious danger in allowing that single group to represent the period's activism.

Challenging empire in Montreal, I hope to demonstrate, was not the effort of a small group of isolated revolutionaries. Rather, it became a mass movement through which countless individuals came to see themselves as historically and politically consequential, providing a framework through which democracy was re-imagined as encompassing individual and collective sovereignty and social solidarity.[19] Activists worked in their local communities, created daycares and medical clinics, formed organizations in defence of the rights of tenants and the unemployed. Groups formed many different political parties, staged mass demonstrations, organized within their unions, and founded publications devoted to political analysis and poetry. Women challenged the everyday dismissals and devaluation they experienced not only in wider society but also within left-wing organizations themselves, Caribbean activists challenged racism, and thousands demanded that economic, cultural, political, and educational structures be brought under democratic control. It is this diversity and depth of political thought and action that this book explores.

This book has three purposes. First, it hopes to point to a new way of thinking about Quebec and Canadian history, one that situates Montreal's political upheavals of the 1960s within a framework of global dissent, insisting that they cannot be adequately understood outside of this larger context.[20] Second, this book attempts to describe something of the different yet overlapping worlds of political opposition in Montreal, thereby rethinking the ways in which different groups and movements during the 1960s interacted and fed upon each other's analyses, learning from each other even if they did not always acknowledge such reciprocity at the time. Sara Evans demonstrated long ago that the roots of the women's liberation movement could be found in the radically democratic (although practically limited) ideals of both the Civil Rights movement and the New Left.[21] Her findings, I believe, can be expanded to show that many other movements of the 1960s – and especially in a city like Montreal – were deeply connected on an intellectual and ideological level. My argument goes further than just trying to demonstrate the relationship between different movements in the 1960s. I argue that in Montreal, radical ideas crossed linguistic and ethnic boundaries, and radical groups benefited from each other's analyses. Such interactions were often fleeting, of course, and temporary alliances generally broke apart as conflicts arose around questions of class, language, and ethnicity. Yet on a more subtle level, the various movements of Sixties Montreal shared a similar grammar of dissent. While each movement had its own complex array of intellectual sources and to some degree needs to be thought of separately, none can be understood completely on its own. What I propose is a re-reading of the 1960s through a different lens, asking whether there is, or can be, a common intellectual history for a wide variety of dissident political movement in a multi-cultural city.

Finally, by looking at the centrality of Third World decolonization to the development of dissent in Montreal, I hope that this study will add new perspectives to the international field of Sixties scholarship, a field which has, with a few important exceptions,[22] remained limited by its near exclusive focus on connections between movements in North America and Europe. In contrast, I argue that the histories of the "First" and the "Third" Worlds are bound up in one another and cannot be untangled. Many dissident movements that emerged in the 1960s in the West, I maintain, are impossible to understand without looking at their connections with struggles and ideas originating elsewhere.

Considering the ways in which the theory of decolonization shaped a variety of radical political movements in Montreal challenges any notion that there can be one single, coherent story of the 1960s. Each movement maintained its own distinct narrative of liberation, but, linked by the flexible language of decolonization, all these narratives overlapped. No one group or movement could ever hold the monopoly on oppositional life. The language of decolonization fused with the politicization of language, sex, race, and class, creating mass movements that, albeit in different forms, continue to this day. If the project of "Othering" is essential to any political position, in Montreal, for the wide assortment of radicals of the late 1960s and early 1970s, this "Other" was, broadly speaking, "empire." Decolonization, in short, acted as a structure of ideas that gave diverse groups and individuals intellectual resources to understand their own conditions in new ways and, in turn, to creatively adapt and reshape those very ideas.[23] When a whole array of radical political movements emerged in the late 1960s – women's liberationists, French unilingualists, Black Power advocates, radical labour activists – they not only accepted the terms of the decolonization debate, but worked to make new space within it for a larger conception of democratic politics.

Exploring the ways in which international theories and ideas were interpreted, applied, and built upon by intellectuals who were situated in Montreal, and therefore affected by the city's unique characteristics, requires
an open and non-reductionist understanding of culture. Cultures are, by
their very nature, hybrid and mixed. As Edward Said demonstrates so ele-
gantly, "the history of all cultures is the history of cultural borrowings," and
all are heavily "involved in one another." Cultures constantly defy patriotic nationalisms that insist on the fundamental differences between peoples.[24] If we accept that culture generally, and political and intellectual ideas
more specifically, are porous and are forged through an interaction of
internal and external influences, then the history of political movements in
Montreal takes on new dimensions. Publicly expressed ideas can never be
the jealously guarded property of one group or another. In Montreal, as elsewhere, the ideas of Black Power were never the sole property of the Black
community, conceptions of women's liberation had an important influence
on many men, class oppression could be understood by sympathetic writers who emerged from the elite and, as so many non-francophones demonstrated in the Sixties, the cultural and material alienation of francophone
Quebeckers could be understood and opposed by those whose roots did not
go back to the founding of New France. It is this mixing of ideas and movements, this constantly metamorphosing counter-hegemonic challenge to
empire, that constitutes the history of postcolonial thought in Montreal.

■ ■ ■

Part 1 of this study, which covers 1963–68, details efforts to construct a new
language of dissent in Montreal. Chapter 1 outlines the project of Quebec
decolonization, and chapter 2 introduces the actors and organizations that
developed the early ideas of Quebec decolonization and explores the importance of Montreal in the construction of their oppositional language. In
Montreal's cafés and meeting places, activists of various political ideologies
argued with, learned from and influenced one another. And in its working-
class neighbourhoods, people organized around issues affecting their daily
lives, from housing to welfare rights. Chapter 3 explores how this alternative vision for Quebec interacted with international ideas and movements.
Activists in Montreal looked to France for inspiration but, often disappointed, they focused their sights on the example of the Cuban revolution, which helped them to understand the interrelated nature of anti-

imperialist struggles. Radicals ultimately looked to the Black Power movement in the United States when striving to reconceptualize themselves and
their place in the world.

After Part 1 explores the conditions and circumstances that led to the con-
ceptualization of Quebec liberation, Part 2 examines the various ways in
which the concept of decolonization fused with the politicization of different social identities to give birth to a variety of political movements which,
while distinct from one another, were also deeply connected. In 1968, as mass
protests and rebellions erupted around the world, students in Quebec's
newly instituted junior college system were enraged over their crowded
conditions and limited prospects at finding university spaces. In the fall
of 1968, major student strikes and occupations broke out across the province. One of the main demands was the construction of a second French-
language university in Montreal, and students began to realize that their
particular demands would need to form part of a broad movement for
social change. At almost the same time, activists in Montreal organized
the Congress of Black Writers at McGill University, a conference that
brought many of the world's most important activists and writers – including C.L.R. James and Stokely Carmichael – to Montreal. Both the struggle to oppose structural racism and attempts to challenge the cultural and
economic power of the English language exploded in the spring of 1969.

First came the revolt over race. When students at Sir George Williams
University determined that their charges of racism against a biology professor were being inadequately addressed, they staged an occupation of
the university's computer centre. Lasting roughly two weeks, the occupation ended with the blows of riot police, the arrest of nearly one hundred
activists, and the destruction of two million dollars worth of property. An
intense backlash against Montreal's Black activists (although roughly half
of those arrested were White) swept across the city. Chapter 4 describes
how, in the aftermath of the "Sir George Williams Affair," a cultural renaissance took place in the Black community, one that witnessed the birth of
new media, new forms of community action, and new interpretations of
race and racial oppression. Montreal's Black activists drew on their own
readings and interpretations of empire and race, but they also moved closer,
both ideologically and politically, to other movements operating in the
city.

One month after the Sir George Williams Affair, in March 1969, 10,000
to 15,000 students, workers, and activists staged the largest street demon-

stration since the end of the Second World War. The protesters marched towards McGill, demanding that the university, the traditional bastion of anglophone privilege, serve the francophone working class. In the build-up to and the aftermath of the protest, activists used the language of decolonization to challenge the unquestioned power of English in economic life. Chapter 6 maintains that arguments about linguistic alienation and cultural domination were deeply indebted to analyses of capitalism and colonialism in Quebec. For the activists and thinkers of the Opération McGill français movement, having more French-speaking managers and technicians would do nothing to ameliorate the conditions of workers. Only a holistic program of social change could bring about the required transformation in power relations. The ultimate effect of Opération McGill was therefore the popularization of an argument about language that placed linguistic devaluation within a political economy of empire.

While radicals spoke about different forms of exploitation and alienation, they remained blind to a form of oppression that reached into the heart of their own organizations. Learning from movements throughout the world that rhetorically, metaphorically, and actually excluded women from meaningful political roles, most activists in Montreal portrayed politics as a male preserve, and the process of decolonization was seen as a way to overcome the emasculation wrought by colonialism. But in the fall of 1969, women began organizing consciousness-raising groups, discussing their oppression as women, and articulating the necessity to join together in an autonomous political movement. Before long, the Montreal Women's Liberation Movement had been organized and, in November 1969, English- and French-speaking women joined together to take to the streets in chains to denounce a new "anti-protest" law passed by Montreal's municipal authorities. In the aftermath of the protest, the two groups joined to form the Front de libération des femmes (FLF), an organization that situated the liberation of women within the larger world of anti-imperialist politics. Chapter 5 charts the development of women's liberation in Montreal, arguing that, by drawing on both an international language of feminism and on ideas of Quebec decolonization, theorists of women's liberation did not operate in opposition to the left, but rather worked from the inside to widen its horizons.

During the tumultuous year of 1969, Black activists, advocates of French unilingualism, and women's liberationists all burst onto the political scene. But they were not alone. Chapter 7 argues that it was also during 1969 that the radical wing of Quebec labour – represented most clearly by the Montreal Central Council of the CSN – decisively entered the ranks of oppositional movements in Montreal. When long-time labour activist Michel Chartrand was elected as president of the Central Council, an organization that represented the 65,000 CSN workers on the territory of Montreal, the lines that separated labour and the left began to blur.

The politicization of social class, however, was not only occurring within the ranks of organized labour (and the CSN itself had begun moving to the left in 1966). Chapter 7 details how, in poor and working-class neighbourhoods throughout Montreal, individuals had begun the process of organizing citizens' committees to demand redress of specific grievances that affected daily life, and by the mid- to late-1960s a whole series of parallel institutions had emerged, including citizens' health and legal clinics, consumer co-operatives, newspapers, and libraries. By the end of the decade, many activists in both community organizations and within the labour movement had begun to recognize the need to organize along class lines in order to take political power. Joining together with intellectuals and students, they formed the Front d'action politique (FRAP), a radical political party that hoped to take power at the municipal level. The FRAP represented the coming together of the politics of citizens' committees and the politics of labour around a larger project of building working-class power. Workers, the FRAP maintained, were perpetual renters in a city that they themselves had built, and it was time that they transformed the city according to the needs and aspirations of the majority of its inhabitants.[25]

Just as FRAP was campaigning in its first municipal election, however, the left was sent into profound disarray as a result of the October Crisis. In the face of the state's crackdown, during which hundreds of activists were arrested and the homes of thousands searched, few organizations dared to voice their opposition publicly. Chapter 7 examines in detail the lead-up to and the events of the October Crisis, and explores the actions and ideas of the FLQ, as well as the reactions of the labour movement to the crisis.

In the face of the repression engendered by the FLQ's actions, Quebec's three main labour unions, the Confédération des syndicats nationaux (CSN), the Fédération des travailleurs du Québec (FTQ), and the Corporation des enseignants du Québec (CEQ) attended an important joint meeting, accelerating the inter-union solidarity that had been gaining momentum in the previous years, and presaging an era of radicalization that was to come. In the spring of 1972, Quebec's public and para-public sector workers, pitted in a major confrontation with the provincial government, staged a general strike that lasted until the government passed back-to-work legislation. When a judge sentenced the three union presidents – Marcel Pepin, Yvon Charbonneau, and Louis Laberge – to one-year prison sentences for having advised workers to ignore injunctions limiting their right to strike, 300,000 workers throughout the province walked off the job in one of the most dramatic general strikes in North American history. I argue that the May 1972 general strike resulted from the interaction of local grievances and a language of dissent that had now spread far beyond the confines of Montreal, and that identified the Quebec Liberal government as the defender of American imperial capital.

In many ways, May 1972 represented the high point of anti-imperialist activism in Quebec. And yet, by the end of the strike, it was clear that the idea of decolonization was losing ground, becoming less and less appealing to those concerned with social justice. Activism certainly did not die down in Quebec in the 1970s, and intellectuals who deplored the power of American imperialism still abounded. But the idea of decolonization had given way to a variety of different frameworks. There are many reasons for its lost appeal, at least some of which were inherent in the contradictions of the movement itself. Decolonization had always relied on a heavily gendered language that appealed to a robust masculinity, a language that, while attempting to empower marginalized people, excluded women from political roles. And it also relied on metaphors of race and of victimization, metaphors that were unsustainable when faced with the rise of Black Power activism in Montreal and Aboriginal activism throughout the continent. At least partly because of its reliance on gendered and racialized concepts, the language of decolonization was inherently unstable, revisable, and, ultimately, disposable.

PART ONE
1963–1968

ONE

EMPIRE, DEMOCRACY, AND MONTREAL

Few eras of the past live on into the present like the 1960s. In recent years, election campaigns in France and the United States have been fought over the legacy of the period, while students have drawn explicitly on the period's rhetoric in their various campaigns. For the political right, the decade of the 1960s marks the moment during which morality and authority gave way to permissiveness and disorder. For the left, it was a time when great hopes collapsed into bitter disappointment. In Quebec the memory of the 1960s has received a somewhat different treatment. Loosely referred to as the Quiet Revolution, the 1960s are primarily remembered, at least in popular representations, as a time when a traditional and religiously dominated society underwent an intense period of modernization, and when francophones, making use of the Quebec state, gained control of their own society. Not only did the political apparatus of the province become the primary instrument defending and maintaining a distinctive culture, but a new Québécois identity – centred on territory and language rather than on religion and ethnicity – was born. Historians have produced detailed and persuasive studies arguing that the 1950s were neither as repressive nor the 1960s as transformative as they are often portrayed, but scholars have had little success in altering a firmly anchored popular perception.[1]

The prevailing narrative of the 1960s can be contested on the grounds that it describes as a profound rupture what was really just an accelerated period of change. But equally as important, the narrative of the Quiet Revolution needs to be challenged for what it ignores, suppresses, and pushes to the margins of historical memory. Seeing the 1960s in Quebec only through the lens of capitalist modernization is to succumb to what Kristin Ross has called "a teleology of the present."[2] From this perspective, the roots of Quebec society today can be found in the social and political movements of the 1960s. Looking back vertically from the perspective of the present downplays the alterity of the past and the different alternative social imaginaries that fuelled so much of the period's dynamism. As the editors of a recent collection of writings on postcolonialism point out, "historical transformation cannot simply be understood as progression or decline. Earlier periods are more than simply precursors to later periods, and they must be understood in their own terms."[3] After sketching some of the characteristics of 1950s and 1960s Quebec, this chapter will explore the meaning of the project of decolonization, and will end with a brief discussion of the urban context in which it was forged.

■ ■ ■

The years following the Second World War were ambivalent, years of vast economic expansion and chronic poverty, restrictive moral codes and all-night jazz clubs.[4] Quebec, like Canada as a whole, experienced important economic and demographic growth. From 1951 to 1961, the province's population grew by 26.7%, and low unemployment, coupled with a steadily expanding economy, provided a sense of security which eased the lingering memory of the Great Depression. Between 1946 and 1960, Quebec received 400,000 immigrants, most of whom settled in Montreal with the goal of making a better life for themselves and their families. In the 1930s only a minority of people had access to hot water, telephones, or consumer goods such as radios, household appliances, and cars, but in the prosperous 1950s such goods became commonplace.[5] In 1952, the French-language public television station Radio-Canada began broadcasting, and it would come to play an important role in creating a new sense of culture and community throughout the province.[6]

The optimism and prosperity of the 1950s were not equally shared, and individuals' experiences differed greatly depending on gender, ethnicity, class, and region. Francophones with equal competencies to anglophones earned less, and men earned more than women. The widely cited statistics of the Royal Commission on Bilingualism and Biculturalism – a commission established by the federal government in response to the nationalist upsurge of the 1960s – provided statistical proof of the discrimination that many francophones had been experiencing for years. In 1961, a 35% difference in average income separated anglophones and francophones, and statistics which correlated income with ethnicity found that francophones ranked twelfth of fourteen ethnic groups in the province. 56% of the Montreal region's best-paid workers were anglophones, although they made up only 24% of the labour force. And while 78% percent of francophones earning over five thousand dollars needed to speak English on the job, an ability to work in French was required for only 14% of anglophones in the same wage range. Although francophones comprised the vast majority of Quebec's population, they controlled only 20% of its economy. And the province – which represented 27% of Canada's population – contained 40% of the country's unemployed workers.[7]

In Montreal's low-income francophone neighbourhoods, rates of infant mortality had long surpassed those of the English-speaking neighbourhoods on the west side of the city, and the rest of Canada in general.[8] In companies owned by non-francophones, a survey conducted by the CSN in 1965 found, despite the fact that over 90% of the workforce primarily spoke French, workers needed to use English with their bosses 50% of the time.[9] Ambitious French Canadians needed to learn English to advance economically, although the reverse was far from being the case.[10] Even the custom guards who presided over the border between Quebec and the United States, a 1951 report showed, often only spoke English.[11] The Royal Commission on Bilingualism and Biculturalism found that with the economic expansion of the post-war years, discrimination took on new forms, and French Canadians faced greater obstacles in the workplace in 1961 than they had in 1941.[12] Outside of Quebec, francophones were up against even greater odds. Senior posts in the federal civil service were largely closed to francophones, as were most senior jobs in finance and industry.[13] Although the divisions were by no means absolute, linguistic and class alienation fused together in the minds of many, giving a potent force to the revolts of the 1960s and early 1970s.

It was in Montreal, with scarcity and wealth inscribed upon the very geography of the city, that many French Canadians came to realize the extent of the cultural and material oppression they faced. In 1960, for example, Charles Gagnon, who would go on to become one of the most well-known advocates of Quebec decolonization, moved from Le Bic – a small town on the Saint Lawrence River – to Côte-des-Neiges, a region close to the campus of the Université de Montréal. At first, the wealth of the city's residents amazed him, but once he left the mountain and travelled down to the French-speaking working class districts, he found the familiar material and cultural deprivation he had known growing up. This contact with the suffering of ordinary citizens was one of the inspirations that led Gagnon, and others like him, to engage in political activities.[14] Poverty in the city at the time was considerable; a 1965 study demonstrated that over a third of Montreal's population was destitute,[15] and a similar proportion of apartments downtown was considered uninhabitable.[16] During Expo '67, City Hall erected boards alongside the Jacques-Cartier Bridge so that tourists would not see the slums below.[17]

The conflation of class and ethnicity echoed the way many people understood the power relations that shaped their lives. Yet statistics that correlated income with ethnicity also demonstrated that two groups earned even less than French Canadians: Italians (whom I will discuss in Chapter 6) and Aboriginal peoples. The history of Aboriginal groups in Quebec and their relationship with larger society is shaped by varying degrees of racism and paternalism, as well as cultural mixing and resistance. Indigenous people living in Quebec were denied the right to vote in federal elections until 1960, and in provincial elections until 1969.[18]

From 1870 to 1960, the demographic weight of Aboriginal people continued to decline, and by the beginning of the 1960s Quebec's roughly 21,000 Aboriginal people represented only 0.4% of the province's population.[19] As the relative population declined, so too did the proportion of Aboriginal people who lived in close proximity to Quebec's main population settlements, thereby rendering them less and less visible.[20] But numbers alone were not responsible for their exclusion from conceptions of the French-Canadian nation. According to Claude Gélinas, intellectuals of the post-confederation era generally saw Aboriginal peoples as belonging to a prehistoric era. Even as late as 1950, a prominent French-Canadian could describe the land that French settlers had colonized as "nearly empty."[21] Native peoples were not only believed to have lived a history cordoned off from Quebec's francophone majority, but had often been portrayed as obstacles in the way of the province's development.[22] The consequences of this exclusion from any conception of the "nation" – an exclusion that was inherited by Montreal's anti-colonial writers of the 1960s – would be felt throughout the late 1960s and especially in the 1970s, when Aboriginal people increasingly began to make their own demands for autonomy and self-determination.[23]

Whether left- or right-wing, religious or secular, the intellectual world of the 1950s was a world dominated by men. Women writers and activists made important contributions, of course, but the public sphere in which they operated was profoundly gendered. According to the dictates of conservative French-Canadian nationalism, women's patriotic duty was served not through political or economic citizenship, but through motherhood. Women were the "producers" of the national community, the bearers and not the makers of national identity.[24] French-Canadian women were seen as the guardians of language and tradition, and as the pillars of survival for francophones in North America.[25] In 1950s Quebec, authority remained in the hands of men. Nonetheless, there were always women who defied expectations and actively took part in the public sphere. In 1952, for example, the mostly women workers at the Montreal department store Dupuis Frères went on strike, eventually winning a collective agreement substantially improving their wages and working conditions. Women were also involved in social, political, and artistic and cultural issues, they made effective use of birth control, and their presence on the job market grew.[26]

■ ■ ■

Politically, the 1950s were dominated by the figure of Maurice Duplessis. Duplessis' Union Nationale party first came to power in 1936, was defeated three years later, and returned to power in 1944, where it remained until the 1960 provincial election (Duplessis died in 1959). While his rhetoric was that of classical liberalism, Duplessis ruled the province with an iron fist, relying on political corruption to ensure re-election while opening the province's natural resources to a flood of American investments. The government made use of restrictive laws to intervene in labour conflicts, using the provincial police to protect the interests of capital and crush the resistance of striking workers. According to his critics, Duplessis worked to maintain a power structure that systematically discriminated against French Canadians, keeping them in inferior positions at all levels of society.

While the government's power was maintained by a bloc of interests that included monopoly capitalists as well as the traditional *petite-bourgeoisie*, the hierarchy of the Catholic Church wielded important influence in maintaining the conservative nature of Quebec's intellectual and institutional structures. Duplessis himself spoke the language of traditional French-Canadian nationalism, emphasizing the rural roots and Catholic nature of the French-Canadian people, and defending Quebec's autonomy in the face of the federal government. "At a time when there was no more than a handful of communists in the entire province of Quebec," Susan Mann writes, "Duplessis postured as the protector of Quebec against communism, materialism, atheism, and class warfare."[27] Through a well-oiled system of patronage, favouritism, and political repression, and the use of a gendered language of female domesticity, Duplessis became the powerful *chef* of the province. And he became the most prominent defender of the nation, supported by a network of right-wing intellectuals who defended the traditional family, denounced feminism, and advocated the maintenance of structures of authority.[28]

But movements of opposition to the Duplessis regime began to take shape.[29] Liberals coalesced around the journal *Cité libre*, arguing that if Quebec was to integrate fully into mainstream North America, it would need to overcome the handicap of clericalism and the ideology of nationalism. Another group collected around the journal *L'Action nationale* and *Le Devoir*, the newspaper of the intelligentsia. This group worked to oppose conservative French-Canadian nationalism with a modern vision of the future. It privileged Quebec's urban rather than its rural experience, and advocated the building of a modern nation-state, in which Quebec City would become a national capital. The neo-nationalists advocated, in Michael Behiels's words, a secular state "devoted to the socioeconomic, cultural, and political aspirations of Quebec's francophone majority." Rather than socialism, neo-nationalists promoted the development of a mixed provincial economy "with an increasingly francophone-dominated private sector working in cooperation with an interventionist state."[30] From the 1960s to today, all provincial governments of Quebec have been shaped by neo-nationalism, their ideological outlooks crucially indebted to its modernizing program of development.

It would be wrong, however, to juxtapose the emergence of a new secular intelligentsia against a universally reactionary Catholicism. Recent works by Michael Gauvreau, and Jean-Philippe Warren and E.-Martin Meunier, have demonstrated the intellectual diversity of pre-1960 Catholic thought. They have highlighted the dynamism within Catholic thinking, and have shown the importance of an anti-clericalism within Quebec Catholicism that set the groundwork for many later changes. The origins of this renewed Catholic thought can be found in attempts by Catholic thinkers to find a way out of the economic catastrophe of the Great Depression of the 1930s, and on the insistence of the necessity of renewing Catholic values from below, by "rechristianizing" society through the establishment of Catholic Action youth movements. Thousands of youth were attracted to the idea of finding a new, "pure," more "authentic" version of Catholicism that would be free from hierarchical traditionalism.[31]

The intellectual ferment created a pluralism within Catholic thought in the province, and in the post-war years the corporatism of the 1930s was reinterpreted "in a more liberal, humanist, social-democratic direction."[32] This left-wing Catholic personalism helped social democratic ideas make inroads in Quebec in the 1950s. An insistence on the absolute value and autonomy of the human person had an important impact on the province's Catholic trade union movement, a movement that grew increasingly militant as it began waging conflicts against the power of the provincial state. Promoting democracy rather than corporatism, Catholic labour leaders also advocated a much clearer distinction between the temporal and spiritual spheres than that which prevailed in the province.[33] By the 1950s, a great deal of ideological diversity existed within Quebec society in general. Progressive intellectuals, academics, and trade unionists all worked within left Catholic traditions, many emanating from France, which provided them with the intellectual tools to challenge the spiritual and material devastation of liberal capitalism, and many began offering critiques of clericalism from within the Catholic tradition itself.

Throughout the 1960s, left-wing Catholic figures would become important to community organizing in Montreal's poor neighbourhoods, and by the late 1960s left Catholic traditions emanating from Latin America were also having a significant impact. In the summer of 1967, Gustavo Gutiérrez, the Peruvian theologian and theoretician of liberation theology, gave a summer seminar at the Université de Montréal. And it was in Montreal, he would later claim, that he developed ideas of liberation theology that would have such a powerful resonance in many parts of the world.[34] Even before the influence of liberation theology, however, Catholic missionaries had been bringing a certain form of internationalism to Quebec society, a form of internationalism that was, according to one observer, marked by a mixture of racism, paternalism, and human solidarity.[35] Since the nineteenth century, French-Canadian missionaries operated in various parts of the world,[36] a trend that only increased in the aftermath of the First World War. With the establishment of foreign mission societies, hundreds of nuns and priests from Quebec began to head out every year to work

in Africa and Asia and, somewhat later, in Latin America and Haiti. By the
eve of the 1960s, thousands of missionaries from Quebec were being re-
cruited and sent around the world.[37] And when these missionaries returned
to Quebec, they brought with them their new understandings of the world.
Pierre Beaudet, a future important intellectual of the left, recalls first learning about the slums of the Third World, and of the resistance that was taking shape there, from missionaries at his college.[38]

In the early 1960s, many facets of the world appeared to be changing
simultaneously. Transformations within the Catholic Church ushered in by
Vatican II coincided with the Civil Rights movement in the United States,
decolonization in Africa and Asia, and the rise of second wave feminism in
North America and Europe. In Quebec, shifts in the global realm coincided with the death of Maurice Duplessis in 1959. When Jean Lesage's Liberal Party came to power the following year with a reformist program, a
wave of pent-up anger unleashed both energy and optimism across the
province.

The province that the Liberal Party inherited in the early 1960s was full
of contradictions and, despite having a history of modernization stretching back to the nineteenth century,[39] it shared traits with societies classified
as both "developed" and "underdeveloped." Quebec produced 90% of all
of Canada's iron ore but, by 1960, 90.3% of this ore was being shipped out
of the province in its raw form, generally to the United States. Despite
Quebec's large mining industry, only 4.3% of Canada's steel was produced
in the province, which did not even contain a single blast furnace.[40] Even
in sectors where natural resources were *not* being exported in raw form, such
as forestry, only 4.8% of the pulp and paper industry was controlled by
French Canadians, with foreign companies controlling nearly 42%.[41] Foreign corporations controlled 86.5% of the primary metals industry. By
1961, only 2.2% of mining production was in French-Canadian hands.[42]
Despite these statistics, however, it should be remembered that Quebec
did have a strong balance of trade in many industries (such as chemical
products, transportation equipment, textiles and clothing),[43] and that Quebec's economy also relied on the exploitation of other regions in Canada,
such as the Atlantic provinces and the West,[44] as well as other parts of the
world.[45]

By the end of the 1950s, there was agreement among many different sectors of Quebec society on a broad program of reform. A major goal of
what became known as the Quiet Revolution was to fully integrate Quebec

in general, and francophone Quebeckers in particular, into the North American economy.[46] Economic planning was needed, many argued, so that francophones could gain greater control over the province's economy, and to ensure that more of the province's resources were processed in Quebec.[47] Whether the primary impetus behind the reforms of the 1960s came from a new middle class or from an alliance of classes, the objectives of the Quiet Revolution remained the same: the political modernization of the province, the creation of new social and economic opportunities for francophones, and the elevation of francophones to the upper levels of the Quebec economy.[48] The Quebec state – now conceived of as a national state – became the primary instrument of development.

For those living through the period, the Quiet Revolution was often experienced as a great moment of transformation. From 1960 to 1966, six new ministries and eight public enterprises were created and the provincial civil service grew from 29,298 to 41,847 employees. In the decade following 1961, mass attendance in the Montreal diocese dropped from 61% to 30%.[49] In the excitement and intellectual fervour of the early 1960s, newly released books attacking traditional social structures caused sensations. In the highly controversial *Pourquoi je suis un séparatiste*, Marcel Chaput argued that for francophone Quebeckers to control their own society, they needed to form an independent state.[50] And Jean-Paul Desbiens – a teacher and member of a religious order who wrote under the pseudonym "Brother Anonymous" – penned a stinging and irreverent attack on the Catholic-dominated Quebec education system. The book, *Les insolences du Frère Untel*, sold over a hundred thousand copies.[51] Within a matter of a few years, the provincial Liberal Party had instituted hospital insurance, passed new labour legislation, re-established a Ministry of Education and, declaring that the era of economic colonialism had come to an end, nationalized hydro-electric power.[52] It was on this shifting landscape that young dissident writers began developing their ideas of decolonization.

THE IDEA OF DECOLONIZATION

Studies of the 1960s in Quebec have generally been framed within the context of the province's history. Seen from this angle, the social conditions of the 1950s and the particularities of Quebec society provided the backdrop for the explosion of political activity in the 1960s. This interpretation speaks to an important dimension of the political activism of the period, and the changing political, economic, and demographic structures of Quebec provided the ground on which later revolts would develop. But Montreal did not live the Sixties on its own, and in addition to understanding the local environment, it is also necessary to look across borders in order to situate political developments in the city within the larger world of global dissent. When leftists in Montreal began reading and interpreting Marx and Freud, Fanon and Memmi, the works of French existentialists and the advocates of women's liberation, they did so alongside activists throughout North America, Europe, and the Third World.

In the 1960s, across North America and Europe, cultural mores were overturned, political truths challenged, and the numerous and demanding members of the baby-boom generation burst onto the political scene. While many countries experienced an upsurge of militant unionism in the 1960s, images of White middle-class student radicals dominate representations of the decade. The New Left, characterized by its rejection of American imperialism and the socialism of the Soviet Union, and by its desire to end both individual and national alienation, became the hegemonic force on the left in many Western countries. While activists in Montreal shared much with others across North America and Europe, they remained, in many ways, distinct.

Like other North American activists, Montrealers sympathized with and supported struggles taking place elsewhere, and were greatly affected by the Vietnam War. And like many activists around the world they were young. Especially when it came to student politics at the end of the decade, it would be impossible to deny a generational dimension to the New Left.[53] Yet the political revolts of the 1960s, while they need to be situated in the context of changing demographic and educational structures, cannot be reduced to generational explanations alone. Many of the early architects of the language of Quebec decolonization, for example, were born in the 1920s and 1930s, and had come of age long before the 1960s began.[54] And the politicization of the late 1960s had an important cross-generational dimension to it, sometimes even affecting entire families.[55] As Fernand Dumont remarked in the aftermath of the October Crisis of 1970, "obsessed as we were with the spectacular revolt of the young, we had not taken note of the suppressed revolt of the adults and the old."[56]

In addition to demographic changes in Quebec society, activists in Montreal were deeply affected by the global geo-political changes of the postwar era. Radical Montrealers, like Black activists in the United States, drew correlations between their conditions and those of the peoples of the Third World. "Decolonization" generally refers to the period following the Second World War when nations in Africa and Asia began achieving political independence. The term "Third World" became commonplace during this period, referring, as Vijay Prashad reminds us, not to a geographical place, but to a political project. Caught between the polarized sides of the Cold War, he argues, "the peoples of Africa, Asia, and Latin America dreamed of a new world."[57]

The term "Third World" was coined by Alfred Sauvy in 1952, with specific reference to the "Third Estate" of the French Revolution. Like the Third Estate, the Third World was poised to take its rightful place in the world.[58] Largely as a result of decolonization, the concept of empire had become increasingly discredited in the years following the Second World War. "By the 1970s," Frederick Cooper argues, "colonialism had been banished from the realm of legitimate forms of political organization. What remained 'colonial' in world politics passed itself off as something else."[59] In the 1960s, therefore, there was much to gain for Montreal activists in naming their condition "colonial" and conceptualizing their movement as one of *de*colonization.

The claim that Quebec formed a colonized society derived from two different interpretations that, in practice, often co-existed and informed one another. In the first version – more prevalent among radicals throughout the early 1960s – French Canadians became colonial subjects when Great Britain defeated France on the Plains of Abraham in Quebec City in 1759. After the Conquest, the story went, British settlers assumed key roles in the administration of the colony, relegating French Canadians to second class citizenship, a status that was perpetuated and formalized by Canadian Confederation in 1867. But the Conquest of 1759 was far from being clear proof of French Canadians' colonial status; before 1759, after all, New France was itself composed of Europeans and European descendents who had settled on previously occupied land, yet this contradiction mattered little for the early architects of Quebec decolonization. By the second half of the decade, however, references to the Conquest had declined dramatically, giving way to a new but related way of conceiving empire, one that would place an overwhelming emphasis on the grip that American imperialism held over the province.

While the political movements of the 1960s in Montreal incorporated many elements of traditional French-Canadian nationalism, they also drew heavily on a Third World nationalism that differed greatly from its European form. If it is true, as Benedict Anderson argues, that anti-imperial nationalisms of the twentieth century had a "profoundly modular character," drawing inspiration from earlier forms of nationalism,[60] it is equally true that they differed from earlier models in important respects. "Forged in opposition to imperialism," Prashad explains, "this nationalism created a program and agenda that united people on a platform of sovereignty in all domains of life."[61] Of all the various writers involved in Third World liberation, activists in Montreal looked above all to Jacques Berque (whom I will discuss in chapter 3), Albert Memmi and Frantz Fanon. Memmi, in his most well known work, *The Colonizer and the Colonized*, speaks of the ways in which colonialism created insurmountable divisions between human groups. To justify their superiority, colonizers systematically devalue the colonized, rejecting their culture, stripping them of their language and their history. The colonial situation works to "manufacture" the colonialists and the colonized, isolating them into "airtight colonial groupings" from which they cannot escape. Colonization not only occurs on the political and economic levels, Memmi argues; it reaches deep into the psychological realm, and racism becomes internalized by the colonizer and the colonized alike.[62]

Memmi's vivid dissection and analysis of the colonial situation had a powerful resonance with Montreal radicals, but the path towards liberation that he envisioned remained somewhat unclear.[63] For a vision of a future postcolonial society, many radicals turned to the works of Frantz Fanon, finding in *The Wretched of the Earth* the means of reconciling their feelings of national alienation with their socialist convictions. Engagement with the book helped them articulate the necessity of resisting neo-nationalist narratives of modernization. Fanon's work operates on the terrain of the nation, outlining the cultural degradation wrought by colonialism, but it goes much further, warning of the disastrous consequences of an outlook that remains purely national in scope and does not proceed to a deeper project of human emancipation. While *The Wretched of the Earth* is a hybrid text combining philosophy and imaginative story, argumentative essay, psychological case study, and nationalist allegory, it also acts, as Edward Said points out, as a "visionary transcendence of history." The work begins by dramatizing a Manichean split between the settler and the native, then proceeds to chart the birth of an independence movement, and finally moves on to outline the transformation of "that movement into what is in effect a trans-personal and trans-national force."[64]

The opening chapter lays out in vivid detail the trauma and violence of colonization. In contrast to traditional Marxist understandings of capitalism, according to which power is lived in the temporal sphere by workers who spend an increasing amount of their labour-time producing for the profit of capitalists, Fanon describes how power relations in colonial societies are lived spatially.[65] Natives live in dark and cramped quarters, physically removed from the decadent neighbourhoods of the colonizer. The colonized are cordoned off, hemmed in, removed from their land and subjugated not only as workers, but also as a subject race. Through the process of colonization, cities are segregated and lines of demarcation drawn between natives and settlers. Understanding the social struggle as one between capital and labour alone, Fanon writes, cannot do justice to the particular forms of oppression caused by colonialism: "When you examine at close quarters the colonial context, it is evident that what parcels out the world is to begin with the fact of belonging to or not belonging to a given race, a given species. In the colonies the economic substructure is also a superstructure [...] This is why Marxist analysis should always be slightly stretched every time we have to do with the colonial problem." Decolonization, according to this initial sketch, is nothing more than "the replacing of a certain 'species' of men by another 'species' of men."[66]

Almost as quickly as Fanon builds up his portrait of the Manichaeism dividing colonial society, he begins to undo it, to draw a more subtle and complex portrait of the colonizer and the colonized. Although an initial reading of the colonial situation points to two undifferentiated categories – the colonizer and the colonized – Fanon proceeds to demonstrate that the "colonized" society itself is made up of differing interests. The activist struggling for independence begins to realize that, "while he is breaking down colonial oppression," he is simultaneously "building up automatically yet another system of exploitation," a system which rests on the class divisions within the colonized. The activist comes to understand that the interests of the national bourgeoisie, and the limited independence which it advocates, are not her own. The bourgeoisie of a colonized country, a bourgeoisie which, lacking the capital to initiate local economic development, does not even fulfil its function in the development of capitalism, works towards a narrow independence which preserves the colonial structures of the past under the guise of neo-colonialism. The poverty-stricken people, Fanon writes, begin to realize the hollowness of a political independence that does not radically alter power relations, of a nationalism achieving only formal sovereignty while leaving colonial hierarchies in place. In other words, they "pass from total, indiscriminating nationalism to social and economic awareness." As the categories break down, the colonized begin to realize that many colonizers take side with the natives, and that many of the "sons of the nation" sacrifice the common good of the people for their own personal gain.[67] Rather than leading in the direction of liberation, the nationalist narrative merely reinforces imperialism's hegemony.

Fanon goes on imaginatively to chart the rich possibilities of a counter-narrative of liberation, one "set in motion by fugitives, outcasts, hounded intellectuals who flee to the countryside and in their work and organization clarify and also undermine the weaknesses of the official narrative of nationalism."[68] By leaving the city behind, renegade intellectuals come into contact with the people, learn from them, and put their technical and intellectual capacities at their service. This "true" liberation movement attempts to forge a national consciousness – which Fanon insisted was not nationalism – "the only thing that will give us an international dimension," a prerequisite for what he at one point called "the assumption of responsibility on the historical scale." Because the building of a nation "is of necessity accompanied by the discovery and encouragement of universalizing values," "it is at the heart of national consciousness that international consciousness lives and grows."[69] This process of national liberation relies upon the active participation of the colonized who, through a massive collective act of refusal, develop new ideas and outlooks, becoming active agents in the construction of a new world. Rather than seeking a national hero or a great leader, Fanon insists that radical intellectuals need to work with the people in a project of political education, a project that will open minds, awaken spirits, allow the birth of intelligence and, drawing here upon the words of Aimé Césaire, "invent souls."[70] A new postcolonial society would only be sovereign if made up of free and responsible individuals: "Yesterday they were completely denied responsibility; today they mean to understand everything and make all decisions."[71] In other words, new subjects needed to be born.

The importance of Fanon to the history of political movements in Quebec is multi-faceted, as are Fanon's ideas themselves. Fanon has often been understood as a mindless promoter of violence, as someone who felt that violence could cleanse the colonized of their internalized feelings of inferiority. Such facile characterizations belie the subtlety of his ideas. As a clinical psychologist, he sought to diagnose and explain the dehumanizing effects of colonialism, arguing that the violence of the colonial system became internalized by the colonized, often resulting in fratricidal destruction. He describes how the direction of violence begins to change in the period immediately preceding decolonization, as the colonized begin turning towards their oppressors. As Fanon saw it, this initial phase of decolonization is a reversal of the Manichean world created by colonialism, before the development of a mutation of consciousness. This mutation, Nigel Gibson argues, results from a critique "of politics based on violence alone."[72] Anticolonial violence is contradictory in that it is both Manichean and dialectical, and while it "indicates the end of colonial rule" it does not in itself "constitute a program." Rather than being an answer, "violence becomes a problematic that needs to be worked out."[73]

Fanon believed that violence was inevitable if a subjugated people was to regain its independence, and declared (wrongly) that "decolonization is always a violent phenomena."[74] But he did not promote violence for its own sake, recognizing its destructive consequences.[75] Although the violence of decolonization could be understood, he wrote in A Dying Colonialism, "we do not on this account justify the immediate reactions of our compatriots."[76] Fanon took into account the importance of local context, arguing that the counterviolence of the colonized would be proportionate "to the violence exercised by the threatened colonial regime."[77] Yet even with these qualifications, Fanon's theories leave many questions unanswered. Could violence really lead to freedom? And, if so, at what cost and with what consequences?

The Wretched of the Earth emerged from the lived reality of the Algerian revolution, but the power of the book lay in Fanon's transposition of this unique experience to a general theory of the colonial condition, one that appealed to liberation movements around the world.[78] And just as Fanon developed a general theory out of his specific experiences in Algeria, his readers in turn applied this general theory to their own particular situations. Arguably more important than Fanon's intended meaning, therefore, was the way in which he was understood. In Montreal, some undoubtedly read Fanon as legitimizing their belief that decolonization needed to come about through violent means, or even, although it was rare, that violence itself could act as a cathartic force.[79] Such interpretations rested on a deeply flawed interpretation of Quebec society and on an overly mechanical mapping of anti-colonial theory onto it. Montreal had witnessed neither the brutal colonial terror of Algeria nor the death squads of Latin America. It had its share of secret police activity, raids, and armed interventions, but with the exception of the War Measures Act there was never a complete collapse of civil liberties.

Though some used Fanon to legitimate armed struggle, this was certainly not the only or most important reading of his work. Writers stressed over and over again the need to adapt his theories to the specific realities of Quebec society. As Jan Depocas wrote in *Parti Pris*, Quebec might not be a province like the others, but neither was it a colony like those in Africa or Latin America. To attempt to create a Cuba or Algeria in Quebec would be to have "neither read Fanon nor to have decolonized."[80] And when Quebec's three main labour leaders cited *The Wretched of the Earth* in 1971 for its usefulness to an understanding of power relations in the province, it was certainly not with the intention of promoting wanton violence.[81] They, like so many others, were drawn to Fanon for his powerful description of the colonial condition. Arguably more important than Fanon's position on violence was his preoccupation with the nefarious effects of the corrupt nationalist bourgeoisie, which acted as the central concern of *The Wretched of the Earth*.[82] Montreal writers therefore drew on Fanon to draw lines between themselves and more mainstream nationalists, as well as to understand the internalized feelings of inferiority of colonized people.

Like anti-colonial writers around the world, intellectuals in Montreal also drew on Marxism. Refusing orthodoxy, they saw Marxism as a flexible body of ideas that needed to be continually reshaped according to the needs and aspirations of the colonized. According to Robert Young, the Marxism of anti-colonial movements "emphasized what one might call the untranslatability of revolutionary practices, the need for attention to local forms, and the translation of the universal into the idiom of the local."[83] This "Third World Marxism" therefore needed to be adapted to and renewed by Quebec's specific historical circumstances and by its unique logic. In response to Pierre Trudeau, who continually argued that Quebec was neither Cuba nor Algeria, and could therefore not draw on their examples, Montreal poet and theorist Paul Chamberland argued that the authors of *Parti Pris* understood Quebec's particular nature better than anyone. What Trudeau refused to recognize, he wrote, was that "by applying them to our situation, we are transforming the very meaning of the terms 'colonization' and 'decolonization.'"[84] Anti-colonialist and anti-imperialist ideas in Quebec did not remain static. By the late 1960s and early 1970s, most authors took a more active interest in economic and structural explanations of imperialism, drawing heavily on Andre Gunder Frank and others.

In the international upheaval of the 1960s, Montreal leftists drew heavily on Third World decolonization movements, but their understandings of these movements were largely read through the prism of French exis-

tentialism, and especially the works of Jean-Paul Sartre. In the crisis-rid-
den atmosphere of post-war France, Sartre emerged as a larger-than-life figure, advocating individual responsibility in the face of human tragedy.[85]
Sartre's formulation of existentialism posited that existence preceded
essence; in other words, human action was guided by the particular
choices of free individuals rather than some pre-existing notion of human
nature. The individual therefore "is not fixed but in a constant state of
self-transformation and self-production, playing an active part within
the masses as a conscious collection of individuals who make history."[86]
By emphasizing freedom and responsibility, by maintaining that meaning could only be forged through human action, and by attempting to
outline a new and radical vision of humanism, Sartre encouraged a
sense of optimism that individuals, despite the limitations of their own
particular circumstances, could actively shape the world in which they
lived.[87]

All throughout the 1960s, activists and intellectuals drew on Sartre to create a culture of resistance. They also took inspiration from both the New
Left and the Third World to form a hybrid mixture of ideas and movements. As a perceptive article pointed out in 1964, "French Canada dances
on a tightrope, oscillating between the two types of societies and nations
to which it simultaneously belongs." From a socio-economic perspective,
Quebec was clearly an advanced capitalist society; from a political and cultural perspective, Quebec was colonized. Here, the authors argued, resided
both the originality of Quebec as well as its ambiguity.[88] The explosion of
leftist activism in Montreal during the 1960s and early 1970s was neither
typical nor inconsequential; the city's unique blending of linguistic and
cultural groups, and its imagined geographical position sitting at both
the centre and on the periphery of empire, created a laboratory in which
both New Left and decolonization ideas flourished, acquiring their own
colours and contours. But why were Montreal's particular configurations
so explosive?

MONTREAL CIRCA 1960

For radicals coming of age in the 1960s, the language of decolonization, with
its emphasis on Quebec's cultural and economic alienation, provided a
framework within which they could understand their own experiences.
While many have written about the artistic and theoretical developments

of 1960s Quebec, few have explored the relationship between intellectual ideas, street politics, the city, and resistance. Montreal acted as the site for the vast majority of political confrontations, and it was home to nearly all of the young intellectuals and artists who worked to develop new interpretations of Quebec society. Political groups, even those purporting to be national in scope, often existed only in the city. And in Montreal, unlike many other parts of Quebec, bookstores were scattered throughout the downtown, ensuring that journals such as *Parti Pris* could achieve widespread distribution.[89] The concentration of politicized intellectuals and activists – many of whom had themselves come from elsewhere – and the blending of linguistic and ethnic groups created an explosive climate unique to the city.

Montreal was linguistically and ethnically divided, and these divisions were at least partly represented in its geography. The centre of Montreal was dominated by Mount Royal, on which stood the stately buildings of the prestigious English-language McGill University. To the west of McGill, but still high on the mountain, was predominantly English-speaking Westmount, a neighbourhood that had become a symbol of anglophone domination. In Westmount's imposing mansions lived industrialists and financiers, bankers and professionals, and the neighbourhood was dotted with beautiful parks and well-kept lawns. Heading straight down the mountain from Westmount, one entered a completely different world, the predominantly working-class and francophone neighbourhood of Saint-Henri, immortalized in Gabrielle Roy's novel *The Tin Flute*. In Saint-Henri, located in close proximity to the factories and smokestacks that lined the Lachine Canal, apartments were cramped and crowded together, and green space hard to find. Further still down the hill, on the other side of the Lachine Canal, was the ethnically diverse but uniformly poor working-class neighbourhood of Pointe Saint-Charles. And along the close-by rue Saint-Antoine, adjacent to the headquarters of the Canadian Pacific Railway, lived Montreal's Black population. It was in the Saint-Antoine district that many of Montreal's legendary jazz clubs were situated, including Rockhead's Paradise, a club founded by Rufus Rockhead with money that he had earned working on the railway.[90] But despite Montreal's vibrant jazz scene, Black Montrealers, many of whom worked as sleeping-car porters or domestic servants, were segregated from the rest of Montreal by discriminatory housing and employment practices.[91]

Saint-Laurent Boulevard ran down the centre of the city, separating the largely francophone working-class east from the more affluent and largely

English-speaking west, although these divisions were by no means absolute. The street itself, colloquially called "The Main," became the home of many successive waves of immigrants, and for much of the twentieth century was associated with Yiddish-speakers. Although Montreal's Jewish population had increasingly adopted English, in many ways it remained culturally distinct from Anglophone Montreal, and faced prejudice from both the city's French- and English-speaking populations.[92] In addition to Westmount, west Montreal also consisted of the middle-class and largely English-speaking neighbourhood of Notre-Dame-de-Grâce. To the north of downtown, on the other side of the mountain from Westmount, sat the bourgeois neighbourhood of Outremont. Home both to the French-Canadian bourgeois class – a class composed mostly of professionals, doctors, lawyers, and notaries – and many members of Montreal's Jewish elite, the tree-lined streets and spacious houses of Outremont stood second only to Westmount in their opulence. Outremont contrasted sharply with the francophone neighbourhoods of east Montreal where, in districts like the Plateau Mount Royal, Hochelaga Maisonneuve, and Rosemont, chronic poverty and unemployment cast a shadow over the daily lives of their residents.

While living patterns often seemed static and fixed, Montreal was a city that was both expanding and undergoing a process of dramatic transformation. Although in retrospect it is clear that during the post-war period Montreal was slowly losing its place as the Canadian metropole, as financial transactions, head offices, and people moved west to Toronto, during the 1960s Montreal remained the most populous and high-profile city in Canada. Montreal mayor Jean Drapeau personified the many contradictions and possibilities of the era. According to historian Paul-André Linteau, Jean Drapeau "presided over the decline of Montreal while giving it the illusion of grandeur."[93] And, while working to give Montreal an international profile, he ruled over the city in an autocratic fashion, remaining insensitive to the many communities disrupted by his drive for urban development.

It had taken three hundred years for Montreal's population to reach a million inhabitants, but only thirty years for the metropolitan region to double in size, achieving a population of just over two million by 1961. The dramatic increase in the population resulted from migration from the countryside to the city, a significant post-war baby boom, and a massive influx of new immigrants, mostly from Europe. Immigrants played an increasingly important role in Montreal society, changing the way in which this society came to see itself. In 1951, only 12% of the city's inhabitants were born outside of the country; this figure had risen to 17% by 1961. At the beginning of the 1960s, 64.2% of the metropolitan region of Montreal was made up of people of French origin and 17.9% of British descent, with Jews and Italians making up the largest minority groups.[94] By 1971, the percentage of residents who were of neither British nor French origin had grown to nearly 25% of the Island of Montreal.[95]

From the years following the Second World War until the late 1960s, the city also experienced significant economic growth. In the 1960s, this growth fuelled dreams of grandeur on the part of city planners and municipal authorities, and massive construction projects, like the building of an extensive metro system and the construction of a site for the 1967 world fair, symbolized this vision of unlimited possibilities. In many ways Expo 67, the most spectacular aspect of the Canadian centennial celebrations, represented, as one author puts it, an "energetic commitment to transnational urban modernism." On one of the very first days after the fair's opening, a staggering 569,500 people visited the site, easily breaking previous records for single-day attendance at such fairs. By the time that the fair had come to a close, over fifty million people had made their way through its exhibits.[96]

The millions of people who visited Expo 67 came from around the world, and most left the city unaware of the seething discontent below the event's pomp and ceremony. Among the various displays stood the Indian Pavilion, a building that portrayed the impact of colonialism on Native populations, provoking a public unused to seeing history through the eyes of the marginalized.[97] And before long, many of the workers who had been responsible for building the fair would form political organizations to attempt to dislodge mayor Jean Drapeau from power, contesting the very modernism that Expo celebrated so triumphantly.

Throughout the 1960s, Montreal was being transformed, as author Hubert Aquin stated in 1963, "at a staggering pace."[98] In the 1960s city planners had forecast that the urban population would reach 4.8 million by 1981, and they built accordingly.[99] Montreal was undergoing an unprecedented period of prosperity, but many felt that this modernization was headed in the wrong direction, and with the interests of only a tiny segment of the population in mind. It is indicative of the tensions opened up by Montreal's expansion that the city's many building sites acted not just as symbols of capitalist modernization, but also as stocks of explosives for the Front de libération du Québec (FLQ).[100]

The changes in the physical and human makeup of the city greatly affected the nature of French-Canadian cultural life. While the countryside acted as the mythical home for earlier generations of French-Canadian nationalists, the new forms of nationalism of the 1960s found their expression in the urban environment. Cities, of course, act not only as empty spaces in which actors operate, but their structures, institutions, and landscapes actively contribute in the production of knowledge, ideas, and culture. Between 1931 and 1961, the number of francophones living in Montreal doubled, and the city's rapid growth made it a venue in which French-speaking artists could both meet one another and reach out to a mass audience. According to one author, these changes created "an *ébullition culturelle*, a surge in cultural activity marked by the launching of new French-language publishing houses and theaters, and a proliferation of French-language literature, theater, music, journalism, and critical analysis that turned Montreal into a city of francophone intellectual excitement and creativity."[101]

In the city's cafés and meeting places, young intellectuals and artists came into contact with one another, collectively shaping new lines of thought. Writing in the literary journal *Liberté* in 1963, Luc Perrier argued that Montreal acted as a common site of meaning; the city's streets and buildings were not important because of their beauty or historic value, he wrote, but because they existed as the physical spaces in which the city's inhabitants interacted, as the locations of friendship and solidarity.[102] And, as cultural alienation and marginalization were grafted onto the urban landscape of Montreal, an important goal of radicals was to transform the city, believing that through it they could transform society as a whole. To achieve their goal, they set out to build a mass movement of political resistance.

TWO

THE ANTECEDENTS

Political activism in Montreal reached new heights in the 1960s, but intellectual and psychological challenges to structures of power had begun much earlier. From the labour radicals, socialists, and anarchists of the late 19th and early 20th centuries to the Communists and social democrats during the 1930s, dissent played an important role in the political life of the city.[1] By the end of the 1950s, many cracks in the ideological structure had begun to widen. Rumblings could be heard in working-class neighbourhoods, where some of Montreal's poorest citizens would organize community-run health and legal clinics in the next decade. Beat culture, jazz, poetry and theatre created an atmosphere of excitement that spilled out from new avant-garde cafés into the city streets. At Le Mas, a third-floor loft on Saint-Dominique Street just above Sherbrooke, young francophone poets, artists, and *chansonniers* began meeting to discuss politics, poetry, music, and art. They interacted with the jazz musicians who played through the night, and two different expressions of rebellion collided.[2] And in the Librairie Tranquille, situated on Sainte-Catherine Street in the heart of downtown, francophone poets, writers, and painters would regularly gather to talk about the state of Quebec society and possibilities for its future.[3]

Despite this bubbling underground energy, an entire generation experienced the 1950s as a time of repression and isolation. In the 1950s many books were still banned, reading Marx in public drew hostile glares[4] and, according to one young intellectual, the "fear of living" was a daily experience.[5] In the late 1950s, poet Gaston Miron would sit for hours at a restaurant on the corner of Montreal's Carré Saint-Louis with the young Pierre Vallières. Depressed about the state of society, they would talk about poetry and decolonization, dreaming of going to France and leaving Montreal behind them. While these two writers – both of whom would help define the new terms of political resistance in the coming decade – dreamed of leaving, a third, Raoul Roy, was busy laying the foundations for a new socialist movement in the province.

Montreal was a complicated place in the 1950s, and Raoul Roy an equally complicated figure. Born in 1914 in the small rural town of Beauceville, Roy grew up on a farm as the oldest of thirteen children. Aside from a grade eight education, Roy was an autodidact, and he jumped from job to job during the 1930s and 1940s, moving to Montreal, then back to his home region, then back to Montreal again. His political trajectory took him from sympathizing with fascism in the 1930s to joining the Communist Party in the 1940s. Roy's reasons for leaving the Communist Party are unclear, but he did so at a moment when the party lost the majority of its French-Canadian members, who had been accused of "nationalist deviations."[6]

Although Roy was the first to promote the idea of socialist decolonization for Quebec, the concept of decolonization had already been circulating for a few years. In 1957, a small group of right-wing nationalists formed the Alliance laurentienne, one of Quebec's first separatist organizations. Through the pages of its journal, *Laurentie*, the group promoted a form of decolonization that hoped to by-pass democracy and consolidate a nationalist Christian social order based on corporatism.[7] A more influential voice was that of André Laurendeau, editor of the province's most prestigious French-language newspaper, *Le Devoir*. In the late 1950s, Laurendeau consistently made use of metaphors comparing Quebec to colonized societies, famously declaring in 1958 that premier Maurice Duplessis was a *"roi nègre,"* ruling Quebec on behalf of foreign colonial interests in a fashion similar to that of African leaders.[8]

Roy's left-wing project differed from those of *Laurentie* and Laurendeau. He saw socialist decolonization as a way that French Canadians could build a new society free from cultural and material alienation. Roy almost single-handedly founded the *Revue socialiste* in 1959; working tirelessly day and night, he wrote nearly all of the articles and produced the journal himself. And in its pages he argued that, being a colonized nation, French Canada needed to look to Algeria and Cuba for inspiration in overcoming imperial domination. A lengthy hundred-point manifesto accompanied the journal's first issue and, while it dealt with everything from secularization to unilingualism, its very first point coloured all the others: "Humanity is divided by two constant and entangled struggles: vertically between subjugated or oppressed peoples and imperialist or expansionist nations, and horizontally between exploited workers and bourgeois or directing classes." Although these two struggles often varied with intensity, the journal argued, they sometimes – as was currently the case with French Canadians – converged into a single battle opposing a proletarian nation and a foreign bourgeoisie.[9]

This was the major innovation of the *Revue socialiste*: it provided a socialist analysis that forcefully argued that French Canadians formed an oppressed and colonized population. The idea of the French-Canadian "ethnic class," despite its lack of nuance in conceptualizing power relations in the province, would achieve prominence among radicals for years to come. In the early 1960s, Roy introduced his idea of socialist decolonization into Quebec's public sphere and, at least partly through his efforts, a nascent left began to emerge. In the smoke-filled backroom of a café that he ran on avenue Christophe Colomb – Le Mouton pendu – Roy would lecture to groups of young followers, some of whom would be among the first members of the Front de liberation du Québec (FLQ) and *Parti Pris*.[10] Roy also offered a book service that sold radical literature such as Frantz Fanon's *The Wretched of the Earth*, and in 1963 he reprinted Albert Memmi's *The Colonizer and the Colonized* for greater distribution in Quebec.[11]

Roy's politics remained contradictory. He argued that socialism would allow Quebec to take full control of its own science and culture, would make the full development of the individual possible, and would usher in a new and better humanism. And he wrote that French-Canadian workers needed to express solidarity with all oppressed groups in North America, including American Blacks and Canadian Natives. Yet, in the same breath, he vehemently denounced immigration and maintained an exclusionary nationalism that did not acknowledge the multi-faceted nature of Montreal itself. As the bourgeoisie promoted immigration to enlarge the labour pool, drive down wages, and assimilate French Canadians, he argued, French Canadians had the right to defend themselves, both as workers and as members of a specific ethnic group. Immigrants were tools of the imperial power and a future independent Quebec would strictly control immigration and issue work permits and identity cards. Rather than declaring solidarity with all members of society, Roy argued that socialists needed to demand the repatriation of those French Canadians who, as a result of high unemployment, were "scattered throughout all of North America."[12] And while younger thinkers were vehemently anti-clerical and demanded the independence of the territory of Quebec, Roy refused to attack Catholicism, and he maintained his desire for the liberation of the ethnically based "French-Canadian people."

Ultimately, the analyses of a younger and more educated generation moved further and further away from Roy's influence. But in its day, while the *Revue socialiste*'s circulation hovered from a few hundred to a little over a thousand,[13] the ideas that it advanced catalyzed the formation of two groups that drastically altered the political and cultural landscape in the 1960s: the FLQ and *Parti Pris*, and had an important impact upon a third, the Rassemblement pour l'indépendance nationale (RIN). Once the RIN became an official party in 1963, it acted as the main political advocate of independence for Quebec. Although it never received more than 10% of the popular vote (in the 1966 provincial election, it received 7% of the vote across the province and 10% in Montreal), the RIN both excited and frustrated those on the left. The RIN could be respected or it could be hated, but it could not be ignored. Formed initially by a group of roughly twenty professionals and intellectuals, the organization quickly acquired the label of "bourgeois nationalist."[14] At first, the RIN steered clear of making statements on any social issues at all, let alone demanding social revolution. The group advocated national independence to the exclusion of any other political ideology, be it the corporatism of the Alliance laurentienne or the socialism of *La Revue socialiste*.[15]

The RIN remained a common front of diverse ideologies, but its discourse moved steadily to the left as the 1960s progressed. It did not take long for a flood of students to join the older and more established members of the group, and the students, along with the Montreal section in general, continuously worked to adopt Marxist analyses and to discard leaders like Marcel Chaput who prioritized national over social liberation.[16] When André d'Allemagne – widely recognized as the party's most influential intellectual[17] – published *Le colonialisme au Québec* (1966), presenting a program of political and economic decolonization, it was clear how far left the RIN had drifted. D'Allemagne argued that "cultural and linguistic survival cannot be separated from economic and political power." And in an independent Quebec, economic and political power would need to be equitably distributed throughout society, not remaining in the hands of a French-Canadian elite. The Quebec government alone had the power to introduce state planning and put an end to economic colonialism, but to do so it would need to extract itself from the British North America Act.[18]

Throughout the 1960s d'Allemagne and the RIN were identified as reformist, yet the line between reformist and radical was continually shifting. The lines separating the left of the RIN and the extra-parliamentary left were so slim that, in the late 1960s, many individuals from *Parti Pris* – the most influential socialist journal of the period – joined the RIN in an attempt to instil in it the idea that sovereignty needed to be achieved through the efforts and in the interests of the working class. Deep tensions resided at the heart of the party, and when the popular nationalist René Lévesque quit the provincial Liberal Party in 1967 to create his own movement, which would soon become the Parti Québécois (PQ), the RIN split apart. The left wing, which had opposed a possible merger with Lévesque's movement, was expelled, and the remaining party dissolved itself and the majority of its members entered the PQ.[19]

If the RIN – with ideas that at times coincided with and at times challenged those of the overtly socialist writers of the liberation movement – represented the reformist wing of Quebec national liberation, the FLQ stood at the opposite end of the spectrum. The founding of the FLQ goes back to clandestine discussions among renegade RIN members in the early 1960s, before being formally established by Raymond Villeneuve, Gabriel Hudon, and Georges Schoeters in February 1963. The FLQ was never formally a party but rather an informal network; throughout the years of its existence, there were many different waves of activists who declared themselves to be fighting in its name. The three founders represented among themselves the diversity of FLQ adherents. While Villeneuve and Hudon were both young (nineteen and twenty-one respectively) and motivated by a combination of socialism and an especially deep-felt nationalism, Schoeters, age thirty-three, was a Belgian-born immigrant to Quebec. He had met Fidel Castro in Montreal in 1959, travelled extensively within Cuba, and drew his motivation from Third World Marxism. Cuban and Algerian flags and pictures of Castro and Che Guevara hung on the walls of his apartment on Côte-des-Neiges Boulevard.[20]

The FLQ first burst onto the political scene when, on 7 March 1963, explosions tore into the icy calm of the Montreal night. On the walls of the targeted army barracks three letters, F.L.Q., were painted in red, announcing the birth of the armed wing of the Quebec liberation movement. In the coming months more barracks would be attacked, and mailboxes in the upper-class and English-speaking neighbourhood of Westmount would be bombed. The 1963 bombings marked the beginning of a seven-year period during which the FLQ would be responsible for a series of such explosions, a period which came to a dramatic end with the kidnapping of British diplomat James Cross and the murder of Quebec cabinet minister Pierre Laporte in October 1970. In response to the kidnappings, the federal government sent the army into Montreal, enacted the War Measures Act, made hundreds of arrests and undertook thousands of searches. While the FLQ had a brief history following the October Crisis, the police and military actions crushed the group so thoroughly that it ceased to exist in any meaningful sense.

Few could honestly argue that Quebec faced the same type of repression as colonial nations in Africa, Latin America, or Asia, and the destructive actions of the FLQ were intensely controversial. Labour leaders consistently denounced the FLQ, as did many writers and activists who insisted on the importance of community organizing, and those who advocated working through the electoral system.[21] The FLQ did, however, represent something of the atmosphere of Sixties Montreal. In its focus on "risking it all," its glamourization of the guerrilla fighter, its belief that dramatic actions could spark a revolution, it is not difficult to see a romantic and masculine conception of politics, one which was fed by both the larger activist movement and portrayals of redemptive violence in some of the literary works of the period.[22]

But even if it at times received the support of other elements on the left, the FLQ was never composed of more than a small minority. There was no shortage of other groups working to develop new terms of opposition with different ideas of political praxis.[23] A literary avant-garde formed around the journal *Liberté* in 1959, for example, and an older generation of academics and trade unionists came together in 1964 to form *Socialisme 64.*[24] And different Quebec student bodies united in 1964 to form the Union générale des étudiants du Québec (UGEQ), a body that became increasingly radical as the years advanced.[25]

■ ■ ■

While the city's cafés and universities overflowed with intellectual and artistic energy, the rumblings of revolt could also be heard in its most disadvantaged neighbourhoods. Saint-Henri and Pointe Saint-Charles, located in the southwest part of the city, were traditionally working-class neighbourhoods, home to a population that was of largely French-Canadian and Irish descent. Throughout much of the twentieth century, workers from these neighbourhoods laboured in the factories that bordered the Lachine Canal, many leaving school to begin factory work at a young age. These neighbourhoods had been home to important labour battles stretching back to the nineteenth century, but by the 1960s the region had been going through a period of deindustrialization and decline. By 1961, four out of ten families in Pointe Saint-Charles were living on social assistance.[26] In Saint-Henri 41.6% of residences were considered to be in need of repair, as were 35.9% of those in the Pointe.[27] The 1960s, elsewhere a time of economic expansion, did not treat these neighbourhoods well. From 1966 to 1974 the rate of people living on social assistance in Pointe Saint-Charles and Saint-Henri tripled, while population numbers themselves declined as many left for greener pastures.[28]

The neighbourhoods were poor, but in the 1960s they were also becoming sites of resistance, and they would eventually inspire grassroots initiatives across the city. At the beginning of the 1960s the Conseil des oeuvres de Montréal began to hire "social animators" to organize the residents of south-western Montreal. Premised on the belief that citizens could be mobilized to resolve problems relating to their daily lives, social animation sought to break down feelings of apathy and isolation, and to build grassroots democracy. In 1963, for example, a group of parents in Saint-Henri got together to demand that a new school be built to replace a dilapidated and dangerous one. Out of the parents' committee came a host of others, organizing popular education courses, fighting unjust zoning laws, and demanding more democratic forms of urban renewal.[29]

The activity in Saint-Henri catalyzed the emergence of similar groups in close-by Pointe Saint-Charles. Before long, the Fédération des mouvements du Sud-Ouest, a group with a more clearly defined ideology, emerged with the intention of coordinating the various neighbourhood movements that were now spreading in all directions.[30] As the decade progressed, a whole array of popular institutions began to emerge. Community activists drew inspiration from Saul Alinsky, and worker-priests in the neighbourhoods invested themselves in the cause of empowering the poor and dispossessed.[31] In Pointe Saint-Charles, citizens began organizing consumer co-ops and collective kitchens, fighting for greater community control over streets and schools, and forming organizations to fight landlords and welfare agents. In Saint-Henri a citizens' bookstore was opened, and citizens began to understand not only the structural roots of poverty but also their own potential to shape the world around them.[32] By the late 1960s, citizens' committees were emerging in the neighbourhoods of Saint-Jacques and Hochelaga-Maisonneuve in east Montreal, as well as elsewhere throughout the city, and citizens began thinking seriously about how to oppose the structures of power that shaped their lives. Soon they would join together with each other as well as with representatives from the labour and student movements, as well as with radicalized intellectuals, to found a municipal political party to challenge Jean Drapeau's hold on municipal power.

In 1960s Montreal, women were generally expected to be responsible for the private sphere, which involved tasks like dealing with landlords and welfare agents, and seeing to the safety of children. As such, activism around these issues generally fell to them. Women formed the majority of those in community groups and citizens' committees; in the process, many became more conscious of the multiple forms of oppression they faced.[33] As a woman of the Hochelaga-Maisonneuve citizens' committee put it, through community activism, power and authority were being demystified and therefore challenged and contested.[34] According to women activists from Pointe Saint-Charles, grassroots politics helped break the isolation of daily life, allowing them to develop skills and to "assert themselves as people and as women."[35]

The organization of citizens' committees in Montreal's poorer neighbourhoods happened at the same time as a radicalization of class in other sectors of society. By the middle of the decade there was a sharp rise in the number of strikes. An average of 67.6 strikes and lockouts per year for the period covering 1961–65 more than doubled to 143 per year for the period from 1966–70.[36] Construction workers brought entire projects to a standstill to demand wage increases, and longshoremen walked out on the Montreal docks over working conditions.[37] At *La Presse*, Montreal's largest newspaper, employees went on strike for seven months in 1964, and other strikes seemed to be constantly breaking out, demonstrating the increasing class militancy of the 1960s that would eventually lead to a wave of militant strikes in the 1970s.

The increasing militancy of the working class also began to be articulated by the leadership of the province's labour movement. Throughout the early 1960s, the movement had been a key player in the Quiet Revolution,[38] but in the coming years labour moved steadily to the left, becoming a staunch critic of successive Quebec governments. CSN president Marcel Pepin announced a decisive shift in the organization's orientation with his "moral report" of 1966, and two years later he launched his famous call to arms, calling on the CSN to open up a second front. Labour activists, he argued, could not restrict their activity to collective bargaining (the "first front"), as too many aspects of workers' lives could not be dealt with within the confines of collective agreements. Price increases, poor housing conditions, exploitation through credit, unemployment and inflation were all problems that called for the opening up of a "second front" in which workers would organize *outside* of the workplace as consumers, renters, and parents.[39] In the late 1960s, the CSN began organizing around housing and living conditions, and it also denounced the Vietnam War as well as imperialism in Quebec. By the late 1960s and early 1970s, radicalization had spread throughout the labour movement as a whole, to the Fédération des travailleurs du Québec (FTQ) as well as to the province's teachers' union. Quebec became, in the words of one labour historian, "the syndicalist centre of direct action in North America."[40]

The 1960s also witnessed the birth of new organizations demanding women's rights. In 1960 some Montreal women, like long-time labour activist Simone Monet-Chartrand, joined the Voice of Women, an organization that denounced nuclear proliferation, advocated greater female participation in politics, and argued that it was up to women, in their roles as mothers and educators, to defend the universal values of justice, love, and liberty.[41] And in 1966 long-time activist, suffragist and social democrat Thérèse Casgrain founded the Fédération des femmes du Québec (FFQ), the first mass-based second-wave feminist organization in the province.[42] In the late 1960s, the women's liberation movement burst onto the political landscape, drawing its energy and inspiration not only from women who came before them but also from the structures of dissent that had been developed by the left since the beginning of the decade.

The politics of people like Thérèse Casgrain had roots that stretched deep into Montreal's past. Although Canada's main social democratic party, the Co-operative Commonwealth Federation, traditionally appealed more to anglophones than to francophones, throughout the 1950s many French Canadians played important roles in the Quebec wing of the party. Poet

Gaston Miron and labour organizer Michel Chartrand ran as CCF candidates. Yet when the New Democratic Party was founded as the CCF's successor in 1961, it did not take long for factional debates among the party's Quebec wing to split the party in two, creating the Parti socialiste du Québec, which had a short and marginal existence.[43]

To a greater degree than the NDP, the world of activists opposing nuclear arms sparked the imaginations of young English-speaking radicals. In the late 1950s and early 1960s, a number of anti-nuclear groups emerged, some new and some having roots in communist and socialist parties.[44] The influence of the Campaign for Nuclear Disarmament, formed in Britain in the late 1950s, quickly spread to Canada through the influence of Dimitri Roussopoulos, who returned from studying in England in 1959 to become one of the leading activists in the city.[45] In the fall of 1961, Roussopoulos and his colleagues in the Combined Universities Campaign for Nuclear Disarmament founded *Our Generation Against Nuclear War*, a journal that attempted to challenge the militarist culture that, they argued, was leading the world towards nuclear annihilation.

This group not only used the journal to provide "alternative solutions to human conflict, eliminating war as a way of life,"[46] it also engaged in non-violent protests and brought international activists and intellectuals to the city. In May 1963, a group of American pacifists organized a Quebec-Washington-Guantanamo Walk for Peace "to oppose nuclear weapons testing, nuclear missiles, racial discrimination, and the Cuba travel ban/trade embargo, and bring Canadian and US peace activists into closer cooperation." As the group walked from Quebec City to Montreal, its members were harassed and even arrested. Once they arrived in Montreal, they worked with local peace groups and stayed at the home of Michel Chartrand, a veteran labour organizer and printer who would become one of the most outspoken radical leaders of the late 1960s. He provided meals and accommodations for the marchers, and printed their material.[47]

Montreal's anglophone peace activists not only engaged with their counterparts in Britain and the United States; they also increasingly came to reflect upon their own existence as anglophones in Quebec.[48] Frequenting cafés and reading radical francophone literature, English-speaking activists became influenced by the intellectual and political events taking place all around them. Anti-nuclear activists joined with francophone groups to protest at La Macaza Air Force base in 1964, and in 1968 the anti-nuclear radicals joined with UGEQ to organize a massive rally to simultaneously support the American Civil Rights movement and denounce the Vietnam War. *Our Generation Against Nuclear War* increasingly became an important site of translation, a place where English-speaking radicals at home and abroad could learn of developments taking place in Quebec. In 1966, the journal announced a major change in orientation, dropping its subtitle "*against nuclear war*" to become *Our Generation*. The editors wrote that they intended "to concentrate more substantially on the total implications of pursuing peace *and* freedom."[49] In its very next edition, the journal declared in an editorial that the social developments in Quebec were going to become "a permanent feature of the journal." Revealing a debt to French-language publications, *Our Generation* argued that from "the vantage point of an English-language journal in the heart of Québec," it was clear that "a realistic policy on Québec is integral to the programme of the *new radicals* in Canada." This policy was as important as a "correct policy towards the demand of the Negro people for their human rights in the US is for the new left there."[50]

The journal stopped short of advocating separatism, but events in Montreal were clearly having a profound effect on its ideology. From 1966 onwards, the journal began publishing translations of the works of French-speaking academics,[51] publishing in-depth analyses of Quebec society,[52] and covering the developments of other social movements in the province.[53] Through their interactions with other individuals and organizations in Montreal, the writers and activists of *Our Generation* began sharpening their anti-imperialist and anti-colonial analyses. In a 1967 reversal of the position that it had defended in the early years of the decade, the editors argued that the major task facing them had become "the fight against continentalism in Canada as well as colonialism in Québec."[54]

Intellectual ferment was not only expressed in the city's new radical journals; it also took shape in avant-garde cafés where young intellectuals could feel themselves escaping a world of stifling conformity.[55] The Swiss Hut and the Asociación Española, situated on Sherbrooke Street close to Bleury, were frequented by those involved in many of Montreal's various oppositional currents, both anglophone and francophone, anarchist and communist, social democratic and revolutionary. For francophone radicals who had been confined to the eastern part of the city, going to these places represented a symbolic burst westward, bringing them into contact with a whole new array of people. The Asociación Española, with its red-and-white tablecloths and lively flamenco performances, was a favourite club of

Spanish immigrants, including some Spanish anarchists who had come to Montreal in the aftermath of the Spanish Civil War.[56]

By the middle of the 1960s, a group of Haitian poets began meeting on Monday evenings at the Perchoir d'Haïti, a Haitian restaurant on Metcalfe Street. The restaurant had also become something of a meeting-place for bohemian Montrealers, and well-known poets like Gaston Miron and Paul Chamberland began attending the Monday events. Poetry readings became moments of interaction between Haitian poets and their local counterparts. Haitian poets learned of a nascent world of radical Quebec poetry and Quebecois artists were introduced to the poetry of the francophone Caribbean, including that of Aimé Césaire and René Depestre.[57]

Pouring into the cafés, universities, and meeting places were individuals from the city's many leftist organizations, each informed by distinct reading lists, theoretical orientations, and publications. English-speaking activists rubbed shoulders with francophone advocates of national liberation. Refugees from the Spanish Civil War interacted with Latin American and Caribbean immigrants. In the early 1960s, the various poles of dissent remained largely separate from one another. As the Sixties progressed, however, as I will argue throughout this book, they generally moved in similar directions, and the various movements increasingly came to be intertwined. Hovering over all of the conversations of leftists throughout the city was Montreal's relationship to empire. And in developing the terms of anti-colonial and anti-imperial ideology, one political grouping played a role like no other.

PARTI PRIS

Of all the groups and individuals working to define the project of Quebec decolonization, *Parti Pris* would have the greatest impact on the formation of a larger language of dissent. The idea of founding the journal emerged out of the discussions of a small group of young Montrealers. Jean-Marc Piotte and André Major met growing up on the rough streets of east Montreal, and the two talked for hours about philosophy and literature, poetry and politics. At the beginning of May 1963, Piotte moved out of his family home into an apartment in the east-end with Major and another friend, André Brochu. Paul Chamberland, who studied philosophy with Piotte, lived across the street. Frustrated with the state of Quebec society, the iconoclastic authors – after seeking out the help of another young writer, Pierre Maheu – set out to publish a journal that would combine culture and politics. They felt that they were experiencing a profound rupture with a static French-Canadian past.[58]

For the writers of *Parti Pris*, who considered themselves to be the voice of a new generation, the Catholic Church was one of the primary mechanisms through which the colonial power maintained control over the local population. As Paul Chamberland explained, the "theory of socialist decolonization necessarily implies an end to clericalism, because as a system of exploitation clericalism is an integral part of Quebec's colonial structures, and this is true from no matter what angle we examine it, be it economic, political, social or ideological."[59] Clericalism was seen as a profoundly conservative force preventing the French-Canadian population from creating its own future.[60]

It would be wrong, however, to conflate *Parti Pris*'s deep anti-clericalism with a rejection of religion by the left in general. As I discussed earlier, left Catholicism, including that emanating from Latin America, played an important role in the development of dissident culture in Quebec throughout the 1960s.[61] Much of the organizing which took place in poor communities in Montreal was initiated by religious groups,[62] and many of those who became activists in the 1960s had deeply religious backgrounds: Pierre Vallières and Michel Chartrand, two of the most prominent leftists of the entire period, had each at one point joined religious orders.[63] Nonetheless, *Parti Pris*'s attacks on the religious structures of Quebec society were unrelenting.

As students who had just arrived in university when the provincial Liberals came to power in 1960, and when major changes in Quebec's institutional structures were beginning to take place, the authors of *Parti Pris* lived with the confidence of youth, believing that they could influence all aspects of life.[64] The writers came from different backgrounds – some from the working-class streets of east Montreal, others from the bourgeois neighbourhood of Outremont – but they were all convinced that they could transform social structures. They even saw themselves (wrongly) as the first generation of socialist intellectuals in Quebec, declaring with typical bravado: "If a few socialist political parties have existed in Quebec's past, there have never been any socialist thinkers."[65] Such professions of rupture always conceal as much as they illuminate. While the writers of *Parti*

Pris worked to imagine new forms of democracy for the province, they relied nonetheless on the intellectual structures of the world in which they lived.[66] The writers, for example, emerged out of a patriarchal society that systematically minimized and devalued women's roles as political actors, and in many ways they reproduced these structures within their own organizations and texts.

Although women's lives were changing, mainstream Quebec culture continued to idealize wives and mothers, portraying the home as a woman's proper sphere of activity. It was not until well into the 1960s that the province's labour unions abandoned their rhetoric of the "natural order" that relegated women to the home,[67] and it was not until 1964 that married women achieved the right to act in a legal capacity independently of their husbands.[68]

For all of its revolutionary rhetoric, *Parti Pris* formed a part of this gendered world. In the very first issue of *Parti Pris*, Pierre Maheu argued that liberation was necessary so that Quebeckers could become "men" and positively assume their liberty.[69] And through the journal's intellectual work, Maheu argued, it would be possible to create the conditions that would permit the establishment of "authentic relations between men."[70] Maheu's use of such highly gendered metaphors not only excluded women from any active role in the movement, but also portrayed them as inactive figures upon which male liberation would depend.[71] Throughout its existence, the journal published only twelve short articles by women,[72] and its authors consistently imagined the nation as a brotherhood or fraternity. Despite the humanistic desire to deconstruct systems of domination, to empower the marginalized and forge a new ethic of human solidarity, the left's language of democratic participation therefore remained profoundly circumscribed.

Parti Pris had many shortcomings, but it did embody the atmosphere of revolt and impatience felt by many young people. It is a testament to the journal's importance that many of the women who would go on to form the women's liberation movement were introduced to radical politics through the journal, and in the meetings and courses it offered. Nicole Thérien, for example, recalls first learning about history, economics, and politics through *Parti Pris*'s public meetings. Compared to her early religious education, she considered that *Parti Pris* acted, along with the labour movement, as her first real school.[73] It was at least partly out of the analyses of *Parti Pris,* and the frustration engendered by its exclusion of women, that Montreal's specific manifestation of feminism would become both possible and necessary.

Parti Pris emerged from the historical conditions of the early 1960s, and, through its activities and intellectual work, it played a central role in creating a new language of resistance.[74] The journal was an immediate success, and its editors were catapulted overnight from obscurity to relative fame.[75] A whole generation of activists would come of age reading the journal and attending the meetings it organized.[76] As Pierre Maheu would write many years later, the success of *Parti Pris* was due in part to an intellectual climate that was "ripe for the expression of these ideas."[77] After only three months, the journal counted 500 subscribers and a circulation of 3,500.[78] Nine months later, the journal's subscribers had grown to 800 and the print-run to 4,000, sizeable enough to be a major influence upon intellectual circles.[79] The writers and artists of *Parti Pris,* by working both to analyse the cultural deprivation of colonialism and to actively create a new culture, tapped into a sentiment of unrest, one which until that point had not been fused with the revolutionary aspirations of youth.[80] The writers of *Parti Pris* therefore challenged not only conservative French-Canadian nationalism, but also *Cité libre* and the dissident liberal intelligentsia that came before them.[81]

The journal saw its task as one of helping the budding revolutionary class to achieve self-consciousness, and it forged a vocabulary in which the particular experience of French-speaking Quebeckers could be understood. Readers encountered new words and ideas in its pages: Quebeckers were *alienated* and *dehumanized,* and the role of the intellectual was to *demystify* and create an *authentic* culture of resistance, one in which the colonized would become the active subjects in the creation of the future. A desire for liberation, in the widest possible sense, acted as the central motivating drive of *Parti Pris,* and to achieve liberation it was first necessary to overcome alienation. Perhaps *Parti Pris*'s greatest importance was its insistence that French-Canadian alienation was the material and psychological consequence of colonialism. Because of colonization, the journal argued, francophone Quebeckers were alienated on a political, economic, and cultural level.[82]

Parti Pris's political project revolved around three interrelated demands: secularization, independence, and socialism. Although two factions would eventually form within the journal – one advocating a tactical alliance with the bourgeoisie to achieve independence before moving on to socialism, and the other maintaining that socialism and independence needed to come about at the same time – everyone agreed that independence for its own sake, unaccompanied by social revolution, would lead nowhere. Quebec's political independence had to form part of a comprehensive transformation that would affect all spheres of life, from poetry and literature to cinema and sexuality. *Parti Pris* therefore did not only contain discussions of politics and philosophy: the journal printed creative works alongside discussions of political strategy and analysis. Literature, and culture generally, were deeply constitutive of this leftism, and were central to the new world of freedom and creativity that needed to be built.[83]

For this reason, *Parti Pris* both reflected and formed an important part of a cultural efflorescence. Throughout the decade, Quebec's filmmakers and novelists, playwrights and poets, went through a cultural renaissance. Michel Tremblay brought the experiences and language of working-class women to the stage with his play *Les Belles-soeurs*, shocking Montreal's theatre world when it was produced at the Théâtre du Rideau Vert in 1968. And at the National Film Board, which moved its technical installations to Montreal in 1956, an iconoclastic "Équipe française" took shape and began – in defiance of the management of the board – to experiment with form and content.[84] Filmmakers opposed the very criteria being defended by the NFB management, challenging the standards of the organization and denouncing the superficial nature of the society in which they lived.[85] All of this cultural excitement found its way into the journal's pages.

Within its first year of existence, *Parti Pris* had expanded to become a publishing house and, shortly afterwards, a political movement. Les Éditions Parti Pris published literary works and essays as well as working documents for the revolution: tracts for political education, personal accounts, studies of various aspects of political life, and sociological and economic analyses of Quebec society.[86] To portray the harsh reality of poverty and cultural degradation in the province, it published works written in *joual*, the urban slang French of east Montreal, and sought to build a literature of struggle.[87] A whole new generation of literary figures felt that writing in *joual* allowed them to express their anger and frustration while, as Sherry Simon points out, turning a "negative condition into one full of hope." Novels such as Jacques Renaud's *Le Cassé* and the poetry published in issues of *Parti Pris* caused a sensation, turning urban slang into a weapon of liberation.[88] Gérald Godin, one of the most ardent defenders of the use of *joual* in literature, wrote that Quebec writers needed to refuse to use proper French, which would merely gloss over the decayed language of the people. It was better to be proud of a mistake, he argued, than humiliated by a truth.[89]

Through the journal, the group hoped to demystify Quebec's ideological structures: "our critical work will tear apart established myths, we will attempt to destroy, by discovering their inner contradictions, official rules and morals, in order to make possible the establishment of authentic relations between men."[90] And through its numerous public meetings, reading groups, discussions, and street protests, the editors hoped to foster an ongoing dialogue between readers and writers. The journal encouraged readers to see the publication as their own, and the relationship between theory and praxis pointed in both directions. *Parti Pris*'s first manifesto, published in September 1964, summarized the history of the emergent left and came to the conclusion that its various organizations were plagued by the same problem: "we are fascinated by and enthusiastic about the idea of revolution because we feel a real necessity for it, but we don't have the concrete means to achieve it and, up to this point, we have not worked seriously to acquire them." The journal therefore argued that it would need to work towards the creation of a revolutionary party,[91] and, with this in mind, it acquired an office space on Bellechasse Street in the francophone working-class neighbourhood of Rosemont. The journal's editors hoped that the space would become the location of an emerging revolutionary network: a place where they could organize public forums and assemblies, and hold meetings of *Parti Pris*'s new political club.[92] And by the mid-1960s, they had begun laying the groundwork for what would become the first serious attempt to build a revolutionary party, the Mouvement de libération populaire (MLP).

The MLP was the result of the convergence of the Groupe d'action populaire and the Trotskyist Ligue ouvrière socialiste with the Club Parti Pris and the activists that circulated around *Révolution québécoise*, a journal founded in 1964 by Pierre Vallières and Charles Gagnon. Vallières, a twenty-six-year-old journalist who had been born into a working-class family in east Montreal, had spent most of his youth in the muddy streets of the suburb of Jacques Cartier. Gagnon, for his part, was a twenty-five-year-old teacher who had moved to the city in 1960 from Le Bic. The two writers, who met while working with the liberal political journal *Cité libre* in the early 1960s, shared the goal of ameliorating the cultural and material degradation that surrounded them. In 1965, after Vallières had been fired from his editorial position at *Cité libre*, he, along with Gagnon and a few others, founded *Révolution québécoise*, a political journal which placed the struggle for independence more firmly within a Marxist framework, and which challenged *Parti Pris* from the left. Through their analyses in *Révolution québécoise*, Vallières and Gagnon resituated ideas of Quebec decolonization by placing an overwhelming emphasis on American economic imperialism, a move that would have important consequences for the development of the movement as a whole.

The MLP's manifesto, published in the September 1965 edition of *Parti Pris*, laid the foundation for dissident politics in the province for years to come. The document provided nuance and depth to earlier and more simplistic formulations of decolonization. It rejected, for example, the idea that francophone Quebeckers formed an ethnic class: "Between the resident of Outremont and that of Saint-Henri, even if both are ethnically francophone Quebeckers, there are still differences of which each is well-aware."[93] And the manifesto not only outlined the changes in class structure as a result of the Quiet Revolution, it also grappled with Quebec's unique situation of being an industrialized colony. Because Quebec's economy was controlled by English-Canadian and American capital, the province was an underdeveloped region of North America. American interests were imposed through the intermediary of the government in Ottawa and, although participating to a certain degree in North American prosperity, Quebec workers were exploited as consumers, excluded from political and economic power, and culturally degraded. If the Quiet Revolution witnessed the rise of a new bourgeoisie in Quebec, the manifesto argued, independence would now need to be won not through a tactical alliance with this bourgeoisie, but through the efforts of the working class.[94]

The MLP offices were situated on Carré Saint-Louis in the centre of Montreal. The organization planned to support workers' struggles and hoped to implant itself in working-class neighbourhoods.[95] Yet just as the MLP seemed to be getting off the ground, attracting a couple of hundred members, it broke apart into differing factions. Vallières, the movement's only full-time employee, was partly responsible for its demise: while working for the organization he had also begun clandestinely forming the basis of a new version of the FLQ.[96] A few members followed him, while others either joined the RIN in the hope of pulling the party further to the left, or turned to the Parti socialiste du Québec, which would soon no longer exist.[97] Although the attempt to form one unified party advocating Quebec decolonization had failed, the analysis of society put forth and popularized by the MLP manifesto would shape political movements in Quebec until at least the end of the decade.

■ ■ ■

Throughout the 1960s, debates raged about whether Quebec needed to achieve independence before proceeding to build socialism, or whether independence and socialism could be achieved through the same process. Some felt that a short-term tactical alliance with the French-Canadian bourgeoisie could spur the movement, while others felt that any such alliance would compromise the entire project. Activists were divided on whether it was necessary to build a party – and once again split as to whether the party should be Leninist or social democratic – or whether the masses needed to take control of all social institutions. Yet, despite these long-standing arguments, francophone intellectuals in Montreal had much in common, and they all agreed that they were living in a colony and that Quebeckers needed to develop an autonomous voice of resistance.

One overriding concern informed the project: the demand to become the active subjects rather than the passive objects of history. In the late 1950s, Albert Memmi had argued that one of the most devastating effects of colonization was the removal of the colonized from history, the stripping of their ability to play "any free role in either war or peace," and the denial of "all cultural and social responsibility."[98] For the colonized, "[p]lanning and building his future are forbidden."[99] In the 1960s, people the world over were asserting their right to be the active creators of the world in which they lived. This struggle was not conceived of as an attempt to go back to a previous age of glory before colonization or to turn back the forces of modernity. Rather, activists and intellectuals worked to construct a *counter-modernity*, an alternative society in which citizens would be able to control the forces that shaped their lives.

Authors began arguing that citizens needed to rise up and take control of the city in which they were living. When discussing Montreal, Luc Perrier argued that is was "up to us to impose our tastes, our preferences, and our personality." And it was up to the city's citizens to transform it, to reorient it, and to humanize it.[100] Yves Préfontaine wrote that "I think that we can, that we have to reinvent the city."[101] And this drive for control spread outwards to society as a whole. Since the Conquest of 1759, André d'Allemagne maintained, French Canadians had stopped being subjects of their own history. But now things had changed: "the colonized were no longer demanding favours but, rather, responsibility and therefore power." Once Quebec had been liberated from the oppression of colonialism, it would become "a blank page upon which everything is yet to be – and on which everything can be – written."[102] Charles Gagnon wrote in 1966 that the time when French-speaking Quebeckers would ask others to take care of them was over; from now on, he argued, it would be up to them to take care of themselves.[103]

In the pages of *Parti Pris* Paul Chamberland wrote one of the most articulate statements of the existential responsibility and drive of the colonized:

> decolonization has never been a movement based upon reason:
> it is the result of a decision, which is at first unsubstantiated and
> then becomes justified through analysis. ... [The person who makes
> history] makes it in opposition to the supposedly objective common
> sense, which actually is only the falsely universal truths and values
> of the oppressor. The person who makes history – the proletarian,
> the Black, the Algerian, the South American – only believes the truth
> inherent to his own project: he actively perceives, as if contained
> within his very being, the new possibilities heralding the dislocation
> and rearrangement of current realities. It is he who becomes the
> active force, the centre and heart of history. This force overcomes
> all intellectual understandings of power relationships.[104]

Chamberland was not alone in articulating existentialist ideals. Pierre Vallières was also discovering that truth and freedom did not stand "outside our history, outside our past, present, and future." "I was coming to understand," he continued, "that they are born, live, and die with us; that we affirm their reality and power through action, through practice, through continual transformation of the world." To decide to live was to agree to "take responsibility for a collective history that is being made and at the same time always remains to be made, that is ceaselessly made, unmade, and remade, according to our knowledge and abilities, to our struggles, passions, hopes, interests, needs, and choices." Society therefore needed to be organized in such a way that it would enhance freedom, and for this to happen workers would need to gain control over "economic and social policy."[105] The future would be open, everything could be created, and history could be written anew.

And yet, despite the desire to deconstruct systems of domination, to empower the marginalized and forge a new ethic of human solidarity, until the late 1960s the movement, in all of its various manifestations, remained remarkably silent on one crucially important issue. Francophone Quebeckers were themselves the descendents of Europeans who had pushed Aboriginals to the margins of society and relegated them to subordinate status. Therefore the natural starting point for anti-colonial analysis in the province, one would have thought, would have been a critical reflection upon Quebec's *own* process of colonization.

Yet Aboriginals are, with a few rare exceptions, almost completely absent from the early writing about Quebec decolonization. In order to imagine themselves as the indigenous population, Quebec liberationists needed to ignore the existence, both past and present, of Aboriginal communities in the province.[106] True, some radical activists evoked romantic visions of Natives.[107] André Major claimed Indian ancestry,[108] and Raoul Roy felt that francophone Quebeckers were legitimate Natives because of the *métissage* in the colony's past.[109] But in nearly all historical portraits, the perspectives and existence of Native communities were systematically ignored. Pierre Vallières barely mentions Natives in his analysis of Quebec history, and when they do appear, they are divorced from any relation to the present.[110] The absence of Natives in the imagination of the theorists of decolonization was so complete that Jacques Godbout could joke at the thought that Quebeckers could themselves possibly be thought of as exploiters: "of whom?" he asked, "the Eskimos?"[111] Throughout the early to mid-1960s, virtually all of Montreal's radical francophone writers, reading their society through the lens of an anti-colonial theory that highlighted the Manichean nature of empire, internalized these divisions while ignoring the possibility that the Aboriginal populations in Quebec could have their *own* claims of colonization, their own grievances, and would eventually develop their own terms of resistance.[112]

The language of decolonization therefore simultaneously opened up new possibilities and reinforced existing structures of thought. When many different groups began emerging in the late 1960s – women's liberationists and racial minorities locally, and Aboriginal groups across the continent – radical francophone theorists would be forced to re-examine their previously held conceptions of themselves and their movement. Unlike earlier radical portrayals of Quebec history, Léandre Bergeron's 1970 *Petit manuel d'histoire du Québec* explores the complexities and multi-layered nature of colonization in Quebec, and he discusses the marginalization of Native populations in the province's past. And unlike his own *Nègres blancs d'Amérique*, Vallières's 1971 *L'urgence de choisir* discusses, albeit briefly, women and women's liberation as well as the exploitation of Aboriginal peoples. But in the early to mid 1960s, these openings had not yet appeared.

By the late 1960s and early 1970s, social forces demanding greater democratization of social structures – that now included many new segments of the population – were propelled by an unparalleled momentum. Some saw this activity as the result of the anxieties of youth, or as the predictable consequence of increased social permissiveness. Others, pointing to the growing wave of international dissent, blamed foreign agitators. In reality, the growing unrest in Montreal was the result of a local movement that had begun years earlier. But this movement grew not only out of local conditions and circumstances; it was also forged with a deep knowledge of political, intellectual, and social developments around the world, and through an engagement with a transnational language of dissent.

THREE

THE INTERNATIONAL DIMENSION
OF RESISTANCE

If the ebullient cafés of Montreal provided the setting in which ideas of decolonization were forged, it was on the scale of the world that they were dreamed. Throughout the 1960s, international literature filled the shelves of Montreal bookstores and the private homes of individuals, and scores of visitors – including many of the most important political theorists of the era – passed through the city, exchanging insights and inspiration.[1] Groups and individuals on the left sent copies of their material to like-minded organizations around the world, from Havana to Buenos Aires to Berkeley.[2] Hubert Aquin travelled to Africa and then to Europe to do research and meet with many of the leaders of African decolonization,[3] while other activists travelled to Latin America, France and the United States. The very foundation of decolonization rested on a reading of the local situation through the lens of international movements, giving individuals the belief that they were part of a movement of world-wide dimensions.

Many Quebeckers argued that their ultimate goals and objectives could not remain limited to cultural affirmation, but that they needed to proceed through national liberation to achieve a general emancipation of humanity. Always aware that people in other oppressed countries were engaged in similar struggles,[4] activists of the 1960s believed that internationalism could best be achieved through the development of a national consciousness. Writers regularly argued that the development of a "national self" would lay the groundwork upon which Quebeckers could move on to "universalization,"[5] and that the "struggle for national liberation" signified the end of their current isolation.[6] It was *through* national liberation, the argument went, that activists in the province could play a role in the creation of a truly global movement.

Internationalism was therefore not merely one aspect of a larger ideology, but stood at the very core of the political project. Activists and writers worked to expand the geographical frame of reference within which Quebec's politics were generally understood; rather than seeing the plight of francophone Quebeckers as an internal problem that could be solved by appealing to local leaders for redress, they endeavoured to take their grievances to the world stage.[7] Looking closely at the response to the Algerian war in Quebec newspapers and journals, Magali Deleuze demonstrates that an international awareness existed in Quebec before the 1960s.[8] And Daniel Gay has argued that throughout the 1950s and 1960s, political and economic figures looked not only to France, but also to Latin America, where with a mixture of solidarity and condescension they sought to expand their own economic and political interests.[9] What was new about the anti-colonial movement during the 1960s was not being *influenced by* international events, but believing oneself to be *part of* a global struggle of resistance, one that had its origins and found its most dramatic expression in Cuba and the political struggles of American Blacks. But before going on to look at the influence of these two different sites of engagement, it is necessary to examine the complicated relationship that Montreal writers and activists maintained with France.

THE PROMISES AND PITFALLS OF THE FRENCH

In the turbulent aftermath of the Second World War, France, despite its unstable governments, was an important cultural centre. Tremendous creativity existed alongside the dislocation caused by the breaking up of the country's colonial empire, a disintegration that had its most painful expression in the drawn-out violence of the Algerian War. The bitter experience of the Algerian War tore French society apart at the seams.[10] Intellectuals in Montreal kept a close watch on these developments, and Algerian decolonization became an important influence on young radicals.[11] Although all of France, including those on the left, appeared to have their hands bloodied by the bitter fighting, a small but influential group of French intellectuals began speaking out openly in defence of Algeria's right to self-deter-mination. Of these intellectuals, few influenced Montrealers more than Jean-Paul Sartre and Simone de Beauvoir, especially through *Les Temps modernes*, the publication with which the two philosophers were intimately associated. Because Paris acted simultaneously as an intellectual capital and a site of resistance, it was irresistible for young Montrealers. And so they travelled in significant numbers to Paris to study and take part in French intellectual life. Their pilgrimage highlights the ambiguity of Quebec's political positioning; although it was conceptualized as a colony of either English Canada or the United States, in many ways it was Paris that acted as its imperial metropole.

One of the most important cultural figures in 1960s Paris was writer, translator, and publisher François Maspero. Maspero opened a bookstore in Paris's Latin Quarter in the mid-1950s, and a few years later he founded Les Éditions Maspero, a publishing house with a list that would come to include Frantz Fanon and French-language translations of Amílcar Cabral, Che Guevara, and Malcolm X. Les Éditions Maspero, publishing books that were distributed and read around the globe, remained an indispensa-ble resource for the French-speaking world, significantly expanding the range of anti-imperialist writers available in French. As Kristin Ross explains, in "these years dominated by the decomposition of the European empires, Maspero's bookstore and press took up the task of representing the image of an exploded world where Europe is no longer the center."[12] In the book-store one would find, side-by-side, books of theory and personal testimo-nials, the poetic and the political.[13] For Montreal radicals, Maspero's publishing house was a crucial conduit between their own movement and other decolonization struggles, and it became the natural choice when they began searching for a publisher for their own works. Maspero published *Les Québécois* – a book of *Parti Pris* articles – and the French edition of Pierre Vallières's explosive 1968 *Nègres blancs d'Amérique*, thereby making the works of the Quebec liberation movement widely available to the French-speaking world. From 1956 to 1975, Maspero also maintained his book-store, "La Joie de Lire," situated on rue Saint Severin. At the lively and crowded store, the various factions of the French left would meet with individuals from all parts of the world, sometimes even using the space as a refuge from police clubs during protests.[14] Young Quebeckers studying or travelling in France came to the store to exchange ideas.

Anti-imperialist French intellectuals also travelled to Montreal, both to teach and to learn from the local situation in the city. In 1962 Jacques Berque, Islamic scholar, professor at the Collège de France, and well-known decolonization theorist, accepted an invitation from the Department of Anthropology of the Université de Montréal. While there, Berque took a keen interest in intellectual and political currents in the city. He became friends with the poet Gaston Miron.[15] And to the great pleasure of Montreal activists, Berque published a major article in the anti-imperialist *France Observateur* on "Les révoltés du Québec."[16] Because of the ambiguity that surrounded the province's status as a colony, international legitimacy was both incredibly valued and hard to attain, and Berque's endorsement lent much-needed academic prestige to the framework outlined by Montreal radicals.

Yet, despite Berque's approving articles and the important relationship between François Maspero and Montreal writers, the relationship that Montreal radicals had with France remained fraught with tension. While certain prominent French radicals were sympathetic to Quebec liberation, most of the French left was more skeptical, denouncing the movement for its nationalism and refusing to see its legitimacy.[17] This compounded the many negative experiences that francophone Quebeckers had when travelling to France, where their high expectations were met with bitter disappointment. Pierre Vallières described his three months in Paris as "a veritable hell."[18] Vallières admitted that he did learn a great deal in France – he met North Africans who influenced his thinking[19] and, by working with Italian and Spanish labourers, he learned about the daily humiliation of manual labour[20] – but not through his interactions with the French left. Jean-Marc Piotte, for his part, found that Quebeckers were not well liked by Parisians, who treated them as if they were worthless.[21] After having lived for a year in Paris, he moved to London, ironically finding himself far more at home among the English than he ever had among the French.[22]

The troubled relationship between radicals in Montreal and those in France would be plainly visible on the occasion of French president Charles de Gaulle's visit to Canada in 1967. On 24 July, de Gaulle stood before a cheering crowd on the balcony of Montreal's City Hall. After delivering a speech about the energy, enthusiasm, and atmosphere of excitement that reigned throughout the province, he responded to the cheering of the crowd by dramatically declaring, "Vive le Québec libre." The exact meaning of de Gaulle's words remains obscure, but they were clear enough to infuriate federal officials in Ottawa. In Montreal, however, many people were ecstatic, hearing what they wanted to hear – a ringing endorsement of Quebec liberation (rather than recognizing the limited form of independence de Gaulle surely had in mind).[23] For Gilles Bourque, the speech represented a crucially important act in the process of decolonization; de Gaulle "illuminated Quebec," placing it in the international arena and revealing it to itself, forcing everyone to take a position on its future.[24] Pierre Renaud and Robert Tremblay argued that, with de Gaulle's speech, "the struggle for Quebec liberty is known around the world."[25] *Parti Pris* even printed a portrait of de Gaulle on its front cover and, declaring ambiguously that "France and Quebec share a common destiny," dedicated the issue to the journal's French comrades.[26]

De Gaulle's enthusiastic reception served to underscore the lines of demarcation between the French left and that in Quebec. Although associated with right-wing and anti-democratic politics in France, de Gaulle's speech made him a hero for Montreal dissidents, and they became increasingly frustrated with many French leftists' refusal to recognize the importance of Quebec independence. Gilles Bourque wrote that the "French left is for the Quebec left what the USSR is for South American guerrillas: a force of inertia."[27] Vallières felt that the problem resided in the fact that the "French left imagined that de Gaulle had himself initiated the national liberation struggle in Quebec, without even taking the time to consider the fact that if de Gaulle had cried 'Vive le Québec libre,' and if his words had such a resonance, it was because a national liberation movement had already existed – even if people outside of Quebec had not yet begun to talk about it."[28] Montreal radicals had hoped that the French left would help to propel their movement to the international arena, but they were left disillusioned. Although briefly excited by the events in Paris of May–June 1968, ultimately they looked elsewhere for inspiration.

CUBA, ANTI-IMPERIALISM, AND THE DREAM OF THE THIRD WORLD

For those in search of an alternative model of development in the 1960s, Cuba became a beacon of hope, demonstrating that even small nations could triumph over the seemingly invincible power of imperialism. No event since the Russian revolution of 1917 had so transformed the political climate and inspired the hopes of leftists around the world as the Cuban revolution. Images and ideas emanating from Cuba reverberated from Mexico City to Paris, and from Harlem to Montreal.

The Cuban revolution can be said to have begun when, on 26 July 1953, a year after president Fulgencio Batista had returned to power by way of a coup d'État, a group of rebels led by Fidel Castro launched an attack on the Moncada fortress just outside of Santiago de Cuba. In 1953, Castro was a twenty-six-year-old lawyer, well-known in his student days as a great orator and athlete, a man born into a wealthy family who, upon first glance, seemed to have the background and training to engage in a conventional career as a member of Cuba's ruling class. When Batista's coup upset his hope of running for election under the banner of the Ortodoxo party, he organized a group of rebels to overthrow the government. The attack failed, many of the rebels were executed, and Castro himself was sentenced to fifteen years in prison on the Island of Pines. After being released as a goodwill gesture by Batista in May of 1955, Castro fled to Mexico where, along with comrades including the Argentinean Ernesto "Che" Guevara, he began making plans to return to the island to lead an armed insurrection. And when they finally did return, in December of 1956, they waged a guerrilla campaign in the Sierra Maestra mountains in the eastern part of Cuba. Despite countless setbacks, the movement gathered momentum over the next two years. By New Year's Day 1959, Batista had fled, the army had been defeated and, shortly afterwards, crowds filled the streets of Havana to celebrate the end of Batista's rule and the arrival of the new revolutionary regime.

Images of Cuba's bearded rebels, portrayed as fighting a heroic battle against tyranny and injustice, circulated around the world.[29] Yet when the rebels came to power in 1959 their social and economic program was, at best, unclear. Castro had declared humanism the guiding principle of the revolution, and he immediately set out to initiate a vast program of land reform. The program expropriated large estates and turned roughly 40% of the island's farmland into individual plots for Cuba's landless peasants.[30] Although the revolution enjoyed wide popular support at home, it was raising eyebrows abroad. The United States government became increasingly disenchanted with Castro, and Castro, in response, became more defiant, deciding to exchange sugar for oil with the Soviet Union. Despite the menace of the United States, the revolution continued in earnest. In 1961, declared the "Year of Education," the country set out on a vast campaign that had the objective of eliminating illiteracy in one year. A hundred thousand student teachers, many of whom were teenagers, headed out to the countryside armed only with uniforms and oil lamps. The early years of the revolution were filled with experimentation and setback, but its symbolic power – demonstrating that a small but determined nation could stand up to the world's greatest economic and military power – resonated with progressive intellectuals and activists throughout the world. Cuba moved steadily into the Soviet camp, yet it also stood for something new, acting as the voice of the postcolonial Third World.

Many of the most well-known leftist intellectuals of the period, from Jean-Paul Sartre and Simone de Beauvoir to C. Wright Mills, Claude Julien, and Paul Sweezy, visited the island, recording their thoughts and communicating Cuba's atmosphere of freedom and experimentation to the world. In his quickly-written and fast-selling *Listen, Yankee: The Revolution in Cuba*, C. Wright Mills assumes the voice of a Cuban explaining the revolution's imperatives to an American audience, making clear the "distinct possibility" that what "the Cubans are saying and doing today, other hungry peoples in Latin America are going to be saying and doing tomorrow."[31] Sartre's book about Cuba – entitled simply *Sartre on Cuba* – detailed the country's pre-revolutionary dependency on the United States and the tyranny of the sugar quota, which, by imposing a single-crop economy, worked to preserve feudal relations on the island. He described in vivid detail the energy of the revolution, the young rebels who barely slept, his meeting with Guevara at midnight and his tour of the countryside with Castro. But Sartre went further, explaining that through the process of actively creating and taking control of their society, the Cuban people had become citizens, awakened to responsibility, and created individual and national sovereignty; they had, in short, changed "even the very notion of man." "The Cubans must win," Sartre dramatically declared, "or we will lose all, even hope."[32]

Throughout the 1960s, Cuba symbolized the possibility of Third World revolution. It stood for creating an alternative to American-led capitalism and the racism and inequality inherent to it. In the years after the revolution, however, Cuba worked extremely hard to court the support of both the Canadian government and the country's business community.[33] On 26 April 1959, just months after assuming power, Castro came to Montreal, where he spoke to leading business figures at a banquet sponsored by the Jeune chambre de commerce. Official diplomatic and business relations aside, the example of Cuba filled many Quebeckers with hope. As early as

1960, Raoul Roy argued that the significance of the Cuban revolution resided in its destruction of a myth according to which the struggle against economic dictatorship was doomed to failure.[34] From Guevara, activists were also beginning to believe that they could not sit back and wait for the right conditions for social transformation, but that these conditions needed to be actively fostered.[35]

The Cuban revolution differed from the decolonization of Africa in that it pitted rebels against their own ostensibly sovereign government. The battle was not against foreign forces but against a government beholden to foreign economic interests. The writings of Fidel Castro,[36] and especially the socialist humanism of Che Guevara,[37] convinced many that Third World socialism wore an entirely different face than its Soviet counterpart. And the 1966 Tricontinental conference in Havana marked what seemed to be the dawning of a new era, the first time, as Robert Young explains, that "the three continents of the South – the Americas, Asia and Africa – were brought together in a broad alliance to form the Tricontinental," an event marking "the formal globalization of the anti-imperial struggle."[38] Because of the global reach of American imperialism, the success of the Cuban revolution depended upon the various anti-imperialist struggles taking place everywhere, including Quebec. Vallières wrote in 1967 that "Imperialism has not only linked us all in our servitude, but it has also made us interdependent in our efforts to conquer our liberty and our selves. We will either all become free together, or we will together remain slaves of the American Yankee." And, from this perspective, he argued that the best way to support Cuba was "to foster the struggle against imperialism and capitalism in our own respective countries."[39]

In the first half of the 1960s, Vallières had been instrumental in building this larger systemic analysis of imperialism, an analysis that modified the way in which radicals situated themselves internationally. When *Révolution québécoise* appeared in 1964, it emphasized the transnational nature of struggle. It is instructive to listen to a critique of *Parti Pris* published in the journal, a critique in which the author attempted to resituate the "imperial capital" of Quebec:

> We should never forget that secession will only be meaningful if it eliminates or greatly weakens foreign control over the Quebec economy, if it eliminates what you, comrades of "Parti Pris," call the economic alienation of French Canadians.

As Latin America demonstrates, Washington controls virtually all the national bourgeoisies of the Western Hemisphere. The weaker they are, as much internationally as nationally, the more they need to rely on Washington and the more they become dependent upon American capitalists, who even resort to "military aid" to prop up the political power of these national bourgeoisies when their own power is challenged by progressive forces.

"In the Quebec of 1964," the article argued, "the number one enemy is no longer Ottawa, but Washington."[40] The critique articulated by *Révolution québécoise*, one that drew heavily on Marxism and insisted that power lay in the hands of American imperialists rather than politicians in Ottawa, profoundly transformed the geographic boundaries that had earlier confined ideas of Quebec liberation. Cuba was not the only inspiration for this subtle yet profound transformation, but the Cuban example was crucial in reinforcing this new interpretation, surfacing again and again as the primary example of the imperative of global anti-imperialist struggles.

Under the new rubric of anti-imperialism, intellectual work and activism underwent an important shift. Internationalism was no longer associated with an understanding of solidarity in a parallel struggle; rather, political activity in Quebec formed part of a larger global movement against imperialism. In each year following the publication of *Parti Pris*'s 1965–66 manifesto, the tendency to focus on American imperialism became more pronounced. In the second half of the 1960s, writers like Philippe Bernard maintained that Quebec liberation not only ran parallel to, but was deeply integrated with, the struggles of Black Americans. Bernard articulated much of the sentiment of *Parti Pris* in general by arguing that it was the responsibility of all advocates of Quebec liberation to assist American army deserters, support the Black Power movement, be in solidarity with Vietnam, and encourage all other manifestations of liberty in opposition to imperialism.[41] For Gabriel Gagnon, because the United States was the most important enemy in North America, all challenges to American hegemony furthered the cause of building an alternative society. Far from being limited to Quebec, therefore, the struggle for decolonization was actively being forged "in the outskirts of Chicago, the rice paddies of Vietnam, and the *Maquis* of the Andes."[42]

Cuba had more than just symbolic value; many individuals travelled to the country, interacted with Cubans,[43] and learned a lot from their concrete engagement with Third World socialism. As Richard Gott writes, "Havana in the 1960s, like Paris in the 1790s and Moscow in the 1920s, became for a brief moment a revolutionary Mecca, the epicentre of a changing and optimistic world."[44] Many Montreal radicals travelled to the country, some for political conferences or to discover the revolution for themselves, others in forced exile as a result of illegal political activity. In the early 1960s, labour organizer and printer Michel Chartrand travelled to Cuba to gain a better understanding of the country and its development. Chartrand spoke admiringly of trailers crossing the countryside to show movies to the rural population, and of the Cuban government's program to bring rural people to the city to take courses in ceramics and attend the ballet.[45] And he drew clear parallels between Cuba and the situation in Quebec. The introduction of socialism in Quebec would begin, he argued, with the nationalization of natural resources, and "will extend to education and hospitals, and so on." The only difference with Quebec was that "we are white people, so it will be a little more difficult for the USA to push us around."[46] Many other radicals travelled to Cuba – Eric Hobsbawm, for example, recalls encountering young Quebec revolutionaries when at the Havana Cultural Congress of January 1968,[47] and Nicole Thérien, one of Montreal's earliest women's liberationists, learned in Cuba that socialism did not necessarily imply the liberation of women[48] – but they left few traces of their travels, aside from reports by the Canadian intelligence service.[49]

In the first decade of the revolution, Cuba advanced in an almost experimental way, giving support to different revolutionary movements around the world. The revolution meant many things to many people, but among its most important gestures were its broad declarations announcing an end to racism in Cuba itself, and its open courting of Black activists in the United States. Discrimination against Blacks was rife in pre-revolutionary Cuba. Blacks were excluded from White-only beaches and White-only clubs. The new revolutionary government quickly set out to put an end to such policies. Operating on an integrationist logic, however, it failed to take into account the power of racism as a cultural system that could not be undone merely by abolishing laws. The government did not allow the development of Black organizations that would work towards eliminating the cultural structures of racism. Despite its mixed record on race, however, Cuba's triumph over the colossal powers of imperialism and its pronouncements on behalf of the marginalized and oppressed ensured that the revolution would have a profound impact on Black thinkers in the United States. Castro worked hard to reach out to American Blacks, even famously staying at Harlem's Theresa Hotel when in New York City for the opening session of the United Nations in 1960. And he welcomed a continuing stream of Black revolutionaries and exiles who were eager to receive Cuba's support and encouragement.[50]

Black Americans compared their situation with that of colonized subjects,[51] yet Cuba raised interesting questions for those thinking through the relationship between race and revolution. In the minds of the vast majority of those engaged in the wave of decolonization in the post-war period, "empire" had become inextricably intertwined with "race." Frantz Fanon had argued that colonialism created a Manichean world separating the White colonizers from the indigenous population.[52] Malcolm X, for his part, spoke of "dark mankind['s]" movement of liberation, composed of the world's "non-white" peoples, be they "black, brown, red or yellow."[53] Yet Cuba was composed of *both* Blacks and Whites, of the descendents of slaves as well as of Spanish settler colonists (and, of course, of millions who fit into neither category). Because of its position as a victim of American imperialism and its active efforts to forge a movement on behalf of the world's dispossessed, many African Americans, demonstrating the flexibility and malleability of racial metaphors, recognized Castro as on the right side of the world's racial divide. Robert Williams's *The Crusader* initially described Castro as "colored,"[54] and Stokely Carmichael, after giving a stirring speech in Cuba on the combined struggles of Black Americans and the Third World, told *Time* magazine that "Castro is the blackest man I know."[55] Legendary Black American literary and political figure, LeRoi Jones (later Amiri Baraka), evinced much of the same sentiment when writing that, during his visit to Cuba, he had grown "even blacker" under the hot Cuban sun.[56]

Much of Cuban identity, of course, is premised on the impossibility of racial essentialisms. For many, the very defining feature of the country – or even of Latin America as a whole – is its *mestizaje*, its fusing of the culture and identity of slaves, Aboriginals, and settlers. But racialized power relations remained all too present in Cuban society, despite the fact that the spirit of the revolution demanded that the privileged attempt to see the world from the perspective of the marginalized; that they see, in the words of the great Cuban essayist Roberto Fernández Retamar, history from "the *other* side, from the viewpoint of the *other* protagonist."[57] Following José Martí, Retamar argued that, as the country's racial and ethnic minorities were the most oppressed, revolutionaries needed to join with them in sol-idarity. In support of his view, Retamar quoted Che Guevara in a speech that he gave at the University of Las Villas on 28 December 1959. Guevara stood before the distinguished professors of the university and beseeched them to leave their privileges aside, imploring them to "become black, mulatto, a worker, a peasant."[58]

Radicals in Montreal watched events in Cuba with unprecedented inter-est. The Cuban revolution had opened a whole new world, transforming their understanding of the anti-imperialist struggle, and providing them with a concrete example of a post-imperialist and postcolonial present. They too wanted to "become Black," to join in common cause with op-pressed peoples everywhere. Yet they realized that they were not Latin Americans, that their situation differed greatly from that of Cuba, and that they would need to look elsewhere to build a new identity of resistance. Many in Montreal were coming to realize that, unlike Cuba, they were sit-uated at the very centre of the empire, and that for solidarity they would need to look to other North American minorities, and especially to Amer-ican Blacks.

BLACK POWER, RACE, AND THE NORTH AMERICAN REVOLUTION

More than anyone else, it was Charles Gagnon and Pierre Vallières who were responsible for bringing the Quebec liberation struggle to the world stage. On 25 September 1966, wanted by the police in Canada,[59] Vallières and Gagnon emerged from hiding and appeared before the television studios of the United Nations headquarters in New York City. The United Nations, as flawed as the organization may have been, had come to be seen by the Third World as a body in which it was possible to wield some influence.[60] Malcolm X had even famously urged Black Americans to stop appealing to the American government for the protection of their civil rights, but rather to elevate their struggle by bringing the American government before the United Nations for its fundamental violation of African Americans' human rights.[61] And so, deeply influenced by both Malcolm X and the countries of the Third World, it is no surprise that the two Quebec revolutionaries ended up at the United Nations. Speaking before the international media, they announced their plans to begin an indefinite hunger strike with the goal of bringing the world's attention to the plight of francophone Quebeckers, their struggle for liberation, and the existence of "political prisoners" in Quebec.[62] When they returned the following day, they attempted to make their way onto the international territory of the United Nations but were prevented by scores of police and journalists, and were finally arrested on charges of illegal entry into the United States.[63]

The desire to attract international attention to Quebec's situation, along with a deep fascination with the Black Power movement, led the two writers to New York in the first place, and it was while imprisoned in the Manhattan House of Detention for Men that Vallières wrote *Nègres blancs d'Amérique: autobiographie précoce d'un "terroriste quebecois,"* a work that would do more than any other to focus international attention on Quebec's struggle and bring an internationalist perspective on dissent to Quebec. Vallières worked day and night non-stop, standing up in his cell, writing with worn-down pencils on lined paper that rested on a folded piece of wool. He divulged the story of his life in all of its fragility, complete with contradiction, desire, and uncertainty. The manuscript was disguised as notes for his trial and was given to his lawyer, who in turn handed them over to Gerald Godin of the Parti Pris publishing house. When the book was released in the spring of 1968, it caused an immediate sensation. Fearing its potential to ignite revolutionary fervour, police seized all of the copies held in bookstores and libraries, including the legal deposit at the National Library. But this attempt at repression only added fuel to the fire, and the book was reprinted many times underground, becoming an immediate best-seller.[64]

Part political manifesto, part autobiography, *Nègres blancs* was international in both content and form. Vallières took his lead more from the *Autobiography of Malcolm X* than from Quebec's intellectual tradition, composing a tell-all autobiography that explored various forms of oppression through the narrative of his own life. In the years leading up to their appearance before the United Nations, Vallières and Gagnon – like many other Montreal leftists – had become fascinated with the Black Power movement in the United States. Drawing on the revolutionary literature of the time – from Marx to Mao, Fanon, and Guevara – Vallières believed that those who were the most exploited represented, at the same time, the greatest hope for the future of humanity.[65] And by employing a highly racialized metaphor as a title, Vallières sought to position Quebeckers as being among the wretched of the earth.

■ ■ ■

Vallières, however, was not the first Montreal writer to draw on racial metaphors when referring to francophone Quebeckers. During the Sixties, Montreal was awash in a sea of racial metaphors: francophone Quebeckers were the "nègres blancs," the "indigènes," their leaders the "roi nègres." Well-versed in Sartre and Fanon, local writers employed a language of victimization that borrowed heavily from the Third World. As Jean-Paul Sartre said in the opening lines of his preface to the *Wretched of the Earth*, "Not so very long ago, the earth numbered two thousand million inhabitants: five hundred million men, and one thousand five hundred million natives."[66] According to the intellectuals who worked in the early 1960s to construct ideas of Quebec decolonization, francophone Quebeckers were the "natives," and francophone workers the "indigenous labourers" who were colonized by an external power. Already in 1959, Raoul Roy was warning that the anglophone bourgeoisie wanted to keep French Canadians in inferior jobs, as a sub-proletariat, or as Canada's *"nègres blancs."*[67] Members of the early FLQ argued that the federal government had created Quebec as a giant Native reserve in which the colonized had neither power nor authority.[68] In the mid-1960s Gérald Godin maintained that Quebec writers who refused formal French to write in *joual* – colloquial street French – were like "African graduates of the Sorbonne" who had "broken with French and now speak the language of their tribe or their country."[69] And Gilles Bourque argued that Blacks and Quebeckers had a common struggle: as internally colonized groups, they both worked to destroy the system "at its very heart."[70]

Racial metaphors first came to widespread prominence when, in 1958, André Laurendeau compared premier Maurice Duplessis to a "roi nègre," ruling Quebec as local African leaders ruled on behalf of their British colonial masters.[71] The concept of the "roi-nègres" – described by *Parti Pris* as "subjugated intellectuals, profiteering notables, a whole network of people with the one and only goal of keeping the population in ignorance for as long as possible, trading natural resources with the colonizer as secretly as possible, and signing centralizing agreements"[72] – would become a standard trope of the era. Racial categories are, of course, never stable or self-evident, and are always open to a wide variety of meanings. Norman Mailer wrote about how many young Americans in the 1950s turned to the cultural codes of Black America in their search for the "hip," becoming, in his words, "White negroes."[73] Jerry Farber's *Student as Nigger* galvanized students throughout North America when it was released in 1969. And many scholars have investigated the way that various immigrant communities attempted to secure cultural and material advantages by becoming "White."[74] When Quebec radicals appropriated racial metaphors in the late 1950s and early 1960s, it is reasonable to assume, following David Roediger, that they did so not as an act of solidarity with the marginalized, but rather as "a call to arms to end the inappropriate oppression of whites."[75]

As Montreal radicals worked to place Quebec in the worldwide decolonization movement, it became evident that the province differed from most decolonizing nations in one crucial respect. Rather than being an indigenous population, or a population whose ancestors had been sold into slavery and forcefully displaced from their home of origin, French Canadians were, although rarely theorized as such, themselves the descendents of White settler colonists. How could such a population draw on a literature, and imagine itself as part of a global movement, that had explicitly stated its objective to be overcoming and displacing White power? In *Nègres blancs*, Vallières is the first to grapple with this question, and he does so through an extensive engagement with the ideas of the major personalities of the Black Power movement in the United States.[76] Already in 1964, in the pages of *Révolution québécoise*, Vallières and Gagnon were attempting to introduce Malcolm X and the Black liberation struggle to Quebec. In November 1964 the journal included an interview with Malcolm X, announcing at the same time a plan to bring Malcolm X to Montreal, a plan thwarted, presumably, only by Malcolm X's assassination.[77]

Vallières also learned from Black Power on a theoretical level. From James Boggs, a Detroit-based African-American theorist, Vallières came to understand the ways in which Black oppression and marginalization were rooted in the injustices of the capitalist system. And from both Frantz Fanon and Malcolm X, Vallières learned how racial categories were maintained by a society in which Whites kept their power through the dehumanization and cultural degradation of Blacks. Such works made it clear that racial essentialism hid a structure intent on maintaining White privilege.[78] During the 1960s, many writers, including those who directly influenced Vallières, used the word "Black" as a flexible metaphor, some using the word to describe peoples of colour throughout the world, from Asia to Latin America, and some to designate the vanguard of the world revolution. In *Afro-Orientalism*, Bill Mullen outlines the ways in which many writers, mostly coming from the radical African-American tradition, have opted for a "strategic antiessentialism" on questions of race, giving the term "Black" "relational *political* (as opposed to racial) meaning."[79] During the 1960s, writer after writer argued that to be "Black" was not only to be colonized, but also to be on the side of humanity which was poised to create a new world.

If whiteness was synonymous with power and privilege, and blackness with marginalization and oppression, Vallières clearly saw Quebec as an anomaly, sharing a similar place in North American society as American Blacks. Vallières was profoundly marked by his reading of Fanon: "By awakening the idea of *négritude*, by plumbing the depths of its humanity, ('of higher quality' than the Westerner, Sartre insisted), Fanon was also inviting us to become *nègres*, inheritors of the anger of the humiliated, of the poor and maimed: to become '*nègres blancs*.'"[80] Vallières had learned from Fanon, but also from Aimé Césaire, the great poet and co-founder of the *négritude* movement, a movement which sought to valorize Black history and culture, rejecting the demands of assimilation and persistent cultural denigration by the White world. Years later, in a documentary which appeared in the early 1990s, Césaire admitted to have first laughed at the prospect of a White population employing the concept of *négritude*, but he eventually came to see that Vallières and other Quebeckers had understood the *négritude* movement at a profound level.[81] As Césaire would later reflect, "Our movement was based in fact apparently on race but it went beyond that, beyond race. There was a cry, a universal human cry. It is not a triumphant glorious negritude. It isn't that. It is negritude trodden on. The trodden-on Negro. The oppressed Negro. And it is the Negro rebel. That's what negritude is. Our negritude. It is a humanization. And that is why there can be a White negritude, a negritude of the people of Québec, a negritude of any color. That is the basic notion."[82]

Vallières's choice of title was therefore informed theoretically by the ideas of *négritude*, Malcolm X, Stokely Carmichael, and the emerging Black Power movement in the United States.[83] He looked to them for their potential, arguing that it was "in the interest of all the other niggers, all the other exploited people, including the Québécois, to unite with the American blacks in their struggle for liberation." Like American Blacks, Quebeckers were brought to the Americas as "servants of the imperialists," imported as cheap labour and, with the exception of the colour of their skin, "their condition remains the same." And Quebeckers were not the only "nègres blancs" in North America; they were joined by the vast array of immigrant communities living in substandard conditions as members of the working class.[84]

Vallières was far from alone in his fascination with Black Power. Charles Gagnon collected literature produced by the various strands of the movement[85] and, partly through his engagement with Black Power, sharpened his analysis of Quebec's role in the larger North American revolution. In *Feu sur l'Amérique, Propositions pour la révolution nord-américaine*, a manifesto written in prison in August and September 1968, and seized by police before it could be published,[86] Gagnon disregarded the Canadian border and envisioned francophone Quebeckers as one colonized group among many on the continent. When the North American bourgeoisie talked about their high standard of living, Gagnon argued, it was forgetting "the shanty towns of Mexico, the ghettos of Watts and Harlem, and the slums of Saint-Henri and Mile-End (Montreal)." It was ignoring the chronic poverty that afflicted so much of the continent, having particularly devastating effects "in the regions inhabited by French Canadians, Mexicans, Aboriginals, Acadians, Puerto Ricans, and Blacks." Perhaps most importantly, it was being wilfully blind to the reality that North America had become "the land of White Anglo-Saxon racism." In 1968, Gagnon believed that "class" alone could not explain either the full dimension of oppression nor the real-life axis upon which individuals organized for liberation. We now know, he argued, that "being a Black proletarian in North America is not the same thing as being a White proletarian; being a French proletarian is not the same thing as being an American proletarian," and "being a *Québécois* proletarian is not the same thing as being an (English) Canadian proletarian."[87] Because imperialism exploited people on the basis of "race" and nation, and set different groups against each another, it was precisely around national liberation struggles that the oppressed needed to organize.[88]

Throughout Gagnon's text, the "racial" category of "blanc anglo-saxon" is continually highlighted, constructed as the Other against which various political movements could mobilize. Gagnon argued that daily life in North America pressured everyone, regardless of his or her race or culture, to adopt the cultural mores of the dominant group. Drawing on the language of one of the most explosive poems of the era, one that had debuted only a few months earlier,[89] Gagnon argued that everyone had "to speak white" and "be white."[90] Because of this added dimension of oppression, revolutionary fervour did not originate among the White English-speaking working class, but at the margins, among impoverished people who belonged "to oppressed national groups, victims of White Anglo-Saxon racism." Even though Amerindians, Acadians, and Puerto-Ricans would play an important role, true possibilities of revolution lay with three groups: Quebeckers, Blacks, and Mexicans. In contrast to the high standard of living among Anglo-Saxons, minority groups lived in conditions that more closely resembled the Third World and comprised a Third World living in the very centre of the empire, one which needed to recognize its historical destiny and fight American imperialism from the inside. According to Gagnon, the creation of a North American common front became the crucial task of the moment.[91]

When Vallières and Gagnon headed to New York in the summer of 1966, it was with the idea of making contacts, forging links, and establishing connections with oppressed minorities, and especially with those involved in the burgeoning Black Power movement. In New York, Vallières recalls wandering the streets and holding discussions with a variety of activists, thinking hard about how a unified theory could be forged from the various struggles of Blacks and Whites, workers and students, women and men, flower children and those who advocated armed revolution.[92]

But his experience in New York deeply shocked him. Fascinated with the emergence of Black Power, he hoped to make alliances with American Blacks; in New York, however, he found that they knew nothing about Quebeckers. Rather than looking north, they looked "to Cuba, Latin America, Africa, or Asia." They felt closer to "Peking, Cairo, and Algiers than they did to Montreal and Quebec City." Vallières felt that Black radicals saw all Whites in North America in the same light, making little distinction between different groups. At first sight, according to Vallières, a White Quebecker was merely one more White North American, not a "'nègre blanc.'"[93] Although writing in French, Vallières claims that his title came to him spontaneously in English: *White Niggers of America*. He wanted, more than anything, to pierce the "wall of indifference and disdain" separating Americans from the movement for Quebec decolonization.[94]

And to some degree he succeeded. His book was published in many world centres and reviewed in many of the most important newspapers.[95]

In the *New York Times*, Christopher Lehmann-Haupt argued that *Nègres blancs* will likely "take its place alongside the writings of Malcolm X, Eldridge Cleaver, Frantz Fanon, Che Guevara and Régis Debray; for it is an eloquent revolutionary document that clutches one's throat like a drowning hand."[96] Nicolas Regush, a journalist who had been born in Montreal but was living in the United States, came across *White Niggers of America* while living in New York City, and he was so moved by the book that he decided to become Vallières's first biographer.[97] Vallières himself boasted of receiving the support of, among many others, the *Monthly Review*, Youth Against War and Fascism, the Black Panthers, and various other Black Power representatives.[98]

The greatest show of support came by way of a telegram at the beginning of 1968. Only a day after Vallières's trial began, Stokely Carmichael, one of the most important Black leaders in the United States, wrote to him and Gagnon: "Courages nos frères, SNCC [Student Nonviolent Coordinating Committee] experiences government chicanery and deception daily. We refuse to be divided from our brothers in the FLQ by malicious lies. We support you in your trial. Your experiences are no different from those of true patriots everywhere and at any time who resist against tyranny. We are confident of your complete vindication. Nous Vaincrons."[99] And when Martin Luther King was assassinated just a few months later, Vallières and Gagnon sent their own letter to Carmichael declaring: "The time has come for Black Americans and white niggers of Quebec and America to unite their forces to destroy the capitalist and imperialist Order which assassinates those who choose to break the chains of slavery and liberate humanity from oppression, exploitation and all forms of enslavement. We are uniting with you to avenge the heroic death of Reverend King, Malcolm X, and all those who paid with their lives, their passion for justice, freedom, equality, brotherhood and peace. [...] Vallières and Gagnon, on behalf of the white niggers of Quebec."[100]

■ ■ ■

Nègres blancs profoundly shook activists and writers living in Montreal. In the years following the book's publication, references to the concept of "nègres blancs" multiplied, reshaping the way that many conceived of oppression and liberation. As Gilles Dostaler wrote in the pages of *Parti Pris*: "The title of the book, one must concede, is a revelation. We are *nègres*, like all other victims of imperialism, in the same way as those who have started

to weaken the giant: the twenty-two million Afro-Americans. Regardless of
the opinions of our friends from the publication 'Indépendantiste,' all of the
nègres of the world, of all colours, today have one common enemy."[101]
Pierre Renau and Robert Tremblay were so convinced by the metaphor
that they published a chronology of the Quebec liberation struggle in
which, each year beginning in 1963, developments in Quebec were juxta-
posed with the development of the American Civil Rights/Black Power
movement.[102]

Reading the cultural degradation of francophone Quebeckers through
the lens of anti-colonial resistance and Black Power also had a powerful resonance among poets and song-writers. On 27 May 1968, Quebec's most
well-known poets and *chansonniers* gathered together at the Théâtre Gesù
to raise money for the defence of Vallières and Gagnon. Many believed
they were being tried not for their actions, but for their ideas,[103] and the
evening of performances was entitled "Chants et poèmes de la Résistance."
The evening opened – in front of a capacity crowd of 700, with over 100 people turned away due to lack of space – with a report about Vallières's trial,
followed by a reading of the names of all of Quebec's "political prisoners."
Poets Gaston Miron and Paul Chamberland read their work, and the music
of *Jazz Libre* filled the air. According to *Le Devoir* reporter Jacques Thériault, "Songs, poems, and free jazz followed one another at a dizzying and
solid rhythm: each number, each silence, each act formed a crucial element of a moving evening."[104]

It was in this atmosphere that the best-known poem of the period
debuted. An energetic audience listened as Michelle Rossignol read Michèle
Lalonde's "Speak White":

...
speak white and loud
qu'on vous entende
de Saint-Henri à Saint-Domingue
oui quelle admirable langue
pour embaucher
donner des ordres
fixer l'heure de la mort à l'ouvrage
et de la pause qui rafraîchit
et ravigote le dollar [...]

Lalonde composed the entire poem in one long night in the month of May

1968, just after the release of Vallières's book. She believed that, for Quebeckers, the French language was their *blackness*. "Speak White" was the command of the coloniser to the colonised, the command of the British in west Montreal, of White Americans in the United States, of the British colonizers in Africa and of the French in Algeria.[105] And if all colonized people shared a similar cultural degradation and humiliation at the hands of the colonizer, then they also shared a common basis upon which they could unite in opposition.

...

speak white
c'est une langue universelle
nous sommes nés pour la comprendre
avec ses mots lacrymogènes
avec ses mots matraques

speak white
tell us again about Freedom and Democracy
Nous savons que liberté est un mot noir
comme la misère est nègre
et comme le sang se mêle à la poussière des rues d'Alger
    ou de Little Rock

speak white
de Westminster à Washington relayez-vous
speak white comme à Wall Street
white comme à Watts
be civilised
et comprenez notre parler de circonstance
quand vous nous demandez poliment
how do you do
et nous entendez vous répondre
we're doing all right
we're doing fine
we
are not alone

nous savons
que nous ne sommes pas seuls.[106]

■ ■ ■

The ultimate effect of Vallières's book was to rally support for the plight of francophone Quebeckers, to place their struggle in the larger context of the decolonization movement, and to tap into a universal identity of suffering and resistance.[107] His greatest achievement was to express the pain and humiliation felt by francophone Quebeckers by offering a piercing look at the cultural alienation of the working-class family.[108] It is undoubtedly his description of the alienation of everyday life, and his attempt to link this pain with that of other exploited peoples around the world, that had such resonance with his local readership. Yet in Vallières's anger and frustration, he argued that the only remedy was to take action, and for him this meant that it was necessary to take up arms to incite revolution. In calling for "action" at all costs, he articulated not only the masculine bravado of the era, but also what one young activist, in retrospective, calls the impatience and arrogance of his generation.[109]

Nègres blancs also contains profound contradictions, typical of its place and time, which were all too apparent to Black and Aboriginal activists even then.[110] Intent on affirming solidarity with oppressed groups elsewhere, Vallières marginalizes other oppressed groups within Quebec itself. Not only does he ignore the active role of Aboriginal groups in Quebec, but he also denies the very existence of Blacks in the province: "French Canadians are not subject to this irrational racism that has done so much wrong to the workers, white and black, of the United States," Vallières argues, but they can take no credit for this, as "in Quebec there is no 'black problem.'" [111] In fact, at the time that Vallières's book was going to print, the Black population of Montreal numbered roughly 15,000 individuals who were waging constant struggles against discrimination.[112]

Vallières, of course, was hardly alone in his silence on the Black population within Quebec; he reflected the general lack of concern across the left. With the exception of Monique Chénier – who noted in 1965 that many on the left were in solidarity with Blacks who lived "far away," while being blind to discrimination in their own province[113] – most writers ignored the oppression of other groups in Montreal. It was not until 1968 that *Parti Pris* published an article on Montreal Blacks. The article, written by Robert Tremblay, demonstrated the extent of the separation between *Parti Pris* and the Montreal Black community, describing Black immigrants who came to Montreal during the nineteenth century while ignoring both the Black population of New France and saying little about those of West

Indian origin who were currently forming political organizations in the city.[114] Tremblay argued that "Montreal is a city of subtle discrimination, a situation which is tolerated at the moment but which will quickly become unsustainable if the Black population grows to significant levels."[115] It was just this sort of attitude, which downplayed discrimination and spoke of the Black population of Montreal as negligible, that would soon be challenged in no uncertain terms by Blacks themselves.

Rue Saint-Hubert, 1961. Note the prominence of English. Archives of the City of Montreal, VM94, A32-11

Placards after a protest following the assassination of Martin Luther King Jr. (4 April 1968). Note the variety of messages, including a prominently displayed picture of Malcolm X. *La Presse*, 8 April 1968, Pierre McCann

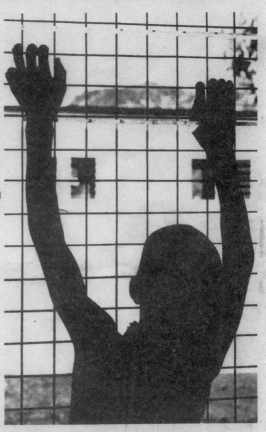

congress of black writers
congrès des écrivains noirs

towards

the second

emancipation

the dynamics

of black liberation

❖

vers la seconde

émancipation

dynamique

de la libération

noire

october 11th-14th, 1968
students union and leacock building
mcgill university
montreal, canada

**souvenir
program**

The cover of the program of the Congress of Black Writers, held in Montreal from 11–14 October 1968. Alfie Roberts Institute, Montreal

Above: Captivated McGill students watching a debate between Stanley Gray, Principal H. Rocke Robertson, and the Dean of Arts. McGill University Archives, PR000407, Chris Payne/*McGill Reporter*; *below*: A crowd of students and workers in front of the Roddick Gates at McGill University during the Opération McGill français protest on 28 March 1969. *La Presse*, 29 March 1969, René Picard

A poster, circa 1973, announcing an evening of solidarity with the Vietnamese. Note the broad range of groups participating in the event. Centre de recherche en imagerie populaire, UQAM

Above: A meeting during the Common Front strikes of 1972. Archives de la csn. Photo: René Derome; *below*: Quebec labour leaders march with supporters to turn themselves in for their prison terms in May 1972. Archives de la csn. Photo: René Derome

Poster announcing a demonstration for 1 May 1973. Centre de recherche en imagerie populaire, UQAM

PART TWO

1968–1972

FOUR

MONTREAL'S BLACK RENAISSANCE

"Black Power" had been inspiring dissidents in Montreal since the mid-1960s. But in the fall and winter of 1968–69, in the movement's cafés and avant-garde papers, in the teach-ins and cramped apartments, a new topic began creeping into conversations. Those who had considered themselves the left, and who had compared their plight to that of American Blacks, were surprised by the sudden explosion of Black activism in the city. In the years leading up to the 1960s, discrimination ensured that Black Montrealers remained segregated in substandard living conditions and concentrated in unskilled and low-paying jobs. Montreal's Black population – with its history stretching back to the seventeenth century – had always found ways to resist racism, but now something new was taking place. From the perspective of Montreal's Black population, the 1960s, with political organizations continually being formed, public protests abounding, and a whole series of international conferences taking place, was a watershed in political organizing.[1]

In the second half of the 1960s, Black activists transformed Montreal into a major centre of Black thought, where many of the worlds leading Black intellectuals converged with local activists to discuss the global context of race and imperialism. When an occupation of the computer centre at Sir George Williams University in February 1969 ended badly with the blows of riot police, the destruction of $2,000,000 of property, and scores of arrests and criminal charges, a new era of Black activism began. The event reflected the heated atmosphere of the late 1960s, and in response to the open hostility that Blacks faced after the event, many members of the community began meeting regularly to discuss the need for autonomous institutions, sparking a political renaissance in the community.

The powerful surge of Black activism in Montreal cannot be understood outside of the larger international context of Black militancy in the late 1960s. Many activists were, after all, recent immigrants from the Caribbean who had come to Montreal to study, and all were profoundly influenced by the movement taking place in the United States. Although they framed their struggle in global terms, they also operated in a politically charged milieu. So even if they had wanted to, it would not have been possible for Montreal's Black activists to remain indifferent to the decolonization movement unfolding all around them. The emergence of Black activism, I will therefore argue, operated simultaneously on many levels, generated many diverse meanings, and constituted a movement that was not only international in scope, but one which was also deeply imbedded in the lived realities of Montreal.

BLACK MONTREAL AND THE 1960S

While the Sir George Williams Affair of 1969 acted as the immediate spark that set off a Black renaissance in the city, Black opposition to racism originated deep in the city's past. From the everyday forms of resistance employed by the slaves of New France, to the organization of a division of the Universal Negro Improvement Association in 1919, to the unionization of the largely Montreal-based sleeping car porters of the Canadian Pacific Railway during the Second World War and the efforts of the Coloured Women's Club of Montreal, Montreal's Black residents had never accepted the racism and segregation they faced on a daily basis.[2] Yet racism persisted, limiting their employment prospects and the areas of the city in which they could live, and ensuring their psychological and cultural segregation from mainstream society. Walking into downtown restaurants and cafés would often be a humiliating experience for Blacks, as they were met with cold looks and sometimes refused service altogether.[3] White passengers on public transit would refuse to sit beside Black people, bars and clubs sometimes turned them away, and they were almost always forced to work in jobs far below their skill level.[4]

Throughout the 1950s and early 1960s Montrealers were increasingly becoming fascinated by the growing Civil Rights movement in the United States, and Montreal's main civil rights organization, the Negro Citizenship Association, began denouncing continued discrimination and, in the mid-1960s, founded the journal *Expression*.[5] From its beginning in 1965, the journal opposed racism and advocated a lobbying campaign to the provincial and federal governments that aimed at both more comprehensive anti-discrimination legislation and a stronger enforcement of the laws already in place. While the Negro Citizenship Association worked for civil rights, a new energy began to sweep into the city, capturing the imaginations of many young Blacks, and especially students of Caribbean origin who had recently arrived in the city. Montreal's Black population had always included people of different origins, so it would be wrong to draw too clear a division between the community's various components.[6] But in the 1960s, it was Caribbean students – often intent on returning home to pursue political activity after their studies – who introduced anti-colonial ideas into Black Montreal, at first upsetting many established members of the community, but ultimately deeply affecting the way in which the community conceived of itself and understood its relation to the rest of Quebec society and the world at large.[7]

Increased immigration from the Caribbean began in the mid-1950s with the West Indian Domestic scheme that allowed single women to immigrate to Canada if they agreed to act as domestic servants for about a year. And, while Britain began restricting non-white immigrants in the early 1960s, Canada began to undo some of the more overtly discriminatory aspects of its own policy, a process that would lead to its 1967 point base selection criteria. As a result of the changes, the makeup of immigrants to Canada began to change. From 1966 to 1972, the proportion of immigrants from Latin America, the Caribbean, Africa and the Middle East rose to 23% (it had been 4.5% from 1940–50). Immigration from the English-speaking Caribbean rose from representing 1% of Canada's immigration in 1960 to 10% in 1971.[8] Often, in historian Dorothy Williams's words, the new immigrants brought "different values which did not quite mesh with Montreal's old stock black community," but eventually "these newcomers used their energies to refashion old community associations and create new ones."[9]

In the mid-1960s a group calling itself the Caribbean Conference Committee on West Indian Affairs formed the basis of a new Black intelligentsia in the city. It worked to develop new analyses of colonialism and neo-colonialism in the Caribbean, laying much of the groundwork for Black politics in Montreal in the late 1960s and early 1970s.[10] As recent immigrants to Canada, group members felt alienated from the larger society. While their focus remained the future of the Caribbean, the committee also strove to oppose the daily realities of discrimination in Montreal, fully aware, as one member put it, that they were continuing in a tradition of what others in the city "had done before."[11]

Troubled by the continued subjugation of their countries of origin by dominant Western powers, even after formal political independence had been achieved, the group set out to organize a series of international conferences to analyse both the history and the present-day realities of the Caribbean. Robert Hill, one of the group's most important members, recalls that the conference committee was formed at a time when recuperating Black history was seen as a revolutionary gesture. For its very first conference in 1965, the committee hoped to bring Aimé Césaire to Montreal but, when Césaire could not attend, Barbadian novelist and poet George Lamming took his place.[12] Lamming's speech revealed his profound belief in the possibilities opened up by the process of decolonization. He congratulated the young activists, assuring them that the effects of their work were being felt around the world.[13] In the exciting aftermath of this first conference, C.L.R. James was invited to Montreal for another conference the following year. He would not only come to the 1966 conference, but also became deeply involved with the committee, staying in Montreal for prolonged periods throughout the winter of 1966–67, and greatly influencing their intellectual work.[14]

Although Black nationalism – rather than the more theoretical work of the Conference Committee – would come to play an increasingly important role in Montreal, the effects of the group's activities continued to be felt. Perhaps even more important than its intellectual achievements was the sea change the Conference Committee represented. By bringing together individuals who were both theoretically informed and highly committed to social justice and democracy, the committee began an ongoing discussion about the structural roots of racism and economic exploitation. Although the committee itself disbanded before the emergence of Black Power in Montreal at the end of the decade, the ideas it had developed in preceding years laid much of the groundwork for the movement.

The end of the 1960s was a turbulent time for Blacks in North America.

Because of the persistence of racism despite the legal victory of the American Civil Rights Bill, many young African-Americans – like Martin Luther King himself – began rethinking the analyses and strategies of the Civil Rights movement.[15] In popular representations of the period, the Civil Rights and Black Power movements are often portrayed as being mutually exclusive, the former advocating racial integration and an end to legal segregation, the latter advocating racial pride and separation. What this perspective ignores are the ways in which the two movements emerged in response to similar problems, reflected the same pursuit of freedom, and, perhaps most importantly, the ways both changed as the 1960s progressed.[16] Popularized by Stokely Carmichael in 1966, the term "Black Power" generally refers to attempts to overcome the psychological and material consequences of being Black in a society marked by institutionalized racism. Rather than appealing to the moral conscience of White America, the Black Power movement "affirmed black people, their history, their beauty, and set them at the center of their own worldview."[17] In response to racism, the argument went, Black people needed to organize independently and affirm their own priorities and needs. The earlier hope of integration into White society gave way to the idea of Black community-building, one that meant moving beyond the narrow individualism that characterized mainstream society. It also meant transforming blackness from a source of shame into a source of pride.[18]

The movement in the United States had a profound effect on politics in Montreal. No one single event, of course, marked the end of the Civil Rights era. But, in the minds of many, the assassination of Martin Luther King on 4 April 1968 put an end to hopes of peaceful racial integration. King's assassination sparked a wave of violence that swept across most major urban centres of the United States. Many took to the streets in anger and, in the days of rioting that ensued, the National Guard was mobilized, curfews were established, forty African Americans were killed and another twenty thousand arrested.[19] In Montreal, while the actions were less dramatic, the anger was just as intense. Citizens organized a street protest to denounce the racism of both the United States and Canada. A crowd of six hundred gathered at the Hall Building of Sir George Williams University, and as the march proceeded to Dominion Square, it swelled to over 2,000 protesters. Many sang the Civil Rights anthem "We Shall Overcome," and a large picture of Malcolm X was carried at the front of the march. Protesters carried signs reading, "Shake off your chains," and "Vive le pouvoir noir." One speaker spoke with approval of Stokely Carmichael, the figure most closely associated with Black Power, and another yelled out: "For 400 years, we've been exploited. We've been beaten. We've been shot." This exploitation did not only occur in "Raceland, U.S.A.," he argued. Blacks had also been discriminated against and exploited in Canada. Now, he continued, "is the time to put an end to the discrimination, the exploitation, the degradation."[20]

The pages of the Negro Citizenship Association's *Expression* also revealed a more pronounced mood of anger. An editorial published right after King's assassination argued that if Montreal continued along its present road, it was "almost inevitable" that the city would witness fierce rioting in the years to come. If nothing was done, the journal warned, "Our ghettos will grow; we will fester under your noses; and, the dirty dunghills that you have created will, one day, explode with the thunder of many suns into your clean, unconcerned, lily-white faces." The editors warned that they were "tired of writing useless letters" to government officials and, presaging the uncompromising attitude to come, thundered that Blacks "are no longer duped" by "clever lies." "Behind the false facade of pleasantness, we can glimpse the murderous teeth of discrimination, we can spy the diseased head of prejudice, we can smell the putrid odour of their rotting and bankrupt souls."[21] This rage would soon be expressed by the city's Congress of Black Writers.

THE CONGRESS OF BLACK WRITERS

By 1968, Black Montrealers were searching for new ways to overcome racism. Two conferences took place in the fall, both indirect successors to the conferences on Caribbean affairs. The first, held from 4 to 6 October 1968, dealt specifically with local problems. Held at Sir George Williams University, the conference featured speakers who discussed everyday problems of discrimination in housing and employment, the paucity of opportunities for marginalized people, and the social and cultural alienation of Blacks in Canada.[22] Many of the speakers reflected the mood prevailing in the city. John Shingler, a professor of Political Science at McGill University, argued that merely integrating into the larger capitalist system is to "entirely to miss the point of human liberation."[23] And in his keynote address, Howard McCurdy spoke of the necessity for self-respect, arguing that it was necessary to get to "the roots of our blackness." Black Power meant, he maintained, "black solidarity" in Canada and throughout the world.[24]

The Congress of Black Writers, held at McGill from 11 to 14 October, was considerably more controversial. Dedicated to the memory of Malcolm X and Martin Luther King, and organized by a younger crowd of mostly students, the congress had the goal of fostering a "second liberation" for Blacks.[25] In the week leading up to the event, *Le Quartier latin*, the student newspaper of the Université de Montréal, wrote that it formed a logical continuity with the Congrès des écrivains et artistes noirs held in Paris in 1956, in Rome in 1959, and in Dakar in 1966[26]; the *McGill Daily* called the event the "largest Black Power conference ever held outside the United States."[27] Co-chairs Elder Thébaud, a Haitian postgraduate student at McGill, and Rosie Douglas, a McGill graduate student from Dominica who had previously been involved in the Caribbean Conference Committee, and who acted as a link between the two different cohorts of Black activists in the city,[28] explained the goals of the event:

> In the face of this total colonial stranglehold, it is clear that the task of self-liberation involves much more than freedom from economic and social oppression. Genuine freedom can only come from the total liberation of the minds and spirits of our people from the false and distorted image of themselves which centuries of cultural enslavement by the white man have imposed upon us all. The struggle for liberation of black people is accordingly not only an economic or political question, but also a cultural rallying cry, a call to re-examine the foundations of the white man's one-sided vision of the world, and to restore to ourselves an image of the achievements of our people, hitherto suppressed and abandoned among the rubble of history's abuses.
>
> It is in this context that this Congress of Black Writers hopes to make its contribution. Here, for the first time in Canada, an attempt will be made to recall, in a series of popular lectures by black scholars, artists and politicians, a history which we have been taught to forget: the history of the black man's own response (in thought and in action) to the conditions of his existence in the New World; in short, the history of the black liberation struggle, from its origins in slavery to the present day. For the sake of to-morrow's victories, it is imperative that we take another look at the events of yesterday, in the

Congress, black people will begin to rediscover themselves as the
active creators, rather than the passive sufferers, of history's events;
the subjects, rather than the objects, of history. It is only when we
have rediscovered this lost perspective on ourselves that we can truly
begin to speak of emancipation; it is only when we have returned
to our authentic past that we can truly begin to dream about the
future.[29]

The congress brought many of the world's most important Black intellectuals to Montreal: Michael X, leader of the Black Muslims in England;
Walter Rodney, prominent West Indian intellectual; and American activist
and intellectual James Forman. The congress also featured both Trinidadian
activist and intellectual C.L.R. James and Halifax-based activist Rocky
Jones.[30] Jones, the only African-Canadian to speak, endorsed an alliance
between Blacks in Canada and other marginalized people in the country,
including Natives and francophone Quebeckers.[31] Eldridge Cleaver, the
Black Panther Information Minister and author of *Soul on Ice*, hoped to
attend, but was stopped because of his troubles with Californian law.[32]

While the conference caused much excitement, it was, as David Austin
points out, "a product of its time, full of machismo and male bravado."
"Tellingly," he argues, "women activists and writers were conspicuously
absent from the roster of speakers, despite the fact that, behind the scenes,
women played a crucial role in organizing the congress."[33] While some recognized the problematic gender politics of the conference, others denounced the continual reference to violence as a legitimate political weapon.
One prominent Caribbean intellectual, Lloyd Best, felt that the conference
was pitched at an "absolutely scandalous" intellectual level, dividing the
world simplistically into "cowboys and Indians."[34] Other members of the
Black community felt ambivalent, recognizing the importance of the event
while remaining uncomfortable with its tone and approach.[35]

The conference's various speakers lectured on African history and African
civilization and on the necessity of fostering a pride in the beauty of Blackness. James Forman, drawing on Fanon, denounced African bourgeois
leaders as opportunists who had only their own interests in sight.[36] The
biggest event of the conference was undoubtedly the appearance of Stokely
Carmichael, the Trinidadian-born, American-raised civil rights and Black
Power activist. After waiting anxiously in the Union Ballroom at McGill University, the overflow audience of 2,000 – mostly made up of White stu-

dents – stood in disbelief as Carmichael stepped onto the stage. He began by outlining the colonization of Black people throughout the world, and vividly described its devastating effects.[37] He insisted on the need to globalize Black struggle, calling on people the world over to "create their own legitimations."[38] The electrified crowd repeatedly interrupted Carmichael, who spoke for over an hour, with cheers and applause.[39] The power of his speech brought seasoned activists "close to tears," and had a profound effect on C.L.R. James.[40]

Carmichael's speech was powerful, but it was also controversial. He made no secret of the way he felt that power needed to be achieved: "I don't think that white Canadians would say that they stole Canada from the Indians (laughter). They said they took it – and they did (applause and laughter). Well then, it's clear that we can't work for these lands, we can't be for 'em, so we must take them. Then it's clear that we must take them through revolutionary violence."[41] Carmichael's uncompromising militancy embodied the spirit of the conference: a new climate of anger that would lead, at least in part, to the Sir George Williams Affair.

Although Montreal's English-language newspapers denounced the gathering at McGill, many White activists attending the conference were fascinated by this local manifestation of Black Power. Among these were Stanley Gray, a lecturer involved with student politics at McGill[42] and Gérald Godin, the radical poet and director of the Parti Pris publishing house. Godin had long drawn on racial metaphors to describe the oppression of French Canadians, and had even argued just two years earlier that francophone Quebeckers were "the Blacks of Canada."[43] But now, in the margins of his souvenir program, Godin began to make connections between the oppression and alienation of French Canadians and that of Blacks *in Canada*. When listening to Halifax-based activist Rocky Jones plead for Canadian Blacks to join forces with francophone Quebeckers and Aboriginal peoples,[44] Godin wrote "that's the way I feel," transcribing Jones's attempt to convey the psychological impact of racial oppression. He went on to draw similarities between Blacks and francophone Quebeckers, adding a message of his own: "that's the way French Canadians feel."[45] Godin was so moved that he started planning to make a movie about Canadian Blacks.[46]

The congress undoubtedly had its greatest impact on a new generation of Black Montrealers. According to Barbara Jones, for them it was an "edifying experience," and they came to realize that their only hope lay "in a new era of black militance and a new humanism."[47] Dennis Forsythe has recorded that many people claimed the conference was the biggest event of their lives, and that it demonstrated "the emotional intensity of Blacks crying out in the wilderness." He observes: "The overall effect on the Black psyche was to inculcate a feeling of exhilaration and uplift; we had been christened in the holy cause. We now saw ourselves as makers rather than takers of our history. We saw ourselves as part of a great struggle, a historic struggle, from which we derived a peculiar feeling of exhilaration, uplift and pride, and a sense of power. We were sanctified as the makers of our own destiny."[48]

At the congress, according to Forsythe, as Blackness became "a symbol of rightness," then "the Whites present had to be, by definition, symbols of evil." Much controversy broke out at the conference when some wanted to exclude White people from sessions, while others wanted to ensure that White people did not wear Malcolm X buttons. Many speakers shocked the largely White audience by referring to Whites as "pigs" and "oppressors."[49] For the first time, many Whites felt "distrusted, excluded, [and] ignored."[50] Conference co-organizer Rosie Douglas noted that because there were Whites in the audience, "the speakers found themselves having to justify the need for liberation." He argued that it was therefore necessary to make a compromise: Whites were allowed in, but after every session there was an exclusively Black caucus.[51] In the months to come, the pent-up frustrations of Montreal's Black population would head towards a dramatic collision with one of the city's most important institutions.

THE SIR GEORGE WILLIAMS AFFAIR

The influx of Black Power ideas into Montreal had a great impact on the political dynamic of the city, but it was not until January and February of 1969 that this new militancy would be translated into action at Sir George Williams University.[52] The origins of the conflict dated back to the end of the 1967–68 school year, when a group of West Indian students accused biology professor Perry Anderson of racial discrimination in grading and academic incompetence. On 29 January 1969, after months of heated controversy, the students felt that their charges were not being adequately addressed. Roughly two hundred protesters overtook a hearing into the matter, and then proceeded to the ninth floor of the Hall building to occupy the university's computer centre.[53] Tensions grew to a climax on the fourteenth day of the occupation when, feeling betrayed by the administration and cornered by the police, the students barricaded themselves in the computer centre. Realizing that the riot squad had been called in, the students threw paper and computer punch cards out of the ninth-floor window. Riot police broke down the doors and, in the confusion that ensued, a fire broke out and computers were destroyed.

In the end, ninety-seven protesters were arrested, criminal charges were laid, and the damage totalled over two million dollars. Rosie Douglas and Anne Cools were seen as the ringleaders, and they each served significant jail time for their actions.[54] The media broadcast news of the event around the world, and protests against symbols of Canadian power erupted throughout the Caribbean. Students at the Cave Hill campus of the University of the West Indies in Barbados mounted a "symbolic burial of Anderson and the racist institution of Sir George Williams University,"[55] and the visit of Canadian Governor General Daniel Roland Michener to the West Indies on a "good-will tour" set off a series of mass protests – he was even blocked by students from entering the University of West Indies St Augustine campus – contributing to a period of political unrest that nearly toppled the government of Trinidad.[56]

The Sir George Williams Affair has generally been left out of narratives chronicling political developments in Montreal during the 1960s. It has been seen as either an aberration or, at best, a matter of secondary importance to the struggle between two linguistic groups. When it is remembered, it is generally portrayed as an event having relevance only for Black Canadians, and as a conflict that had little impact outside of the circles of Black Montreal. Such representations distort both the impact of this event on other sectors of society, and the ways in which the protest formed part of a larger atmosphere of revolt that prevailed in the city. In addition, this interpretation overlooks the fact that the occupation had the support of many White students at the university, and that they actually formed the majority of those present.[57]

Black students, most of whom had come to Canada from the Caribbean to study, were keenly aware of both the international context and the local environment in which they lived.[58] Alfie Roberts, a member of the Caribbean Conference Committee and a participant in the Sir George Williams Affair, was aware of being part of a larger movement that affected nearly all aspects of life in Quebec. In 1962, the same year that he immigrated to Montreal from his native St Vincent and the Grenadines, Roberts read

Marcel Chaput's *Pourquoi je suis séparatiste* and realized that many people in Quebec were making claims to independence similar to those being championed by the nations of the Third World. Roberts described the meshing of international and local developments when he arrived in Montreal:

> So all of this was happening and there was a certain conjuncture
> of events. We are talking about the agitation, the effervescence, the
> emerging to the fore of the problems that Black people were having
> and were publicly agitating to have redressed in the United States; we
> are talking especially about the Cuban Revolution in 1959 with its
> bearded, olive green-clad combatants filling the newspaper pages and
> the works of guerrilla warfare by Che Guevara making the rounds;
> we're going back to Nkrumah in 1957 – the independence of Ghana;
> we're talking about Guinea in 1959; the works of Fanon. All of this
> had a tremendous impact on what was happening here in Quebec
> and I walked into all of it.[59]

Roberts argued that the many Black conferences of the 1960s could be considered as "a Black complement to the ongoing Québécois Quiet Revolution." When the Sir George Williams Affair erupted in February of 1969, Roberts continued, it "announced loud and clear that Black people were here, and not only below the tracks, but inside the whole society." The event, Roberts explained, must be understood as coinciding with the "tremendous worker unrest" that prevailed in the province of Quebec at the time.[60] True, Roberts was something of an exception among those involved in the Sir George Williams Affair. He had arrived in Canada relatively early and was not a student at the time of the event. But the young students who were radicalized by the affair also came to recognize the importance of the local situation. The Sir George Affair – with crowds of White people yelling "burn, nigger, burn" during the fire, and with the Black students being locked up separately from the White students once they had been arrested[61] – provided many with a dramatic example of the discrimination that they faced more subtly on a daily basis.

As Paul Gilroy has argued, racism needs to be understood not as a static essence that exists unchanged through history, but rather as a process, as something which gains new characteristics and dimensions at different moments. Understanding racism depends on our "capacity to comprehend political, ideological and economic change."[62] Racism, to put it another way, does not "move tidily and unchanged through time and history. It assumes new forms and articulates new antagonisms in different situations."[63] The events of February 1969 grew out of tensions caused by racial injustice in Montreal and throughout the world. Local events acquired their meaning when they were read through larger narratives of anti-colonialism and anti-imperialism, as well as the Civil Rights and Black Power movements. And the Sir George Affair itself played an important role in causing many Montrealers to embrace Black Power as an intellectual framework.

The confrontation at Sir George also changed the way in which some francophone intellectuals thought about race. Gestures of support came from many in Quebec nationalist circles. During the occupation, a scheduled "Quebec Week," which was to feature many prominent nationalist figures, was cancelled in support of the occupation.[64] Student groups across the country came out in support of the occupation and against institutionalized racism. After the forced expulsion from the computer room and the vast property damage that ensued, however, many supporters disappeared. The students' society at Sir George Williams University attempted to distance itself from the events of 11 February, even firing the editor of *The Georgian*, the university's main student newspaper, and there was a backlash against those involved in the demonstration among the university's student body,[65] including some Black students.[66] Nearly all of the main anglophone student organizations abandoned the protestesters, and many faculty members did so as well (although some Black faculty members supported the students).[67] Nonetheless there was some support from francophone circles. The Montreal Central Council of the CSN called for the release of those being held in prison, declaring that the mainstream media "tends to forget that the material mess caused by the occupation of SGWU is nothing in comparison with the problem of racism."[68]

In the university newspapers, individual students wrote angrily about the events at Sir George. Speaking on behalf of students at the Université de Montréal, Romeo Bouchard wrote that as both francophone Quebeckers and as students they were "brothers twice over" of the Black students at Sir George.[69] One author in *Le Quartier latin* wondered whether, by "blaming the ferocity of a cornered animal, we come to forget the ferocity of the animal that corners," and went on to question the operating priorities of the modern capitalist system: "These charred IBM computers acted as the very symbol of a consumer society that turns its universities into depersonalizing factories, manipulating and shaping humanity to its own needs." Those "who idolize the dollar as the Supreme Dispenser of peace and happiness are enraged to see $2 million go up in flames," yet these same people do not shed a tear when "the human spirit is suffocated in the cold bowels of the machine."[70] Jacques Maassen articulated the same sentiment in the pages of the *McGill Daily*, arguing that the very fact that such "havoc" was caused over "the destruction of a few computers" demonstrated "the corrupt sense of values infused into us by our 'great society.'" The destruction of a computer, he argued, was a symbolic act against "the image of the progression and evolution of this society."[71]

In the hall outside of the large courtroom where the arrested students were to appear, amongst the bright and colourful dashikis, many people wore "McGill français" buttons. A petition was passed around stating that "black students and French students are more or less fighting for the same things."[72] And a reverend who had travelled all the way up from Harlem for the trial distributed leaflets that had been given to him outside. The leaflet read:

WE THE SUPPORTERS FOR ALL PEOPLES DEMAND THAT THE STUDENTS WHO ARE BEING ILLEGALLY HELD WITHOUT BAIL BE RELEASED IMMEDIATELY.

THE ALLEGED DAMAGE DONE TO THE COMPUTERS READ TO THE AMOUNT OF TWO MILLION DOLLARS WHEREAS THE AMOUNT OF DAMAGE MANIFESTED BY INSTITUTIONALIZED RACISM IS INCALCULABLE.

NOT EVEN IN RACELAND, U.S.A. WOULD THIS GRAVE INJUSTICE BE COMMITTED.

WE WANT JUSTICE.

And, on the reverse side of many of the leaflets:

NOUS LES NÈGRES BLANCS D'AMÉRIQUE SOUTENONS NOS FRÈRES.[73]

MONTREAL'S BLACK RENAISSANCE

By bringing questions of racism and immigration to the forefront of public discussion, the Sir George Williams Affair challenged many of the established truths of the Montreal left, but its most important and lasting impact was on Black Montreal. When Black activists and their supporters decided to take over the computer centre, they did so with the belief that the computer symbolized not only capitalist modernity, but also the ravages that Western imperialism had wrought on the poor nations of the world. Through the control of technology, capitalism was transforming the world's population into consumers, and they conceived of their efforts as an attempt to bring democracy to the community, the country, and the world.[74] After the destruction of the computers and the riot squad's forceful removal of the students, various segments of Montreal's Black population came together as a community.[75] According to Dennis Forsythe, the affair was "a major event in the metamorphosis of Black people."[76] In the pages of *Expression*, the journal of the Negro Citizenship Association, an editorial argued that the events "had a profound influence on that institution and the entire Montreal community." It had become clear that Canada, "riddled with paradoxes and contradictions," was a country that championed "equality for all races" yet "condone[d] in silence the unequal treatment of its non-white peoples: the Indians, the Eskimos, the Japanese, the blacks." In the context of the heated aftermath of the Sir George Williams Affair, the battle for equality "can be considered nothing less than a revolutionary struggle to reformulate the basic and fundamental concepts, value judgments, and ways in which each racial group perceives the existence of all others."[77]

Black activists decided that they needed to move out of the university milieu and begin organizing the community in its entirety, especially those, like domestic servants, who were the most vulnerable. Alfie Roberts started the Caribbean International Service Bureau, which organized a conference, started a day care, and published a special issue of the *McGill Free Press* entitled "The Black Spark."[78] According to Leroy Butcher, Black activists and intellectuals were teaching people that they had the right to do things for themselves, and that they needed to believe in themselves and be proud of their history.[79] Members of the Black community began meeting on a weekly basis at what became known as the "Thursday Night Rally." The rallies started after the Sir George Affair, when semi-weekly gatherings were held to relay information about the arrested students. As the meetings evolved, they became a forum for broad community discussions about race and racism. Before long, guest speakers were regularly being invited, and a crowd of up to 175 people would commonly turn out for the event.

Historian Roy States gave lectures on international Black history and on the history of Blacks in Canada. Films featuring the Black struggle were screened, speakers lectured on Africa and South America, and discussions about books like *Malcolm X Speaks* and *Soul on Ice* took place among young people struggling to find their place in the world.[80]

If uncompromising militancy and a belief in violence as an appropriate means of social change led in part to the destruction of the computer centre, the racist backlash after the event instigated the creation of a range of new organizations and institutions. The creation of communications media such as Black Is Television and, slightly later, *The Black Voice* were matched by new community organizations such as the Côte des Neiges Black Community Association, the Lasalle Black Community Association, the Black Coalition of Quebec, the Notre-Dame-de-Grace Black Community Association, the Quebec Black Board of Educators and others.[81] Other activities emerged, such as the Congress of Black Women, as well as Cultural Youth Workshops and Black Youth TV, and a group of university students formed the Black Action Party and set out to provide afro-centric education for Black youth. Initiatives of grassroots organizing and alternative media proliferated, becoming a crucial element of Montreal life in throughout the 1970s.[82]

One of the most important legacies of the Sir George Williams Affair was UHURU (Swahili for "freedom"), a newspaper that became the dominant voice articulating Black activism in the city.[83] The paper began as a bulletin of the Feb. 11th Defence Committee and, through its very existence, was seen as a concrete demonstration of Black Power ideals.[84] It provided a medium free from White control through which Black intellectuals were able to challenge the assumptions of Western society and develop their own understanding of themselves and of their community.

The paper, while always controversial, was an immediate success. Its circulation of roughly 3,000 nearly matched that of *Parti Pris* of the mid-1960s,[85] and the editors felt that the "demand is even more pressing."[86] UHURU even received a letter of congratulations from Stokely and Miriam Carmichael, thanking the paper for the service that it was rendering "to the Black world."[87] On 30 November 1969, over 300 of its supporters celebrated the opening of its new office on 2554 Saint-Antoine. On the ground floor of an apartment building in the city's traditional Black neighbourhood, the office was identified by a big sign that hung in its window. The interior of the building matched its austere exterior. The walls, plastered with posters, were adorned with a painting, a map of Africa, and a donated electric clock; a picture of Eldridge Cleaver hung on the door to the toilet. In the combined workroom and library, the journal's writers sought to develop their own understandings of the origins of, and alternatives to, the injustice that surrounded them.[88]

Although those who wrote for UHURU articulated a variety of ideological positions, they agreed on a few central points. Chief of these was the conviction that to be Black was to be colonized, and therefore to be on the side of those who were involved in the worldwide struggle against empire. And Montreal's radical Black writers – building on the work and insights of the Caribbean Conference Committee[89] – were at the forefront of developing analyses of Canada's imperialist role in the Caribbean. While many in the wider circles of the left saw Montreal as a colonized city, Black writers began considering its role as an imperial metropole which undoubtedly formed part of the West, and which therefore held its share of responsibility for the misery inflicted upon the poor nations of the world.[90]

Black writers in Montreal would continue seeing their condition through an anti-imperialist lens, analysing universities like Sir George Williams as institutions that fulfilled a "colonial role of conditioning young people (Bible in hand) under the guise of progress, civilization, democracy and christianity."[91] Viewed from this angle, the Sir George Affair was an "unavoidable confrontation between colonizer and colonized."[92] Because capitalism had historically required slave labour, it was argued, racism and capitalism were connected. But it was not capitalism per se, but colonization – theorized explicitly as the experience and legacy of African slavery – that gave the Black liberation struggle "an autonomous vitality of its own."[93] Frantz Fanon's *Black Skin, White Masks* acted as a key work for Montrealers who sought to understand the meaning of racial oppression. Fanon had outlined ways in which notions of Black inferiority and White superiority had infused and shaped cultural systems and individual perceptions. For Fanon, "White" had come to represent morality, beauty, intelligence, rationality, and respect; "Black," on the other hand, symbolized "the lower emotions, the baser inclinations, the dark side of the soul."[94] Fanon helped to elucidate the "black sickness of mind," the "acquired belief" in "inferiority based on the enforced values of a white society" that so many Blacks had experienced.[95]

Maurice Tremblay, for example, wrote movingly in UHURU about how he devalued himself as a Black person growing up in Montreal, and about

the psychological trauma of constantly living under the gaze of White society. For Tremblay, the Sir George Williams Affair was a turning point.
When the administration remained deaf to the students' concerns, and
when the crowd yelled "let the niggers burn" as the fire broke out in the computer centre, he began to understand that the task at hand was *not* to emu-
late White society but to celebrate and "rejoice in Black Identity."[96] Like
many other writers in *UHURU*, Tremblay had become convinced that Blacks
in Montreal could no longer allow their self-perceptions to be forged by others. Writers in *UHURU* varied in the meaning they assigned to being Black.
Some defended an essentialist position, arguing that Blacks formed a proud
race that had been destroyed,[97] while others gave a political and ethical
definition to the word. But uniting the various attempts was the belief that
Blacks *themselves* needed to do the defining, needed to come together and
establish their own terms of reference.

As compared to those of many American cities, Montreal's Black community was extremely small, numbering no more than about 15,000 at the
end of the 1960s.[98] And they were deeply aware that there was little hope of
advocating complete separation from larger society.[99] Perhaps for this reason, pan-Africanism took on a heightened importance for Black activists
in Montreal. Rosie Douglas explained the appeal of Stokely Carmichael's
vision in this regard: Carmichael saw Pan-Africanism as the "highest political expression" of Black Power, and believed that "African people on the
continent or scattered all over the world must define their working political framework in a manner which will enable us in our day to day struggle to relate our common heritage to the racist oppression which we all
face irrespective of our socio-economic status."[100] As more and more Blacks
in Montreal began to see the world this way, there was a great surge of
interest in all things African. Groups began organizing cultural events like
the "Journey back to Africa" and articles featured "authentic" African fashion. News of the "first real Afro-American wedding in Canada" even
adorned the front page of the paper.[101]

BLACK INTELLECTUALS AND MONTREAL

UHURU may have framed its struggle as between Black and White, but such
a clear dichotomy ultimately could not hold given the complexities of
empire in Canada. From its very beginning, *UHURU* acknowledged a ten-

sion between the conflation of the "colonized" with "Black," and the recognition that not all of those who were colonized were of African origin. In an issue arguing that the dominant legacy of the Sixties was the challenge to White supremacy, Asian and Latin American anti-imperial resistance was cited alongside struggles in Africa, the Caribbean, and Black North America.[102] And, perhaps not surprisingly, Black Power advocates in Montreal reached out to Native Canadians in their first attempt to build solidarities across different movements.

The first non-Black person who lectured at a rally of the Black community at the UNIA Hall was Henry Jacks, an Aboriginal man from Vancouver. In UHURU, Edmund Michael compared the plight of Aboriginals and that of Blacks. Henry Jacks, Michael wrote, "has had to endure very much the same type of humiliations and dehumanization that the black man has had to endure in this country."[103] "We as black people here in Canada," Michael continued, must "turn a sympathetic eye to the plight of the red man and vice versa for, just as he is kept in place on his controlled reservations and in the ghetto and are always regarded as 'those damned Indians,' so too are we regarded as 'those damned niggers,' by whites." It was necessary for Black activists to make contact with Native groups, for "after all it is they who were the original owners of N. America and we as black people were forced to work and build it all for the white people, who are our oppressors." He called on his readers "to develop the consciousness of our fellow blacks, while the reds strive to re-educate their people, and in this way, we can co-operate with each other in areas which can rebound to the mutual benefit of both peoples who constitute the 'wretched of the earth'."[104] Another article mocked Cardinal Leger's plea for Catholics to conduct missionary work in Africa and argued that, in "view of the treatment meted out not only to Blacks in Canada but also to the indigenous Indians, one wonders whether Cardinal Leger and the Church should not transfer their missionary activities to the Canadian scene."[105] Following and extending the logic of Black Power, UHURU advocated Native control over Native communities. UHURU also covered the rising tide of militant Native activism in the United States,[106] and clearly saw Red Power as a natural ally of Black Power.

But Montreal also differed from other North American cities in that radicals of the *majority* population claimed to be colonized by a foreign power. Montreal's Black activists therefore faced a situation in which many in the White population surrounding them had drawn on the very same literature of Third World liberation and Black Power as they did to theorize themselves as being culturally, economically, and psychologically dominated by an imperial system of power. This basic fact of Montreal life in the 1960s could neither be ignored nor dismissed; at press conferences and in interviews, Black activists were repeatedly asked about their position on the "Quebec situation."[107] Still, as late as 1968, many Black leaders refused to acknowledge the legitimacy of the movement in Quebec. When three organizers of the Congress of Black Writers, Rosie Douglas, Keith Byrne and Elder Thébaud, were interviewed by the *McGill Daily* just before the opening of the congress, Douglas stated that one of the important landmarks of the event was that it brought both French- and English-speaking Blacks together in the same forum.[108] But when the interviewer of the *Daily* pushed further, asking about the "significance" of the bilingual nature of the conference, clearly implying that it was related to its location in Montreal, Thébaud merely reiterated that it was significant in that French- and English-speaking Blacks were getting together. That Quebec itself was bilingual, Thébaud stated, was of little importance. The interviewer then pushed further: "some Québecois draw an analogy between the situation of the Blacks in the world and that of French-speaking Québecois. Do you [think that] the analogy is valid, and if so, do you see the possibility of co-operation between Québecois and blacks?" Thébaud remained intransigent: "Quebeckers like to call themselves the *nègres* of Canada, but we would like to highlight the fact that of all races, the black race has been the most humiliated. We therefore need first to organize among Blacks who have been divided by the colonizer. Collaboration between Blacks and oppressed Whites is desirable, but this is not the task of the moment." Thébaud and Douglas were adamant that it mattered little that the congress was being held in Montreal. When asked if it was important for people in Canada and Quebec to hear speakers on the subject of racial discrimination, Thébaud responded again: "No," it was important for "people generally." It was "incidental" that the congress was being held in Montreal, and it "could have been held anywhere."[109] Rosie Douglas quickly added that the congress could have been held "on Mars" for all that it mattered.[110]

■ ■ ■

It is not difficult to understand why Black activists would have been hesitant to recognize the political claims of French-speaking Quebeckers. Black people had been enslaved by French colonists from the earliest days of settlement, and they had been marginalized and debased ever since. They had been subject to the discrimination and racism of French- and English-speaking Montrealers alike, and it is easy to see how the struggle for Quebec liberation, which up until the late 1960s had been predicated on the language of francophone victimization, could be seen to be of little concern for them. With the rarest of exceptions, francophone intellectuals ignored the presence of Montreal's Black population.

The first opening towards mutual recognition came in the aftermath of the computer centre incident and amidst the vicious language debates that were tearing the city apart. As mentioned earlier, the Montreal Central Council of the CSN publicly declared its support for the students and denounced the attitude of the courts in which they were being prosecuted.[111] And in the years following the Sir George Affair, Black intellectuals arrived at a deeper understanding of the complex power relations of Montreal society. In 1970, those responsible for the Thursday night rallies decided to set up a political committee to develop an analysis "of the political situation in Quebec."[112] They also recognized their ambiguous situation in the language wars, and of the danger that they might be unwittingly drawn into the debate as tacit supporters of "English rights." When an English-language school attempted to use Black children to bolster their arguments for English-language education, *UHURU* reacted angrily. If "the white English at the Royal Arthur School want to fight the white French," the paper asked, "why use blacks to fight their war?" In educational debates, as in all other aspects of life, Black people needed to "act on decisions made by themselves and by their own initiation."[113] Racism, another article argued, existed in both francophone and anglophone communities, and it was necessary that Blacks abstain from the language wars, demanding that "both English and French be taught to our children."[114]

While *UHURU* always maintained that Blacks were the object "of discrimination from both English and French," the paper did recognize that Blacks and francophones were oppressed by the same forces in the province. In English-controlled companies, an editorial argued, "racist hiring policies ... have existed for years," and "French speaking Quebecois find it very difficult to make any headway in the economics of their country." It was therefore "difficult if not impossible to understand how blacks (the object of discrimination from both English and French) can find themselves doing any better than the French if at all as well."[115]

The 1970 provincial election campaign was the first in which the Parti Québécois (PQ), the new provincial sovereignist party that had been founded in 1968, fielded candidates. The PQ's social democratic platform captured the hopes of a wide variety of activists, from labour unionists to members of neighbourhood citizens' committees. Opinion in the Black community was divided over the election and the significance of the PQ. In an official editorial, *UHURU* noted that during the election, which ended up bringing the Quebec Liberal Party to power, "the white anglo-saxon (English speaking) voters panicked at the thought of independence in Quebec, not understanding what it is all about, fearing reprisals, loss of influence, and against the French majority assuming their rightful positions of responsibility (economic and otherwise) in their own province." When it came to the PQ, the editorial explained that their "platform is clear cut and should be viewed without fear since it simply calls for [francophone] Quebecers [to take] control of Quebec, which is the ambition and right of all nations and peoples." It even suggested that "Blacks must if they intend to stay in Quebec make up their minds to adopt at least a working knowledge of French."[116]

When Dennis Forsythe published *Let the Niggers Burn!* in 1971 about the Sir George Williams Affair and its aftermath, the very first sentence of the book – "Something happened here in Montréal on February 11th, 1969, which for different reasons neither Blacks nor Whites will ever forget" – reveals an important change in the dialogue between Black and francophone activists. Unlike most anglophones, Forsythe used the French spelling of 'Montréal,' thereby recognizing the primacy of the French language in the city.[117] For Forsythe, it was crucially important to understand that "Quebec is a tension-ridden environment, and that this state of affairs has increased over the last few years. Quebec, and Montreal specifically, is like a machine creaking at its seams, as witnessed by the increasing frustrations and resentment expressed by almost all segments of the society. In the last three years policemen, teachers, taxi-drivers, post-men, anti-poverty groups, students and women have all entered the 'long march' here in Quebec."[118]

According to Forsythe, one had to realize that, as "conservatism, capitalism and imperialism, to an even greater extent, do not respect national borders; so neither can radicalism respect frontiers." But although an incident such as the Sir George Williams Affair "could have occurred in many other places; that it erupted in Montreal, and at Sir George Williams University, is due to specific situational factors that emerged in Montreal."[119] While struggling with key questions of empire, imperialism, and colonization, many other Black Montrealers came to understand the cultural and material oppression of French-speaking Quebeckers. Some, like the writers of the Caribbean International Service Bureau, even began seeing the French-Canadian working class, who they hoped would intervene "on the side of black and oppressed people in their struggle for a new society," as potential allies in the political struggles in the years to come.[120]

■ ■ ■

Black writers introduced new analyses of race, community development and democracy into the public sphere, adding and contributing to the complex and hybrid mixture of ideas and movements. In ways that were at times complex and at times contradictory, a new generation of Black intellectuals challenged dominant understandings of colonization, and worked to reclaim the meaning of Blackness through a process of psychological, economic, and political decolonization. Yet Black Power in Montreal, like the larger world of Montreal radicalism of which it formed a part, rarely even recognized one of its most central contradictions. While advocating liberation for all human beings, Black Power was theorized as a "struggle for manhood,"[121] both explicitly and implicitly excluding women from any active role. Winston Franco argued that "there are some black people who cannot see the institutionalized racism of our society." This was not such "a strange phenomenon," he continued, "since people who lose their balls in their infancy find it impossible to remember what it felt like to have had them."[122] Omowale wrote that "the dignity and manhood of black students at Sir George Williams University, was belittled in every way possible."[123] During one of the demonstrations of the occupation, Rocky Jones challenged the masculinity of White men, calling them "pansies, because they won't even fight for white folks."[124] And in the surge of Black Power activism after the event, one author wrote in UHURU that the "Black Man is the personification of strength, power, peace and love; the 'Father of Civilization,'" and even the very "essence of Manhood."[125]

But while Black men were called forth to reclaim their virility, Black women were expected to assume a passive role. True, women had been involved in Black politics from the start. The 1967–68 *Caribbean Conference*

Bulletin highlighted the work of Anne Cools, Bridget Joseph, Gloria Simmons, and Jean Depradine as "the living indication that the Caribbean woman will be in the forefront of the movement for a new Caribbean."[126] More often than not, however, women were valued only as the reproductive force of the nation, a position sometimes advocated by women themselves.[127]

This was typical of left wing politics in the 1960s. While theorizing national liberation, male activists were blind to the oppression many women experienced in their traditional roles. But at the end of the 1960s, Black women began speaking out against the sexism of a movement that was ostensibly going to bring about "liberation," mostly through letters to the editor and to the advice column of *UHURU*, and surely in many heated arguments in meeting places and private homes. Letter after letter complained that Black men continued to believe in the myth of White beauty. In addition, the men thought that being seen with a White woman was a symbol of success. Black women felt that they were perceived as slowing the progress of their husbands. Black men's search for White women, their "reaching out after whiteness," often affected Black women "to the point of trauma."[128] Many were left "sad and confused" with the hypocrisies of the movement.[129]

Black women argued that racism, with all of its devastating implications, did not operate in isolation. For one woman it was clear that "our so-called black brothers" did not seem to be practising what they preached. "These brothers," she argued, "have no morals, no manners, no etiquette, they treat the sisters like dirt." She had even come to believe "that all this black power bit is a farce."[130] Black women, another author wrote, experienced the same devaluation by Black men as Black men did from White society. "So that what he [the Black man] termed as 'violence' on the part of the white man," she argued, "he viciously practices in turn on the Black woman."[131] Anne Cools, who was both a member of the Caribbean Conference Committee and a participant in the Sir George Williams Affair, was one of the loudest voices to speak out. Through her work, she helped to build a new militancy among women, a militancy that was capturing the imaginations of women across North America.[132] In Montreal, as across the continent, individuals began recognizing the need to extend organizing and cultural self-affirmation to women. When they did so, Montreal politics would never be the same again.

FIVE

QUÉBÉCOISES DEBOUTTE!

On the evening of 28 November 1969, two hundred women – many wearing chains to symbolize their oppression – charged out of their meeting-place on Saint-Laurent Boulevard into the middle of the street, where they sat down in a circle and waited to be arrested. The hundreds of riot police who were waiting outside arrested 165 of them and in less than an hour the street was open to the regular flow of traffic. The protest, although small in size and relatively short in duration, was loaded with meaning. That fall, a spirit of revolt had been spreading throughout various sectors of Montreal society and the city's streets had become the primary space where dissident groups expressed their voices. The city's administration, claiming to be acting in the interests of the "silent majority," had passed Regulation 3926, effectively banning public protests. Although many groups and individuals were quick to denounce the law, the women gathered on Saint-Laurent Boulevard were the first to defy it.[1]

This demonstration acted as a watershed in feminist mobilization. Women on Montreal's English-speaking university campuses had already been reading feminist literature and meeting together, and had even formed the Montreal Women's Liberation Movement (MWLM). But in the lead-up to the protest, and during the protest itself, many anglophone women close to the MWLM joined with francophone women from leftist groups, unions, and citizens' committees, to create the Front commun des Québécoises, a loose organization that had no leader, spokesperson, or official ties to any feminist organization. And in the aftermath of the protest, English- and French-speaking women came together to form the Front de libération des femmes du Québec (FLF), a group that would become the public voice of women's liberation in Montreal. Many of the ideas and arguments that the FLF would later popularize were first articulated in relation to the 28 November protest. In response to the municipal administration's claim to be acting on behalf of the "silent majority," the women argued that they represented "the point of view of the largest silent majority which exists in the world, that of women."[2] They were taking to the streets to contest the convention of female passivity. By "relying on an old prejudice which dictates that men, embodied by the police, are the protectors of women," they hoped to disarm the established system of power.[3] And by claiming the right to protest, the women were asserting their right to think and act as citizens, and therefore challenging the traditional hold that men claimed over political participation.

The women saw their action as having a significance far beyond the interests of one social group. By defending their right to think, to disagree, and to protest, they saw themselves as fighting on behalf of "all of Quebec society."[4] Radical women in Montreal, like Black women in the United States, differed from many other North American feminists in rejecting the idea that "woman" was a universal category. They argued that in their province, women were marginalized both as women and as Quebeckers, and therefore their fight needed to be framed in the terms of radical humanism and universal emancipation. What was at stake, as one group put it, was "not only our liberation, but also the liberation of all our people, and of all the peoples of the world."[5] By challenging the language of the left on its own terms, women therefore worked to conceptualize liberation in deeper and more all-inclusive terms.

Any nuanced and large-scale study of the ways in which second-wave feminism transformed Quebec culture will have to consider the countless women – many of whom did not form part of feminist organizations – who challenged the structures of their everyday lives, transforming institutions and altering urban landscapes.[6] They fought for equality and recognition in workplaces and unions, and they questioned their most intimate relationships.[7] A more inclusive approach and an expanded understanding of politics will also allow scholars to explore the ways in which the province's diverse communities, such as Montreal's Caribbean activists, building on

Black women's long history of resistance to both racism and sexism, learned from and contributed to the development of Quebec feminism.[8] Finally, the role that lesbians and transsexuals have played in challenging the gender norms and hierarchies of exclusion in public spaces, hierarchies which were often inscribed in the very logic of the early women's liberation movement itself, will need to be highlighted.[9]

But this is not my goal. In this chapter, I want to explore the ideas that the women's liberation movement introduced into Montreal's public sphere, and the ways in which these ideas built upon and shaped the larger language of opposition.[10] From its beginnings, women's liberation in Montreal was a hybrid movement that combined the insights of the nascent women's movement in the United States (and, somewhat later, France) with conceptions of decolonization that were being developed in the city.

CHALLENGING GENDER IN THE 1960S

Beginning in the early 1960s, there was a resurgence of a feminist consciousness in Montreal, as women began arguing that the right to vote – which had been the object of a long and arduous political battle – did not, in itself, guarantee full political citizenship or equal rights. Women's lives were changing dramatically during the period. Quebec's birth rate was dropping, births out of wedlock were increasing, and married women were coming to occupy a greater role in the workforce.[11] In 1966, one-third of women aged twenty-four to thirty-four were in the paid workforce, and this number jumped to 39.9% by 1971 and continued to climb. Despite newfound economic independence, however, many opportunities for individual self-development were blocked by the persistence of sexism. Although entering the workforce in record numbers, women, for the most part, were marginalized in "women's professions," and were often expected to work in the paid labour force during the day while remaining responsible for housework in the evening.[12] The labour movement remained mostly male, although women were increasingly present in large numbers, and it was not until the very late 1960s and early 1970s that labour organizations began to seriously integrate feminist issues into their activities.[13]

Women did not sit idly by as society was changing around them. In 1960 some, like long-time labour activist Simone Monet-Chartrand, joined the Voice of Women, a peace organization that denounced nuclear proliferation, advocated greater female participation in politics, and argued that it was up to women, in their roles as mothers and educators, to defend the universal values of justice, love, and liberty.[14] Others challenged the structures of their everyday lives, rejecting the gender codes inscribed in their families and personal relationships. A major turning point came in 1965 when, on the twenty-fifth anniversary of women's right to vote in provincial elections, Thérèse Casgrain organized a conference. Five hundred women from diverse sectors of Quebec society discussed issues ranging from divorce to contraception, from discrimination in the workforce to maternity leave. They resolved to create a new feminist organization in the province, and the following year the Fédération des femmes du Québec was formed, uniting women's groups of many different kinds, and marking the beginnings of second-wave feminism in Quebec.[15]

In the face of persistent discrimination, women from both English Canada and Quebec began demanding a Royal Commission on women's inequality. In February 1967, the federal government yielded to their demands by establishing the Royal Commission on the Status of Women.[16] The various individuals and groups who came before the commission demanded pay equity, equal opportunities in the workplace, maternity leave and day care, reintegration and retraining for mature women, the valorization of women's unpaid work in the home, and an end to a system which gave drastically different opportunities according to one's sex. Their briefs collectively articulated the concerns of second-wave feminism: the need to overcome individual and social alienation, the necessity for self-actualization, and the importance of women's meaningful participation in society. Both Betty Friedan, author of *The Feminine Mystique*, and Simone de Beauvoir, author of *The Second Sex*, had argued that because women had been taught that fulfilment could only be achieved through their role as mothers, they were systematically excluded from responsibilities of political citizenship. Because women were discouraged from developing their full creative potential, they did not see the future as an open realm of possibility that could be forged through their actions. Women, in other words, were taught to be the objects rather than the subjects of history.[17]

In their testimonies before the Royal Commission, women were demonstrating that they refused to accept a passive role.[18] And one step in becoming fully autonomous and responsible human beings was having control over one's own body. In the hearings of the Royal Commission, women

repeatedly argued that they needed to gain greater control over their sexuality, and that the ability to control their own fertility was a central fac-
tor in emancipation. The Marriage Counselling Centre of Montreal
demanded daycares and legalized abortion, and argued that medical schools
needed to teach doctors to be more sensitive to sexual health issues.[19] The
Medical Students' Society of McGill University, speaking to issues directly
affecting "the freedom of women in society," argued that laws needed to be
adapted to the mores of a rapidly changing society; contraception and sexual education needed to be made widely available, and abortion should
be legalized.[20] For Montreal's Centre de Planification familiale, birth control was the cornerstone of all of the changes in the status of women
throughout the past few years. While it was clear that "our society was constructed by men and for men," the arrival of new forms of contraception
profoundly altered the political and social landscape; for the first time in
history, women could separate sexuality from reproduction, could rely on
reason rather than tradition to weigh options and choose which one to
follow.[21]

The Royal Commission brought together a myriad of disjointed senti-
ments and experiences, experiences not yet united in any holistic program
of social change. Such a program would emerge from the analyses of
women's liberation that first emerged in the city's English-speaking university campuses. In 1968, the pages of the *McGill Daily* – a paper that was
widely read and one of the most important voices of anglophone student
activism – was publishing new voices of women who were being influenced by the women's liberation movement. The front page of the 1 November 1968 edition of *The Review*, the *McGill Daily* supplement, featured a
graphic picture of a young naked woman being held down by barbed wire,
and the lead article sarcastically mused about the socially prescribed roles
that women were expected to fill.[22] Other articles urged that women's
liberation must form part of the larger radical awakening taking place in
the city.[23]

Women's liberation was also emerging as a theme within New Left circles in the rest of Canada, and women tried to find novel ways of incorpo-
rating feminism into Marxist frameworks. Margaret Benston's widely
circulated "Political Economy of Women's Liberation," for example, sought
to outline the function of housework within capitalism, and the essay had
an important underground life before being published in the *Monthly
Review* in 1969.[24] All of these developments had a deep resonance at McGill.

To build a women's liberation movement based on the working class, Myrna Wood and Kathy McAffee argued in the *McGill Student Handbook* in 1969, women needed to fight not only for equality with men, but also for access to child care, birth control, abortions, and self defence. This was "not so much an academic question," the authors maintained, but "an inescapable empirical fact; women must fight their conditions just to participate in the movement."[25]

One of the first major texts of the movement was the *Birth Control Handbook*. The publication of the handbook by the McGill Students' Society in 1968 deliberately defied a Canadian law that prohibited the distribution of information on birth control and was considered, from the outset, as "a political act."[26] First distributed to students at English-language universities, the publication became increasingly popular and successful, and other schools and organizations began ordering copies. Its phenomenal success was a testament to the pent-up demand for information about contraception. By the summer of 1969, nearly 50,000 copies had been sold, and this number increased to a quarter of a million by 1969–70, and to nearly two million by 1970–71.[27]

A decisive moment for feminist organizing came when well-known American feminist Marlene Dixon obtained a teaching post in the Sociology Department at McGill University in 1969. She began giving courses in the sociology of women that directly addressed questions relating to the women's movement such as imperialism, labour, and women's work.[28] Partly as a result of her influence, English-speaking university students founded the MWLM in October 1969.[29] The group's members – many of whom had fled the United States with male draft dodgers – were deeply shaped by American feminist theory.[30]

The development of the women's liberation movement in anglophone Montreal was linked to the collective awakening of women across North America.[31] Susan Brownmiller, speaking of the beginnings of women's liberation in New York City, recalls meetings that at times "took on the flavor of a tent camp revival, a hallelujah chorus."[32] In Montreal, the MWLM was attracting members by the dozen, holding meetings in the fall of 1969 and the winter of 1970 on Thursday nights at the University Settlement on Saint-Urbain Street. The meetings had no hierarchy and no leadership, so the topics and format of discussions were determined by all participants.

From these meetings, smaller "consciousness-raising" groups were formed.[33] Discovering their common experiences of discrimination and alienation, women were beginning to see the political nature of personal problems. Housework and birth control, sexual satisfaction and ideas of feminine beauty were all recognized as political issues.[34] Women began to realize the systemic nature of their personal problems and to think collectively about the possibilities of building a different future.[35] Because oppression was inscribed in the cultural codes of daily life, it was necessary to begin creating "an entirely new culture," and to do this, women needed to realize their "full potential for being strong, effective, complete human beings."[36]

English-speaking feminists in Montreal knew from the very beginning that their cause was intimately related to other liberation movements. Marie Henretta opened the first issue of the *Montreal Women's Liberation Newsletter* with a statement that clearly drew on other struggles that had engulfed the city (and the world). In "Imperialism in the Home," she argued that,

> For the wife without an independent source of income, marriage is a minute system of imperialism. Not only does the husband own and control the family property; not only has he legal power over his wife and children; not only does he direct the labour of his domestic slave, his wife, for his own benefit; but he also engages in a psychological stance as 'lord and master'. He must not only be admired, his commands must be obeyed – his own low status in the world and his cowardice in accepting the humiliations there, are purged when he heaps more of the same shit on his wife. Vicariously, he becomes the "boss," the "dictator" – he feels the thrill of domination.

To end sexist oppression, women were beginning to realize that they needed to struggle "for a revolution that is both feminist and socialist," a revolution that would create a society "in which there will be equal human beings," and "in which all share freely."[37]

The authors of the *Birth Control Handbook*, Donna Cherniak and Allan Feingold, also attempted to place the struggle for women's rights in the framework of a democratic awakening taking place across the globe. They saw the importance of their handbook as far more than the dissemination of medical information. Theirs was a project that sought to decentralize structures of power by placing expert knowledge in the hands of the oppressed, providing "men and women with the information they need to control their own bodies."[38] Birth control therefore had a "radical potential," was crucial "in the redefinition of women," and could help empower women to "write our own history and to create a future adequate to our needs." Because all forms of oppression were linked, and because the liberation struggles of all marginalized peoples were inter-connected, women's liberation could lead to the undermining of dominant structures of power. From "the understanding of one's own oppression as a woman," the authors argued, "comes a better understanding of the oppression of others also enchained in master-slave relationships." The authors therefore explicitly theorized their project as forming one part of a larger movement of resistance to imperialist systems of power,[39] and as part of an ongoing search for "new methods of governing ourselves."[40]

In addition, the authors of the handbook were sensitive to the fact that they were anglophones living and writing in a city with a francophone majority. The front cover of the handbook proudly bore a stamp declaring that the production had been carried out by workers affiliated with the CSN, the union most closely associated with labour activism at the end of the 1960s. Although writing in English, the authors wrote both "Montréal" and "Québec" in French, symbolically declaring that they believed French to be the public language of the city. But, more importantly, the handbook was translated into French as *Pour un contrôle des naissances*, and the tasks of writing a new introduction and distributing the document were given to the FLF. By 1971, 200,000 copies of the French-language edition had already been distributed.[41]

As anglophones, the members of MWLM were aware that in Quebec the English language was associated with imperial domination. And at its Thursday night meetings, in addition to discussing the economic exploitation of women and problems relating to the nuclear family, the group explored the specific history of women in Quebec. The organization agonized about its relationship to other movements in Montreal,[42] and worried greatly about poor rural women in Quebec and their access to reliable contraception.[43] Given that the MWLM was founded in the fall of 1969, the exact moment that the city's political foundations were being shaken by the linguistic debates (to be examined in the following chapter), it is no surprise that its role within Quebec society preoccupied the group. Some members began working with women in the Quebec labour movement. In the meetings that ensued, anglophone women began talking with francophone women about holding an all-women's protest to denounce the city's increasingly repressive political climate.[44] The initial link came between Naomi Brickman, a McGill student, and Nicole Thérien, an activist and employee of the CSN. Thérien had been involved in leftist movements throughout the 1960s, and had even travelled to Cuba during the summer of 1969, where she realized that socialism did not necessarily entail the liberation of women. The two activists met in the Milton-Park citizens' committee in the fall of 1969, and organized an informal group of women composed of activists in the CSN and at McGill. Out of this group came the idea of organizing an all-women's protest to denounce the anti-demonstration by-law passed by the municipal government.[45]

After the 28 November protest, a group of women decided to establish the FLF, and its first meetings were held in the library of the CSN on Saint-Denis.[46] According to Martine Lanctôt, among the francophones "women who were the most likely to join the women's liberation movement were precisely those who were involved in the political struggles of the era, and those involved in the nationalist movement. They were not very concerned about the struggle for the liberation of women. It was the anglophone feminists of Montreal who would encourage the francophone women to join the struggle for women's liberation."[47] Ultimately, the FLF set its goal as the liberation of women through the creation of an independent and socialist Quebec.

After the FLF was formed, it collaborated with the MWLM. The profits earned by the sales of the *Birth Control Handbook* provided money to open a Women's Centre located on Sainte-Famille Street in downtown Montreal. The Centre housed the MWLM, the FLF, and an abortion counselling service that had previously been run out of the apartment of the *Handbook*'s authors.[48] Walking through the door of the Sainte-Famille centre, one was immediately struck by a sign reading "Québécoises deboutte" hanging at the entrance, and by the poems and feminist slogans adorning the walls.[49] The FLF and the MWLM jointly ran the abortion referral service in 1970, until it was finally taken over by the FLF in 1971.[50] The collaboration between the two organizations, and between anglophone and francophone activists more generally, shaped the early years of women's liberation in Montreal.

It created a unique understanding of women's oppression, although tensions and conflicts often arose between the two groups.

The FLF continually tried to reach out and make headlines and change the public language of dissent that prevailed in the city. The FLF fought to lay claim to the city and widen the sphere of female political participation. Members of the group plastered "Québécoises deboutte!" stickers around Montreal and occupied taverns that did not permit the entry of women.[51] In these ways it challenged a gendered urban geography, laying claim to public space for women. In one of its most daring activities, vividly described in the work of Marjolaine Péloquin, an FLF cell occupied the jury boxes of a Montreal courthouse during a hearing for Lise Balcer, one of the witnesses in the trial of FLQ member Paul Rose. Because women were not allowed to sit as jurors in Quebec, Balcer refused to testify as a witness and was found in contempt of court. When she was in the witness box explaining the reasons for her refusal, seven FLF women from the audience charged to the front of the courtroom, took over the jury benches, and began yelling "discrimination!" and "la justice c'est de la merde!"; they brought feminism into the headlines, as they had intended, but in the process were sentenced from one to two months each in prison.[52]

In addition to trying to publicize these and other forms of discrimination, the FLF worked to develop a new interpretation of the world to voice the concerns of Quebec women. Women, the FLF argued, had never had a say in major decisions that affected their daily lives, and they were given "an education which prevented them from becoming full and equal human beings." In the summer of 1970, the FLF announced that some of its members were planning to found a newspaper "exclusively devoted to women, and centred on the various aspects of their oppression." Finished were the days of having "feminine" pages in mainstream papers. From now on "Quebec women will have an entire newspaper to themselves." It was up to women themselves to determine their own conditions of existence, to determine how to use their bodies and what to make of their lives.[53] The newspaper that the group published was distributed by Arlette Rouleau and Andrée Bérubé, two women who hitchhiked throughout the province with copies of the paper on their backs.[54] Through the FLF, the women's liberation movement became highly visible in Montreal, ensuring that its analyses and critiques would have a significant effect on wider structures of dissent.

CHALLENGING THE GENDER OF DISSENT

The women who formed the FLF came from diverse backgrounds; while some came from the largely English-language women's liberation movement, others had been active in the various groups of the Montreal left, and especially in the CSN. Women had been involved in various facets of oppositional politics throughout the 1960s,[55] but by the end of the decade the way they conceived of their participation in the larger movement began to change. Women in progressive political organizations all across Montreal were beginning to defy the expectation that they perform secondary roles, such as typing, making coffee, and preparing food. They began accusing male theorists of not taking gender oppression seriously, and of continually brushing aside women's experiences and concerns. The MWLM wrote of the "schizophrenia" of radical groups that called "for the liberation of all oppressed peoples," yet oppressed "the women right among them."[56] Radical women began, in short, to turn the language of emancipation back on the movement itself, because they realized that if women were to become free political subjects, they would need to develop their own terms of reference and their own autonomous voice of resistance. Following the example of other marginalized groups, women argued that they needed to break away, organize independently, and create free social spaces of their own. Women began making their own analyses of their place in the larger struggle as well as of their needs as women in the movement.

In *Personal Politics: The Roots of Women's Liberation in the Civil Rights Movement & the New Left*, Sara Evans demonstrates how women's liberation in the United States was born out of the discrepancy that female activists felt between the New Left's "egalitarian ideology and the oppression they continued to experience within it." But the New Left did much more "than simply perpetuate the oppression of women"; it also created arenas in which women could develop new senses of themselves and, by "heightening women's self-respect, it allowed them to claim the movement's ideology for themselves." The radical democracy of the New Left therefore "carried over into an unequivocal assertion of sexual equality," and women began taking their demands beyond a formal equality of "rights" towards a more comprehensive conception of empowerment.[57] The women's liberation movement in Montreal similarly emerged out of the wider structures of the left. By working in the various political groups of

the period, women gained confidence and experience in political organizing and, perhaps more importantly, they began learning new ways of seeing both themselves and the world around them.[58] When radical women
began defending their specific rights as women, therefore, it was from
within – and not in opposition to – the language of anti-colonialism. With
such hybrid influences, this coming together of American women's liberation theory with the terms and vocabularies of the Montreal left, women's
liberation in Montreal began to take on its own shape.

The FLF was the most prominent group attempting to articulate the
new terms of women's liberation, but it was not alone. A group of women
from Montreal also published the *Manifeste des femmes québécoises* in 1971.
The book's editor described the work as one of self-definition, a process that
always preceded self-determination.[59] The authors had clearly thought
about the left's project, and about both its potential and its serious limitations. It was not a coincidence, the authors argued, that, although women
had been involved in the Quebec liberation movement from the very beginning, nobody ever remembered the *names* of women activists. "It seems that
in the minds of everyone," the authors argued, "national liberation implies
the liberation of women." And they went on: "We have all, for the most
part, been active in a variety of groups with rather ambiguous positions on
the question of women. The 'Marxist' theory of these groups can be
summed up quickly: the capitalist system oppresses men and women. Men
oppress women because they are colonized. If we change that system, men
will be decolonized and they will stop oppressing women. Splendid. Here
is an easy evasion of the question of women, of their specific oppression,
and of the struggle that they need to wage. Such a theory encourages passivity and a wait-and-see policy. We, the women of these movements,
engaged in the big struggle against the common enemy, have been unable
to articulate how this enemy oppresses us."[60]

The experience of previous socialist revolutions had demonstrated that,
as the liberation of women was far from being an automatic outcome, it was
necessary for women to work to develop their own terms of analysis.[61] But
this severe criticism of the left did not change the fact that, for the manifesto's authors, the liberation of women was impossible without national
liberation. Women therefore had a responsibility towards the larger movement to deepen its understanding of freedom.

While male revolutionaries had *Nègres blancs d'Amérique* and *Le Petit
manuel d'histoire du Québec*, the manifesto argued that women, with the

exceptions of the report of the Royal Commission and the texts of French feminist Simone de Beauvoir, did not have any tools of analysis to outline their own specific terms of oppression. Women's oppression, the authors argued, needed to be understood as affecting all aspects of daily life. But women now needed to move *beyond* discussions of their daily lives, as a "growing awareness of the necessity for liberation needs to lead to collective action." The women spoke of their coming to consciousness, of the way in which they learned that their oppression, though distinct from other forms of exploitation, could be analyzed using the tools of historical materialism. They had come to learn that the liberation of women implied the transformation of the capitalist system. And they realized that, although French and American feminism had provided much of the theoretical basis upon which Quebec feminism was founded, it was now time to situate their struggle "within a framework of social and national liberation," and to define their own specific terms of reference.[62]

For the authors of the *Manifeste*, women, by outlining their own terms of oppression and their own understandings of liberation, could significantly deepen the movement and help in their own way to liberate "all the peoples of the world." And, following the line of argument familiar to both Black activists and the intellectuals of *Parti Pris*, the authors argued that they needed to begin "by denouncing the ideologies ... that reinforce our inferior status, and by creating a new culture of women, a culture in which women will be in solidarity in the struggle for liberation." It was, after all, only through struggle that the new woman could be forged.[63]

The *Manifeste des femmes québécoises* articulated many of the intellectual arguments that were being developed by the FLF. In its first widely distributed text, the FLF outlined its goal of creating "solidarity among all Québécoises" which would allow women "to articulate together the meaning of our liberation."[64] A first step in this liberation was working to understand the world in their own terms. The women of the FLF were tired of being continually told that their liberation was implicit in Quebec's national liberation. From its outset, the FLF saw its struggle as forming an essential element of Quebec's national liberation, which, it believed, also acted as the condition for women's emancipation. The FLF's slogan clearly revealed the primary tenets of its ideology: "NO LIBERATION OF QUEBEC WITHOUT THE LIBERATION OF WOMEN, NO LIBERATION OF WOMEN WITHOUT THE LIBERATION OF QUEBEC." The group therefore situated its project as one of deepening and expanding the idea of liberation being articulated by the left. "The liberation of women," an FLF bulletin declared, "will not be achieved by oppressing other groups or individuals, but forms part of a process of liberating all human beings. Roles must not be reversed, they must be transformed."[65]

The FLF's debt to the decolonization movement is clearly revealed in the introduction to the French edition of the *Birth Control Handbook,* in which the group vehemently denounces the Catholic Church's teachings that sexuality was "impure" and that it was the duty of Quebec women to reproduce and perpetuate the "race." The FLF argued instead that the Church worked to keep women in ignorance about contraception, ensuring that they continued to produce a steady stream of cheap labour for the province's industries.

Theoretical inspiration for the group's ideology was acknowledged with lengthy quotations by two very different authors, Emma Goldman and Pierre Vallières. The FLF approvingly quoted Goldman declaring that women should have the free choice to bear children when they wanted them, and that only this would ensure that children be raised with love.[66] More surprising was the group's reliance on Vallières's discussion of his mother in *Nègres blancs d'Amérique.* From a contemporary perspective, Vallières's denunciation of his mother – blaming nearly all of his problems of adolescence on her domineering tendencies and holding her responsible for imposing clerical repression on the family – strikes the reader as approaching misogyny in its virulence.[67] But at the time, Vallières's argument that "capitalism and religion have mass-produced mothers like mine"[68] was understood by radical women as a damning indictment of the ways in which the combined forces of capitalism and colonialism stripped individuals of their humanity. It was in this context that he was cited, and the introduction went on to argue that access to contraception provided the first step towards women's liberation, as the "control of one's own body" provides the condition for "the control of one's individual and collective existence." Rather than providing cheap labour for industry, the children that Quebec women conceived of their own free will would grow to swell the ranks "of those who are currently fighting for a more just way of life in a liberated Quebec."[69] "We believe that women will not be able to truly liberate themselves," the FLF declared, "unless their liberation forms part of a larger process of social liberation writ large, which will itself only be possible if it includes the participation of women at all levels."[70] While it was imperative that feminists fight for women's emancipation, Quebec women could not forget that they also needed to join "the struggle for the national liberation of the Quebec people, without which their liberation would be illusory."[71]

The FLF attempted to create a flexible structure that reflected its principles. It remained open to women from all backgrounds and, while promoting ideas of socialist decolonization, was always home to a diverse range of ideological tendencies. Like other women's liberation organizations throughout the continent, it was decentralized and anti-hierarchical, and opposed to fixed doctrine.[72] And through its engagement with anti-colonial ideas, the FLF placed itself in an international context. From the beginning, Véronique O'Leary and Louise Toupin maintain, Quebec feminists "felt very close to women involved in Third World liberation movements."[73] Seeing Quebec as a colonized nation was the beginning point of the FLF's social analysis and, like earlier decolonization theorists, the women of the FLF believed that it was through their work in Quebec that they could best participate in a larger international movement. When writing to American feminists, they explained the reasons why they were not able to participate in activities of international solidarity: "We believe that the best way to join in your struggle and that of the women of the world is, for the moment, to devote all of our energies to struggle for the liberation of Quebec women."[74]

Because Quebec women were exploited on a national level by colonization, on an economic level by capitalism, and on a social level by patriarchy, it was imperative that *all* social structures be transformed. For the FLF, the economic exploitation of Quebec women was shaped by the interrelated forces of American imperialism, colonialism, and capitalism.[75] In its 1971 *Bulletin de liaison*, the FLF clearly outlined the interrelated nature of its program. According to its authors, the group was struggling "For independence, because we are not only women, but *Québécoises* and as *Québécoises* we are colonized. For socialism because, even if the exploitation of women predates capitalism ... we live today in a capitalist system which depends upon the exploitation of women."[76] To free themselves from exploitation, the women of the FLF believed that it was necessary for feminists to advocate national liberation and socialism. Building upon the analyses of Black Power, many argued that the FLF needed to work towards "reconquering our dignity as human beings."[77]

The FLF maintained that it needed to work on behalf of those who were most marginalized, to reach "women from poor communities, as they have

no material comforts to lessen their hardship, and because they have nothing to lose and everything to gain."[78] Some women involved in the Théâtre
radical québecois went to Saint-Henri to be of service to the local citizens'
committee.[79] Seeing themselves as forming a part of the struggle for Quebec liberation, members of the FLF did not primarily identify as women but
rather as *Quebec* women. Feminists working in this framework challenged
the universal idea of sisterhood being developed by feminists elsewhere, and
instead focused on the ways in which a confluence of systems of oppression marginalized women.

Because of their belief in the need for national liberation, the women of
the FLF had a turbulent relationship with English-speaking activist groups.
The group, for example, refused to participate in the abortion caravan to
Ottawa. In a May 1970 press release, the FLF explained its refusal to participate: "Comrades, we refuse to go and protest in front of the Canadian
Parliament when we do not recognize the authority which it claims over
Quebec. We are, however, in solidarity with the women of Canada, because,
as women, we suffer the same oppression … We have the same dreams: we
want to bring the world from fatalism to freedom."[80]

In addition to distancing itself from English-Canadian feminist organizations, the FLF's belief in the centrality of national liberation led it, in
the fall of 1970, to exclude anglophones from its ranks, breaking apart the
alliance that had been responsible for the group's very origins. Véronique
O'Leary and Louise Toupin recount how the francophone women of the
FLF were worried about the imbalance that existed between English- and
French-speaking members of the group. It was during a two-day meeting
in the Laurentians, they recall, that the francophones decided to exclude the
anglophones. "Among the reasons put forward," O'Leary and Toupin state,
"was the argument that the anglophones, because they had access to a wide
array of American and British documentation on 'Women's Lib.,' exerted
an ideological control over the FLF, giving the group an American orientation that had little regard for the specific realities of Quebec." The existence of an increasing body of English-language feminist literature
emanating from the United States and Britain therefore threatened the
francophone members of the FLF.[81] Many francophone women began seeing the anglophones' imparting of their knowledge and opinions as a reflection of "a thoroughly colonial attitude." Hoping to create a movement
based both on an international awareness of women's oppression and a
firm understanding of specific issues relating to Quebec women, the FLF felt

that the movement must be composed only of francophones. The anglophone members of the group, comprising about half of the total membership, were shocked by their exclusion from the organization that they had helped to form. Many of these women, "deeply integrated into the francophone and separatist community," were hurt and upset by their exclusion, and decided to give up feminist activity altogether.[82] In February 1971, the FLF decided that it would only conduct abortion counselling in French, and the francophone women moved out of the shared house on Sainte-Famille Street.[83]

The split between anglophones and francophones in the fall of 1970 was only the first of a series of divisions that would surface within the group. By 1971, the FLF was divided into many "cells," each with its own unique take on effective political action, its own rationale for women's liberation, and its own understanding of the conditions of women's oppression. The two poles of the group, represented by "cellule II" and "cellule X," reflected many of the debates that were shaping the women's liberation movement across North America. Cellule II highlighted the ways in which the oppression of women was intimately related to capitalism and the family structure, and it argued for the close collaboration with mixed (male and female) groups. Cellule X, for its part, while recognizing the material nature of exploitation, considered patriarchy to be a primary system of oppression and therefore insisted on complete autonomy from male groups, and it oriented its activities around shock actions of cultural demystificication.[84] Discussions between these disparate factions consumed a great deal of time throughout the spring and summer of 1971, creating an atmosphere of intellectual excitement while simultaneously draining the energy of many. In the summer, many of the women who situated women's oppression economically decided to leave the group, returning to the Marxist left from which many of them had emerged.[85]

Despite the ideological divergences that were clearly beginning to prevail, the group's various factions all maintained that the emancipation of women could only be achieved through a comprehensive program of national liberation. Cellule II argued that the "complete integration of women into the struggle for national liberation" was not only "an essential element of that liberation," but was also crucial for "the abolition of our own particular exploitation." Liberation would, after all, remain incomplete if it did not include "all Quebec men and women."[86] Another group argued that the FLF needed to focus on one objective: "the struggle for the sexual, social, political and economic liberation of the Quebec woman in order to achieve her individual and collective self-determination."[87] And cellule X, the defender of an autonomous women's movement and the group that went the furthest in identifying the common plight of all women under patriarchy, still argued that the FLF "needs to form part of the struggle for Quebec independence and social revolution."[88]

■ ■ ■

In two turbulent years of existence, the FLF had staged many demonstrations, opened a day-care, and published the first edition of its newspaper. Although it had never attracted a large membership, probably never surpassing sixty members organized in independent cells, it had a large impact on the feminist movement.[89] It politicized the question of gender discrimination and brought feminist demands for equality into mainstream discourse. In the spring of 1971 the group received a flood of new members,[90] yet just as it seemed to achieve real success, it started to come undone.

By the fall of 1971 many members had left the group and, just as it was losing speed, the group underwent a shock with the death of one of its members, twenty-eight-year-old Michèle Gauthier, on 29 October 1971. Along with a group of friends, she had attended a protest march in defence of a group of locked-out workers at the newspaper *La Presse*. As the protest of 15,000 marched towards the section of town that had been barricaded by police, the police charged the crowd, arresting 200, injuring 190, and causing the death of Michèle Gauthier.[91] Her funeral, held on 2 November in a small village twenty-five miles southeast of Montreal, attracted thousands of mourners. The pallbearers represented Montreal's atmosphere of revolt. The coffin was carried by Quebec's three major labour leaders, Marcel Pepin, Yvon Charbonneau, and Louis Laberge, a locked-out *La Presse* worker and a student of CEGEP Vieux-Montréal, as well as a representative of the FLF.

In the tense atmosphere pervading the city, Gauthier became a martyr representing the senseless human costs of capitalism.[92] Members of the FLF produced a tract denouncing the collusion of capital and the state, and reaffirming its belief that it was more necessary than ever for Quebec women to organize themselves in their workplaces, neighbourhoods, and everywhere else.[93] But the shock of Gauthier's death occurred at a time of general demobilization for the FLF. Despite the apparent vitality of the group the previous spring, by the fall of 1971, internal divisions, the heavy nature of abstract theoretical discussions, and a drastically reduced membership discouraged the few remaining activists, and they decided to dissolve the group. While some returned to the mixed groups of the left, others went on to form feminist organizations with different ideological orientations and organizational structures.[94]

Throughout the 1970s, the women's liberation movement helped to catalyze an enormous array of feminist initiatives that were collectively transforming the everyday lives of men and women in Montreal, as well as throughout Quebec in general. Women's committees emerged in unions and began to play an increasingly important role in shaping union policy. The Parti Québécois established a committee on the status of women in each riding, and large numbers of women were attracted to the party, seen to be an important vector of change throughout much of the 1970s. Outside of formal party or union structures feminists began to organize battered women's shelters and theatre troupes, and by the mid-1970s Montreal had a vibrant francophone feminist bookstore and publishing house. One of the most important initiatives of the early 1970s was the creation of daycares – already by 1973, according to Micheline Dumont, Montreal had 250 daycares, many of which were run by parents. By the end of the 1970s, she states, feminism had, in one way or another, touched all women in Quebec.[95]

Not all of these developments occurred solely because of the women's liberation movement, but through its activism and writings the movement boldly introduced new ideas into Quebec's public sphere. And from its beginnings, feminism in Montreal was inextricably linked both to the left and to the analyses of empire circulating in the city. The movement was always mixed, fluid, in constant mutation and intensely creative. Like all movements, of course, it had its shortcomings, including its silence on questions of homosexuality and race.[96] And the split between francophone and anglophone feminists in 1970 had a lasting impact on feminist politics throughout the 1970s, demonstrating how fragile and fleeting such alliances could be. How and why language could have such a divisive force, and could become symbolic of larger systems of power, is the subject to which we now turn.

SIX

THE LANGUAGE OF LIBERATION

Beginning in the early 1960s, language dominated political debate in Montreal. Questions of language rights and of linguistic devaluation, of the cultural and imperial power of the English language, and of the necessity of building a new francophone culture of resistance, stood at the very centre of the political movements of the 1960s. In 1969 these questions exploded.[1] The first mass demonstration over "language rights"[2] took place on 28 March 1969, marking the beginning of a new era in which linguistic struggles would be played out on the streets of Montreal. The protest began when a crowd of 10,000 to 15,000 protesters carrying placards reading "McGill aux Québécois!" and "McGill aux travailleurs!" began marching west towards Montreal's most prestigious university. In the heated political atmosphere of 1969, McGill, standing on Mount Royal and dominating the city's urban landscape, had come to be seen as a symbol of imperial domination. In the months leading up to the demonstration, many had demanded that the university shed its colonial identity by becoming a French-language institution serving the province's working class. As the day of the protest approached, the rhetoric from both sides grew increasingly polarized, the army was put on alert, and everyone braced for the inevitable confrontation.

Leading the march were two figures who had become prominent in the provincial media: recently fired McGill professor Stanley Gray and nationalist leader Raymond Lemieux. Because of the increasingly violent nature of demonstrations, the city's municipal authorities feared the worst; 2,707 security officers were deployed, hundreds of police were arrayed inside McGill, and many more were waiting in full riot gear at the headquarters of the provincial police, the city police, and the RCMP. The covers of utility holes on the streets around McGill were welded in place and, during the demonstration, the crowd was circled by police helicopters and watched from rooftops. As the protesters reached the front entrance of the university, a group of counter-demonstrators yelled insults and sang "God Save the Queen." By 10:30 p.m., the riot squad had already divided the crowd into three groups and, although many scuffles and arguments broke out, the protesters never did succeed in taking over the university. A few fires burned throughout the evening but, by midnight, "Opération McGill" had come to an end.[3]

Opération McGill français represented an important moment in the development of oppositional politics in Montreal. It was the first in a series of mass demonstrations that made the claim that cultural deprivation could only be reversed if the root problems of capitalism and imperialism were opposed. Or, to put it another way, if an alternative North American society based on social justice and human dignity was to be built, the cultural and economic power of the English language would need to be overcome.

The question of language rights does not, of course, belong solely to the left. The defence of the French language and the fear of assimilation and cultural devaluation have been constant themes throughout Quebec history. But the defence of linguistic rights became a left-wing question when the devaluation of language was linked to larger analyses of capitalism and colonialism, and when its remedy was seen to require a reshaping of society in general. Opération McGill français, planned by the left, played a decisive role in articulating and popularizing a leftist interpretation of language rights. The movement itself was the product of an alliance of individuals and groups from many different backgrounds. Anglophone socialists from McGill preoccupied with building a working-class revolution joined with Quebec nationalists concerned primarily with questions of linguistic survival. The radical wing of the labour movement joined with Quebec students. Tensions remained, of course, for such coalitions are always temporary and fragile.

In this chapter I will argue, first by looking at Opération McGill and then by exploring the massive street protests in the fall of 1969 over the province's proposed language legislation (Bill 63), that the linguistic explosions of the late 1960s were characterized by a mixing of people and ideas, of issues and analyses which defy the classifications in which they have so often been understood. Out of the street protests and political debates emerged an analysis that placed conceptions of language firmly within a political economy of empire.

ORIGINS AND EXPLANATIONS OF
THE "LANGUAGE QUESTION"

The struggle for the French language has a long history in Quebec. Various organizations such as the Société du bon parler français, the Comité permanent de la survivance française (which later became the Conseil de la vie française) and nationalist organizations such as the Ligue d'action nationale and, most importantly, the Société Saint-Jean-Baptiste, promoted the use of the French language in business names, labels, and signs, and steadily worked to defend French-Canadian cultural rights more generally. In the mid-1950s, a conflict broke out over the new name for a Canadian National Railways (CNR) hotel in Montreal. Nationalists proposed "Château Maisonneuve," but the CNR held firm to its idea: "The Queen Elizabeth." In 1962, CNR president Donald Gordon did not help matters by declaring that, while it was true that no senior post in the organization was occupied by a French Canadian, this was due to the simple fact that none was sufficiently qualified. Students burned an effigy of Gordon, and linguistic tensions grew. Throughout the 1960s, political parties in Quebec placed a new emphasis on language. The RIN had demanded that French be declared the sole official language in Quebec and, in its official 1966 election platform, the Quebec Liberal Party made the proposal that French should be the language "with priority" in the province.[4]

During the 1960s the question of language motivated much political activity and critical reflection. Writers had denounced the cultural and economic power of the English language. They had spoken eloquently about the need for francophones to build a culture of resistance, and had attempted to valorize the spoken French of the Quebec working class. Many agreed that French in Quebec was, as the famed 1965 *Parti Pris*/MLP manifesto put it, a "decomposing language."[5] The manifesto continued by arguing that "there is much to do to protect national culture: the creation of a Quebec press agency and a Quebec film board, measures to protect national art and literature, aid to French-language bookstores." But the most important measure, the precondition for all of these different endeavours, was the establishment of "French unilingualism: that is to say that French be recognized, at all levels, as the only official language of Quebec."[6]

Many authors have sought to uncover the reasons for the explosion of linguistic nationalism at the end of the 1960s, and for the provincial government's decision to begin legislating language rights. Some historians have argued that, as Quebec became both more modern and secular, language became the main distinction between Quebec and the rest of North America.[7] Others have attempted to demonstrate that, as the language question facilitated a critique of capitalism, the language policies enacted by the Quebec government served specific legitimating purposes within the capitalist system.[8] These explanations certainly contain many elements of truth. Until recently, few authors have dealt explicitly with the intellectual arguments that were made in defence of the French language generally, and of unilingualism specifically. In this respect, the works of Karim Larose have significantly added to our understanding of this often-misunderstood concept. For Larose, unilingualism became a priority for intellectuals who sought to promote a distinctly francophone North American culture.[9] Yet at the end of the 1960s, the mass protests advocating unilingualism also had other origins and, I will argue, they cannot be separated from the diversity and complexity of political life in Montreal.

LANGUAGE AND SCHOOLING IN 1960S QUEBEC

Debates over language and schooling have a long history in Quebec. The origins of the explosions of the late 1960s stretch back to at least the end of the Second World War, when Montreal was increasingly becoming a cosmopolitan city. From 1951 to 1961, Quebec received 195,000 immigrants, the vast majority of whom settled in the Montreal area and integrated into the city's anglophone community.[10] Sixty thousand of the city's new immigrants were of Italian origin, and by 1961 Montreal's Italian population numbered 108,552. The community had a long history of living alongside and interacting with the city's French-Canadian population – until the Second World War, Italians generally sent their children to French Catholic schools, and they intermarried with French Canadians to a far greater degree than they did with anglophone Montrealers.[11]

By 1961, however, Italian parents (like the parents of other immigrant groups) were sending their children to English-language Catholic schools over 70% of the time.[12] In Montreal during the 1950s and 1960s, English was not only the language of economic power, but also of social mobility. Often leaving impoverished lives in their home countries, immigrants were eager to increase their standard of living, and learning English not only provided them with greater earning power, but it also gave them the tools to move elsewhere in North America.[13] In addition to these economic factors, and despite the efforts of many within the Catholic school system, immigrants often faced hostility from principals and other officials, so sending their children to English-language schools seemed a better choice.[14]

It was in this context of economic and ethnic relations that conflicts in the Montreal suburb of Saint-Léonard – situated between downtown and the industrial east end – took shape. In November 1967, the Catholic School Board of Saint-Léonard decided that French would be the exclusive language of instruction for the children of immigrants living under its jurisdiction. Low housing costs had drawn many lower middle-class families to the new suburb and, by the end of the decade, the neighbourhood was made up of a majority (60%) of individuals of French-Canadian origin, with a significant minority (30%) of people of Italian descent. Before 1967, the Catholic school board had been offering bilingual schools for Italian children that taught 60% of the time in French, and 40% in English, and parents reacted angrily to the new restrictions against English-language schooling. In April 1968 the school board, unprepared for the backlash that its new restrictions elicited, decided to delay the implementation of the new policy by one year. But it was too late; Saint-Léonard had already become a symbol of the anglicization of immigrants in the province, and a new organization, the Mouvement pour l'intégration scolaire (MIS), had been formed to defend French-language schooling in the district and throughout the province.[15]

Before long, the MIS, led by Saint-Léonard architect Raymond Lemieux, an American of French-Canadian origin who had returned to Quebec, had a membership of over 3,000 and a large public profile. Throughout the late 1960s, the MIS became closely allied with left-nationalist groups, deployed shock-troops to demonstrations and, echoing Che Guevara, outlined its goal of creating "10, 20, 50 Saint-Léonard crises."[16] In the Saint-

Léonard Catholic school board election of June 1968, the MIS presented a slate of candidates and, after winning a resounding victory, declared that French would be the only language of instruction in all schools that fell under the board's jurisdiction. With linguistic tensions reaching a fever pitch, Premier Jean-Jacques Bertrand announced in November of 1968 that he would introduce legislation that he hoped would put an end to the crisis. "Bill 85" stated that, while French would be the "priority" language of the province, all parents would have the right to choose whether their children would be instructed in either French or English.[17] While Quebec's politicians were scrambling to contain the crisis in the halls of the National Assembly, however, linguistic unrest had already spilt into the streets.

■ ■ ■

The language crisis of 1967–8 began in elementary schools; in the fall of 1968, it was the state of post-secondary education that ignited a related dispute. Expenditures on education rose dramatically during the 1960s, going from 23% of the provincial budget in 1959 to 35% in 1969.[18] According to Jean-Philippe Warren, for the first time in Quebec history, the majority of those under the age of twenty were in school, which had the effect of conflating the categories of "youth" and "student."[19] In 1967, the Union nationale government opened the first seven CEGEPS – new junior colleges that would replace the province's antiquated classical college system – and in September 1968, sixteen more CEGEPS were created. By the late 1960s, 100,000 students studied in the province's CEGEP system, and the expansion of the education system became one of the main pillars of the Quiet Revolution.[20]

In September 1968, standing before an audience at Laval University, Quebec government officials made an announcement that sent shockwaves throughout the CEGEP system: 20,000 CEGEP students, they declared, did not find university places for the fall of 1968, and for the fall of 1969 the problem would only get worse. In the eyes of many, the promise of the Quiet Revolution, that francophones could improve their social and economic status through new educational opportunities, did not appear to be materializing.[21]

In October, Quebec students, having watched students and workers in France bring their country to a standstill just months earlier, took to the streets and occupied their schools. For two weeks, the CEGEP system stopped functioning. Students barricaded themselves inside their buildings, hanging portraits of the world's best-known revolutionaries, from Lenin and Marx to Castro and Mao. Students wrote tracts, demonstrated in the streets, organized teach-ins and performed revolutionary theatre. In one of the more dramatic occupations, students at the École des Beaux-Arts took over their institution and proclaimed a republic. As the red flag flew above, those inside exercised their creative faculties and put art in the service of humanity.[22]

The occupations of the fall of 1968 died down, but the resentment among the student population remained. Students kept demanding that education be less repressive, and they wanted to be provided with money to attend university, as well as opportunities to use their skills once they graduated. They also demanded that a new French language university be established in the city (while McGill, Sir George Williams University, and Loyola College all served the city's less populous English-speaking community, Montreal's only French-language university at the time was the Université de Montréal).[23]

It would not take long for resentment over the inadequacy of the French-language education system to be directed against the grandeur of McGill. On 21 October 1968, 5,000 to 10,000 students had marched through the McGill campus chanting "étudiants-ouvriers," before making their way to the Université de Montréal to hear speeches by student leaders.[24] And then, on 3 December 1968, activists close to the MIS stormed the McGill campus and proceeded to occupy its computer centre. The occupation – which took everyone by surprise – was meant as a protest against Jean-Jacques Bertrand's proposed guarantee of English-language schooling rights in the province. Principal Rocke Robertson called in the police, and the riot squad stormed the building at 1:00 am. The eleven students inside had enough provisions to stay for a week, but their barricade of a door opening to the exterior did little to protect them, and the police had no trouble in clearing them out.[25] The occupation, along with the earlier CEGEP strike, brought Quebec politics directly onto the campus of McGill.

Before the 1968–69 school year, student politics at McGill comprised the same mixture of local issues and universal causes that was capturing the imaginations of students across North America and Europe.[26] The student population had grown from 8,795 in 1960 to 12,728 in 1965, with the majority of the new students enrolling in the humanities and social sciences.[27] In the mid-1960s, the *McGill Daily*, under the editorship of Patrick MacFadden, had begun to publish articles about the Vietnam War and liberation movements in the Third World, and the *Daily* soon became the home of a nascent McGill left.[28] Throughout the 1960s, the *Daily* not only acted as the most influential critical voice at the university, but it also achieved an important influence over Montreal's English-speaking activists more generally. Many McGill activists were "red diaper babies" who had grown up in the dynamic world of Jewish Montreal, and had faced the discrimination of French- and English-speaking Montrealers alike.[29]

Strongly influenced by European Marxism, activists placed their hopes in the working class, and they advocated the transformation of the school into a "critical university" organically connected to the needs and aspirations of the majority of citizens. Rather than fostering critical consciousness, it was argued, the university moulded students to the demands of capitalist society, creating the functionaries and technicians of exploitation. The task for radicals was therefore to grab hold of the university to bring the forces of modernity under democratic control and, by uniting theory and practice, put the university at the service of "the people."[30] The idea of the critical university was that student radicals should ally themselves with broader movements of social change.[31] Many activists at McGill were acutely aware of their relatively privileged position at the heart of Quebec society. In February 1967, the McGill student body even narrowly voted – after two unsuccessful attempts – to join UGEQ.[32] But it was not until the 1968–69 school year – when McGill itself became the object of unrelenting attacks and denunciations – that the university became part of a city-wide movement of social upheaval.[33]

In September 1968, the atmosphere at McGill – like that at universities around the world – was tense. In France, students, who were quickly joined by workers, nearly succeeded in toppling the French government. Police had to break up an occupation at New York's Columbia University, and similar revolts on other campuses throughout North America were being met with similar repression. McGill's Radical Student Alliance (RSA) was doing its best to ensure that this insurrectionary energy would fuel student politics on campus. After fierce debate, the RSA even came to support Quebec independence, arguing that the sovereigntist movement could be likened to the efforts of Third World nations to free themselves from colonialism.[34]

Of all the radical personalities who emerged on the McGill campus at the time, it was Stanley Gray – a young lecturer in the Department of Political Science, and Economics – who captured the most attention, becoming the intellectual leader of a new group of students who would put Quebec at the centre of their political ideology. Gray had grown up Jewish in Montreal's Mile End, and his father had been a member of the Communist Party of Canada. No stranger to the prejudices of English-speaking Montreal, Gray nonetheless enrolled at McGill in the early 1960s where he became active in the Combined Universities Campaign for Nuclear Disarmament. After earning his D. Phil. at Oxford, Gray returned to McGill in the fall of 1967, and would soon be at the very centre of one of the biggest controversies that the university had ever witnessed.[35]

September 1968 also marked an important moment for the *McGill Daily*. In the fall of 1968 Mark Starowicz took over as editor, and McGill's role in Quebec society became centrally important to the newspaper's coverage. For example, when John Ross Bradfield, Chairman of the Board and Chief Executive of Noranda Mines, received an honourary doctorate from McGill, Starowicz lambasted both the company and the university. Contrary to what the university claimed, Starowicz argued, the event made it clear that McGill does "take political stands."[36] And it was therefore the task of student radicals to take political stands of their own. Student activists at McGill – a school which seemed, in the eyes of many, to be a bastion of anglophone privilege – had come, by the fall of 1968, to believe that a democratization of society required a radical questioning of their own institution. In the coming school year, the *Daily* would become the chief organ of anglophone radicals who had decided to join the larger movement of opposition in the city.

Opération McGill was not just one more sixties demonstration; in the months leading up to the march, previously separate movements and organizations converged. In this sense, the lead-up to Opération McGill shared many characteristics with other revolts taking place around the world, and with France's May '68 in particular. According to Kristin Ross, May '68 can be seen as a "crisis in functionalism," as a time when the movement "took the form of political experiments in *de*classification, in disrupting the natural 'givenness' of places."[37] In the union of intellectual and worker rebellions, Ross argues, lay "the verification of equality not as any objective of action, but as something that is part and parcel of action, something that emerges in the struggle and is lived and declared as such."[38] In a similar way, students in Montreal were no longer defending only student rights. Some anglophones, albeit representing a minority of McGill students, had joined the opposition to the cultural and economic power of the English language, and workers took their demands outside of the workplace to the front gates of the university. While it is true that in the years immediately preceding Opération McGill workers and students had sometimes joined together in demonstrations and on picket lines,[39] it was only in the months leading up to the march on McGill that the logic which kept various movements separate began to unravel. Activists argued that McGill, having its roots in nineteenth-century British colonialism, had become an institution dominated by American capital, training those who would go on to work for the American and English-Canadian companies operating in Quebec. To the eyes of the young activists, the school had come to symbolize much more than a prestigious site of "anglophone" education; it was a symbol of both the privileges of settler colonialism and of the technocratic and inhuman nature of American imperialism.

The battle over McGill was therefore not only about schooling rights; it was also a fight concerning foreign control of the economy and public space in the city. Rather than merely writing political tracts from a distance, the protesters took their grievances over the state of Quebec society to the heart of its most venerable institution. On the Monday following the event, an article in Le Devoir openly mused about the necessity of limiting protests to certain areas of the city.[40] And in the period leading up to the march, Montreal police planned to prevent marchers from coming onto the McGill campus and to make it extremely difficult for protesters to gather anywhere near the university. According to Don Mitchell, social justice and rights to urban space "are not determined in the abstract, but rather in practice."[41] In this sense, the conflict over McGill was, at least to some extent, a conflict over who owned and controlled Montreal itself. Protesters denounced the university's isolation from the interests of the majority of citizens and, in their eyes, to protest anywhere else would have merely reinforced McGill's lack of accountability to the Quebec people.

The first organizational meetings for Opération McGill, bringing together anglophone radicals and the largely francophone organizations of the extra-parliamentary opposition, began in the aftermath of the MIS protests on McGill campus in the fall of 1968.[42] Francophone radicals felt that challenging the hegemony of McGill allowed them to attack many symbols at once: the legacy of colonialism, the injustices of capitalism, the present-day dominance of the English language, anglophone control over the Quebec economy, and the inadequacy of the francophone education system. It allowed them to link opposition to colonialism with the opposition to hierarchies in the educational system, and to combine these struggles with the issue of access to university for francophones.[43] At the same time, some anglophone students had come to see that, if they wanted to forge a working-class movement, they would need to join forces with francophone groups.[44] Before long, in schools and CEGEPs around Montreal, hundreds of committees sprang up, and many began predicting that the demonstration would be the largest in the history of Quebec.[45] The coalition received the support of the Mouvement de libération du taxi, citizens' and workers' committees, the Comité Vallières-Gagnon, the Chevaliers de l'indépendance and, most importantly, the Montreal Central Council of the CSN (representing the CSN's 65,000 Montreal workers).[46]

From its origins as a confessional Catholic union, the CSN had always paid special attention to the French language. Although the initial motivation for establishing the union was religion rather than language, from 1921 until 1969 the union consistently passed resolutions advocating the defence of French language rights in a bilingual Canada.[47] But upholding Canadian bilingualism is a far cry from supporting French unilingualism. By the late 1960s, the question of French unilingualism had been explicitly placed in the larger framework of the struggle over power in Quebec, and it quickly became a central platform in the fight for decolonization. As I will recount in more detail in the following chapter, the election of Michel Chartrand to the presidency of the Montreal Central Council of the CSN at the end of 1968 marked an important moment for Quebec labour. Opération McGill was, in fact, the Central Council's first major demonstration. In the weeks leading up to the march on McGill, Chartrand invited Gray to speak before a General Assembly of the Central Council. In an explosive hall packed with workers, Gray outlined the case against McGill, the destructive power of imperialism, and the need for decolonization. And he watched as huge piles of the newspaper *Bienvenue à McGill* were devoured by the anxious audience. In the period leading up to the protest Gray, Michel Chartrand, and Raymond Lemieux, toured the province, being greeted by enthusiastic crowds everywhere that they went.[48] On 26 March 1969, just two days before the protest, flyers announced a "teach-in" to be held in the ballroom of the University Centre featuring talks by, among others, Léandre Bergeron, Michel Chartrand, Raymond Lemieux and, of course, Stanley Gray.[49]

While the growing coalition prepared for the march, the university administration became increasingly concerned about Gray's presence on campus. On 11 February 1969, the same day as the Sir George Williams Affair, Gray was given notice that he was being fired from his job at the university. Although the reason cited for his dismissal was his disruption of a Board of Governors' meeting, many believed that the real reason was Gray's effort to bring student activism off the McGill campus and into the city.[50] Gray's termination hearings demonstrated both the new coalition and the new lines of opposition that were being drawn. While some members of the English-speaking establishment wondered why McGill had hired "such a dirty, unkempt creature" in the first place,[51] the CSN assigned two of its staff lawyers, Jacques Desmarais and Robert Burns, to Gray's defence; both refused to speak English at the hearings.[52] Michel Chartrand issued a statement supporting Gray, declaring that, from "its behavior, it is becoming simpler to visualize McGill as some university in South Africa."[53]

Many members of the English-speaking community condemned the movement.[54] Its organizers and sympathizers were routinely harassed by police, residences were put under surveillance, cars were followed, and arbitrary arrests were made. On 18 March the police arrested, among others, Mark Starowicz and Robert Chodos from the *McGill Daily*, Louis-Bernard Robitaille from *La Presse*, Stanley Gray, and an assorted group of activists that included CSN militants, members of the Mouvement de libération du taxi, a professor, an unemployed man, and a bureaucrat – all of whom were returning from an assembly of the Montreal Central Council.[55] In the week leading up to the protest, many of the main organizers had to go underground to avoid police harassment.[56] The movement received scorn from many of the city's mainstream nationalists, including the editorialists of the province's major newspapers. Claude Ryan, editor of *Le Devoir*, for example, argued that the English-speaking community in Quebec merited its own schools, not only because its numbers warranted them, but also because of its very long, distinguished, and honourable tradition.[57] To the movement's organizers, that the majority of French editorials denounced the demonstration merely proved the alternative nature of their project.[58] But it was not only the city's newspapers that kept their distance from the movement. All the main political parties, including the newly formed Parti Québécois and its leader René Lévesque, distanced themselves from the protesters.[59] Even the Société Saint Jean Baptiste de Mon-

tréal, the traditional mouthpiece of French-Canadian nationalism, and
one of the most ardent defenders of linguistic rights, decided that it would
have nothing to do with the march.[60]

THE ARGUMENT

The distance between Opération McGill and the mainstream nationalist
movement was at least partly a product of the latter's reaction to the militant tone and uncompromising attitude of the mostly young activists
organizing the protest. The organizers of Opération McGill spoke a language
of absolutes, one very much shaped by the certainties of youth. But there
were ideological divisions as well, as Opération McGill explicitly framed its
struggle as one of overcoming not only linguistic, but also economic power.

In the middle of February 1969, the *McGill Daily* published Stanley
Gray's "McGill and the Rape of Quebec," an article which, reprinted in
publications throughout the province, played a central role in shaping the
ideology of the movement. The article was indebted to the language of
Quebec decolonization, inheriting both the insights and limitations of the
larger movement. Gray's very title reveals his reliance on the heavily gendered language of decolonization that had been characteristic of the movement since its beginning. Gray not only spoke of the "Rape of Quebec," but
also of how "the university's academics act as the intellectual whores of
the Establishment."[61] Gray was not alone in using gendered metaphors in
his attempt to highlight power relations in the province. Mark Starowicz,
for example, caricatured the administration's pronouncements in defence
of the university as an attempt to pose "the spectre of McGill the innocent virgin standing naked before thousands of sexually depraved sepa-
ratists."[62] By using gendered metaphors representing women as either
passive victims or as "whores," these writers tried to deconstruct systems of
power and oppression, but in doing so they relied on a gendered language
that embedded new forms of exclusion.

"McGill and the Rape of Quebec" not only addresses the role of the
university in society, but also strives to expose the democratic potential
dormant in its structure. The article begins with the premise that for the
past two hundred years Quebec has been colonized, its natural resources
owned by British and then American capital, and its people exploited by foreign elites (with the collusion of local leaders).[63] And there was perhaps

no better symbol of this foreign domination, Gray argued, than McGill University. The McGill Board of Governors personified Quebec's ruling corporate elite, representing corporations that had "a relationship to Quebec similar to that of the United Fruit Company to Latin America banana republics – absentee owners of the economy, plundering the nation's natural resources and taking the profits out of the country."[64] That Quebec's richest and most important institution functioned in English was not an accident of history, Gray argued: the English language had been imposed on Quebeckers by "military conquest, political colonization and economic domination." Colonialism had ensured that the "two major contradictions operating within Quebec society – the class conflict pitting workers against the interests of private profit, and the national conflict pitting the nation on the bottom against the nation on top – are thus integrally related." Echoing the simplistic Manichaeism of *La Revue socialiste* in the late 1950s, Gray argued that when workers went on strike against major corporations, "the French are almost wholly on one side and the English almost wholly on the other." In Quebec, there were two forms of exploitation – class and national – but these two different forms of domination were fused together, and McGill, Gray maintained, was "on the wrong side of both."[65]

Gray's analyses of Quebec society and of McGill's role within it were repeated by student publications throughout the city, from the *McGill Daily* to the papers of francophone CEGEPs. When, in March 1969, Maurice Roy of the Université de Montréal's *Le Quartier latin* telephoned Mark Starowicz to inquire into the *Daily*'s position on the upcoming demonstration, for example, he was both surprised and pleased that, while the *Daily* supported a French-language McGill, Starowicz made a point of indicating that "it was not merely a linguistic question: the editors of the *Daily* are demanding a socialization of McGill." If it was a question "of creating a second 'Université de Montréal,'" Starowicz was reported to have said, they would no longer take part. The editors of the *Daily*, Roy wrote, "define themselves as indépendantistes and socialists, and are unable to disassociate the two concepts."[66]

Because of its function as a training centre for the managers of American capital, the CEGEP students at College Sainte-Marie in Montreal argued, "McGill has become the bastion of Canadian and American imperialism." As the university was guilty of "the exploitation of thousands of Quebec workers and entire populations," and formed an important part of the American military industrial complex, it became clear that the liberation of Quebec workers "passes through McGill."[67] For J.-P. Dallaire of *Le Quartier latin*, McGill had become the symbol of a "colonial minority," and it was becoming more and more clear that the university was an obstacle to any progress of the Quebec people.[68] In a future independent and socialist Quebec, McGill would not only have to become a French-language institution, but revise its relationship with the population.[69]

In a widely-circulated document signed by many of the groups involved in organizing Opération McGill[70] – a document which became something of a manifesto for the movement[71] – the current inequities of the Quebec educational system were traced back to the Conquest of 1759. Because of the fortune of the English-speaking bourgeoisie, the quality of English-language universities was far superior to that of their French-language counterparts, which reflected "the painful history of a defeated, conquered and dominated nation." The statistics seemed to speak for themselves: although francophones made up 83% of Quebec society, of Quebec's six universities, three were English. Anglophones comprised 17% of the population, but they occupied 42% of all university places and received 30% of Quebec government grants. McGill had a research budget equivalent to the budgets of the Université de Montréal and Laval combined, and its library – not accessible to the general public – had the best collection of Quebec literature in the province. McGill's tuition was two hundred dollars more than that of other universities and, to top it all off, the document argued, the school regularly awarded honourary doctorates to Anglo-American financiers who were responsible for the exploitation of the Quebec people.[72]

Of all the documents, papers, and flyers produced by Opération McGill, the most important was *Bienvenue à McGill*. Originally conceived as a French edition of the *McGill Daily*,[73] the paper was funded by the "comités d'actions" of a number of CEGEPs, and by the Montreal Central Council of the CSN. Over 90,000 copies were printed and were distributed in schools, factories, metro stations, and political meetings.[74] This paper, more than any other document, spoke for the movement, outlining the reasons why students, workers, and activists needed to take to the streets in protest. McGill needed to be opposed, the paper argued, because it was the living symbol of the two hundred years during which Quebec had been exploited by imperial powers. In support of this argument *Bienvenue à McGill* reprinted Michèle Lalonde's poem "Speak White," and to demonstrate its internationalism, the paper reprinted a letter of solidarity from the national bureau of the German S.D.S. (Sozialistischer Deutscher Studentenbund), the main organization of the German New Left, which stated: "Today, in the context of international interdependence, international solidarity is not only a question of moral sympathy towards people who are struggling for their liberation. The victory of the Vietnamese is also our victory, the repression against movements in Quebec is also repression against us. The S.D.S. movement has followed the development of an anti-imperialist consciousness in Quebec with much interest, sympathy, and solidarity. The National Bureau of the S.D.S. therefore expresses its total support of the struggle of the *Québécois* against Anglo-Saxon cultural imperialism."[75]

In its attempt to reach a wide constituency, *Bienvenue à McGill* reached out to workers, printing a message by Michel Chartrand about the need to restructure Quebec's economy, and arguing that if McGill were simply to become another French-language university, little would change. The university system itself needed to be radically democratized, and put to the service of ordinary people. Chartrand's argument was taken up by Gray who emphasized the enormous potential that the university possessed. If the university was put in the hands of the people, he argued, it could become "a centre of research and teaching which would help give the population the means of taking control of its own destiny." But if McGill did not change, did not democratize, "an increasing number of *Québécois* will perceive it as a threat to their self-realization, as an obstacle to their liberation."[76]

The protest at McGill articulated a complicated mix of national and social demands, so it would be wrong to attribute it to either nationalism or socialism alone. One of the major points of contention around the event was its very name. Many were dismayed when the socialistic Opération McGill gave way to the more nationalistic "McGill français."[77] When the organizers of the protest allowed the media to present the event as more focused on language than class, they faced a revolt from francophone students and workers, who had become angry by the downplaying of the class-based struggle of the movement's origins.[78]

Most people at McGill did not support the protest or the larger politics of anti-colonialism in Quebec,[79] of course, yet an important consequence of Opération McGill was the radicalization of a new generation of anglophones who would continue to defend the cause of Quebec decolonization. Many of the radical writers from the *McGill Daily* went on to found *The Last Post*, an English-language journal which sought to connect readers with the radical political movements in Quebec, hoping to be a Canadian version of *Ramparts*. The journal stands alone as the one major English-

Canadian publication to be born out of the struggle for Quebec decolonization. For the Quebec student movement, which had played such an important role in politicizing questions of language and education, and which had
exploded onto the scene in the fall of 1968, 1969 would be the beginning of
its unravelling, as it was crushed under the weight of its own voluntarism
and the polarizing nature of its own rhetoric.[80]

In many ways, Opération McGill français was just another ephemeral
protest of the 1960s: a protest that brought diverse groups together temporarily, but which did not lead to any lasting political organization. Yet,
the protests around McGill had brought questions of language, power,
economics, and education to the centre of political discussion, and contributed much to an atmosphere that would bring tens of thousands to
the streets in the fall of 1969.

BILL 63, DECOLONIZATION, AND NATIONALISM

The MIS/Ligue pour l'intégration scolaire (LIS)[81] organized public meetings
and demonstrations to discuss the language of schooling in Saint-Léonard
throughout 1969. On 10 September, as the LIS decided to march through the
neighbourhood demanding that the language of education be French, Italian demonstrators lined the roads yelling insults. Before long a riot broke
out; fifty people were arrested, one hundred were injured, and for the first
time since 1957 the Riot Act was read in Montreal.[82]

With linguistic tensions growing more pronounced by the day, Quebec's Union Nationale government realized that it would need to enter
into the explosive debate. On 23 October 1969, Bertrand presented his solution to the linguistic crisis, Bill 63. Many features of the Bill were intended
to promote the French language; immigrants would be encouraged to learn
French, an "Office de la langue française" would be established, and all
graduates from Quebec schools would be expected to have a working
knowledge of the language. But these elements did not ease the worries of
Quebec nationalists, when compared to the Bill's one key provision: all
parents in the province – francophones included – would be able to choose
whether their children would be educated in either English or French.[83]
By guaranteeing English-language schooling rights, the government was
seen to be giving a privileged place to the language of the dominant class.
Because it was unrealistic to expect immigrants to choose to educate their

children in a language that would ensure economic marginalization, Bill 63 was seen by many as "one more step in the direction of the cultural genocide of the Quebec nation."[84]

Virtually all the opposition movements in Montreal began to mobilize against the bill. Labour unions, student groups, and extra-parliamentary organizations began moving into action. But unlike the lead-up to Opération McGill, this time protest would not come from the left alone. Both the PQ and the Société Saint-Jean Baptiste joined the ranks of opposition and, on the first Saturday after Bertrand unveiled Bill 63, over 600 individuals representing a wide variety of groups gathered in a common front. Over one hundred groups came together to form the Front du Québec français (FQF), and they decided that they would organize a week of protest to mobilize public opinion against the passing of the Bill.[85] Within days, streets across the province were filled with protesters forming the largest popular mobilisation since the conscription crisis of the Second World War.

The FQF's main spokesperson was François-Albert Angers, president of the Société Saint Jean Baptiste de Montréal. Angers declared that the struggle against Bill 63 was a new Battle of the Plains of Abraham, and he affirmed that Quebec premier Jean-Jacques Bertrand was a new General Wolfe. By giving English equal legal status to French, he argued, the National Assembly was de facto legislating anglophone superiority. From its very beginnings, the FQF outlined its demands in purely linguistic rather than social and economic terms. As a solution to the language problem, the FQF demanded that the government present the population with a comprehensive policy and that it proclaim French unilingualism at all levels.[86] While many groups involved in the protests saw them as evidence of a mass desire for change, it was the FQF that succeeded in becoming the main voice of opposition to Bill 63.

The FQF – bringing together groups from both the right and the left – spoke in a language of nationalism that blurred class distinctions and relations of economic power. There is no better expression of this outlook than François-Albert Angers himself, speaking before the Montreal Central Council of the CSN. Appealing to the CSN workers as the "elite of the working class" and then as "simply the elite of Quebec," Angers argued that "French is the mother tongue of the entire population, and when it is in danger, there are no more workers, no more lawyers, there must no longer be business men, or professors, but there are only francophone Quebeckers, defending their life, their very existence, their right to work in French, to speak French, in the language of their mothers and fathers."[87] For Angers, the linguistic problems in Quebec were the result of conquest, by which one group imposed its language onto another. To anglophones who argued for parents' right to choose, he stated that true linguistic rights were the rights "of a group to conserve its culture in spite of conquests."[88] The only solution was for francophone Quebec to close ranks, ignore distinctions between workers and professionals, put aside questions class and power differences, and fight for the preservation of the nation.

But at the same time another vision was being articulated which considered the interrelationship of class and language, and envisioned social transformation in different ways. Although the FQF was seen as the dominant voice of opposition to Bill 63, the crowds that spilled into Montreal streets in the first week of protests had an agenda that could not be controlled by a single voice at the top. According to one young activist, Bill 63 was denounced because it merely reproduced colonial structures. "At a fundamental level," he argues, "it was not a linguistic question, but a political one."[89] Workers, students, and independent leftists organized themselves to mobilize in the streets. Student and citizen groups worked to mobilize their constituencies, and a coalition of leftist groups even formed a common front of their own, "Front commun contre le Bill 63." This alternative common front ran parallel to the FQF and acted as the main organizational force behind many of the demonstrations during the first week after Bill 63 was unveiled.[90]

The first major protest, held Tuesday 28 October, was organized by the combined forces of student and other leftist groups. Students throughout the province disrupted the regular functioning of their schools by organizing study sessions, but it was in Montreal that the largest and most dramatic protests were held. Ten thousand students marched through the city before converging on the sports centre of the Université de Montréal, where they were met by thousands of others. At certain moments, there were more than 11,000 students packed into an arena that held 4,500; the ice surface and aisles were covered with people and, in the end, over 20,000 students rotated in and out of the arena for a massive "teach-in."[91] Michel Chartrand, Pierre Bourgault, and Raymond Lemieux spoke to the receptive crowd, telling them that their purpose in opposing Bill 63 was to stop English from serving as the "main tool in the oppression of the Quebec people."[92]

On Wednesday 29 October, a coalition of workers' and citizens' committees[93] organized a massive protest that brought at least 25,000 citizens to the streets of Montreal. Protesters met in the early evening at four rallying points, in Saint-Henri, downtown, and in the east and the north ends; they were soon joined by groups of students who had been roaming the city throughout the day, and who had gathered at Parc Lafontaine in preparation for the march. The itinerary of the march reveals much about its underlying ideology. The mass of protesters walked past the main sites of power in Montreal, first to City Hall and then west to Square Victoria, the heart of the city's business district. Standing before offices including those of the Conseil du patronat and the Montreal Chamber of Commerce, the crowd lit a large bonfire and burned Bertrand, mayor Jean Drapeau, and others in effigy. The protesters then marched back along Dorchester and up to Parc Lafontaine, where they lit more fires, burnt more effigies, and then dispersed.[94] By marching through the city's main sites of economic and political power, the crowd demonstrated that their struggle was about more than just language.

While the FQF did not oppose the protests organized by students and workers, neither did it do anything to aid them. Instead, it planned a massive rally in Quebec City on Friday 31 October. The protest, which started out calmly, erupted into violence when protesters began throwing bottles at police. It did not take long for the police to respond with tear gas, and for chaos to ensue.[95] By the end of the unprecedented week of protests, it was clear that opposition to Bill 63 was profound. The groups of workers, students, and leftist organizations did not have a coherent ideology, but, for all of them, Bill 63 fit within a larger conception of the colonized nature of Quebec society. According to a pamphlet issued by a variety of neighbourhood workers' committees, Bill 63, the "Bill of electoral donations," facilitated the exploitation of Quebec workers by the province's anglophone minority.[96]

The newly-minted *Quebec-Presse* – a weekly newspaper founded by the left to provide a counter-weight to the mainstream media – outlined its own rationale for opposing Bill 63. The French language was in danger in Quebec, the paper argued, because francophones increasingly needed to be able to speak English – the language of power and authority – to survive. Reinforcing this unequal power relationship, Bill 63 was designed by either "the conqueror" or "the *roi-nègre*," and was not legislated by "a free government."[97] The editors of the paper recognized that parents could not be blamed for sending their children to English-language schools, because everyone knew that speaking English was economically advantageous.[98] An in-depth and comprehensive understanding of the language problem therefore revealed that focusing only on the language of education was putting the "cart before the horse." Was the problem of language at work, the paper asked, not an effect of social and economic factors?[99]

When the Parti Québécois – with the collaboration of the CSN, the CEQ, the Alliance des Professeurs de Montréal, the FTQ, the Fédération des Sociétés Saint-Jean Baptiste and the SSJB de Montréal – published a special edition of *Pouvoir*, the differing ways of understanding the language problem in Quebec were made apparent. On the one hand, the paper reprinted a speech by Jérôme Proulx, an ex-Union Nationale deputy who left the party when it unveiled Bill 63. Proulx, far from seeing the world through the lens of global anti-imperialism, made ample use of traditional nationalist tropes, speaking of a "betrayal to the direction of history," and about "how there exists only one true loyalty, one solidarity, that which we owe to our nation, our people, ourselves."[100] While the paper printed Proulx's speech, it also published speeches by Raymond Parent of the CSN and Fernand Daoust of the FTQ, both of whom insisted that the struggle for language rights needed to be placed within a larger frame of reference. Parent argued that while the causes of the present linguistic crisis were multifaceted, they included both the power and influence of English Canada and the United States, and the separation under capitalism between "the economic rulers" who were "mostly anglophone," and the "mass of the population." "Taken as a whole," Parent argued, "we believe that the future of a threatened and compromised culture like ours depends on a deeply popular movement, one which is political, economic, and social."[101] Fernand Daoust, for his part, argued that English was the language of prestige and economic power and French the language of unemployment and uncertainty. The FTQ rejoiced in the knowledge that the population "has begun to wake up and that more and more, it has decided to take its destiny into its own hands."[102]

While both the street politics and the political language of opposition to Bill 63 were profoundly influenced by ideas about socialist decolonization, this was not the only theory inspiring the protests. Many, especially those who protested at the National Assembly on 31 October, drew on the tropes of traditional nationalism to denounce the actions of the government. But most were simply caught up in the public expression of outrage; protesters on the streets articulated an ambiguous mélange of nationalism, Marxism, and national liberation. And yet, despite the mixing of perspectives and movements, many voices were left unheard, suppressed, or at the very least pushed to the sidelines. If the language of schooling for immigrants sparked the crisis in the first place, why were the voices of those immigrants – and especially of the many immigrants on the left who formed such an important part of Montreal's radical community – not being heard?

A QUESTION OF IMMIGRANTS?

During the 1960s, conceptions of the nation in Quebec underwent an important symbolic transformation from an ethnically defined "French-Canadian" nation to a more *territorially* defined nationalism, represented by Quebec as a state. With this transformation, Martin Pâquet has argued, came a new political culture and new conceptions of citizenship, as relations between the individual and society increasingly came to be defined in contractual terms rather than organic ones.[103] Rather than seeing immigration as a destabilizing force for the nation, as earlier nationalists had done, many mainstream nationalists in the 1960s began to see immigration in instrumental terms. They came, in other words, to believe that the successful integration of immigrants into the francophone community was essential for the survival and development of the nation.[104]

The struggle against Bill 63 revolved specifically around the language in which new immigrants would be educated. It was a fight over which linguistic community in Montreal, the French or the English, would, in the face of a dramatically declining birth-rate, continue to grow.[105] Leftists in Montreal consistently included immigrants in their descriptions of the oppressed in Quebec. The problem they saw was not that immigrants were refusing to integrate into a new society, but rather that they were integrating, for reasons of economic necessity, into the language and culture of the dominant power.

At the same time that debates about the place of immigrants in Quebec society brought Montreal to a standstill, however, many immigrants themselves were demanding that their voices be heard. On 12 November 1969, Kimon Valaskakis, a self-declared "néo-Québécois," published a moving article in *Le Devoir* in which he described his interpretation of the debate around Bill 63. Valaskakis was encouraged to see a "long oppressed popu-

lation deciding to take to the streets to demonstrate its desire to avoid fad-
ing away," and he was convinced that the "neo-Quebecker certainly needs
to assimilate into the *québécois* milieu." Nonetheless, despite the excitement of the moment, he worried about the near unanimous response of
civil society to Bill 63. He objected to both nationalist arguments and to the
left-wing rhetoric which too easily conflated language and class on two
grounds: "1) not all of the exploited are francophones; 2) not all francophones are exploited." To the contention that language was an arm of domination, Valaskakis responded that this argument did not take adequate
account of the political, economic, and military dimensions of domination,
against which speaking French offered little protection. And it was not just
francophones who were poor: the two ethnic groups that ranked below
them, Italians and Natives, were predominantly English-speaking.[106]

What made Quebec unique, for Valaskakis, was that it escaped the prison
of monolithism that entrapped so many other societies. Montreal symbolized "a veritable mosaic of nationalities, ideas, and points of view. Here
we have an open society, and therefore a rich and fertile one. Here we have,
in opposition to the old European capitals, a human dimension which is
a language without nationality, an aggregate of values, a free spirit." But
Montreal was not only different from Europe – it was also an alternative to
the rest of North America. "This character," he argued, "exists only because
of francophone Quebec culture which, through its vitality, has foiled North
America. And it is this same society which can either remain multi-dimen-
sional or itself become monolithic." He worried that nationalism had the
potential of denying Quebec's diversity, and that, if this were to happen, the
"transatlantic and multicultural symbiosis of Quebec will be eliminated. The
American melting-pot will be neutralized, but only to be replaced by a
new French-language one. Individualities will be broken, dissidents will
be treated as foolish and a monolithism as ruthless … and as ugly as its
American version will transform us." "We can therefore ask ourselves," he
wrote, "what would be the interest of being 'melted' in French rather than
in English?" During their struggle for liberation, he concluded, Quebeckers should adopt a form of nationalism which was polyvalent and flexible,
one which would undergo perpetual questioning and renewal, and work to
create "the first technologically advanced society which would not be one-
dimensional."[107]

Valaskakis's intervention, coming just weeks after the beginning of the
protests against Bill 63, was prescient and insightful. A struggle for identity

that positioned francophones as the victims in Quebec's historical drama, and which drew a clear line between English capital and French labour, was bound to fail. Life in Montreal was too multifaceted to ever contain only one movement of political opposition with one axis of oppression. In the radical rhetoric of opposition to McGill or to Bill 63, those on the left often set francophones – seen to be a colonized ethnic class that carried the hopes of a future based on justice and liberty – against the province's English-speaking minority, portrayed as a parasitical class of settler colonialists and capitalist imperialists. But in between, as the object of struggle, as the silent partner which both sides hoped to "integrate" or "assimilate," were Montreal's immigrant communities, almost by definition excluded from the debates. When a group of anglophones who had been radicalized through Opération McGill headed out to Saint-Léonard with the intent of inform-ing the Italian community about the Quebec liberation struggle, for exam-ple, few thought of seeking out the perspectives of immigrants themselves.[108] The independent voices of these communities, although they were begin-ning to be more loudly articulated, rarely factored into the debates.

Soon these voices would be too loud to be ignored. Haitian emigré groups began publishing newsletters, participating in debates at the Uni-versité de Montréal, and appearing on Radio-Canada to discuss their efforts to bring social justice to Haiti.[109] African groups advocating anti-imperial-ism and decolonization began publishing newspapers and bulletins.[110] Mon-treal's Vietnamese community organized marches and demonstrations to oppose the war being waged on their country of origin, and exiles from South Africa organized resistance to the Apartheid regime that ruled with brutal terror.[111] As the vast coalition of francophone radicals attempted to claim public space in the city, therefore, new groups of radical immigrants protesting against the exclusion of minorities from society's larger struc-tures began to emerge. They were intimately involved with the struggles tak-ing place in their countries of origin, yet were also becoming interested in the struggle in Quebec. Many groups even began developing their own spaces of resistance where radical thought could develop. Like the offices of UHURU and the Negro Community Centre for Black Montrealers, a group of self-defined "Afro-Asians" founded the Ho Chi Minh bookstore, and members of Montreal's Arab community established a Palestinian House.[112]

The Afro-Asian Latin American People's Solidarity Committee and the parallel Comité de Solidarité des Peuples d'Afrique, d'Asie et d'Amérique Latine eventually went on to establish a "Third World Centre" on University Street, asserting by its very presence that language issues could not capture the full complexity of life in a cosmopolitan city like Montreal. But the "Third World Centre" also maintained a goal that differentiated it from similar centres throughout North America. It hoped not only to broaden "the base for anti-imperialist work among the Third World people," but also to "play its due role in promoting solidarity between the people of Quebec and the people of the Third World."[113] Already various coalitions of minority groups were claiming to be playing their parts in *both* worldwide anti-imperialist struggle and politics in Quebec.[114] It would be wrong to argue that inter-ethnic solidarity ever became the driving thrust of politics in Montreal, or that all groups united in opposition to empire. But it is true nonetheless that the history of this period is far more complex than is often portrayed. In order to grasp some of its complexity, it is necessary to turn to the community organizing that had been taking place in Montreal's working-class neighbourhoods since the beginning of the decade, as well as to the organization that did the most to open its doors to the multi-faceted world of dissent, the Montreal Central Council of the CSN.

SEVEN

THE CSN, THE FLQ, AND THE OCTOBER CRISIS

In North American radical circles of the 1960s, the labour movement did not have a good reputation. The New Left was generally seen to have occupied a space left vacant by a receding class politics. Where once stood class, the argument went, came a deeper understanding of individual and national alienation, racial oppression, and a new awareness of the political nature of private life. Frantz Fanon had argued that in a colonized society, true hope for revolution lay with the rural masses. The urban working class, "pampered by the colonial regime," had "everything to lose" in the event of decolonization.[1] Malcolm X, for his part, preferred to see the world primarily through the lens of race rather than class, just as Betty Friedan and Simone de Beauvoir did with sex. And Herbert Marcuse discussed the way in which capitalism had come to accommodate industrial workers, buying them off with material abundance.[2] Even when "class" was not written off as a theoretical category, few on the left looked to the North American labour movement for inspiration. Claude Julien argued that, in the United States at least, the major labour unions constituted "one of the pillars of the empire."[3] And Pierre Vallières wrote in 1964 that Quebec unions merely reinforced in workers feelings of "powerlessness, uselessness, and humiliation."[4]

By the end of the decade, such comments could no longer be made, or not in Quebec at least. Organized labour had the wind in its sails. It became the dominant voice of opposition in Quebec and captured the attention of radicals across the continent.[5] Beginning in the late 1960s, labour activists were present at every major demonstration and participated in nearly every major assembly in defence of social justice or in opposition to empire. The radicalization of labour came in many forms and in many places, from the new militancy of the Metallos (steelworkers) to the Mouvement de libération du taxi, a union of the city's beleaguered taxis drivers who roamed the city in packs waiving red flags and openly displaying their allegiance to Che Guevara.[6] More than any other organization, however, it was the radicalization of the Confédération des syndicats nationaux (CSN) that came to symbolize a new era of labour activism.

In this chapter, I will outline the changing nature of activism within the labour movement (and especially the CSN) in the second half of the 1960s, and describe some of the ways in which this political activity intersected with the city's community-based organizing. Organized labour became more militant at roughly the same time as citizens' and political action committees proliferated throughout Montreal's poor and working-class neighbourhoods, and all these movements converged to begin laying the foundations for the Front d'action politique (FRAP), a political party that hoped to challenge Jean Drapeau's hold on power in the city's 1970 municipal elections. Just as activists from many different backgrounds and orientations were investing their hopes in the FRAP, the kidnappings (and later murder) committed by the FLQ, and the political repression that it engendered, transformed the political climate of the city, creating a context in which the labour movement began to see itself as the primary vehicle promoting democracy in the province.

THE CSN AND THE SIXTIES

While other North American minorities rarely had large institutions to represent them, the CSN gave French-speaking Quebeckers a powerful organization through which they could make demands for both cultural and economic democracy.[7] The CSN originated in the Catholic clergy's attempt to counter the influence of American-based unions in the early twentieth century.[8] In the post-Second World War era, it grew increasingly militant, engaging in a series of bitter strikes. By 1960, the union had shed its religious character and changed its name to reflect its new identity as a national labour organization. Throughout the 1960s, the CSN grew at a remarkable rate, mostly due to the rapid unionization of Quebec's public sector workers. By 1966, the union represented 190,454 individuals, more than double the 90,733 of 1960,[9] and many began seeing the enormous potential that such a rapid growth entailed.

A decisive turning point came at the union's 1966 convention when Marcel Pepin, newly elected as president, delivered a moral report entitled *Une société bâtie pour l'homme*. The moral report of the CSN president is a highly significant document which, written collectively and approved by the executive, outlines the ideological parameters for the organization as a whole.[10] When Pepin delivered this speech, people knew immediately that the CSN had taken a turn to the left. In the years to come, his reports were reprinted and circulated many times, becoming the objects of numerous discussions.[11]

Une société bâti pour l'homme denounced the inhumanity of the capitalist system, in which workers were forced to sell their labour as a commodity. With this report, the CSN began distancing itself from the reformist platform of the Quiet Revolution, a separation that would become increasingly marked.[12] Pepin argued that monopoly capital, having no consideration for the public interest, subverted democracy, dehumanized workers, and stifled social progress. And it was up to workers to help in bringing basic principles of humanism and democratic participation to society as a whole.[13] At the CSN's October 1968 convention, Pepin would outline the organization's new political strategy, launching his famous call for the CSN to open up a "second front." For Pepin, too many aspects of workers' lives could not be dealt with through collective bargaining alone (the "first front"), and it was up to the labour movement to take its struggles into working-class communities, to forge parallel institutions, and to build democracy from below. Labour activists, in other words, now needed to open up a second front to organize workers outside of the workplace as consumers, renters, parents, and citizens.[14]

Pepin's reports had an enormous impact on the Quebec labour movement. In the late 1960s, at the instigation of labour activists, political action committees began to emerge in neighbourhoods and municipalities.[15] As workers had been shut out of the power structures that controlled their lives, many argued, it was necessary to use the labour movement to organize workers outside of the workplace.[16] Political action committees were therefore designed to be sites where workers could actively participate in building a more democratic society.[17] CSN activists Paul Cliche, Pierre Vadboncoeur, and André L'Heureux assumed the responsibility of the CSN's political activities, and they set to work to build programs of popular education and political activism. During strikes, they would distribute information explaining the political dimension of the conflict, and they educated workers, intervened in the media, and organized political campaigns around issues such as health insurance.[18]

Pepin's reports spoke to the hopes and aspirations of a growing number of activists who were hoping that labour would play a larger role in politics. The second half of the 1960s witnessed an important increase in workplace conflicts, and in 1969 alone more than 103,000 workers took part in more than 160 work stoppages across the province.[19] In February 1968, a few months after UGEQ had organized a protest that saw 5,000 people protesting in front of the American consulate, the CSN condemned American actions in Vietnam.[20] Discussions within the union also included the influence of imperialism in Quebec.[21] With both his 1966 and his 1968 reports, Pepin had brought the CSN significantly to the left, a move that, while creating some discontent,[22] generated excitement throughout the movement. It was in this context that the Montreal Central Council of the CSN emerged as the organization's radical wing.

THE MONTREAL CENTRAL COUNCIL

At the CSN's 1968 convention Michel Chartrand, recently returned to the labour movement after a long absence, worked to organize all the Montreal delegates at the convention into a single bloc. When the convention came to a close, he emerged as the clear voice of the Montreal unions and, before long, was elected as president of the Montreal Central Council. When Chartrand returned to the labour movement he did so as an elder statesman, a veteran of the struggles that had shaped Quebec for the previous thirty years. Politicized during the Depression and the conscription crisis of the Second World War, Chartrand joined the labour movement in 1949 during a divisive strike in Asbestos, Quebec, and he then went on to work throughout the 1950s for both Catholic and American-based international unions. By the early 1960s, while remaining politically active in social democratic politics, most notably as the founding president of the Parti socialiste du Québec, he left the labour movement and returned to his trade as a printer, founding Les Presses sociales.[23] Although he remained formally outside of the ranks of organized labour, Chartrand continued to meet with many of his former colleagues associated with the left wing of the labour movement at the Press Club on Saint-Denis.[24] Chartrand was a complicated figure who was well known for oratory and rhetoric but his fiery statements at times inflamed passions rather than spurring debate. Yet Chartrand's ascendancy to the presidency of the Montreal Central Council altered the nature of labour activism. Disorganized and lacking political energy before 1968,[25] the Central Council, representing the roughly 65,000 workers in unions affiliated to the CSN on the territory of Montreal (roughly one third of the CSN's total membership),[26] quickly became alive with activity. At its general assemblies, crowds of people – ranging from unemployed workers to McGill professors – packed into a primary school on De Lanaudière Street in east Montreal.[27] Although Chartrand and Pepin developed a fierce rivalry, the Central Council became the most important advocate of Pepin's idea of the "Second Front."[28]

The Central Council's general assemblies were open forums, and dissent and disagreement abounded. When the Central Council decided to support French unilingualism, to take just one example, fierce debate broke out between francophone and Italian construction workers.[29] Despite their often acrimonious nature, the assemblies generated an enormous amount of excitement throughout political circles in Montreal. The Central Council opened its assemblies and conventions to leftists of all backgrounds, and provided moral and material support to groups across the city. In 1969 alone, the Central Council supported – both financially and otherwise – the legal battles of Pierre Vallières and Charles Gagnon, participated in many street protests, helped to organize Opération McGill français and the battles against Bill 63, and succeeded in forcing the CSN's confederal council to pronounce itself in favour of unilingualism.[30]

From 1969 to 1972, the offices of the Montreal Central Council became a hub of activity for a wide range of individuals, groups, and ideas. The organization became involved in consumer co-operatives and in protests, and participated in the founding of a mass-circulation newspaper.[31] Perhaps most importantly, it forged a space – in both the physical and metaphorical senses of the word – in which many differing groups could come together and talk about their particular grievances and perspectives. The office, with two small rooms on either side, was situated on the corner of Saint-Denis and Viger, and people on the street below were able to observe the activity taking place above. As Fernand Foisy recalls, the office overflowed with people coming and going throughout the day.[32] In the late 1960s and early 1970s the Central Council advocated a broad project of anti-imperialism and national liberation, one that was focused on both international and local solidarity. It supported the struggle of Palestinians, denounced the US intervention in Vietnam and, in support of struggling farm workers, boycotted grapes from California. In the early 1970s, it supported the liberation struggles of Angola, Mozambique, and Guinea-Bissau against Portugal, the Greek and Spanish people against their own dictatorial governments,[33] and it began making contacts with people of Latin American origin in Montreal.[34] Chartrand travelled to Chile at the end of 1972 to observe firsthand the country's experiments with democratic socialism.[35] By the end of the 1960s, it had become deeply ingrained in Montreal leftism that the movement in Quebec formed part of a larger revolt sweeping the world, and the Montreal Central Council built on these insights.

Although leftist organizations considered themselves internationalist in scope, they had traditionally ignored Montreal's own immigrant communities. The Central Council attempted to overcome this ingrained paradox. It actively courted the participation of people of all origins and provided offices and meeting spaces for a wide variety of organizations, including the Afro-Asian People's Solidarity Committee, the Québec-Palestine Solidarity Committee, and the Mouvement de libération du taxi.[36] It defended the Black and White activists who were arrested during the Sir George Williams Affair, and it printed tracts for the Regroupement des Noirs de Montréal.[37] At its 1969 convention, guests at the front table included not only labour leaders but Dimitri Roussopoulos from *Our Generation*, representatives from the Saint-Jacques citizens' committee, the Jeunesse ouvrière catholique, the Association of Canadian Greeks, the National Labour Confederation of Spain in Exile, members from the Mouvement de libération du taxi, among others.[38] And in his hour-long speech to the assembly, Chartrand endorsed collaboration with "the various groups which are working for the well-being of the population or which are working for the liberation of the population of Montreal."[39] "We will fight," he declared in one of his most often-repeated statements, "alongside all dissidents, protestors, and revolutionaries."[40] And when the Central Council published a brochure explaining the services and resources at its disposal, it stated that "The *Montreal Central Council* collaborates with all Quebec community associations, including those with members who do not speak French. It will soon make a meeting space available to workers from other areas of the world who have chosen Quebec as their adopted homeland."[41] The brochure itself was translated into eight languages: English, French, Italian, Spanish, Portuguese, German, Greek, and Chinese.[42]

REWRITING HISTORY

In the space fostered by the Central Council, the lines separating the labour movement from the left became much more fluid, and radicals from outside the ranks of labour lent their services to the movement in a variety of ways. The effort to rethink Quebec history involved many people, but one in particular, Léandre Bergeron, played a central role in synthesizing disparate views. Born in Saint-Lupic in Manitoba and educated in Winnipeg and France, Bergeron taught at the Royal Military College in Kingston until 1964, and then in the department of modern languages at Sir George Williams University. As a faculty member during the Sir George Williams Affair of 1969, Bergeron, who supported the student occupation,[43] was forced to confront questions of race in Quebec. His first effort at popular education came in the summer of 1969, when he organized a series of weekly courses for the Saint-Jacques citizens' committee.[44] The idea of holding courses for workers was greeted enthusiastically at the Central Council's 1969 convention, and it was decided that the education committee and the political action committee would work together to prepare their implementation. According to the education committee, to understand the contradictory forces at work in present-day society, it was necessary to study the contradictions governing Quebec's past. It was crucial, it argued, that a "colonized population like that of Quebec" learn a history different than that which it had been traditionally taught. It needed to be offered a history shaped by the politics of decolonization, a history that could help it "reinterpret its past, understand its present condition, and change its future." Political education for workers therefore needed to include a study of the ideology of the British colonizers and the collaborationist elite, as well as Quebec workers' various attempts to organize resistance. Limiting political education to the history of the labour movement "would only orient workers towards a corporatist view of society," and limiting the courses to abstract economic theories, not grounded in reality, would be dreadfully boring. The present, the committee argued, needed to be understood within the larger history of anti-colonial resistance.[45]

In November 1969 Léandre Bergeron and Bertrand Lapalme began to teach popular education courses for the workers of the Montreal Central Council. The courses given at the Central Council's headquarters covered Quebec history, nationalism and the class struggle, the history of the Quebec labour movement, capitalism, socialism and communism.[46] While the sessions themselves reached a wide audience, it was the publication of

Léandre Bergeron's *Petit manuel d'histoire du Québec* that did the most to popularize Bergeron's iconoclastic vision of Quebec history. The book built upon notes from his courses and was sold by the Council for fifty cents at its 1970 convention.[47] In the first seven months after its publication, sales had already reached an unprecedented 60,000 and, by 1972, over 140,000 copies had been sold.[48]

In the *Petit manuel d'histoire du Québec*, rather than merely looking to the Conquest, or to the negative effects of "Anglo-Saxon colonialism," Bergeron argues that Quebec's past can be divided into the three different colonial regimes to which it has been subjected, the French, the English, and the American. European explorers did not "discover" America, Bergeron writes, as the land "was already populated by *men*, men of a different colour, yes, but men all the same." Bergeron also highlights the continuing effects of racism which, present during the early years of European colonization, "still permeates much of White society, and will only disappear with the complete liberation of all non-White peoples." Rather than ignoring Natives, Bergeron argued that the "principal characteristic of human society in New France was the domination of the White population over the Red population."[49]

Moreover, in dramatic contrast to romantic versions of Quebec history which, according to Bergeron, glorified "those famous exploiters of the Red man – Dollard des Ormeaux, Jeanne Mance, Maisonneuve, Marguerite Bourgeoys and the rest," his reading traces the ancestors of present-day Quebec back to the "exploited settlers," a group "composed of convicts, vagabonds and the 'king's daughters.'" By identifying the ancestors of modern-day Quebeckers as the "outcasts" and "rejects" of France, Bergeron attempts to demonstrate a continuity of exploitation. Bergeron's terminology speaks to his attempt to read Quebec history through a lens of international revolution. He insists on using the term *Canayen* when referring "to those 70,000 French people of Canada and their descendants." A *French Canadian*, he argues, "is the Canayen who licks the boots of the English or American colonizer," who "is like the American Negro who tries to escape from his identity and hopes to be integrated into White society." Like the African American who refuses integration to become *Black*, the "*Québécois* is the Canayen who rejects colonialism" and who struggles "against the Anglo-American-Canadian domination of Quebec."[50]

By looking at history from the perspective of the marginalized, Bergeron challenges the entire school of neo-nationalist historiography, arguing that the Conquest of 1759 meant "little more than *changing masters*." Rather than being exploited by French merchants and administrators, the Canayens were now exploited by English ones. The Catholic Church, currying favour with the new administration, assumed the role of assuring the subservience of the people, becoming the "negro king" of the province. This complex mix of class and colonialism continued with the rise of the American regime, and especially in the post-Second World War period when American capital stratified Quebec into workers and bourgeoisie. Bergeron argues that even in modern times the upper bourgeoisie is composed almost entirely of anglophones, although francophones are well represented among the middle- and petite-bourgeoisie. The working class, for its part, is composed not only of francophones, but also of Italian and Portuguese immigrants and some English Canadians. Because the vast majority of francophone were workers, however, Bergeron conflates the struggle of Quebec workers with the struggle of the Quebec people, a people now on the march towards liberation.[51]

In many ways Bergeron's reinterpretation of Quebec history emerged out of the structures of the Montreal Central Council, yet it also traced its origins to political education courses given in the Saint-Jacques citizens' committee, demonstrating something of the overlapping worlds of the left during the period. In the late 1960s, the community activism of Montreal's poor and working-class neighbourhoods began to converge with activism generated by the labour movement (with the CSN's Montreal Central Council acting only as the most radical and dramatic example). It was this convergence that led to the founding of a radical municipal party, the FRAP, that was designed not only to give the working class a political voice, but also to democratize all of society's economic, political, and cultural structures. Before looking to the FRAP, however, it is first necessary to briefly consider the community organizations out of which it emerged.

FROM CITIZENS' COMMITTEES TO THE FRAP

The citizens' committees that began taking shape in the early 1960s assumed many different forms and structures. While no two committees looked exactly the same, they did share much in common, as they drew on activists of a variety of different ages and backgrounds and affirmed their independence from political parties. In the early 1960s, citizens' committees were generally organized by "social animators" who had been hired by the Conseil des oeuvres de Montréal, and the animators attempted to organize citizens around local issues, such as the building of new schools, the setting up of culinary classes, or the building of cultural and recreation centres. Committees were set up in Saint-Henri and Pointe Saint-Charles, and then in Mile-End, Saint-Jean-Baptiste, Saint-Louis, Hochelaga-Maisonneuve and elsewhere. The social animators attempted to help citizens overcome the daily indignities of being poor by empowering them around issues such as housing, education, and health care. By the late 1960s, however, many of the organizers involved in citizens' groups had become discouraged with the poor participation of the residents, and began thinking about broadening their scope.[52]

It was also in the late 1960s that radical professionals had joined with community activists to found a network of parallel health institutions, organized and run by the citizens, demonstrating some of the ways that individuals were crossing class and sometimes linguistic and ethnic barriers.[53] In Pointe Saint-Charles, where a mere four doctors served a population of 24,000, a community medical clinic was opened up on the corner of Knox and Charlevoix in 1968.[54] In the impoverished neighbourhood of Saint-Jacques – where more than 16,000 households did not have hot water, 4,500 had neither bath nor shower, and where deaths due to tuberculosis were ten times higher than elsewhere in Montreal – residents, with the help of anglophone medical students from McGill, formed a people's clinic.[55] The clinic's doctors had ideological backgrounds ranging from the ccf to the rin. English-speaking professionals worked in French, and took directions from the largely impoverished French-speaking residents.[56] The clinic set up in a renovated building on Saint-Christophe, and was overwhelmed with residents coming to receive medical care.[57]

Grassroots activism did not only take hold in poor francophone communities. In the neighbourhood lying just east of McGill University, a group of citizens formed a committee that would become the centre of a fierce battle over urban development in the years to come. The neighbourhood was home to an incredibly diverse array of residents, fifteen percent of whom were immigrants, and it had roughly equal numbers of French- and English-speakers.[58] Many Milton-Park students, low-income families, pensioners, and young professionals joined together to fight a major battle – one that would last over a decade – against Concordia Estates, a real-estate developer that planned to destroy many existing residences and replace them with high-rise buildings. According to Claire Helman, opposition to the project grew out of the neighbourhood, which was "the perfect cauldron for mixing people and their ideas."[59] Members of the Milton-Park citizens' committee shared a belief that the marginalized, elderly, and the poor could be empowered to shape the decisions that affected the everyday life of themselves and their community.[60]

Throughout the 1960s, community publications continually emerged. In Saint-Henri, not only was a citizens' bookstore opened, but in December 1967 a group of people formed around "worker-priest" Jacques Couture and founded *L'Opinion ouvrière* as a way for residents to voice their thoughts and opinions. Four thousand copies of the paper's first issue were printed.[61] Other publications – *Le Carré, La Voix populaire, Up to the Neck, Park Extension Community News, Le Va vite, Le Droit populaire, Le Travailleur, The Boiling Pointe, The Poor People's Paper*, etc. – created a whole constellation of publications through which residents could form alternative visions of their society and its possible future.[62] But by the end of the decade, the ideal of participatory democracy had begun to fuse with new understandings of the structural nature of poverty, and many activists focussed their efforts on organizing the working class instead of the indigent, since it was seen to be a more reliable base upon which to found a movement of social transformation. The Saint-Jacques medical clinic and the CAP Saint-Jacques (formerly the citizens' committee), for example, moved out of the impoverished neighbourhood below Sherbrooke Street to the working-class neighbourhood of the Plateau.[63]

The merging of the ideals of popular democracy with a program for working-class power took its most concrete form with the founding of the FRAP in 1970. The immediate origins of the FRAP go back 19 May 1968, when 175 activists representing twenty citizens' committees from across the city met in a Saint-Henri school to discuss their common problems, and their common belief in the necessity of taking political action. Despite the confusion of the meeting, the groups succeeded in drafting a declaration stating that governments could no longer be allowed to continue to act against the interests of the people. If citizens' committees were to have any effect, they would need to co-ordinate their struggles, work with labour activists and, some began to muse, set their sights on political power.[64] The idea of organizing a political party began to spread and, in the fall of the following year, community organizers and activists planned a series of popular assemblies in Montreal neighbourhoods.

The energy generated by community-based activists converged with the drive for political action within the labour movement, which had organized fifteen conferences in regions throughout Quebec uniting representatives of the CSN, the FTQ, and the CEQ. At Montreal's conference, activists from student and community organizations joined with labour organizers to found the FRAP. The party's manifesto, issued in May 1970, outlined the radical nature of the party's new program, premised on the belief in the necessity of representing workers politically and on the idea that, through taking power in Montreal, the economic heart of Quebec, they could contribute to changing society as a whole. The political action committees that made up the FRAP would not only work to contest municipal elections, but also to democratize neighbourhoods, workplaces, and services.[65]

As a broad common front, FRAP meant different things to different people. For community activists the party represented an unprecedented attempt to unite across neighbourhoods, and to join with the labour movement to challenge the structure of municipal power. For students, who were "accepting less and less to be reduced to passive and powerless consumers in a society in which they do not control," the party offered the possibility of joining with other movements throughout the city.[66] And for labour activists, the FRAP acted as an attempt to provide the working class with a political voice.[67] The CSN released a full-time employee to direct the FRAP's election campaign of 1970, and it provided facilities where it could meet. The Montreal Central Council, for its part, provided the party with a substantial financial contribution.[68]

The FRAP's 1970 publication *Les salariés au pouvoir!*, a document outlining the party's political program and philosophy, described the marginalization of workers and the distance that separated them from society's decision-making structures. While workers throughout Montreal lived in poor housing, with chronic debt, and with the realities of plant closings and unemployment, the FRAP argued, the City of Montreal chose to devote its energy to investing in mega-projects of prestige, from Expo '67 to the construction of Place des Arts.[69] And in Montreal – as in Quebec as a whole – workers occupied subordinate positions in industries controlled by Americans and English-Canadians, and the living conditions of workers, made up largely of francophones but also of immigrants, continued to deteriorate despite the city's prosperity.[70]

In Montreal, where seventy-five per cent of families were renters, forging democracy necessarily entailed a program of urban renovation, including the construction of public housing, parks, and daycares. If the FRAP came to power, the party promised that citizens would control urban planning through public assemblies, power would be decentralized, and development would no longer be controlled by the private sphere. Citizen-run community health clinics would be established and, in addition to having abortion services, they would become centres of popular education. Discrimination based on religion, race, or the presence of children would no longer be tolerated in the housing sphere,[71] and inequality for women in the municipal public service would be eliminated, with free twenty-four-hour daycare provided for all. Artistic and cultural institutions would be decentralized throughout the city, the site of Expo '67 would become a popular university, police budgets would be cut, and the riot squad dismantled.[72]

FRAP's program was vast and, even for the most ardent socialists, somewhat utopian. What the party did do, however, was hold out a vision of what it called a "form of democracy that would be lived in the everyday."[73] By uniting many of the different facets of the left in the late 1960s, many believed that the FRAP represented the emergence of a strong and coherent movement, one based on the twin poles of working-class political agency and grassroots democracy.[74] The FRAP was in the midst of its first municipal election campaign when the attention of the city was diverted, and its political climate transformed, by the events of October 1970. To understand what came to be known as the "October Crisis," which began with the kidnapping of British diplomat James Cross by the FLQ, it is necessary to situate it both locally and internationally.

THE OCTOBER CRISIS

At the end of the 1960s, the international order was profoundly shaken by a rising tide of global dissent. In 1968, as war raged in Vietnam and protests continued against it, cities across the United States exploded in riots in the wake the assassination of Martin Luther King. Machine guns were mounted on the White House lawn and the Capitol balcony as flames came within six blocks of the White House.[75] In France, with the memory of the Algerian War still fresh, students and workers took to the streets and nearly toppled the French government, while student protesters in Mexico City were gunned down in advance of the summer Olympic games. In the summer of 1970, the Tupamaros guerrillas staged four kidnappings in ten days in

Uruguay, Argentinean guerrillas kidnapped the country's former president, American Black Panthers were making dramatic attempts to free prisoners, kidnappings were being carried out in Bolivia, and violence was breaking out in Northern Ireland and the Basque Country.[76]

Political violence had also come to Montreal. The destruction of the computer centre at Sir George Williams University in 1969 and rowdy demonstrations in defence of French-language rights spoke to the turbulence of the period. When the city's police force and fire department went on a one-day strike in the fall of 1969, Canadian army troops were deployed to maintain order. Amidst this turmoil, the bombings and robberies of the FLQ continued apace. The FLQ was never a structured organization, but a loose network of individuals that had many different incarnations throughout the 1960s. From 1963 to 1967, groups calling themselves the FLQ had planted thirty-five bombs, a number which increased to as many as sixty bombs for the years between 1968 and 1970. In its first five years, the FLQ had injured four people and caused the death of four others; in the three following years, the FLQ was responsible for two deaths and thirty-seven injuries.[77] Through its various publications, the group reflected at length on its "shock therapy" strategy and on the necessity for revolutionary violence in Quebec.[78] Financing itself through hold-ups, the FLQ claimed legitimacy from its reading of Quebec society through the lens of anti-colonial theory and from the example of other liberation movements throughout the world. In 1970, Carlos Marighella's *Minimanual of the Urban Guerrilla*, giving advice on how to wage an urban revolutionary war, began circulating with its own "Quebec" preface.[79]

The relationship of the FLQ to the labour movement and the left is complicated. Mainstream labour leaders consistently denounced the FLQ. Michel Chartrand and the Montreal Central Council of the CSN, however, well known for its contentious and at times ill-considered positions, played a far more ambiguous goal. One of the most controversial aspects of the Central Council's actions was its tacit support for the FLQ. As mentioned earlier, it actively contributed to the defence of Pierre Vallières and Charles Gagnon, and during the October Crisis Chartrand was often seen speaking alongside members of the FLQ, giving his support to the larger cause. During the crisis, the Central Council even provided office space for FLQ lawyer Robert Lemieux and endorsed the objectives of the FLQ manifesto.[80] The authorities deemed that the lines of collaboration between the FLQ and the Central Council were so close that, on 16 October, Chartrand him-

self was arrested and, on 28 January 1971, the offices of the Central Council were raided and its documents confiscated.[81]

As I have been arguing throughout this book, the FLQ was only one facet
of the political activism of the 1960s in Montreal. Since the beginning of the
1960s, advocates of decolonization had been divided about how to bring
about social change. Some had opted for electoral politics while others
had sought to create a revolutionary party. Others conceived of political
action through cultural production – the creation of poetry and cinema and
fiction – while still others developed consciousness-raising groups for
women or grassroots newspapers and community organizations. Although
many activists opposed the violence of the FLQ, there can be no doubt that
the group benefited from a certain degree of sympathy from many on the
left, and this sympathy fed the FLQ's belief in the legitimacy of engaging in
violent action.

The origins of what became known as the "October Crisis" go back to
the provincial election of April 1970, the first in which the newly formed
Parti Québécois (PQ) participated. The party, and its leader René Lévesque,
had a complicated relationship with the left from the beginning. But the PQ
was the only credible opposition to the province's established parties, and
so few elections were as disappointing for the left as that of April 1970. Just
days before, the Royal Trust Bank staged a campaign of fear, parading nine
Brinks trucks in front of television cameras to give the impression that a
PQ victory would translate into a massive flight of wealth from Montreal
to Toronto, and Quebec's Minister of Justice, Rémi Paul, compared PQ
leader René Lévesque to Fidel Castro. Despite these tactics, the PQ won
24% of the popular vote, yet because of the particularities of the British electoral system it captured only seven of the hundred and eight seats in the
National Assembly.

These disappointing results convinced many that the electoral path to
social change was blocked. There was no shortage of oppositional political groups operating in the city, and activists had formed everything from
grassroots neighbourhood committees to municipal political parties to
Leninist organizations. But some young people drifted to the FLQ. Throughout the summer the bombing campaign intensified, and at the beginning
of September 1970, a group of nine FLQ members held a strategy meeting
to escalate their actions from bombings to political kidnappings. With a
five to four vote, the decision was made to proceed.[82] At 8:20 in the morning of 5 October 1970, a group of four armed members of the FLQ drove a

stolen taxi to the house of British diplomat James Richard Cross on Red-path Crescent in the Montreal neighbourhood of Westmount. After forcibly entering the house, they emerged with James Cross and took their captive to an apartment in Montreal North. Although the Cross kidnapping shocked many, it did not create a crisis in the province. In Ottawa, the official ceremonies and receptions for the opening of the Parliamentary session were not delayed, and Quebec premier Robert Bourassa travelled to New York two days after the kidnapping to encourage American investments in the province.[83]

The FLQ laid out its demands in a communiqué left in an envelope, along with a copy of an eight-page manifesto, at a pavilion of the Université du Québec à Montréal: police searches needed to be stopped, the FLQ Manifesto broadcasted, the twenty-three "political prisoners" currently in jail or awaiting bail released, a plane to Cuba or Algeria arranged, the fired postal workers known as the "gars de Lapalme" rehired, $500,000 in gold provided, and the name of a police informer made public. Overnight, the FLQ was transformed from a handful of disgruntled youths into an important political force. Refusing to name an intermediary for negotiations, it forced the government to negotiate publicly, and by delivering communiqués directly to the media it used the competition between stations for ratings to ensure that its message would be broadcast directly to the population.[84] Through these actions, as Marc Raboy explains, the FLQ "succeeded for a time in publicly imposing a counter-interpretation of social reality, and did so on a grand scale."[85] After repeated communiqués, extensions, responses and counter-responses, the Canadian Minister of External Affairs sought to buy time, and announced that the FLQ manifesto would be broadcast on public television.

Almost as soon as the announcement had been made, journalist Louis Fournier read the manifesto to the audience of Montreal's CKAC radio station, and the following day it was read out on the public television station Radio-Canada. In plain colloquial language, the manifesto spoke of the illusory nature of the existing democratic system and it denounced both the colonialist and capitalist nature of Quebec society. Written in a heavily masculine language addressing itself directly to male workers, the manifesto also denounced Pierre Trudeau for alleged homosexuality. Claiming that the FLQ was merely a group of Quebec workers, the manifesto encouraged workers to make revolutions in their own neighbourhoods and work-places.[86]

Government officials had thought that reading the manifesto out loud would discredit the FLQ, but they were mistaken. Almost as soon as the manifesto was broadcasted, groups and individuals began expressing their support for its objectives, although almost all denounced the group's violent methods. For organizations that supported the manifesto's objectives yet failed to clearly denounce the group's tactics, like the FRAP, the results were catastrophic. FRAP was publicly associated with the FLQ by Montreal mayor Jean Drapeau, becoming discredited in the eyes of the population.[87] On call-in radio stations, many called in to announce their support for the objectives of the manifesto and to denounce the established order.[88] As the days passed, the tension grew and the situation deteriorated. The FLQ gradually abandoned all its demands except one: that its jailed members be released. The government remained firm, refusing to grant even that demand. On 10 October, only forty minutes had elapsed since the government announced its refusal to continue negotiations when another FLQ cell – recently returned from the United States – kidnapped forty-nine-year-old Quebec Cabinet Minister Pierre Laporte, a major political figure in the province. Although completely improvised, the actions of this new cell made the group appear as a disciplined revolutionary force.

The events shook Quebec premier Robert Bourassa profoundly, and the following day the entire cabinet retreated to the heavily fortified Queen Elizabeth Hotel in downtown Montreal. On 14 October, in the face of a clearly deepening crisis and the seeming weakness of the provincial government, a group of sixteen Quebec intellectuals and labour leaders signed a joint declaration urging the Quebec government to negotiate a release of "political prisoners" in order to save the lives of the hostages. Perhaps more importantly, the open letter demanded that it be the Quebec government – which appeared to be wavering and on the verge of collapse – that deal with the crisis. The rigidity and militarism of Ottawa, the group declared, risked reducing "Quebec and its government to a tragic powerlessness." The statement ended with a call for all others who agreed with them to publicly declare their support, and it did not take long for many to do so.[89] Local unions, voluntary organizations, student societies, business groups, and individuals, some from within the Liberal Party itself, quickly stepped forward to announce their support for the declaration. In government circles, rumours began to circulate that the sixteen members who had signed the original declaration were plotting to form a provisional government.[90]

Meanwhile, support for the objectives of the FLQ manifesto grew.[91] While the majority of those on the left strongly disagreed with the violent actions of the FLQ, they read the crisis through the lens of their understandings of power relations in the province. Active support for the FLQ began taking shape on Montreal's university campuses, and on 15 October, 1,000 social science and humanities students at the Université de Montréal voted to go out on strike until the jailed FLQ members were released. At the newly instituted UQAM, an assembly of eight hundred students voted to support the FLQ and to begin a strike to put pressure on the government to negotiate seriously with the FLQ.[92] A group of students also took over the office of the rector of the university and transformed it into a centre of operations, and an assembly of sixty to seventy-five professors announced its support for the objectives of the FLQ manifesto and decided to begin a strike of its own. The administration, not sure how to respond, suspended courses. Critics and supporters of the FLQ alike began to wonder if, in the end, the FLQ's tactics could actually be working. In the province's CEGEP system and high schools, thousands of students began walking out on strike. Leftist figures such as Pierre Vallières, Michel Chartrand, Robert Lemieux, and Charles Gagnon addressed the assemblies.[93]

A major rally had been planned at the sports centre of the Université de Montréal, but the university authorities refused to allow it to take place. Paul Sauvé arena in east Montreal was quickly found as an alternative venue. The curling rink had been rented out to the FRAP, which allowed the assembly to take place once its own event had finished.[94] It was not until late in the evening that the assembly began with a reading of the FLQ manifesto. Once the reading had finished, the 3,000 people who had been waiting for two hours crammed into the curling arena broke into applause. At 10:30, Pierre Vallières addressed them, urging them not to provoke the police and army personnel that were surely waiting in great numbers nearby. Michel Chartrand and Charles Gagnon both spoke as well, but it was Vallières who made the greatest impression. He told the crowd that they needed to avoid falling into the trap of repression, because it was up to each of them to work in his or her own sphere to transform oppressive social structures. Tonight, Vallières told the crowd, each *Québécois* who stands up is the FLQ.[95]

Government authorities were frightened by the situation, and many began to believe that only drastic action could re-establish authority. Municipal, provincial, and federal police forces – along with representatives of MI6 and the CIA – had been collaborating to identify the perpetrators of the kidnappings and to find the hostages. The police had made fifty arrests and carried out nearly one thousand searches, and rumours circulated widely that plans were being made to suspend civil liberties. The statement of the sixteen personalities and the student strikes had deepened the crisis, and the government response came swiftly and decisively. Shortly past one in the afternoon on 15 October, 8,000 Canadian army troops, as requested by the provincial government, began rolling into Montreal, and troops were stationed throughout the city, guarding government buildings and patrolling the streets.

The following day at four in the morning, the federal cabinet declared a state of "apprehended insurrection" and proclaimed the War Measures Act. The Act suspended civil liberties, allowing for warrantless searches and seizures. It authorized arrests and detentions without charge for twenty-one days (and set a period of ninety days before a trial needed to be set), blocked the media from broadcasting or publishing FLQ communiqués, and retroactively declared the FLQ an illegal organization. With these newfound powers, the arrests began. Hundreds of citizens were awakened in the middle of the night to be dragged off with no knowledge of where they were going or of what was taking place. In all, around five hundred people were arrested (the majority of whom would be released without any charges being laid), 31,700 searches, and 4,600 searches with seizure were carried out.[96] The deployment of the army and the enactment of the War Measures Act were two different processes, yet they were meant to act as one. Together they demonstrated that the government had taken control of the situation.

The lists of those who were arrested contained well-known dissident leaders and intellectuals, as well as grassroots organizers in the labour movement, citizens' committees, and legal political parties like the PQ and FRAP. Critical journalists and publishers, poets and singers, soon found themselves behind bars. Dr Bellemare of the Saint-Jacques medical clinic was picked up and brought to jail, never finding out what led to his arrest.[97] The publisher of Parti Pris's publishing house, Gérald Godin, recounted how police arrived at his house at five in the morning, taking him to the headquarters of Quebec's provincial police on Parthenais Street in east Montreal. From his cell, he wrote, he could see "Ontario Street, and St. Catherine, Radio-Québec, the Jacques Cartier bridge, and a part of Man and His World."[98] Poet Gaston Miron and singer Pauline Julien were incarcerated. And along with such well-known figures, hundreds of rank-and-file activists were also arrested in the middle of the night and held without contact with the outside world.

With people randomly missing, and no possibility of confirming their arrests, progressive circles in Montreal were sent into a state of panic.[99] And the repression extended across the country. Police arrested individuals for distributing copies of the FLQ manifesto in Vancouver, and the RCMP ordered the University of Victoria's student newspaper not to publish philosophy professor Ronald Kirby's letter supporting the FLQ. British Columbia's provincial government passed an order-in-council demanding the firing of teachers and faculty who expressed support for the FLQ.[100] Back in Montreal, the arrests and searches seemed so indiscriminate that the police even searched the Westmount home of Gérard Pelletier, Secretary of State and federal cabinet minister. The police later realized that they were searching for another "Gérard Pelletier."[101] To justify the repression, federal cabinet minister Jean Marchand spoke to the House of Commons on 16 October. The FLQ endangered the very existence of the federal and provincial governments, he stated, and had as many as 3,000 members – a drastic exaggeration of the size of the group, which had about thirty-five members on the eve of the crisis. He argued that the FLQ had infiltrated all of Quebec's decision-making bodies, and that without the War Measures Act an insurrection would have begun.[102] At nine o'clock in the evening, Prime Minister Trudeau addressed the country on national television. The terrorists would have stopped at nothing, he argued, and anyone could have been kidnapped at any time. The next victim could have been "a manager of a credit union, a farmer, a child."[103]

The responses to the crisis were multiple and complicated, and both support for and opposition to the government's actions spanned Montreal's linguistic divide.[104] While a frightened public opinion in both English Canada and Quebec supported the government, many grassroots groups in Montreal defended civil liberties. Religious groups stepped forward and, while denouncing the actions of the FLQ, also condemned the government's actions. Six professors in McGill's French department decided to stop giving courses on Quebec literature as an act of solidarity with jailed poet Gaston Miron. The Voice of Women demanded the law be repealed and the prisoners released. Groups around Montreal began to form civil liberties organizations, including students at McGill and at the Université de Montréal, where over a thousand people gathered to found the Comité Québécois pour la défense des libertés.[105] The Ligue des droits de l'homme, Quebec's main civil liberties organization, however, did little to denounce the government's actions during the crisis. The Ligue's inaction remained controversial and, within a few years, the group would be brought under new leadership, and its conception of rights would be greatly expanded.[106]

In the United States, the Student Mobilization Committee, the National Jewish Organization Project, and the Women's International League for Peace and Freedom formed a common front to demand the restoration of civil liberties in Canada.[107] Segments of the English-Canadian left rallied to the cause of civil liberties, as did the New Democratic Party. The Canadian Civil Liberties Association spoke out against the War Measures Act, calling on the federal cabinet to revoke it, and speaking before the Toronto Board of Education to oppose a resolution that threatened the dismissal of teachers expressing support for the FLQ.[108] At Montreal's English-speaking universities, students and professors alike denounced the repression engendered by the War Measures Act.[109] The weekly alternative newspaper *Québec-Presse* launched a call to passive resistance, encouraging citizens' committees and unions to do the same.[110] The Pastoral Council of the Archdiocese of Québec (which represented nearly 1,000 priests), demanded that the War Measures Act be revoked and announced its sympathy for the message of the manifesto. The nineteen parish priests of the Matapédia-Matane Region went one step further, saying that they would respond to the systemic violence of the state with non-violent direct action.[111]

Although many voices were raised in opposition to the government actions, the enactment of the War Measures Act sent the left into disarray. Artists and activists were in jail and the army patrolled the streets. In the week to come, the student movement would all but collapse.[112] The homes of thousands of individuals were raided, documents seized, and lists of names drawn up. The new libertarian publication *Noir et rouge*, to take one example, had just published its third issue dealing with non-violent revolution at the time of the October Crisis. Within hours of coming back from the printers, all of the copies were confiscated by police in a raid on the journal's Saint-Urbain Street office, sending it into financial ruin from which it would never recover.[113]

The enactment of the War Measures Act, accompanied by hundreds of arrests and seemingly random searches, infuriated many. It may have even temporarily increased sympathy for the objectives of the FLQ. But that sympathy quickly disappeared with the news that Pierre Laporte's body

had been found at Saint-Hubert Airport on Montreal's south shore. Laporte's captors had killed him after an escape attempt, an act that was
widely condemned, swinging public opinion decisively into the camp of law
and order.[114] Poet Gaston Miron expressed the opinion of many, declaring
that this "was a stupid and immoral act."[115] The police turned all of their
energy to finding James Cross and capturing those responsible for Laporte's
death. On 3 December, roughly 1,000 police and soldiers surrounded the
apartment in Montreal North where they had located Cross, and negotiations began for his release. Before long, the FLQ Liberation cell released
him in exchange for safe passage to Cuba. On 27 December, the last members of the cell that had kidnapped and murdered Laporte were tracked
down, and the crisis that had begun over two months earlier came to an
end.[116]

On 4 January 1971 the army left Montreal, although the War Measures
Act remained in effect until 30 April. But after this date the repression did
not end. In the early years of the 1970s, a few fleeting FLQ organizations
existed, but to little effect. Security agents, informers, and agent-provoca-
teurs wrote false FLQ communiqués and both encouraged and propagated
terrorist attacks.[117] Federal, provincial, and municipal police forces became
implicated in illegal activities, breaking into the offices of legitimate organizations, stealing membership lists and other documents, and subjecting
groups to electronic surveillance.[118] In September of 1971, the police raided
five avant-garde cafés, photographing everyone on the premises and creating a climate of fear. The police even resorted to picking suspected FLQ
members off the street and keeping them awake at night in hotels, demanding that they become informants.[119] Although the October Crisis was offi-
cially over, it continued to shape the political climate of the city for years
to come.

MEMORY, DEMOCRACY, AND OCTOBER 1970

The dramatic events of the October Crisis have been recounted over and
over again in documentary films, history books, novels, and television
series. Every action of the government and every move of the FLQ has been
scrutinized repeatedly. And in the process the FLQ has grown into a larger-
than-life organization, remembered as being at the very centre of the popular revolts that engulfed the city. At first glance, this attention seems

justified. Yet this study has attempted to contextualize the actions of the FLQ, to demonstrate the group to be but one manifestation of the popular revolts that swept through Montreal during the 1960s. While the labour movement, citizens' committees, FRAP, the women's liberation movement, and other groups were working to transform understandings and practices of democracy during the period, the FLQ formed one controversial manifestation of this popular upsurge.

The FLQ spoke in the language of popular democracy, but its actions demonstrated anything but a belief in popular participation. At the heart of the FLQ mythology lay the image of the solitary urban guerrilla, a member of the revolutionary elite who forgoes the comforts of life for the good of his people – people who themselves are seen to be ignorant and in need of awakening. Membership in this elect group, as Sheila Rowbotham argues (in a slightly different, yet still applicable, context), "will for a start be predominantly male, for if it attracts a minority among men, it fits even fewer women." And, what's worse, "in this critical emphasis on the leadership and on their moments of confrontation, they have nonetheless excluded most people, including most women from their version of history."[120] This heroic vision contains within it in an implicitly gendered understanding of revolutionary activity, one that separates politics from the struggles of women and men to build democracy in their daily lives.

The FLQ therefore represented the limitations of an absolute voluntarism, an excess of the belief in the possibilities of an individual revolutionary agent who can, through sheer will, create the conditions for popular upheaval. Francis Simard was one of the FLQ members responsible for the murder of Pierre Laporte. He recalls being driven by a "will to act," and he describes how the FLQ was living "at gut level."[121] He spoke out against intellectuals who spent too much time theorizing and not enough time in action, and described how "I lived it before I put it into words."[122] It was this prioritization of action over reflection in combination with the legitimization of violence as a political tactic that allowed activists to rationalize the tragic murder of Pierre Laporte.

Although the October Crisis was instigated by the actions of the FLQ, it affected society at large. By focusing too narrowly on the dramatic events of October 1970, we lose sight of the effects of the crisis on both the political culture of the province and the everyday lives of its citizens. And it was precisely on the terrain of everyday life that the crisis had its most profound effects. In his 1974 film Les Ordres, filmmaker Michel Brault displays in detail the effects of the War Measures Act. Brault conducted fifty interviews with people arrested during October, and the film shows the ways in which the characters – all of whom have only tangential relations to political movements – are humiliated by their time in jail. Regular activities of daily life, such as working and spending time with one's family, were disrupted by the intrusions of police into private life. In prison, the arbitrary authority and petty behaviour of the guards reinforced the powerlessness of the prisoners. And when guards are probed for information about why people are being detained, they always respond with the same cold answer: "orders." With such vignettes, Brault captures the crushing weight of repression on the everyday lives of citizens.[123] The same experiences have been recounted by other individuals such as Marjolaine Péloquin, who recalls how the random searches and arrests had their intended effect of silencing the population.[124] And Jean-François Cardin writes of the paranoia that engulfed many in the labour movement in the wake of the arrests.[125]

The October Crisis left a contradictory legacy. Polls that demonstrate widespread popular support for the War Measures Act reveal much, yet they also obscure a great deal. The repression of October had reached into the everyday lives of Quebec citizens, and in the aftermath of the crisis politicization continued on a larger scale than it had before. Roughly 20 to 30% of those arrested during the October Crisis were labour activists, and it was within their ranks that the new mobilization began.[126] Denouncing both the actions of the FLQ and those of the government, the labour movement began seeing itself as the only legitimate force defending democracy in the province.

EIGHT

LABOUR, EMPIRE, AND MAY 1972

With a new social and legal climate favourable to organized labour, created in part by a new labour code giving the public service the right to unionize and strike, the ranks of organized labour swelled to unprecedented levels. Throughout the 1960s there was a continual increase in Quebec's rate of unionization, rising from 29.3% of the workforce in 1961 to 37.6% in 1971.[1] The province's teachers union, which became the Corporation des enseignants du Québec (CEQ) in 1966, went from having 33,840 members in 1961 to 92,888 ten years later,[2] while the CSN grew from 90,733 to 184,925 during the same period. The organization representing international unions in the province, the Fédération des travailleurs du Québec (FTQ),[3] for its part, went from having 201,235 to 364,004 members.[4]

Many individuals who had taken part in the political battles of the 1960s became active players in the labour movement by the early 1970s.[5] And with the dramatic growth of the labour movement came a new sense of social responsibility, one powerfully demonstrated during the October Crisis of 1970.

THE OCTOBER CRISIS AND LABOUR

For the labour movement, the army's occupation of Montreal and the War Measures Act became an important symbol of the colonized nature of

Quebec. Only a day after the enactment of the War Measures Act, the three unions came together to produce a common declaration opposing the suspension of civil liberties and deploring the creation of a military regime "similar to those of banana republics, where military juntas rule as kings and masters." What was remarkable about this joint declaration is that it rejected the actions of both the FLQ and the state, and positioned the labour movement as the defender of democracy in the province. It denounced violence as a political tactic, and rejected the way the government was trying to portray Quebec as being in a state of chaos at the very moment that the province's citizens "had begun to demonstrate the possibilities of democracy in Quebec." The governments knew very well, the unions argued, "that there are a lot more social ills to address than there is anarchy to repress."[6]

Less than a week after the proclamation of the War Measures Act, on 21 October, the CSN, FTQ, and CEQ held an unprecedented joint meeting of their authoritative bodies, and the unions decided to produce a cooperative edition of their respective newspapers, *Le Travail*, *Le Monde ouvrier*, and *L'Enseignement*, which would print their declaration in the face of the crisis. The five-point declaration denounced the FLQ, demanded a repeal of the War Measures Act and announced the labour movement's efforts to secure the release of innocent people, its desire to inform the rank-and-file, and its willingness to work with all like-minded groups. The final point stated the urgent need for an emergency political program of social and political reform.[7]

After the meeting, the unions worked to convey their message to their memberships in all regions of Quebec. The FTQ organized twenty-six information sessions, and the CSN produced a thirty-minute 16mm film of Marcel Pepin calmly explaining the reasons behind the CSN's position.[8] But not all local unions agreed with the common front declaration; almost as soon as it was produced, rumbles of opposition were heard. Opposition was especially strong in the FTQ, where unions representing 37% of the federation publicly disassociated themselves from the common position. In letters to the editor of Quebec's major newspapers, many denounced Quebec union leaders for their stand, and battles also took place within the CEQ and the CSN. But there was also a great deal of support for the position, and the labour movement increasingly came to be seen as the most important agent for social change in the province. By denouncing the actions taken by both the FLQ and the government, the labour centrals began positioning themselves as the defenders of "true" democracy.[9]

This show of strength had a great effect on Montreal radicals. Jean-Marc Piotte, one of the founders of *Parti Pris* who had recently returned to Montreal after studying in Europe, was profoundly affected by the collapse of the left during the Canadian army's occupation of the city. When the three unions joined together to oppose the War Measures Act, he realized that organized labour had become the only real counterweight to the power of the state, and he proceeded to devote his energies to the labour movement.[10] While it is true that the distance separating Quebec's major labour unions had been slowly narrowing throughout the 1960s, and although they had come together on many occasions before the fall of 1970, their response in the face of the War Measures Act, as Jean-François Cardin has persuasively argued, gave them a new image of unity.[11] The process of radicalization for certain elements of the labour movement had begun earlier, of course, but the crisis was a catalyst for the movement's adoption of a more confrontational stance with the government and for its articulation of an alternative vision of democracy.[12]

When this new confrontational stance merged with the grievances of workers throughout the province, the results were explosive. In the early 1970s, workers in Quebec were radicalized to a degree not witnessed in North America since 1919, and the new tone of labour politics got the attention of radicals throughout English Canada and the United States.[13] In this tumultuous period, the speeches of labour leaders and the official documents of the organizations gave voice to the anger of workers, but they did not create that anger. Energy came as often from below as it did from above.[14] There are undoubtedly many reasons for the dramatic radicalization of the labour movement, from the structural changes in the economy to the raised expectations engendered by the reforms of the Quiet Revolution.[15] In addition to these reasons, however, labour's radicalization, I will argue, needs to be situated within the context of the incredible intellectual ferment of anti-imperialist politics of the period. As the labour movement adopted the language of anti-imperialism, it also transformed it, adapting it to its own needs. The new radical analyses developed within the movement spread throughout the province and, combining with a wide array of local grievances, gave shape to one of the most dramatic general strikes in North American history.

In its period of radicalization, the labour movement drew on many intellectual resources. Most of all, it looked to the immense body of theory that had been developed by the oppositional movements in Montreal throughout the previous decade. But as it was doing so, the left was undergoing important transformations of its own.

TOWARDS A POLITICAL ECONOMY OF EMPIRE

The new analyses emerging from the organized labour movement coincided with, learned from, and influenced a transformation in the language of anti-imperialism in Montreal. In 1967, Monthly Review Press published *Capitalism and Underdevelopment in Latin America* by Andre Gunder Frank, an economist who worked at Montreal's Sir George Williams University from 1966 to 1968. The book was published in French the next year by François Maspero. Frank's basic premise was that wealthy nations, and regions at the centre of the economic system, increased their wealth by exploiting those at the periphery, securing primary resources and using them as markets for manufactured goods. These theories of underdevelopment made quick inroads in Quebec.

In the early 1970s, newly-elected Liberal premier Robert Bourassa staged a number of high-profile trips to the United States, working to actively court American investment in Quebec. These trips once provoked hope, one journalist wrote, but now "they simply evoke humiliation."[16] At the same time, socialists were striving to provide economic bases for their arguments about the meaning and impact of empire on the province. In the final years before *Parti Pris* folded in 1968, its contributors, drawing on sophisticated readings of Marxist theory, began shifting their focus away from the subjective experience of colonialism towards concrete analyses of the power of American imperialism in Quebec and around the world. This shift also took place in *Socialisme* in the late 1960s, as the journal began decrying its earlier eclecticism in favour of a more consistent socialist analysis. By the time the journal completed its transformation and became *Socialisme québécois* in 1970, it was attempting to develop a rigorous political economy of imperialism in Quebec.[17] At roughly the same time as francophone leftist intellectuals were debating new analyses of capitalism and imperialism, Montreal's Caribbean thinkers were arguing that Canada, through its role as a major exporter of capital to the Caribbean, acted as an imperial power.[18] And Pierre Vallières, whose *Nègres blancs* had been driven by his *subjective* experience of colonization, reflected something of the new mood when he wrote in 1971 that his decision to join the Parti Québécois was not based on an "abstract" or "theoretical" choice, but on an analysis "of the conditions of exploitation and the interplay of forces that the imperialist mode of production imposes on the Quebec people as a whole."[19]

In the early 1970s many Montreal leftists also began looking with growing interest towards analyses emanating from Latin America. Some travelled to the region themselves, and the influence of the Latin American left was also spread by immigrants to Montreal, who became involved with the labour movement and established a variety of solidarity organizations.[20] In addition to Montreal being the home of francophone radicals and immigrant leftists, many English-Canadian radicals, who were increasingly concerned about American domination and the lack of Canadian sovereignty, also resided in the city.[21] In 1967, *Canadian Dimension*, one of the New Left's most important periodicals, hosted a conference in Montreal entitled "Canada and the American Empire," featuring American political scientist Robert Engler as well as Andre Gunder Frank.[22]

By the early 1970s, Montreal had become a laboratory in which different conceptions of empire and various forms of anti-imperial resistance were being developed. And out of this potent mixture of English-Canadian left nationalism, francophone radicalism, and Caribbean and Latin American economic analyses came one of the most influential anti-imperialist books of the period, Kari Levitt's *Silent Surrender: The Multinational Corporation in Canada*. Levitt had arrived in Montreal in 1960 to accept a teaching post in the Department of Economics and Political Science at McGill. She was the daughter of Hungarian political economist Karl Polanyi, and had grown up as an exile in Vienna and London before becoming involved in socialist politics in Toronto and then Montreal. In the early 1960s she had become interested in Latin American theories of economic dependency and, as her personal and professional concerns drew her to the Caribbean, she travelled back and forth between the region and her Montreal home. In Montreal she became closely associated with English-Canadian left nationalists, Caribbean intellectuals, and francophone labour activists, and the insights of these different worlds flowed into one another.[23] Urged on by her colleague Charles Taylor at McGill, Levitt started studying the effects of foreign investment in Canada.[24] At the same time she worked to analyze the plantation economies of the Caribbean, and she found herself at the centre of the city's Caribbean activist community.[25] Levitt's economic analyses of Canada and the Caribbean soon converged. The first version of her study of foreign investment in Canada, "Economic Dependence and Political Disintegration: the Case of Canada," was published in 1968 in *New World Quarterly*, a West Indian journal of independent criticism.[26]

Before long, this paper was being distributed underground, generating debate among activists across the country.[27] And when a revised and lengthened version was published with a forward by University of Toronto Professor Mel Watkins, it became an immediate success, being reprinted many times in a variety of different editions.[28] Levitt charts Canada's slide into "economic, political and cultural dependence on the United States,"[29] arguing that American multinational corporations had replaced earlier forms of European mercantilism, and that their political and economic influence had stripped Canada of its democratic decision-making capacity.[30] Her plea to curb the power of American imperialism and to bring economic forces under democratic control resonated with the Quebec labour movement.[31]

Levitt returned to Montreal from Trinidad in 1971 and, having just witnessed the Black Power revolts there (themselves partly caused by events in Montreal), she found herself amidst the labour demonstrations taking place in the city. When the French-language edition of Silent Surrender appeared in early 1972, the author's new post-script, "Towards Decolonization: Canada and Québec," reflected the connections she was making between the protests in the Caribbean and in Montreal. With the political movements in Quebec, she argued, the "Third World" had emerged in North America, and the redefinition of "the French Canadian into a Québécois," like the "American Negro into a Black," acted as "the most powerful internal force of change in these two adjoining countries."[32] The new preface captured the sensibilities so well that the Montreal Central Council distributed it at its meetings.[33]

Although Levitt, Vallières, Montreal's Black activists, and the writers of Socialisme québécois had all begun prioritizing economic analyses of imperialism, the most influential anti-imperialist texts of the early 1970s would ultimately emerge from the ranks of organized labour. In 1971, the distance between the labour movement's moderates and radicals was narrowing.[34] Each of Quebec's three main unions developed sophisticated analyses of imperialism that were distributed to tens of thousands of workers throughout the province.

THE MANIFESTOS

Just as new economic analyses of imperialism were playing an increasingly prominent role within the left, a wind of energy swept into the labour movement. Radical intellectuals lent their services to the movement, becoming involved in worker-education programs, circulating documents, and giving lectures.[35] The early 1970s in Quebec witnessed an important number of plant shutdowns and layoffs, and many within the labour movement argued that the government was both powerless and unwilling to intervene, and that only a change in the economic system could reverse the situation.[36] When a conflict broke out at *La Presse*, North American's largest French-language daily newspaper, the new confrontational stance of labour became clear. Because of the paper's importance in shaping news coverage, what began as a lock-out in the summer of 1971 soon grew into a fierce battle for control of communications in the province. The three unions organized a protest for 29 October, and two days before the protest, the paper stopped publication, locked out all of its employees, and blocked access to its headquarters with barricades, armed guards, and police dogs.[37] On the day of the protest itself, after blocking the crowd from walking towards the city's English-speaking west end, police charged the protestors, leaving 190 people injured and one, Michèle Gauthier of the Front de libération des femmes, dead.[38] In the days that followed, not only did thousands of people attend the funeral of Michèle Gauthier, but an increasingly radical labour movement held a massive rally of 15,000 workers on less than twenty-four-hours notice. The crowd, gathering at the invitation of the Montreal Central Council of the CSN, arrived at the Montreal Forum full of rage. The Montreal Forum was chosen not only for its size, but also because it was firmly situated in the western part of the city, and therefore demonstrated the labour movement's resolve to claim its right to the city. Labour leaders and other oppositional figures stood before the crowd and spoke of the colonialist nature of Quebec society.[39]

At an FTQ convention held in Montreal from 30 November to 4 December 1971, one month after the *La Presse* protest, FTQ president Louis Laberge's opening speech set a new tone for the traditionally moderate union; one observer called it "one of the most militant speeches ever made by a modern top-ranking North American trade-union leader."[40] Laberge declared that the events of the past two years had forced all trade unionists "to constantly interrogate themselves without respite," as they had brutally unmasked "a hypocritical society which had heretofore more or less succeeded in hiding its oppression." But Laberge went further, arguing that power operated differently in Quebec than elsewhere. As "a colonized people," Quebeckers had come to realize the "colonial character" of power, a power that operated through the combined effects of economic imperialism and local collusion. They lived in a "colonized country where the government does everything in its power to make life easy for the owners of this country of which we are the lessees." Laberge quoted Fanon, arguing that since the *La Presse* demonstration of 29 October, *The Wretched of the Earth* had "a very acute relevance for the workers in Quebec." The province's politicians and capitalists, and maybe even its labour unions, had played the role of Fanon's "teachers of ethics," blunting the sharp edge of oppression. But now that power had shown its true face, there could no longer be any doubt that Quebec's "weak and dependent political structures exactly correspond to the colonial model."[41]

Laberge spoke of the vast federal and provincial subsidies to multinational corporations, the subordination of the Quebec government to Ottawa, and the human cost of capitalist modernity. Workers could no longer afford to be complacent, he argued, nor could they afford to act alone; it had become more necessary than ever for organized labour to form a broad coalition with non-organized workers, students, teachers and people on social assistance, and to offer an alternative vision of North America. The labour movement, in alliance with other progressive movements, needed to develop a holistic program of social change, one which recognized that it was the whole of the individual – as worker and tenant, consumer and citizen – that needed to be liberated.[42]

At the same convention during which Laberge delivered this speech, the FTQ declared Quebec's right to independence and adopted its mass-circulated manifesto, *L'État, rouage de notre exploitation*.[43] Using comprehensive economic analyses, the manifesto argued that the increasing economic intervention of the Quebec state – far from gradually instituting socialism – actually reinforced the structures of capitalism. And in Quebec, capitalism did not operate as in other areas of North America; being controlled by American and Anglo-Canadian monopolies, it bore "the additional stamp of colonialism." By protecting the interests of foreign capital at the expense of Quebec workers, the state *itself* acted as the "exploiter of the working class," disempowering workers and excluding them from the crucial political decisions which affected their lives. Terms like "free world" hid the fundamental truth that they did not "refer to the freedom of a people," but rather to "the freedom of a privileged class." If Quebec was to become free, it would therefore need to look further than the creation of a French-speaking capitalist class. For a veritable project of economic liberation to take hold, the power of imperialism and its protector, the bourgeois state, would need to be overcome.[44]

The FTQ manifesto sent shockwaves through the labour movement, announcing the radicalization of an organization that had long been synonymous with moderation. At a rally of 10,000 workers at the Montreal Forum in February 1972, the FTQ issued a shortened manifesto that summarized much of *L'État, rouage de notre exploitation*, ensuring a greater mass distribution of its ideas.[45] Meanwhile, two other labour manifestos, one put out by the CSN and the other by the CEQ, were also challenging traditional frameworks of labour politics in Quebec. In the ranks of Quebec's teachers' union, political ferment had been simmering for years. The repression of the October Crisis acted as "a helpful shock, inciting us to discuss real problems," prompting many to question the very meaning of democracy. In January 1971, just months after the proclamation of the War Measures Act, the CEQ began a systematic program of political education, attempting to widen the sphere of union activity by highlighting the political nature of teachers' daily problems. Teachers were becoming increasingly aware that they needed to go beyond collective bargaining, and in February 1971 a special committee began touring the province, meeting with local union members and listening to their problems and concerns. The culmination of the committee's efforts was the writing of *Premier plan: livre blanc sur l'action socio-politique de la C.E.Q.*, a manifesto outlining the possible reach of the CEQ's social and political engagement.[46] At the organization's 1971 convention, the manifesto dominated proceedings.[47]

Premier plan denounced the dehumanization of capitalism and spoke out against the environmental pollution and poor housing that were the by-products of a system that worked individuals to death, destroying everything from self-esteem to sexuality. The manifesto recognized that the economy – "the pivotal point of all political and social struggle" – was dominated by the forces of US capitalism. Workers needed to bring it under democratic control. One of the document's central concerns was to draw common bonds between teachers – the "producers" of ideology – and other workers. Both groups earned wages, the document argued, and neither controlled their working conditions. Lacking control over the workplace and living under the tyranny of the market, both groups had a common interest in building "a democratic, free and equitable society." Teachers in particular had a specific role to play in the larger struggle. Since the education system was designed in the interests of the ruling class, teachers were uniquely positioned to transform it from the inside. Rather than reproducing an ideology dictated from above, they could transform the educational system by placing "its resources and personnel at the disposal of the people so that they could manage their own lives and assume collective responsibility for their political and economic well-being." Teachers could be at the forefront of creating "a free, non-authoritarian, and democratic society in which men and women will unfold into self-actualizing persons." They had the potential of heightening consciousness, developing individual autonomy, and creating new cultural values. The manifesto even suggests that, during strikes, teachers could keep schools open, making them "meeting places where we can discuss with other workers problems that we have in common."[48]

At its June 1971 convention, during which *Premier plan* dominated discussion, the CEQ decided to make a commitment to political work, hiring three part-time and two full-time employees for this purpose. It also decided to print and distribute copies of *Premier plan*. In the end 52,535 copies were circulated and, as networks of activists attempted to implement its recommendations, it became central to the politicization of teachers across Quebec.[49]

In contrast to the CEQ and the FTQ, the process of radicalization had begun much earlier in the CSN. For years it had been thinking about the links between political and economic power, the possibilities of radical democracy, as well as its own unique role in North America. In September 1971, the Confederal Bureau of the CSN adopted the evocatively titled manifesto, *Il n'y a plus d'avenir pour le Québec dans le système économique actuel*, a document that had been prompted by a new wave of lay-offs and plant shutdowns, particularly in the metallurgy industry.[50] Over thirty-two thousand copies of this document, which highlighted the injustices of imperialism in Quebec, were distributed.[51] The organization's more elaborate study, *Ne comptons que sur nos propre moyens*, accepted as a working document in October 1971,[52] became one of the most widely read and discussed labour manifestos in Quebec history. When Marcel Pepin read the document aloud at a CSN meeting, a wave of euphoria swept over the audience and people rose to their feet in excitement.[53] The CSN resolved that the manifesto's insights should be made available to the widest possible audience, and it set out to print tens of thousands of copies and create pedagogical tools for popular distribution.[54]

Ne comptons que sur nos propre moyens addressed the destructive power of American imperialism and argued that, to better grasp its functioning, workers needed to understand the mechanisms of capitalism. The manifesto therefore considered how the stratification of social classes under the capitalist system leads to anarchy, overproduction, and monopoly. It also discussed the way that multinational companies invested in Quebec to take advantage of its natural resources and cheap labour, impeding local development while consolidating their economic empires. It deplored the fact that Quebeckers were expected to sit back and watch silently as plants were closed, workers laid off, and profits flowed south rather than being reinvested in the province. While *L'État, rouage de notre exploitation* and *Premier plan* both argued that the creation of francophone capitalism would not lead to a veritable liberation, *Ne comptons que sur nos propre moyens* took these insights one step further. The CSN manifesto maintained that the Quebec bourgeois class – even with the help of the state – was far too weak to control the province's development. If Quebeckers were truly intent on economic liberation, they would need to look elsewhere. The task of building a truly democratic alternative to capitalism lay entirely in the hands of workers and workers alone. Once they understood the mechanism of capitalist domination they would be able to exercise "their extraordinary capacity to invent."[55]

Ne comptons que sur nos propre moyens created a sensation across the province. Over 75,000 copies were printed and distributed, 44,000 of which were delivered as a special insert in the weekly newspaper *Québec-Presse*.[56] Fifty thousand introductory brochures and other pedagogical tools were circulated by unions[57] and, by the beginning of 1972, the CSN was engaged in a far-reaching debate over the document's arguments and findings.[58] The Montreal Central Council, for example, made the study of the document a priority, and members of political, student, and community organizations, eager to collaborate, came to its offices to get copies for themselves.[59] The debate, which was characterized by a great deal of conflict and disagreement, also generated excitement and energy from the centre of Montreal to the furthest reaches of the province.[60]

FROM THE MANIFESTOS TO THE MAY REVOLT

The mass distribution of the manifestos was a unique step in Quebec history, creating a debate that spread throughout the labour movement. This consultation was taking place at the same time as an attempt by workers in the public and para-public sectors – represented by the three unions that had come together in a common front – to negotiate a collective wage scale for the province.[61] Their demands included a minimum wage of one hundred dollars a week for all public-sector workers, job security, and equal pay for equal work irrespective of region or sex. Specifically designed to influence the wage structure of the private sector – a fact widely recognized by government officials, who were fearful of the economic consequences of the demand – the hundred dollars a week became a rallying cry for the unions. But their first task was to convince the government to agree to negotiate at a single bargaining table, something it had consistently refused to do. Frustrated by the government's intransigence, the unions held a strike vote on 9 March and, receiving a clear mandate, waged a twenty-four-hour general strike on 28 March while beginning preparations for an unlimited general strike.

In the spring of 1972, the atmosphere in the unions was electric. Many realized that the current negotiations carried implications that reached far beyond the public sector. The CEQ, which had situated these negotiations in a socio-political framework from the start, noted a growing grassroots consciousness of economic problems.[62] Marcel Pepin argued that the union movement as a whole was experiencing "labour solidarity unprecedented in the history of the Quebec labour movement."[63] The March 1972 edition of *Le Travail*, the organ of the CSN, stated that with the intense activity within the organization, it appeared "more alive than ever." The labour movement in general was now situated at the heart of current affairs in Quebec, and workers were developing a growing consciousness "of the common causes which are at the root of Quebec workers' problems."[64] The demand for a minimum wage of one hundred dollars a week could not be met, the CSN argued, since the government worked to defend the interests of private companies, a fact that proved the common cause of private and public sector workers.[65]

During the month of March 1972, people across the province were reading the labour manifestos, and discussing the best way to bring democracy to the province. The Syndicat des professeurs de l'université du Québec (SPUQ) demanded that the unions synthesize their three manifestos and explore further the steps needed to truly change society. The results of such an investigation, it argued, would then need to be distributed to all workers, unionized and non-unionized alike.[66] In Granby, union activists gathered to discuss the CSN manifestos in relation to their personal experiences. These workers saw *Ne comptons que sur nos propres moyens* as an "evaluation of our national failure" and, while many different solutions were proposed, most agreed that the ideal would be to create a society with "true popular power, a living democracy."[67] They demanded more information, more political analysis, and more cultural information, "as workers are not less intelligent than others."[68]

The atmosphere of excitement and contestation also infused, although to a lesser degree, private-sector unions. From 25 to 27 March, the CSN's federation of retail workers held its biannual conference. The federation came out in full support of the public sector common front, and argued that it was necessary to take workers' demands beyond collective bargaining and towards more general social change. Private companies, the federation argued, needed to become the collective property of their patrons and be managed by their workers. Though it might be true that a few key sectors needed to come under the control of the state, the state itself should be decentralized to allow for the direct participation of citizens. The federation even offered its own document to complement *Ne comptons que sur nos propres moyens*, one which looked to worker self-management as the solution to the problems plaguing Quebec. In "Pour une société plus juste: le socialisme coopératif," the federation proposed building society in the interests of the whole individual, rather than for the "consumer-object." To do so, it would be necessary to reverse the commodification of social life. Private companies needed to become public ones, or be transformed into worker co-operatives. Unions needed to become schools providing "training in administrative responsibilities" in order to teach workers to manage themselves. Human beings in a democratic community needed to decide what to produce, and both the state and cooperatives needed to yield to their demands. To those who would dismiss it as an organization of dreamers, the federation's members responded that it was "better to be treated as utopians" than to passively accept the status quo.[69]

This energy was felt in all regions of Quebec. Montreal had been the centre of radical politics throughout the 1960s, but the centre appeared to be shifting as other communities imagined new forms of democracy. Not everyone accepted the manifestos, of course, but individuals in the labour movement were engaged in an unprecedented degree of discussion.[70] When an indefinite general strike was finally called on 11 April, public sector workers across the province walked off the job, pushing the province into a major crisis. Before the strike had begun, a series of injunctions were passed to limit the right of nearly 15,000 workers, mostly employed in hospitals, to go on strike. From the perspective of the unions, the injunctions were a serious threat to the public service's newly-established right to strike, and they therefore decided, despite the inevitability of fines and the possibility of jail time, that they would not obey the regulations.

By the second week of the strike, the government passed back-to-work legislation. "Bill 19" threatened heavy fines, the suspension of the right to strike for two years, and the possibility of government-imposed decrees fixing working conditions. Caught off guard, the unions initially announced that they would defy the law but, facing such drastic consequences and unable to consult their 210,000 members adequately, they finally recommended an end to the strike. Some members were bitterly disappointed. A delegation of twenty workers from Sept-Iles – a city which had voted 87% to disobey the back-to-work order – travelled to Quebec City to denounce the decision to go back to work, arguing that the "people doing the striking need to be the ones setting its tone."[71]

On 4 May, the three union presidents were brought before the court in Quebec City, charged with having recommended defiance of the injunctions. The courtroom was filled with riot police and, when the judge did not appear at the prescribed time, the three presidents left the courtroom to be tried in absentia. Before the verdict was announced things appeared calm; for example, on 7 May, Yvon Charbonneau, president of the CEQ, told a crowd of 1,500 in east Montreal that there would be no resumption of the general strike, or at least not until the following school year.[72] But when the judge finally pronounced his sentence the next day – one year in prison for each of the three leaders – the severity of the decision reverberated in labour circles at home and throughout many parts of the world.

As the three presidents began their journey on 9 May to Quebec City to surrender themselves for incarceration, work stoppages began. At the FTQ headquarters, telegrams started to pour in announcing that workers in a dizzying number of factories and institutions had walked off the job. General Secretary of the FTQ, Fernand Daoust, revealed his surprise at the outpouring of anger, stating that the organization could not "do otherwise than pronounce itself in solidarity with these actions."[73] While the FTQ, the CSN, and the CEQ all came to support the insurrection, the initiative and the momentum came from below. The Comité d'information du front commun sent out communiqués detailing the extent of the work stoppages that were read on radio stations across the province.[74] By 14 May, Québec-Presse reported that it was "becoming almost impossible to give the complete list of work stoppages." The strike included workers in both English- and French-speaking institutions, and in the public and private sectors. Federal government employees walked off the job, as did the employees of Montreal's newspapers. Radio stations were occupied and schools and hospitals either closed or were taken over.[75] Young activists in Montreal could not help but recognize that they were no longer at the centre of the popular revolt, that energy and initiative were now coming from elsewhere.[76] The employees of *Québec-Presse* went out on a twenty-four-hour strike, demanding the resignation of the Bourassa government, which, they argued, was "incapable of responding to the veritable needs of workers."[77]

In the Centre-sud, citizens from the neighbourhood began to picket the Maison du Quartier to demonstrate their support and solidarity with the workers of Quebec. They then went to the offices of family services in Centre-sud, before taking to the streets and heading to Notre-Dame hospital, and then to the provincial welfare offices. The community protesters were joined by members of the renters' association, who then headed to the Paul Sauvé arena to take part in a public assembly with thousands of other workers.[78] *Le Va vite*, a citizens' newspaper of the Centre-sud, spoke of its support for the workers, and its desire to end the system of exploitation that made it so difficult for workers to survive. At the present moment, the paper declared, it was not working conditions that they wanted to negotiate, but the liberty of Quebec, and it was in this sense that they were in solidarity with the actions of Quebec workers. The editorial hoped that the common front could eventually work with the PQ to create a Quebec in which workers could live in freedom. And it called out to the workers of Centre-sud – both the unionized and the non-unionized – to join the popular revolt.[79]

Other angry voices demanded to be heard as well. The seven vice presidents and the secretary general of the FTQ insisted that the government take its "inquisition" to its logical conclusion by placing them behind bars as well,[80] and the ten members of the CEQ executive asked to be put in jail with their president.[81] Thirty-six individuals who had earlier been sentenced for having defied injunctions, but who were released after having appealed their sentence, travelled to Quebec City with over one thousand supporters to demand to be incarcerated, stating that they would rather serve their sentences now than wait for the appeals process to be exhausted.[82] At the prison where the three presidents were being held, thousands of teachers from all over Quebec took part in a giant rally dubbed "Opération Woodstock" for its festive atmosphere.[83] The main slogan of the strike, "Ce n'est qu'un debut, continuons le combat," drew both words and inspiration from May '68 in France.[84] Messages of solidarity came from community organizations in Montreal and from labour organizations across Canada and around the world.[85]

While labourers in the ports of Montreal, Quebec City, and Trois-Riv-ières began walking off the job, workers in many regions were shutting down entire cities. On the evening of 8 May, hundreds of workers, the majority of whom were women, gathered at the courthouse in Sept-Iles on Quebec's North Shore. When the police broke up the demonstration, it did not take long before the city of 22,000 was completely paralyzed by a general strike. Air traffic was stopped, workers attempted to prevent fraud by enforcing a price freeze, and the city's commercial establishments were closed, except by order of the common front. The strike coordinating com-mittee met daily, students at the city's CEGEP joined in the common front, and the radio station was occupied.[86] "This station is now in the hands of the workers," came the message on the air, "From now on we'll be broad-casting union bulletins from across Quebec and be playing the music of the resistance."[87] The movement that had begun in Sept-Iles soon spread to other cities, to Port-Cartier, Gagnon, Hauterive, Baie-Comeau, and to Mur-dochville in the Gaspé peninsula.[88] Towns were taken over, and local papers and radio stations around the province came under worker control. In the town of Saint-Jérôme north of Montreal, the radio station was occupied by workers who broadcast themselves chanting "solidarité" as they were expelled by the police.[89]

In response to René Lévesque's claim that the demonstrations were the result of the irresponsibility of labour leaders who refused to appeal their sentences or condemn the uprising, the editorial committee of Québec-Presse argued that, on the contrary, workers had demonstrated an "impres-sive sense of responsibility" in deciding to take over entire towns.[90] The citizens were acting in accordance with a spirit of democracy the govern-ment itself had long abandoned. After the first five days of the uprising, Québec-Presse observed that "Quebec has probably just lived the most dra-matic and intense week of its brief history." Never had so many Quebeck-ers risen "to collectively demonstrate their attachment to liberty and to their rights." "Something has begun," the paper argued, "which no person and no thing will be able to stop: the taste of true democracy."[91]

After the strike had gone on for just over a week, the three unions, act-ing on a renewed hope for a negotiated settlement, issued a joint declaration: "To encourage a return to negotiations, we are appealing to our members who have walked off the job to return to work."[92] But the actions did not come to an abrupt stop. In Thetford Mines and Black Lake, workers remained out on strike for a little while longer. In Mauricie teachers announced a day earlier that they would return to work, but declared that they would take the three pedagogical days allowed by the school board to engage in an in-depth study, not only of the impact of the new regulations and legislation on their working conditions, but also of the possibility of worker self-management.[93] And elsewhere around the province, teachers returned to work, but they too held "internal" actions, including occupations, assemblies, and study days.[94] Despite these last acts of resistance, the strike did, however, eventually come to an end.

■ ■ ■

But why did such a massive outpouring of anger – an outpouring which went far beyond the expectations of labour leaders and government officials alike – spread so quickly and with such intensity throughout the province? The Labour paper *Le Travail* suggested that years "of bullying exploded," and that workers were finally learning to overcome fear and risk security in order to reinvent democracy. They were learning, in short, "to be respected" and "to believe in ourselves."[95] The labour manifestos had circulated to all corners of the province, been read and studied by countless individuals, and ensured that a new language of labour and imperialism, and alternative ways to conceptualize democracy, became widespread.[96] Not everyone accepted the message, of course, and there was a great deal of dissent and disagreement – the manifestos and the strike even caused some lingering wounds to open (as I'll discuss in the conclusion). The events of May did, however, demonstrate an anger and frustration that sprang from citizens who had come to a new understanding of their collective problems. "The anger of Quebec workers is not gratuitous," *Le Travail* reported, as workers had come to understand that the government would not create a wage policy to diminish the differential between the rich and the poor. For the csn, the desire of the provincial government to integrate Quebec into North America – and its complete disregard for the interests and identity of its people – created in workers the desire to create a new and more fully human society.[97] Workers throughout Quebec had, albeit in a sometimes incoherent fashion, begun expressing their belief in the necessity of building a society in which human interests would not capitulate to the demands of profit.[98]

Again and again, it was the mixing of local grievances with a larger interpretation of their structural causes that led to rebellion. When workers occupied the offices of *Québec-Presse*, they took over the PQ executive Jacques Parizeau's column, dismissing him as a representative of the dominant class. In its place, they urged workers throughout the province to create "two, three, many Sept-Iles."[99] Meanwhile in Sorel, workers demanded the resignation of Robert Bourassa, arguing that the "enslaved population which has been terrorized for so long is no longer afraid," and they encouraged everyone to participate "in this movement of pure democracy."[100] The striking workers of Sept-Iles, who set the tone for the uprisings across north-eastern Quebec, published *Le Piochon* from March through May 1972. The paper opened its pages to the thoughts of the rank-and-file.[101] Among other insights, the paper reveals the profound importance of women to working-class militancy. As women were generally underpaid and confined to the lowest positions, provisions of pay equity and a minimum wage of one hundred dollars a week stood to benefit women disproportionately (36,000 of the 40,000 workers who did not earn one hundred dollars a week were women). During the middle of the April strike, women workers at UQAM circulated a declaration that demanded, in addition to an end to the devaluation of women's work, an uncompromising stand on the one hundred dollars a week minimum wage and the continuation of an unlimited general strike.[102] In Sept-Iles, women challenged the traditional masculine rhetoric and explained how they were specifically oppressed by the capitalist system. Michèle Desfonds, writing in *Le Piochon*, demanded that women be paid an equal wage for equal work, and argued that "the government needs to consider women as human beings, and as full and equal workers."[103] Martine Vaillancourt, for her part, vehemently denounced the unequal conditions that women faced in the workforce, reminding readers "to be outraged for women as well."[104]

Women and men joined together to denounce the state of Quebec society. On 28 March, the day of the first twenty-four-hour strike, Carol Leblond evoked the anger felt by workers in the region: "We're on strike today because we're fed up! We're sick of bosses who exploit us non-stop, we're sick of working conditions imposed on us by force … we're sick of salaries that barely allow us to pay the interests on our loans at HFC."[105] Réjean Langlois wrote about the dissolution of the traditional animosity between white- and blue-collar workers, and between the public and private spheres. Teachers and school janitors, workers from Hydro Quebec and hospitals, from the industrial sector and the state-run liquor stores, were meeting and discussing their common concerns at the same assemblies, and were coming to understand their common interests in opposing the same system.[106] Fernand Tardif argued that workers needed to do more than negotiate collective agreements, that they must work to transform a system that was concerned only with profits. As the president of the common front of Sept-Iles, he suggested that workers should make use of the work stoppage to study the capitalist system, and to figure out how they could build something different. He recommended that all members of the common front read the labour manifestos, always keeping the goal of democratic popular power in mind.[107] And he argued that it was time that workers took control of their own destiny, and that they stopped relying on far-away union leaders who were too often corrupted by their proximity to power to be of use.

Many other voices joined in the radical chorus. Martin Poirier denounced government subsidies and the way in which such subsidies helped multi-national corporations exploit Quebec's natural resources while processing them in either the United States or Europe.[108] Fabien Mignault wrote about Robert Bourassa as the "docile servant of the dominant class," but also integrated insights from *Ne comptons que sur nos propres moyens* about government subsidies to American corporations. And he spoke of the "international American fascist Gestapo" before concluding by addressing his fellow workers directly, reminding them of their inherent capacity "to think and to act."[109] Jacques Côté spoke of government subsidies to American corporations,[110] Serge Tremblay denounced the use of these subsidies to create ten jobs while eliminating twenty others,[111] and Viateur Beaupré wrote about teachers' lack of freedom and their subjection to the conditioning of "our modern factory-schools."[112] J.P. Dallaire reminded readers that the role of the ruling order was to manage the profits of foreign capitalists, and pointed out that Quebec unions had joined the global struggle "between people and capital" which was being played out in other places like "Vietnam, Ireland, and Uruguay."[113] It is in the last edition of *Le Piochon*, published on 9 May, the day on which walkouts paralyzed the province, that we can best see the fusing of national and social demands. Some, such as Viateur Beaupré and Jacques Côté, saw the current struggle as the culmination of two hundred years fighting against British colonialism,[114] and Valmore Tremblay highlighted how "Bill 19 was made by a small group of individuals who were elected and manipulated by our large financiers and capitalists who are sold-out to Anglo-Saxon and American interests."[115] Suzanne Cormier, for her part, argued that the strike provided an opportunity to bring "people out of their isolated worlds to create a new mentality, one based on the idea of working for everyone rather than only for oneself."[116]

During the entire period, workers rallied around the slogan, "Nous, le monde ordinaire." Labour activists therefore drew lines of separation between themselves and the province's elite, they struck against local bosses, and they protested against the conditions of their everyday lives. But the defender of the established order, the advocate of increased corporate control of Quebec's economy, was the Quebec state itself. "The state," the title of the FTQ manifesto famously read, "is our exploiter." After the October Crisis, the *La Presse* affair, Bill 19, and the sentencing of the three union presidents, many Quebeckers had lost confidence in their representatives. The modernizing liberal state, built throughout the 1960s by employing a democratic language of equality, appeared revealed as the guardian of imperialism.

CONCLUSION

1 MAY 1973

May first, 1973. The presidents of Quebec's three major unions – Marcel Pepin, Louis Laberge, and Yvon Charbonneau – were still behind bars for their actions during the common front strike over a year earlier. A harsh winter was abating, and a new era seemed to be beginning. Despite May first being the traditional moving day in Quebec (before being moved to 1 July), and despite a Montreal Canadiens playoff final at the Forum, tens of thousands of citizens took to the streets to celebrate International Workers' Day: 3,000–4,000 in Quebec City, 1,500 in Jonquière, 1,000 in Rouyn. In Montreal, 15,000 to 25,000 people – many bussed in from Sherbrooke, Hull and Trois-Rivières – marched in the early evening from Carré Viger to Parc Lafontaine. University and CEGEP students met at Carré Saint-Louis before heading down Saint-Denis to join the demonstration, and many small Marxist-Leninist groups paraded among the groups of workers. As the Centre des femmes was quick to point out, women marched alongside men in solidarity with the struggles of the working class. As the joyous crowd marched, flags and banners in hand, it was becoming increasingly clear that the lines of opposition which had been drawn in the early 1960s, and which had fuelled protest movements in various ways throughout the preceding ten years, had begun to change.[1]

The May Day demonstration of 1973 was far from being Montreal's first. Activists had been taking to the streets since 1906, public assemblies had been held on 1 May throughout the 1960s, and a demonstration of several

thousand protesters had occurred in 1970.[2] Yet, for almost everyone involved, 1973 had a novel feeling. Many declared that, from this moment
on, May Day would become a "New Quebec tradition."[3] The Montreal
Central Council of the CSN loudly proclaimed that the "tradition of cele-
brating May first has begun."[4] The official reason for the protest was to
demand the release of the three union leaders, but many rank-and-file
activists had a message of their own: they wanted nothing less than the
"liberation of the working class."[5] In the days leading up to 1 May, *Québec-
Presse* published a special supplement tracing the history of the labour
movement in Quebec and around the world. And on the day itself, it was
clear that the working class, walking confidently through the streets of
Montreal, would play a central role in the political life of the province for
years to come.

Radicalized in large part through the fusing of class politics with anti-
imperialism, workers throughout the province were questioning the reforms
of the Quiet Revolution and the meaning of democracy. Anti-imperialist
ideas had become central to the ways in which working-class solidarity
and economic democracy were imagined, just as they had played an important role in shaping feminist and linguistic debates, and provided a framework for a rapprochement between Black Montrealers and francophone
radicals. At the time, however, many interpreted the May 1972 strikes as
ending in defeat.[6] Others downplayed the strike's significance.[7] But in retrospect, May '72 represented the extent to which citizens were willing to
challenge the basic operating principles of society. In no other region of
North America did the politicization of class occur with such speed and
intensity, and many looked to Quebec for inspiration. The American journal *Radical America* began publishing substantial articles on Quebec labour
in the early 1970s, even devoting an entire issue to the subject following the
general strike. Native intellectual Howard Adams's account of Aboriginal
liberation, *Prison of Grass*, takes careful note of the transformation of
unions in Quebec and how they differed from others in the country.[8]

Within labour organizations themselves, the radicalization of rank-and-
file workers had both destabilizing and mobilizing effects. If many were
won over to the idea of a necessary class struggle, others remained more
cautious, committed to traditional union practices of collective bargaining
and reformist politics. In the FTQ, there was much internal dissent pitting
radical against more moderate factions.[9] Louis Laberge himself attempted
to curb the memory of the events of May. He published a book arguing that

the conflict's main importance lay in its creation of a favourable climate for collective bargaining.[10] Although a certain degree of dissent existed within the CEQ, Yvon Charbonneau maintained that the union came out of the strike stronger and more united, more resolved in its conviction that teachers formed an important part of the working class.[11] By 1973 the CEQ would begin undergoing important internal changes by accepting many of the tenets of the women's liberation movement, advocating for the liberalization of abortion laws, day-care centres, and salaries for domestic work.[12]

The CSN's Marcel Pepin, for his part, emerged from May 1972 angry and even more convinced of his anti-imperialist position. Labour needed to forge ahead in building an alternative North American society, he maintained, and the ruling regime in Quebec was on the verge of collapse, close to an implosion caused by its own contradictions.[13] The irony is that it was not the Liberal government, but the CSN itself that was in the process of implosion. In the aftermath of the strike, tensions simmering inside the union, and especially among the five-person executive, overflowed. In the split that ensued, the ranks of the CSN shrank from 240,000 to 170,000, 100,000 of whom were public sector workers. However, those that remained in the union were more united, accepting its opposition towards the capitalist system and the state upon which that system relied.[14] The spring of 1972 represented a high point in the unity of the labour movement, but almost as soon as the strikes had died down, the CSN and the FTQ became embroiled in a fierce battle over union raiding in the construction industry, a battle that, in the eyes of many, tarnished the image of the labour movement as a whole.[15]

Outside organized labour, a wide variety of individuals and groups began gravitating to Marxism. In the early 1970s, study groups abounded in which activists sought a clearer understanding of the central contradictions of their society. History students at the newly established Université du Québec à Montréal were required to study Marxist theory,[16] and Marxism became the topic of heated conversations in the city's avant-garde cafés. Influenced by Louis Althusser and Nicos Poulantzas, radicals began turning to structural Marxism. Bookstores and printing presses helped to distribute Marxist reading material, revolutionaries took jobs in factories and hospitals, and thousands of young people offered their services to the "movement," increasingly defined in class terms.[17]

In the early 1970s students and seasoned activists alike sought to overcome the organizational inertia of the left. In bookstores like the Librairie progressiste, situated on Amherst Street in east Montreal, not far from the new campus of the Université du Québec à Montreal, different currents of political opposition confronted one another.[18] After so many years of politicization, many were asking, why did nothing seem to be changing? Some concluded that only a disciplined Leninist party could move ahead with the difficult work of building socialism.[19] Trotskyist groups proliferated in 1970s Montreal, but it was Maoist organizations which flourished, often attracting hundreds of members, publishing weekly newspapers, and playing an influential if controversial role in union and community organizations, making Montreal a Maoist centre unmatched elsewhere in North America.[20]

Young activists and intellectuals had only the most tenuous grasp of the actual dimensions of China's Cultural Revolution, yet they saw in it what they wanted to see: a revolt of the masses against bureaucracy, a desire to renew socialism from below, and the forging of a new relationship between the leaders and the led.[21] Many Quebec radicals discovered Maoism while in France, bringing their Parisian interpretations of Chinese politics back with them to Montreal.[22] Maoist groups expanded outwards across the country, reversing the usual trend of English-Canadian socialists bringing their philosophies to Quebec.[23] By the late 1970s, Maoism was such an important force that En Lutte!, one of the three major Maoist organizations, was printing and distributing as many as 10,000 copies of its weekly newspaper. The group's main rival, the Ligue communiste, had an annual budget varying from $300,000 to $500,000 dollars, fifty employees, and a printing press.[24]

The attraction of so many Quebeckers to Maoism was at least partly a reaction to the disorganization that had come over the left in the aftermath of the October Crisis. Circles of activists, like the CAP Saint-Jacques, which originated in the effort to organize popular clinics in the late 1960s, felt that they lacked the theory necessary to build a program of social transformation. The group turned to a serious study of Maoism in the summer of 1971, and the following year began sending its members into factories.[25] Although many early Marxist-Leninist publications integrated ideas of Quebec's national liberation into their frameworks, by the middle of the decade virtually all were arguing that French- and English-Canadian workers needed to *unite* in opposition to the Canadian bourgeoisie. While maintaining the democratic right to self-determination, Quebec did not need to go through a process of decolonization, they argued, because it was not a colony.[26]

Alternatively, many turned to the Parti Québécois (PQ) with the hope of bringing the party further to the left. Formed after a split of the provincial Liberals, and constituted as an official party advocating "sovereignty association" in 1968, the PQ challenged, frustrated, and inspired leftists from its very beginnings. Although the party incarnated a great deal of popular energy, in the early 1970s it maintained a critical distance from the radicalizing labour movement. René Lévesque had even once declared that he would "rather live in a South American banana republic" than in a province dominated by the "ranting and raving of labor leaders."[27] So when four members of the party's national executive marched with demonstrators demanding the release of the labour presidents on 1 May 1973, many were excited about the potential convergence of the two movements.[28] The party's sizeable left wing exercised an important influence over the party's program and convinced many that the PQ, the sole major political party to be funded only through individual donations, could become an agent of social transformation.[29]

There were never fixed lines between the reform nationalism of the PQ and the extra-parliamentary opposition, and activists moved back and forth between unions, leftist organizations, and the party. Despite – or perhaps because of – its ambiguous character, the draw of the PQ remained strong. Charles Gagnon captured the phenomenon well when he stated that, while nearly everyone criticized René Lévesque, few "could resist his appeal."[30] Organizations that opposed the PQ, denouncing its half-measures and refusal to challenge American imperialism, were forced to recognize that many of their members were working for the party.[31] Posters announcing talks by René Lévesque were plastered in CEGEPs throughout the province,[32] and many of the political action committees that were formed by the labour movement in the late 1960s acted as foundations for PQ riding associations.[33] In December 1971, Pierre Vallières shocked the province by announcing that he had decided to join the PQ.

But Vallières never really did put all of his energy into building the party, and it would not be long before he would become disillusioned with its efforts to appear moderate and responsible by ridding itself of its more progressive elements.[34] He decided instead to head for the countryside, leaving Montreal and its political battles behind him. If Quebec were to be liberated one day, he maintained, it would be the result "of a multitude of small liberations, of 'miniature revolutions' at the grassroots." It was time to stop dreaming of a different future, but to live that alternative in the present, to create new modes of living and thinking.[35] Vallières's decision to leave Montreal was shared by many other activists who, exhausted from years of working for social change, desired only to put the political tensions of the city behind them.[36] In Jean-Marc Piotte's moving oral history, *La communauté perdue*, he writes of the pain and disillusionment that many activists felt when they eventually abandoned politics altogether. When leaving activism behind them, ex-activists often began to question their sense of self, and set out on the difficult task of rebuilding their lives.[37]

By the early 1970s, many of the profound contradictions in the idea of Quebec decolonization, which relied so heavily on gendered and racial metaphors, had become apparent. In Vallières's defense of his decision to join the PQ, published as *L'urgence de choisir*, he recognized that true "popular power is inconceivable without the liberation of women from their specific exploitation."[38] And as he had come to rethink his earlier positions on gender, so too did he reformulate his understandings of race. The idea that Quebeckers could be thought of as "nègres blancs" – a concept which had formed the core of his earlier writings – is abandoned, appearing only once (and cordoned off in quotation marks).[39] Even more significantly, Vallières not only acknowledges the exploitation of immigrants, but also the multilayered nature of colonialism in Quebec. Reflecting a context of increased Aboriginal activism throughout North America, Vallières now spoke of how the "American Indians and the Eskimos of Quebec and Canada" were more exploited than the most downtrodden of francophone Quebeckers.[40]

Throughout the 1960s, the contradictions and ambiguities of Quebec's colonial situation were rarely discussed, but in the early 1970s the multi-layered nature of colonialism in the province could no longer be ignored. Some francophone intellectuals, like Gérald Godin and Gilles Groulx, worked to integrate Aboriginal people into their cinema.[41] Articles in left labour papers began highlighting the plight of Natives,[42] and radical histories of Quebec – like Bergeron's *Petit manuel d'histoire du Québec* – began to make room for the history of the colonization of Aboriginal populations. It was not until a major conflict in Quebec's far north, however, that advocates of Quebec decolonization were forced to deal with the accusation that francophone Quebeckers themselves had become (or had always been) a colonial power. In the early 1960s, the provincial government had increased its presence in the north (which had previously been administered by the federal government). Many believed that this would help Native groups take control of their own educational system, but more than ten years later, the government had done nothing to facilitate Indigenous self-determination. Instruction was not being given in Native languages as promised, Aboriginal teachers were not being trained, local customs were not being observed, and the goal of creating local control over education was not being met. Many believed that Quebec had the responsibility to act differently than other White populations in North America, to treat Aboriginal peoples with respect and dignity, and to facilitate the process of self-determination.[43] But it was not living up to that responsibility and, for some, the original progressive goals set by the Quebec government stood revealed as merely a new incarnation of the same colonialist policy, except that French rather than English had become the language of assimilation.[44]

And so the francophone teachers of the region went on a two-month strike, fighting alongside the Inuit for the preservation of their cultural rights.[45] Working in the north, teaching in French within a system designed for the majority in the south, the teachers – who would have been conceptualized as *nègres blancs* in the mid-1960s – had instead become conscious of their whiteness.[46] The title of the CEQ's report on the question is revealing: *Le Nouveau-Québec, ou comment des colonisés traitent leur colonie ...* It argued that Native populations lived differently from southerners, and had different ways of conceptualizing their past and future. Francophone Quebeckers – "themselves profoundly oppressed in the economic and political spheres" – needed to become conscious "of the colonialist treatment which they are inflicting upon groups of Indians and Esquimaux." The province's teachers' union articulated the distance separating it from the modernizing goals of the Quebec state: "Against the right of states to organize peoples," the union maintained, "we propose the right of peoples to organize themselves."[47]

In the early 1970s, the language of Quebec anti-imperialism was being stretched in many different directions, forced to face internal contradictions and ambiguities that had lain dormant for years. Conceptions of empire and imperialism did not go away in the 1970s, of course, but ideas of decolonization would never again acquire the hegemony on the left that they had in the late 1960s and early 1970s. By 1975, Pierre Vallières himself was forced to concede to the new line of interpretation prevailing in the province: Quebec did not belong to the Third World, he argued, "but to the privileged West."[48]

The arrival of increasing numbers of immigrants from Africa, Latin American, Asia, and the Caribbean complicated broad generalizations conflating race and language. Many Haitian immigrants fought for their lives as they attempted to avoid being deported to their country of origin.[49] And in the aftermath of the coup in Chile in 1973, Chilean exiles developed close relationships with the left, and Quebec-Chile solidarity became an important pole of political life in the city.[50] In the 1970s, Catholic missionaries who had worked in Latin America also returned to Montreal, bringing with them their insights and knowledge of the Third World and forming new solidarity organizations.[51]

Not only did understandings of the relationship between Quebec and empire grow more complicated, but groups that had been excluded from the left began to demand respect for their rights. Being gay or lesbian during the masculine politics of the 1960s presented no small challenge. The FLQ manifesto had, after all, denounced Trudeau for his alleged homosexuality, reflecting something of the homophobia of society at large. But it was also in October 1970 that the counter-cultural journal *Mainmise* published a partial translation of Carl Wittman's "Gay Manifesto," written in the aftermath of the Stonewall riots of 1969, when transvestites, street runaways, and other members of the gay community responded to a routine police raid with several days of street fighting.[52] The manifesto called on homosexuals to overcome their shame, to see homosexuality positively, and to connect their struggle in defense of their humanity with those of women, workers, Blacks, and – in the *Mainmise* edition – those fighting for the independence of Quebec. The journal also launched a call for the formation of a Front de libération homosexuelle québécois.[53]

In March 1971 this front finally took form. In June 1972, just as the group was beginning to take shape, the police raided the opening event at the group's new meeting-place, arresting sixty people and effectively destroying the organization.[54] In the early 1970s, lesbians also began organizing, establishing coffee-houses and political groups.[55] Mass arrests of homosexuals continued in the province throughout the decade, but this repression ultimately spurred an important movement in defense of homosexual rights in the province.[56]

■ ■ ■

The adaptation of anti-colonial ideas to Quebec society was neither clear, linear, nor without significant contradiction. It was a prolonged moment during which conceptions of Quebec identity were at times hardened into rigid categories and at other moments loosened to allow for broad conceptions of solidarity. Francophone and anglophone activists often worked apart from each other, and tensions regularly emerged between the two groups. Yet, as I have attempted to demonstrate throughout this work, the many disparate groups nonetheless learned from each other and were deeply shaped by the local environment in which they operated. Throughout the late 1960s and early 1970s, social groups built upon anti-colonial ideas, stretched and adapted them. Through an active engagement in politics, individuals gained a heightened sense of self and, reading their local struggles through a global lens allowed many, as Greg Grandin wrote in a slightly different context, "to experience the world not in its illusionary static present but as evolving, as susceptible to change through action."[57]

In the 1970s, the language of decolonization no longer had the power and appeal that it did in the previous decade, but politicization continued apace, and it was clear that Quebec society had undergone an important transformation. By the 1970s, the French language was no longer debased in the same manner as it was in the 1960s, gender relations had shifted profoundly, Black people were more able to challenge racism and organize against oppression, and workers were empowered to fight for control of the workplace. Not all of these changes were direct results of the political struggles of the 1960s, but neither were the battles of the period negligible to them. The community activism that had begun in the 1960s spread to all corners of the city, and activists were working to democratize their communities, run medical and legal clinics, create collective kitchens, and fight for tenant rights.[58] Welfare-rights groups denounced the humiliation of being poor and the mistreatment of the indigent by welfare agents, and they demanded government daycares.[59] Black community groups were founded, women organized abortion-counseling centres, shelters, a feminist press, and committees within their unions, and they challenged the gender inequality that remained persistent in all spheres of life. Feminist and anti-racist politics flourished, as did labour politics and Marxist organizations. Progressive Catholics organized in their local communities and drew on left Catholicism to build international solidarity.[60] And in 1976 the PQ came to power with a program inspired, at least in part, by its complex interactions with the many movements and ideas studied in this book.

During the 1960s, ideas that had been developed far away were transposed to the centre of North America. These ideas were reinterpreted – sometimes awkwardly and mechanically, sometimes creatively – by a society undergoing profound demographic and structural changes. Anti-colonial and anti-imperial ideas, though problematic, gave people a new framework within which to understand their reality. The utopias articulated by the political movements of the 1960s and the 1970s have now long faded.[61] But rather than disappearing, the political energies of the movements that envisioned them have been woven into the fabric of Quebec society, deeply altering its nature. The political and social world of today still carries within it their complex legacies.

NOTES

INTRODUCTION

1 Frederick Cooper, *Colonialism in Question*, 188.

2 Kristin Ross, *May '68 and Its Afterlives*, 84.

3 Benita Parry, "Liberation Theory," 141.

4 André d'Allemagne articulated the ambiguity well when he argued that "Aussi, bien que du strict point de vue politico-constitutionnel le colonisateur soit le Canada anglais incarné dans l'État fédéral, dans les faits le colonisateur c'est l'Amérique anglo-saxonne. Le colonialisme, au Québec, est multiple et confus." *Le colonialisme au Québec*, 26.

5 1965 "Preface" Albert Memmi, *The Colonizer and the Colonized*, trans. Howard Greenfeld, xi. The French-Canadian edition of the book includes Memmi's thoughts on Quebec; see *Portrait du colonisé. Précédé du Portrait du colonisateur, et d'une préf. de Jean-Paul Sartre. Suivi de Les Canadiens français sont-ils des colonisés?*

6 Jacques Berque, preface to *Les québécois*, 12.

7 "Sartre Applauds Québécois," *McGill Daily*, 21 January 1971.

8 Aimé Césaire, "Le discours sur la négritude, prononcé le jeudi 26 février 1987," in *Discours sur le colonialisme* (Paris: Présence Africaine, 2004), 81.

9 Canada, Royal Commission on Bilingualism and Biculturalism, "Submission of Miss Kahn-Tineta Horn" *Transcripts of Public Hearings*, 1 December 1965, 4321, 4322, 4323. Seen in Richard Gordon Kicksee, "'Scaled Down to Size,'" 56. For an important look at the history of Aboriginal peoples in the post-Confederation period, see Claude Gélinas, *Les Autochtones dans le Québec post-confédéral, 1867–1960*.

10 While both a Black presence in Montreal and Black resistance to racism stretch back to the seventeenth century, the nature of Black activism in Montreal was altered as a result of increased West Indian immigration in the wake of the revised immigration policies of the 1960s. For a history of Black Montreal, see Dorothy W. Williams, *The Road to Now.* Also see James W. St.G. Walker, *The West Indians in Canada.*

11 As I will discuss later, by the early 1970s Canada's imperial role in the Caribbean was being systematically analyzed and denounced in Montreal's main Black Power publication, *UHURU.* This analysis can also be found in Dennis Forsythe, ed., *Let the Niggers Burn!*

12 For a brief discussion of how imperial metropoles often became centres for the formation of anti-colonial networks, see Elleke Boehmer and Bart Moore-Gilbert, "Postcolonial Studies and Transnational Resistance," 12.

13 Edward W. Said, *Culture and Imperialism,* 17.

14 Edward W. Said, "Travelling Theory Reconsidered," in *Reflections on Exile and Other Essays,* 451–2.

15 Marc Raboy, *Movements and Messages,* trans. David Homel, 121.

16 Robin D.G. Kelley, *Freedom Dreams,* 8.

17 I borrow the conception of being the "makers of culture" from Kelley, Ibid, 2.

18 Both the French- and English-language media played an important role in amplifying and over-representing the importance of the FLQ in the multi-faceted world of political opposition. For the relationship between the media and the New Left in the United States, see Todd Gitlin, *The Whole World is Watching.*

19 I have learned greatly here from Greg Grandin's discussion of social movements in Latin America in *The Last Colonial Massacre.*

20 While no study situates the entire period within a larger international framework, a growing number of works treat more specific questions from an international vantage point. See especially Magali Deleuze, *L'une et l'autre indépendance 1954–1964,* Jean Lamarre, "'Au service des étudiants et de la nation': L'internationalisation de l'Union générale des étudiants du Québec (1964–1969)," as well as the 2009 (Vol. 12, no. 1) edition of *Globe: revue internationale d'études québécoises,* which sheds new light on Quebec's international relations. See especially Michel Lacroix and Stéphanie Rousseau, "Introduction. 'La terre promise de la coopération.' Les relations internationales du Québec à la lumière du missionnariat, de l'économie sociale et de l'éducation." On the historiography of many of the movements of the period, see Sean Mills, "Là gauche montréalaise, le nationalisme, et les années soixante."

21 Sara Evans, *Personal Politics.*

22 See Karen Dubinsky et al., eds., *New World Coming,* Jeremy Varon, *Bringing the War Home,* Robin D.G. Kelley, *Freedom Dreams,* Kristin Ross, *May '68 and Its Afterlives,* Max Elbaum, *Revolution in the Air,* Laura Pulido, *Black, Brown, Yellow and Left,* Cynthia Ann Young, *Soul Power,* and personal autobiographies such as Tariq Ali, *Street*

Fighting Years and Stokely Carmichael and Ekwueme Michael Thelwell, *Ready for Revolution*. Also see Fredric Jameson, "Periodizing the 1960s."

23 I am drawing here on the innovative work of William Sewell who argues that structures can be transposed–not just transferred, but slightly modified when applied in a new setting–from one location to another. These structures provide a set of resources for different groups and individuals. See *Logics of History*.

24 Said, *Culture and Imperialism*, 217, xxv.

25 Le Front d'action politique, *Les salariés au pouvoir!*, 22.

CHAPTER ONE

1 For a look at the Quiet Revolution in popular memory in Quebec, see Jocelyn Létourneau and Sabrina Moisan, "Mémoire et récit de l'aventure historique du Québec chez les jeunes québécois d'héritage canadien-français." For a look at twentieth-century Quebec historiography, see Ronald Rudin, *Making History in Twentieth-Century Quebec*. An overview of how Quebec historians have written about the 1960s can be found in Paul-André Linteau, "Un débat historiographique: l'entrée du Québec dans la modernité et la signification de la Révolution tranquille." Also see Jacques Rouillard, "La Révolution tranquille: rupture ou tournant?" and Yves Bélanger, Robert Comeau, and Céline Métivier, eds., *La révolution tranquille*.

2 Kristin Ross, *May '68 and Its Afterlives*, 6.

3 "Beyond What? An Introduction," in *Postcolonial Studies and Beyond*, 27–8.

4 For interesting looks at Montreal in the postwar years, see Viviane Namaste, "La réglementation des journaux jaunes à Montréal, 1955–1975," Viviane Namaste, *C'était du spectacle!*, and William Weintraub, *City Unique*.

5 Paul-André Linteau et al., *Histoire du Québec contemporain*, 203–5. For an important look at immigrants and Cold War Canada, see Franca Iacovetta, *Gatekeepers*.

6 Linteau et al., *Histoire du Québec contemporain*, 390–3.

7 Marc V. Levine, *The Reconquest of Montreal*, 23–5, Louis Fournier, FLQ, 17–18.

8 For a thorough and nuanced discussion of this phenomenon, as well as of its social and political repercussions, see Denyse Baillargeon, *Un Québec en mal d'enfants*.

9 William D. Coleman, *The Independence Movement in Quebec 1945–1980*, 190.

10 Louis Fournier, FLQ, 17–18. Peter Allnutt and Robert Chodos, "Quebec: Into the Streets," *Radical America* 6, no. 5 (1972): 36–40.

11 Coleman, *The Independence Movement in Quebec 1945–1980*, 194.

12 Kenneth McRoberts, *Quebec*, 65.

13 When the Canadian government wanted to establish diplomatic posts in French Africa, for example, it was unable to do so because it lacked French-speaking diplomats. Robin S. Gendron, *Towards a Francophone Community*, 55.

14 Charles Gagnon, "Je suis né au Bic..." part of which was published in *Magazine Maclean* in July of 1970. Reproduced in Comeau et al, eds., FLQ, 32–3.

15 Marc Comby, "L'expérience du FRAP à Montréal (1970–1974)," in *Contester dans un pays prospère*, 155.

16 Robert Boivin, *Histoire de la Clinique des citoyens de Saint-Jacques (1968–1988)*, 17–18.

17 Ibid., 21.

18 Claude Gélinas, *Les Autochtones dans le Québec post-confédéral, 1867–1960*, 50.

19 Ibid., 27.

20 Ibid., 27–8.

21 Ibid., 59.

22 Ibid., 89, 103–4.

23 See Jane Jenson and Martin Papillon, "Challenging the Citizenship Regime: The James Bay Cree and Transnational Action."

24 Baillargeon, *Un Québec en mal d'enfants*, 27, 31.

25 Ibid., 69.

26 The Clio Collective, *Quebec Women*, 295–303, 318.

27 Susan Mann Trofimenkoff, *The Dream of Nation*, 272.

28 For an important work outlining these developments, see Xavier Gélinas, *La droite intellectuelle québécoise et la Révolution tranquille*.

29 For an in-depth look at the formation of these two different intellectual traditions, see Michael D. Behiels, *Prelude to Quebec's Quiet Revolution*. The following paragraph draws on Behiels's work.

30 Ibid., 274.

31 See E.-Martin Meunier and Jean-Philippe Warren, *Sortir de la 'Grande noirceur,'* Michael Gauvreau, *The Catholic Origins of Quebec's Quiet Revolution*.

32 Michael Gauvreau, "From Rechristianization to Contestation," 809.

33 Jacques Rouillard, "Major Changes in the Confédération des travailleurs catholiques du Canada, 1940–1960," in *Quebec Since 1945*, 111–32.

34 Carolyn Sharp, "To Build a Just Society: The Catholic Left in Quebec," in *Reclaiming Democracy*, 49–50. For information regarding Gutiérrez's stay in Montreal, see Stéphane Baillargeon, "Gustavo Gutiérrez: Le théologien engagé. Un autre regard sur la foi à la lumière de positions socio-politiques," *Le Devoir*, 29 novembre 1993. My thanks to Catherine LeGrand and Fred Burrill for sharing this reference with me.

35 Pierre Beaudet, *Qui aide qui?*, 26.

36 Ibid., 20.

37 Ibid., 41. For important insights, see Catherine LeGrand, "L'axe missionaire catholique entre le Québec et l'Amérique Latine. Une exploration préliminaire." Unpublished manuscript.

38 Pierre Beaudet, *On a raison de se révolter*, 43. For a look at the complexity of the relationship between Quebec and Latin America, see Daniel Gay, *Les élites québécoises et l'Amérique latine*.

39 Rouillard, "La Révolution tranquille: rupture ou tournant?"

40 Coleman, *The Independence Movement in Quebec 1945–1980*, 39, 96–111.

41 Ibid., 39–41.

42 Ibid., 38–9.

43 Ibid., 43.

44 McRoberts, *Quebec*, 20.

45 For just two works exploring the connection between Quebec (as well as Canada) and Latin America and the Caribbean, see Robert Chodos, *The Caribbean Connection*, and Gay, *Les élites québécoises et l'Amérique latine*.

46 See Coleman, *The Independence Movement in Quebec 1945–1980*.

47 Ibid., 116.

48 For an expression of the former interpretation, see McRoberts, *Quebec*. For the latter, see Coleman, *The Independence Movement in Quebec 1945–1980*.

49 McRoberts, *Quebec*, 136–9.

50 See Marcel Chaput, *Pourquoi je suis séparatiste*.

51 Jean-Paul Desbiens, *Les insolences du Frère Untel*. For an important discussion, see Ramsay Cook, *Watching Quebec*, 36.

52 For a look at the way in which one of the most prominent Liberal ministers used the language of colonization and decolonization when speaking of hydro-electric power in Quebec, see René Lévesque, *Memoirs*, trans. Philip Stratford, 168–78. What happened during this period was complex, and had contradictory results. The construction of a secular bureaucracy privileging rationality and professionalization had the effect of replacing many female benevolent societies with male administrators, thereby modernizing patriarchy and reproducing new forms of gender inequality. Baillargeon, *Un Québec en mal d'enfants*, 28. For a discussion of the idea of the "modernization of patriarchy" see Greg Grandin, *The Last Colonial Massacre*, 135. For a discussion of the use of colonial language in the 1950s in the pages of the Liberal party's newspaper *La Réforme*, see Coleman, *The Independence Movement in Quebec 1945–1980*, 97.

53 For a useful look at student politics in Quebec, see Jean-Philippe Warren, *Une douce anarchie*. Also see François Ricard, *La génération lyrique*.

54 This point is made strongly in Alexis Lachaîne, "Black and Blue: French Canadian Writers, Decolonization and Revolutionary Nationalism in Quebec, 1960–1969," 35.

55 For an interesting discussion of one person's experience of the politicization of both herself and her father see Marjolaine Péloquin, *En prison pour la cause des femmes*, 163.

56 Fernand Dumont, *The Vigil of Quebec*, 95.

57 Vijay Prashad, *The Darker Nations*, xv–xvi.

58 As Arif Dirlik explains, "Politically, the idea of the Third World pointed to the necessity of a common politics that derived from a common positioning in the system (rather than some homogeneous essentialized common quality, as is erro-

neously assumed these days in much postcolonial writing)." "Rethinking Colonialism: Globalization, Postcolonialism, and the Nation," 433.

59 Frederick Cooper, *Colonialism in Question*, 33. For another discussion of the new post-war climate favouring human rights, decolonization, and self-determination, see Ken Coates, *Global History of Indigenous Peoples*, 236–7.

60 Benedict Anderson, *Imagined Communities*, 135.

61 Prashad, *The Darker Nations*, 217.

62 Albert Memmi, *The Colonizer and the Colonized*, 56, 74.

63 Memmi argues that he did not conceive of his book as "a search for solutions," but he does hint towards a larger political project. "The liquidation of colonization," he argues, "is nothing but a prelude to complete liberation, to self-recovery." Ibid., 145–51.

64 Edward W. Said, *Culture and Imperialism*, 269–70.

65 On this point, and in the next few paragraphs in general, I am deeply indebted to Ato Sekyi-Otu's reading of Fanon. See Ato Sekyi-Otu, *Fanon's Dialectic of Experience*. I have also drawn insights from Said, *Culture and Imperialism*.

66 Frantz Fanon, *The Wretched of the Earth*, 40, 35.

67 Ibid., 144–6.

68 Said, *Culture and Imperialism*, 272–3.

69 Fanon, *The Wretched of the Earth*, 204, 245–8.

70 Ibid., 197. In *A Dying Colonialism*, Fanon charts how, through the struggle for liberation, a colonized people could reinvent itself, undoing patterns of sexual oppression, learning to adopt and appropriate technology and language to further the process of liberation.

71 Ibid., 94. I have adopted the revised translation found in Sekyi-Otu, *Fanon's Dialectic of Experience*, 207.

72 Nigel C. Gibson, *Fanon*, 113.

73 Ibid., 122. The following paragraph also relies on Gibson.

74 Fanon, *The Wretched of the Earth*, 35.

75 Fanon wrote that "we condemn, with pain in our hearts, those brothers who have flung themselves into revolutionary action with the almost physiological brutality that centuries of oppression give rise to and feed." *A Dying Colonialism*, 25. As Robert Young argues, "the origin of the violence of decolonization is the violence of colonization, something with which Fanon would hardly identify." *Postcolonialism*, 281.

76 Fanon, *A Dying Colonialism*, 25.

77 Fanon, *The Wretched of the Earth*, 88.

78 Young, *Postcolonialism*, 280–3. For an important look at Fanon's life, see David Macey, *Frantz Fanon*, and to understand the international context for his ideas, see Robert J.C. Young, "Fanon and the turn to armed struggle in Africa." A discussion of Fanon's reception among Black Americans during the 1960s can be found in

Micheline Rice-Maximin, "Frantz Fanon and Black American Ideologists in the 1960's."

79 See Pierre Vallières, *White Niggers of America*, 224–5. This theme can also be found in many of the writings of Charles Gagnon. André-J. Bélanger argues that this perspective was absent from the perspectives of the writers of *Parti Pris*. See *Ruptures et constantes*, 191.

80 Jan Depocas, "Le complexe à Maria Chapdelaine," *Parti Pris* 1, no. 9–11 (1964): 37.

81 See Louis Laberge, Marcel Pepin and Yvon Charbonneau, postscript to Robert Chodos and Nick Auf der Maur, eds., *Quebec*, 147–52.

82 Gibson, *Fanon*, 3.

83 Young, *Postcolonialism*, 169. Also see Robert J.C. Young, preface to Sartre, *Colonialism and Neocolonialism*, ix.

84 Paul Chamberland, "De la damnation à la liberté," *Parti Pris* 1, no. 9–11 (1964): 83.

85 For information regarding Sartre's visit to Montreal in 1946 and the controversy it sparked in the province, see Yvan Cloutier, "Sartre en quête d'un éditeur francophone en Amérique."

86 Robert J.C. Young, preface to Sartre, *Colonialism and Neocolonialism*, x.

87 For a riveting account of post-war French politics, and of Sartre and his life companion, writer and philosopher Simone de Beauvoir, see de Beauvoir, *Force of Circumstance*.

88 Emile Boudreau et al., "Matériaux pour la théorie et la pratique d'un socialisme québécois," *Socialisme 64*, no. 1 (1964): 7–8.

89 See Malcolm Reid, *The Shouting Signpainters*, 255.

90 John Gilmore, *Swinging in Paradise*, 163–7.

91 See Sarah-Jane (Saje) Mathieu, "North of the Colour Line," 9–41.

92 Paul-André Linteau, "The Italians of Quebec: Key Participants in Contemporary Linguistic and Political Debates," in *Arrangiarsi*, 186–7. For a recent collection of essays portraying much of the complexity of the relations between Quebec's Jewish and French-Canadian populations, see Pierre Anctil, Ira Robinson, and Gérard Bouchard, eds., *Juifs et Canadiens français dans la société québécoise*.

93 Paul-André Linteau, *Histoire de Montréal depuis la Confédération*, 2ᵉ ed., 540.

94 In 1961, Italians made up 4.8% of the population, and Jews 3.5%. The numbers for the city itself (rather than those for the metropolitan region) follow roughly the same pattern. In 1961 those of French origin made up 66.6%, those of British origin 12.4%, Italians 6.7%, and Jews 3.9%. Ibid., 427–65.

95 Linteau, "The Italians of Quebec," 183.

96 Bryan Palmer, *Canada's 1960s*, 426–8.

97 Myra Rutherdale and Jim Miller, "'It's Our Country': First Nations' Participation in the Indian Pavilion at Expo 67."

98 Hubert Aquin in "L'équipe de LIBERTÉ devant Montréal: (essai de situation)," *Liberté* 5, no. 4 (1963): 278.

99 André Lortie, ed., *The 60s*, 77.

100 Ibid., 107.

101 Levine, *The Reconquest of Montreal*, 43.

102 Luc Perrier, "Connaissance d'une ville," *Liberté* 5, no. 4 (1963): 339–41.

CHAPTER TWO

1 For examples of pre-1960 radicalism in Quebec, see Claude Larivière, *Albert Saint-Martin*, Robert Comeau and Bernard Dionne, *Le droit de se taire*, and Andrée Lévesque, *Virage à gauche interdit*. In the post-war years, strikes often led to violent confrontations with provincial police, most famously in Asbestos in 1949 and in Murdochville in 1957. Jacques Rouillard, *Histoire du syndicalisme au Québec*, 132–8. Also see his essay, "La grève de l'amiante de 1949 et le projet de réforme de l'entreprise."

2 For a description of Le Mas and its role in the history of jazz in Montreal, see John Gilmore, *Swinging in Paradise*, 209–13.

3 See Yves Gauthier, *Monsieur Livre*.

4 See Jean-Marc Piotte, *La communauté perdue*, 14. This is not to say, of course, that Marx was not read and known in the province before the 1960s. Nicole Laurin suggests that in the years before the Quiet Revolution, Marx's most faithful readers were learned religious figures. See "Genèse de la sociologie marxiste au Québec," 184.

5 Pierre Vallières, "La peur de vivre," *Le Devoir* (18 mai 1957) in *Paroles d'un nègre blanc*, 28.

6 Mathieu Lapointe, "Nationalisme et socialisme dans la pensée de Raoul Roy, 1935-1965," 87–90; Henri Gagnon, *Les militants socialistes du Québec*.

7 For reflections on *Laurentie* and the idea of decolonization, as articulated by the right, see Magali Deleuze, *L'une et l'autre indépendance* and Carole Page, "Décolonisation et question nationale québécoise." For a wide-ranging and detailed study of the right of the Quiet Revolution, see Xavier Gélinas, *La droite intellectuelle québécoise et la Révolution tranquille*.

8 André Laurendeau, "Maurice Duplessis à l'Assemblée nationale: la théorie du roi nègre," *Le Devoir* (18 novembre 1958).

9 "Manifeste politique: Propositions programmatiques de la REVUE SOCIALISTE," *La Revue socialiste*, no. 1 (1959): 13.

10 Louis Fournier, FLQ, 18. Also, see Jean-Marc Piotte, *Un parti pris politique*, 13.

11 Lapointe, "Nationalisme et socialisme dans la pensée de Raoul Roy, 1935-1965," 125–7.

12 "Manifeste politique: Propositions programmatiques de la REVUE SOCIALISTE," 22–33.

13 Lapointe, "Nationalisme et socialisme dans la pensée de Raoul Roy, 1935-1965," 103.

14 André d'Allemagne, *Le R.I.N. de 1960 à 1963*, 47.

15 See Ibid., 34.

16 Ibid., 47–56. Chaput, along with many of his followers, quit the RIN in December 1962 to form the Parti républicain du Québec (121). For a new biography of one of the RIN's most defining characters, Pierre Bourgault, see Jean-François Nadeau, *Bourgault*.

17 See Jean-Claude Labrecque, *Le R.I.N.* (Canada: Les Productions Virage, 2002).

18 André d'Allemagne, *Le colonialisme au Québec*, 116, 75, 57–9.

19 See Francis Provost, "Étude sur les dissensions entre la 'droite' et la 'gauche' au sein du Rassemblement pour l'indépendance nationale entre 1966 et 1968."

20 For details about the founding of the FLQ, see Fournier, *FLQ*, 27–39 and Michael McLoughlin, *Last Stop, Paris*, 13.

21 For the labour movement's position on the FLQ, see Jean-François Cardin, *Comprendre octobre 1970*. For a critique of the FLQ from within *Parti Pris*, see Jean-Marc Piotte, "Où allons-nous?," *Parti Pris* 3, no. 1–2 (1965), 64–85. For a discussion of the FLP and its theoretical reasons for distancing itself from the actions of the FLQ, see Pierre Beaudet, *On a raison de se révolter*, 85.

22 For a useful look at the radical literature of the Quiet Revolution, as well as its relationship to Black literature in the United States, see Max Dorsinville, *Caliban without Prospero*.

23 For a more detailed explanation of the diverse French-speaking socialist groups in Montreal, see Luc Racine and Roch Denis, "La conjoncture politique québécoise depuis 1960," *Socialisme québécois*, 21–2 (1971): 17–79.

24 For an excellent look at the two different generations of Marxist intellectuals in Quebec of the 1960s, see Laurin, "Genèse de la sociologie marxiste au Québec."

25 See Jean-Philippe Warren, *Une douce anarchie*.

26 The CourtePointe Collective, *The Point Is*, 31.

27 Donald McGraw, *Le développement des groupes populaires à Montréal, 1963–1973*, 49.

28 Ibid., 50–1.

29 Ibid., 15, 45–7. Further insights can be found in Amélie Bourbeau, "La réorganisation de l'assistance chez les catholiques Montréalais."

30 McGraw, *Le développement des groupes populaires à Montréal, 1963–1973*, 47–9.

31 See Martin Croteau, "L'implication sociale et politique de Jacques Couture à Montréal de 1963 à 1976."

32 For the role of women in community activism, see CourtePointe Collective, *The Point Is*.

33 Ibid., 57.

34 "Le rôle des femmes dans l'animation sociale," *Châtelaine*, 6 juin 1970, 60.

35 CourtePointe Collective, *The Point Is*, 161.

36 Rouillard, *Le syndicalisme québécois*, 207.

37 Bryan Palmer, *Canada's 1960s*, 222–4.

38 Kenneth McRoberts, *Quebec*, 159–60.

39 Marcel Pepin, "The Second Front: The Report of Marcel Pepin, National President, to the Convention of the CNTU, October 13, 1968," in *Quebec Labour*.

40 Bryan Palmer, *Working-Class Experience*, 312.

41 Judy Rebick, *Ten Thousand Roses*, 3–4. Quebec Voice of Women members, Brief to the Royal Commission on the Status of Women, May 1968, 1. Also, see Simone Monet-Chartrand, *Les Québécoises et le mouvement pacifiste (1939–1967)*. For Monet-Chartrand's more general reflections on women's activism, see *Pionnières québécoises et regroupements de femmes d'hier à aujourd'hui*.

42 La Fédération des femmes du Québec, Mme Yvonne R. Raymond, Présidente du comité, Brief to the Royal Commission on the Status of Women, March 1968, 3–4.

43 See David H. Sherwood, "The N.D.P. and French Canada, 1961–1965" and André Lamoureux, *Le NDP et le Québec, 1958–1985*.

44 Palmer, *Canada's 1960s*, 58.

45 Monet-Chartrand, *Les Québécoises et le mouvement pacifiste (1939–1967)*, 41–3.

46 "Statement of Purpose," *Our Generation Against Nuclear War* 1, no. 1 (1961).

47 Bradford Lyttle, unpublished autobiography sent to author, 14 March 2005. My thanks to Mr Lyttle for sharing his unpublished material. The progress of the Quebec-Washington-Guantanamo walk can be followed in *Liberation: an independent monthly*. Interview with Dimitri Roussopoulos, 16 May 2006.

48 Although the journal's content in the early 1960s rarely reflected upon Quebec society, the editors were profoundly marked by living in Montreal. The union organizer Michel Chartrand, for example, acted as the printer for the journal's first issues. And both he and his wife, Simone Monet-Chartrand, had been involved in various aspects of the peace movement and joined the Mouvement pour le désarmement nucléaire (MND) when it was founded at McGill in November 1962. As Monet-Chartrand wrote, "Depuis la déclaration de la Deuxième Guerre mondiale, en 1939, jusqu'à la deuxième Conférence des femmes pour la paix, en 1967, mon journal intime et ma correspondance me permettent de retracer le contexte qui a donné naissance aux mouvements internationaux pour la paix et de me rappeler tous les efforts de coopération et de solidarité venus s'opposer aux forces politiques et militaires qui s'enlisaient dans une guerre froide menaçant la survie de l'humanité." *Les Québécoises et le mouvement pacifiste (1939–1967)*, 13, 46.

49 "Editorial Statement," *Our Generation* 3, 4, no. 4, 1 (1966): 3.

50 "Editorial Statement on Quebec," *Our Generation* 4, no. 2 (1966): 1–2.

51 See, for example, Marcel Rioux, "Youth in the Contemporary World and in Québec," *Our Generation* 3, 4, no. 4, 1 (1966): 5–19.

52 See two articles by Roy Lemoine, "The Quebec Elections: A Reaction, A Pause or Another Step in the Revolution," *Our Generation* 4, no. 2 (1966) and "De Gaulle and the Future of Québec," *Our Generation* 5, no. 2 (1967), and also Jean Laliberté, "Les travailleurs étudiants du Québec; Student Social Action," *Our Generation* 4, no. 3 (1966).

53 See, for example, Evelyn Dumas, "The New Labour Left in Québec," *Our Generation* 4, no. 4 (1967), Robert Favreau, "The Quandary of L'Union Générale des Étudiants du Québec," *Our Generation* 5, no. 1 (1967).

54 "Towards a Peace and Freedom Movement," *Our Generation* 5, no. 1 (1967): 5.

55 Jean-Marc Piotte, *Un Certain espoir*, 34-5.

56 Malcolm Reid, *The Shouting Signpainters*, 40-1. Interview with Dimitri Roussopoulos, 16 May 2006.

57 Vincent Desroches, "Uprooting and Uprootedness: Haitian Poetry in Quebec (1960–2002)," 205; Samuel Pierre, ed., *Ces Québécois venus d'Haïti*, 381.

58 Piotte, *La communauté perdue*, 33-7.

59 Paul Chamberland, "Exigences théoriques d'un combat politique," *Parti Pris* 4, no. 1 (1966): 9.

60 Pierre Maheu, "Laïcité 1966," *Parti Pris* 4, no. 1 (1966): 59.

61 See Carolyn Sharp, "To Build a Just Society: The Catholic Left in Quebec." For an extremely insightful discussion of the relationship between Quebec and Latin America, see Catherine LeGrand, "L'axe missionaire catholique entre le Québec et l'Amérique Latine. Une exploration préliminaire." Unpublished manuscript.

62 The important role of left Catholicism in neighbourhood organizing is often overlooked in political histories of Quebec during the 1960s. See CourtePointe Collective, *The Point Is*.

63 When, after announcing the beginning of a hunger strike at the United Nations, Pierre Vallières learned that a group of Christians from the Université de Montréal declared their solidarity for him, he wrote that "This declaration has been one of the greatest consolations to us during our detention in New York." Pierre Vallières, *White Niggers of America*, trans. Joan Pinkham, 70. Also see Vallières, *Paroles d'un nègre blanc*, and Fernand Foisy, *Les voies d'un homme de parole (1916–1967)*. For an understanding of Vallières's religious convictions, see Constantin Baillargeon, *Pierre Vallières vu par son professeur de philosophie*.

64 Pierre Maheu, *Un parti pris révolutionnaire*, 291-2.

65 Jean-Marc Piotte, "Éditorial: le socialisme," *Parti Pris*, 1, no. 6 (1964): 4.

66 For a full explanation of this theme, see Mathieu Lavigne, "L'idée de décolonisation québécoise." This point is also made in André J. Bélanger, *Ruptures et constantes*.

67 Mona-Josée Gagnon, "Women in the Trade-Union Movement in Quebec." Also, see Lucie Piché, "Entre l'accès à l'égalité et la préservation des modèles."

68 The Clio Collective, *Quebec Women*, 294-302, 321.

69 Pierre Maheu, "De la révolte à la révolution," *Parti Pris*, 1, no. 1 (1963): 12.

70 Ibid., 15. For a discussion of the theme of castration in Maheu's writing, see Bélanger, *Ruptures et constantes*, 149.

71 See, for example, Pierre Maheu, "L'Oedipe colonial," *Parti Pris*, 1, no. 9-11 (1964), 29. The writers of *Parti Pris* reflected well the attitudes of the Montreal left. Stéphanie Lanthier argues that in the radical literature of the 1960s, women are not only excluded from any active roles, but that male writers constructed their mod-

els of national liberation against the submission and exclusion of women. Lanthier found that when women are not symbolically representing either Quebec or anglophone culture, they are absent from all historical analysis. Malcolm Reid makes a similar point in his study of the *Parti Pris* group. "In the *parti pris* world," he argues, "woman remains the beloved, the symbol of the land, the one the revolutionary does not neglect to love well." For a look at the gendered nature of Vallières's discourse, see Katherine Roberts, "'Mère, je vous hais!'," Stéphanie Lanthier, "L'impossible réciprocité des rapports politiques et idéologiques entre le nationalisme radical et le féminisme radical au Québec 1961–1972," 117, résumé, and Reid, *The Shouting Signpainters*, 94.

72 Léon Dion, *La révolution déroutée, 1960–1976*, 141.

73 Marjolaine Péloquin, *En prison pour la cause des femmes*, 218–19.

74 Piotte, *Un certain espoir*, 124–8.

75 Piotte, *La communauté perdue*, 37.

76 For an account of one young activist and his discovery of *Parti Pris*, see Beaudet, *On a raison de se révolter*, 51.

77 Maheu, *Un parti pris révolutionnaire*, 293.

78 Paul Chamberland, "Éditorial," *Parti Pris* 1, no. 4 (1964): 2.

79 "Lettre au lecteur," *Parti Pris* 2, no. 1 (1964): 18.

80 For the experience of the baby boom generation in Quebec, see François Ricard, *La génération lyrique*.

81 Reid, *The Shouting Signpainters*, 258.

82 "Présentation," *Parti Pris* 1, no. 1 (1963): 3. For a discussion of *Parti Pris* and its relationship to socialism, see Pierrette Bouchard-Saint-Amant, "L'idéologie de la revue *Parti Pris*: le nationalisme socialiste," and Reid, *The Shouting Signpainters*, 36–8.

83 For interesting reflections on the relationship between culture and rebellion, see Eric Hobsbawm, *Uncommon People* and Bryan Palmer, *Cultures of Darkness*. In the case of *Parti Pris*, see Bélanger, *Ruptures et constantes*, 150.

84 André Loiselle, *Cinema as History*, 26, 31. Also see, Gilles Marsolais, "L'équipe française de l'ONF (1958–1962)."

85 Marsolais, "L'équipe française de l'ONF (1958–1962)," 13–14.

86 "Manifeste 1964–1965," *Parti Pris* 2, no. 1 (1964): 17.

87 For a document outlining the goals and functions of the publishing house, see UQAM, Gérald Godin fonds, 81p–660:02/12, "éditions parti pris" (1966).

88 Sherry Simon, *Translating Montreal*, 29.

89 Gérald Godin, "Le joual politique," *Parti Pris* 2, no. 7 (1965): 57, 59. Dorsinville, *Caliban without Prospero*, 121. For some, writing in *joual* was a way of escaping their bourgeois origins. For others, a glorification of *joual* was an insult to those who lived in misery and cultural deprivation. Gérald Godin, "La folie bilinguale," *Parti Pris* 3, no. 10 (1966): 57. Charles Gagnon, "Quand le 'joual' se donne des airs," *Révolution québécoise* 1, no. 6 (1965).

90 Maheu, "De la révolte à la révolution," 15.

91 "Manifeste 1964–1965," 9, 15.

92 Ibid., 17.

93 Le Mouvement de libération populaire et de la revue Parti Pris, "Manifeste 1965–1966," *Parti Pris* 3, no. 1–2 (1965): 7.

94 Ibid., 2–41.

95 The MLP's activities are chronicled in the organization's publication *Le Militant*.

96 For more details, see Jean-Marc Piotte, "Charles Gagnon, *Feu sur l'Amérique*," *Bulletin d'histoire politique* 15, no. 3 (2007): 311–18.

97 Interview with Jean-Marc Piotte, 30 October 2006, Montreal.

98 Albert Memmi, *The Colonizer and the Colonized*, trans. Howard Greenfeld, 91.

99 Ibid., 102.

100 Luc Perrier, "Connaissance d'une ville," *Liberté* 5, no. 4 (1963): 341.

101 Yves Préfontaine "L'équipe de LIBERTÉ devant Montréal: (essai de situation)," *Liberté* 5, no. 4 (1963): 296.

102 d'Allemagne, *Le colonialisme au Québec*, 129, 137, 175.

103 André Jacques (Charles Gagnon), "La révolution, c'est une entreprise de construction." *La Cognée* 56 (1 avril 1966), reproduced in *FLQ: un projet révolutionnaire*, 100.

104 Paul Chamberland, "De la damnation à la liberté," *Parti Pris*, 1, no. 9–11 (1964): 55.

105 Vallières, *White Niggers of America*, 200, 19.

106 *Parti Pris* did publish one substantial article on the discrimination against Natives. Camil Guy, "Les indiens du québec: désagrégation culturelle et prolétarisation," *Parti Pris* 4, no. 9–12 (1967): 165–80.

107 See, for example, Jacques Ferron, "Ce bordel de pays: d'un amour inquiétant," *Parti Pris* 2, no. 7 (1965): 60.

108 Reid, *The Shouting Signpainters*, 158.

109 Although Roy's interpretation was idiosyncratic, unlike many others he realized that the paradox of the colonized status of francophone Quebeckers could not be ignored. According to Roy, "jamais les Français, et encore moins les Canadiens français, n'ont 'volé' ce pays aux Indiens. Encore moins les Canadiens français parce que, de par leur ascendance partiellement indienne, ils sont ici depuis toujours et sont ainsi les héritiers des premiers occupants de ce sol canadien, en plus d'en être les défricheurs. Et les Indiens d'aujourd'hui, à part ceux qui ont été enfermés dans les réserves par les Anglo-Saxons, on peut dire que ce sont les Canadiens français." Le Marabout (Raoul Roy), "Indépendantistes victimes de falsifications historiques," *La Revue socialiste* 7 (1963–1964): 58.

110 When describing the experience of French settlers, the only Natives that Vallières mentions are Iroquois "guerrillas." Vallières, *White Niggers of America*, 24. Vallières also wrote that "le FLQ n'est pas le premier à choisir la guerre de guérillas comme stratégie. À l'époque de l'impérialisme français, au XVIIe siècle, les Iroquois et d'autres 'nations' indiennes (Les Cinq Nations) ont, pendant des années, prati-

quer la guerre de guérillas." And he stated that it was necessary "que la métropole envoie à la colonies les moyens militaires d'*exterminer les Cinq Nations pour que cessent ces guérillas ... en même temps que les guérilleros et les nations indiennes elles-mêmes.*" Mathieu Hébert (Pierre Vallières), "Gagner l'appui des masses" *L'Avant-garde* (no. 4, juin 1966). Reproduced in FLQ: *un projet révolutionnaire*, 134.

111 Jacques Godbout, "La haine," *Parti Pris* 2, no. 3 (1964): 21.

112 For a brief but illuminating discussion about Aboriginal activism leading up to Montreal's Expo '67, see Richard Gordon Kicksee, "'Scaled Down to Size.'" For a retrospective critique, see Piotte, *Un certain espoir*, 136–7.

CHAPTER THREE

1 Various groups in Montreal were instrumental in forging international solidarity. To take just one example, the Quebec Student body, UGEQ, helped to organize speaking engagements for student representatives of the Vietnamese NFL, inviting workers and students to come and hear the delegates. Gilles Bourque, "UGEQ," *Parti Pris* 5, no. 2–3 (1967): 51–2. For a look at the international activities of UGEQ, see Jean Lamarre, "'Au service des étudiants et de la nation.'"

2 *Parti Pris* even boasted that the *New Left Review* and the *Revue internationale de socialisme* had asked them for articles about Quebec. "Lettre au lecteur," *Parti Pris* 2, no. 1 (1964): 18. Nicholas M. Regush, *Pierre Vallières*, 112.

3 See Alexis Lachaîne, "Black and Blue," 67.

4 "Manifeste, 1964–1965," *Parti Pris* 2, no. 1 (1964): 17. As the manifesto put it, they were aware that others "osent cette folie avec nous."

5 Camille Limoges, "Éditorial: de l'homopoliticus à nous," *Parti Pris*, 1, no. 9–11 (1964): 5.

6 Paul Chamberland, "De la damnation à la liberté," *Parti Pris*, 1, no. 9–11 (1964): 83.

7 In this sense, they were following in the footsteps of well-known Black American radicals. See *Malcolm X Speaks*, 53–4. For useful insights, see James Tyner, *The Geography of Malcolm X*.

8 See Magali Deleuze, *L'une et l'autre indépendance.*

9 For a wealth of information on the representations of Latin America in Quebec's major newspapers, see Daniel Gay, *Les élites québécoises et l'Amérique latine.*

10 For an account of post-war French intellectual life from the perspective of one of the period's most important protagonists, see Simone de Beauvoir, *Force of Circumstance.*

11 See Deleuze, *L'une et l'autre indépendance.*

12 Kristin Ross, *May '68 and Its Afterlives*, 82. For a discussion between two Quebec intellectuals about their interactions with Maspero, see Pierre Vallières à Jean-Marc Piotte, 20 juillet 1967. Reproduced in Vallières, *Paroles d'un nègre blanc*, 110–11.

13 Ross, *May '68 and Its Afterlives*, 84.

14 Ibid., 82–3.

15 Berque and Miron continued their relationship through correspondence. See ANQ, Gaston Miron fonds, 410/004/033. See also Jean-Christian Pleau, *La Révolution québécoise*, 165–70.

16 Jacques Berque, "Les révoltés du Québec" *France Observateur* (10 octobre 1963). ANQ, Gaston Miron fonds, 410/004/033. Also see Deleuze, *L'une et l'autre indépendance*, 175.

17 See UQAM, Charles Gagnon fonds, 124p–202a/19, Pierre Vallières, "Nous voulons une révolution globale au Québec" in *Combat* no. 8180 (4 novembre 1970). For Albert Memmi's reflections on this phenomenon, see "Les Canadiens français sont-ils des colonisés?" in *Portrait du colonisé*. For a stimulating look at the intellectual exchanges between *Parti Pris* and the French revue *Esprit*, see Stéphanie Angers and Gérard Fabre, *Échanges intellectuels entre la France et le Québec 1930–2000*, 137–53.

18 Pierre Vallières, *White Niggers of America*, trans. Joan Pinkham, 187.

19 Jacques Jourdain, "De Cité Libre à L'urgence de choisir," 21.

20 Pierre Vallières, "Le mythe de l'opulence" *La Presse* (14 août 1963) in *Paroles d'un nègre blanc*, 47.

21 Jean-Marc Piotte, *La communauté perdue*, 43.

22 Interview with Jean-Marc Piotte, 30 October 2006, Montreal

23 There were, of course, those who were not enamoured by de Gaulle's speech, questioning France's economic motives in supporting Quebec independence. See, for example, Luc Racine, "L'inévitable indépendance du Québec: pour qui et au profit de qui?" *Parti Pris* 5, no. 4 (1968): 9–11. By 1970, at least according to the French newspaper *Le Figaro*, many Quebec leftists seemed to have changed their minds and cooled considerably towards de Gaulle. See "De Gaulle vue par les Québécois," *Le Figaro*, 27 octobre 1970, 5. For reassessments of French-Quebec-Canada relations during the period, see David Meren, "Strange Allies" and Robin S. Gendron, *Towards a Francophone Community*.

24 Gilles Bourque, "De Gaulle, politique et stratégie," *Parti Pris* 5, no. 1 (1967): 7.

25 Pierre Renaud and Robert Tremblay, "Les nègres blancs d'Amérique," *Parti Pris* 5, no. 7 (1968): 19.

26 *Parti Pris* 5, no. 1 (septembre 1967).

27 Bourque, "De Gaulle, politique et stratégie," 11.

28 UQAM, Charles Gagnon fonds, 124p–202a/19, Pierre Vallières, "Nous voulons une révolution globale au Québec" in *Combat* 8180 (4 novembre 1970).

29 An excellent study of the way in which Cuba helped to shape the emergence of the American New Left is Van Gosse, *Where the Boys Are*.

30 Richard Gott, *Cuba*, 170. I have drawn on Gott for the details of the revolution.

31 C. Wright Mills, *Listen, Yankee*, 7.

32 Jean-Paul Sartre, *Sartre on Cuba*, 159, 146. See also Simone de Beauvoir, *Force of Circumstance*. For a selection of Sartre's writings published in Cuba, including an interview which he held while in the country, see *Sartre visita a Cuba*.

33 According to Robert Wright, when relations between Cuba and the United States cooled, "Some Canadian politicians and business leaders were unabashed in their enthusiasm for the sudden vacuum in the Cuban market." Robert Wright, *Three Nights in Havana*, 69.

34 Raoul Roy, "La Révolution de Cuba," *La Revue socialiste* 4 (1960): 41-52.

35 Pierre Vallières, *Les Héritiers de Papineau*, 91.

36 See, for example, Fidel Castro, *History Will Absolve Me*.

37 Among the most famous of Guevara's writings was "Notes on Man and Socialism in Cuba." See Ernesto Guevara, *Che Guevara Speaks*.

38 Robert Young, *Postcolonialism*, 192.

39 Pierre Vallières, "Cuba révolutionnaire," *Parti Pris* 5, no. 1 (septembre 1967): 22, 24.

40 Jean Rochefort, "Aux camarades de 'Parti Pris,'" *Révolution québécoise* 1, no. 3 (1964): 13, 15.

41 Philippe Bernard, "Éditorial. Politique internationale: bilan et perspective," *Parti Pris* 5, no. 4 (1968): 6-7.

42 Gabriel Gagnon, "Pour un socialisme décolonisateur," *Parti Pris* 4, no. 1-2 (1966): 52.

43 It was not only in Cuba that Montrealers entered into contact with Cuban officials. In the fall of 1965, a group of Quebec revolutionaries met with Julia Gonzalez, Cuban consul in Montreal. After the Canadian government applied pressure on Cuba, Gonzalez was replaced with a more "neutral" representative. Louis Fournier, *FLQ*, 119.

44 Gott, *Cuba: A New History*, 178.

45 Michel Chartrand, Vernel Olson, and John Riddell, *The Real Cuba as Three Canadians Saw It*, 4.

46 Ibid., 8.

47 Eric Hobsbawm, *Interesting Times*, 258. One Montreal radical, Roger Soublière, wrote of his experiences at the 1968 Havana conference. According to his article, the delegation of fourteen Quebeckers (they were also accompanied by two "Canadians") signed a declaration of solidarity with the struggles of the Third World. Roger Soublière, "Hasta la victoria siempre!" *Parti Pris* 5, no. 7 (1968): 31-2. For interesting reflections on the 1968 conference, and on the experience of foreign radicals in Cuba in general, see Andrew Salkey, *Havana Journal*.

48 Marjolaine Péloquin, *En prison pour la cause des femmes*, 28-9.

49 Canadian intelligence sources have been used most effectively to reconstruct the activities of many Quebec radicals in Cuba in Michael McLoughlin, *Last Stop, Paris*. For one interesting account, see Michèle Tremblay, *De Cuba le FLQ parle*.

50 Cynthia Young, "Havana Up in Harlem." For a brilliant look at the relationship

between one important Black activist and Cuba, see Timothy B. Tyson, *Radio Free Dixie*.

51 Young, "Havana Up in Harlem," 13–14.

52 Frantz Fanon, *The Wretched of the Earth*, trans. Constance Farrington, 40.

53 *Malcolm X Speaks*, 50, 52.

54 Tyson, *Radio Free Dixie*, 221.

55 Seen in Gott, *Cuba: A New History*, 228. A copy of the speech can be found in Stokely Carmichael, *Stokely Speaks*.

56 Young, "Havana Up in Harlem," 22.

57 Roberto Fernández Retamar, *Caliban and Other Essays*, trans. Edward Baker, 16.

58 Quoted in ibid., 45.

59 Fournier, FLQ: *Histoire d'un mouvement clandestin*, 123–4.

60 Vijay Prashad, *The Darker Nations*, 28.

61 See *Malcolm X Speaks*, 53–4. When Vallières arrived in New York everyone was reading Malcolm X and Robert Williams, and he would go on to cite these two authors in his own work. Vallières, *Les Héritiers de Papineau*, 110.

62 See Lettre de Charles Gagnon et Pierre Vallières, rédigée à la suite de leur arrestation à New York, en septembre 1966. "Grève de la Faim pour la reconnaissance 'du crime politique' au Québec (Canada) et du statut de 'prisonnier politiques' pour tous les partisans du FLQ." Reproduced in FLQ: *un projet révolutionnaire*. The letter was also published in the November–December 1966 edition of *Parti Pris*.

63 Vallières, *Les Héritiers de Papineau*, 114–17.

64 Ibid., 126–7, 166.

65 Ibid., 68.

66 Jean-Paul Sartre, Preface to Fanon, *The Wretched of the Earth*, 7.

67 "Manifeste politique: Propositions programmatiques de la REVUE SOCIALISTE," *La Revue socialiste*, no. 1 (1959): 15.

68 Paul Lemoyne, "Travailleurs, aux armes!" *La Cognée* 8 (1964): 3.

69 Gérald Godin, "Le joual politique," *Parti Pris* 2, no. 7 (1965): 59.

70 Bourque, "De Gaulle, Politique et stratégie," 10.

71 André Laurendeau, "Maurice Duplessis à l'Assemblée nationale: la théorie du roi nègre" *Le Devoir* (18 novembre 1958). Also see André Laurendeau, "La théorie du roi nègre – I," *Le Devoir* (4 juillet 1958).

72 "Sur Pierre-E. Trudeau," *Parti Pris* 5, no. 7 (1968): 8.

73 See Norman Mailer, *The White Negro*.

74 See, for example, Noel Ignatiev, *How the Irish Became White*.

75 David R. Roediger, *The Wages of Whiteness*, 68. Noel Ignatiev also notes, when looking at questions of race and ethnicity in the nineteenth century United States, that "in every case, these arguments comparing unprosperous whites with blacks aimed not at broadening the abolitionist vision but at deflecting it." *How the Irish Became White*, 80.

76 While racial metaphors were used in *Parti Pris* and *Révolution québécoise* Gérald

Godin argued that Quebeckers were "les Noirs du Canada," and Jean Rochefort wrote that if American Blacks could produce such a powerful liberation movement, surely "Les nègres blancs du Québec" could do so as well – it was Pierre Vallières who did the most to insert the metaphor into the popular imagination. See Gérald Godin, "La folie bilinguale," *Parti Pris* 3, no. 10 (1966): 56, Jean Rochefort, "Qui sont les traîtres?" *Révolution québécoise* 1, no. 5 (1965): 33.

77 The publication of the interview is a testament to the interconnection of international radical circles during the period. The interview was first published in *Monthly Review*, and appeared in translation in *Révolution*. "Malcolm X parle ..." *Révolution québécoise* 1, no. 3 (1964): 52–7.

78 Key figures in the world of Black Power, such as Malcolm X, began a fascinating reflection on the meaning of racial categories, and especially on the meaning of "whiteness." After returning from his voyage to Mecca in 1964, Malcolm X stated that in "Asia or the Arab world or in Africa, where the Muslims are, if you find one who says he's white, all he's doing is using an adjective to describe something that's incidental about him, one of his incidental characteristics; there is nothing else to it, he's just white." This *meaning* of whiteness, of course, was completely different than the meaning associated to being White in the United States. In America, he argued, when a man "says he's white, he means something else." You can hear in "the sound of his voice – when he says he's white, he means he's boss." *Malcolm X Speaks*, 163.

79 Bill V. Mullen, *Afro-Orientalism*, 78.

80 Vallières, *Les Héritiers de Papineau*, 67.

81 See the footage of Paul Chamberland interviewing Césaire in Jean-Daniel Lafond, *La Manière Nègre, ou Aimé Césaire, chemin faisant* (Canada-France coproduction: ACPAV (Quebec) and RFO (Martinique), 1991).

82 Aimé Césaire, seen in Euzhan Palcy, *Aimé Césaire: A Voice for History, part II* (United States: California Newsreel, 1994).

83 It is interesting to note that when Vallières saw his book advertised under a different title, he immediately wrote to the head of Parti Pris publishing house, Gérald Godin, insisting that his original title be maintained. ANQ, Éditions Parti Pris fonds, MSS-140, 32, Pierre Vallières to Gérald Godin, 24 août 1967.

84 Vallières, *White Niggers of America*, 73, 21, 49.

85 In Gagnon's papers, one can find, for example, issues of *The Black Panther* newspaper, a copy of the speech that Stokely Carmichael gave to the OLAS in Havana in 1967 that attempted to link the Black liberation struggles with struggles in the Third World and, importantly, information on the Sir George Williams Affair. UQAM, Charles Gagnon fonds.

86 See Fournier, *FLQ*, 163. For an interesting look at *Feu sur l'Amérique* and the influence of the American New Left on Gagnon, see Ivan Carel, *"Feu sur l'Amérique."* Also, see Charles Gagnon, *Le Référendum*, 29.

87 UQAM, Charles Gagnon fonds, 124p–203/10, Charles Gagnon, "Feu sur l'Amérique," Propositions pour la révolution nord-américaine. Une Amérique à détruire, une Amérique à bâtir" (August–September 1968), 3–4. This text has recently been republished in Charles Gagnon, *Feu sur l'Amérique.*

88 One hears here an echo of Stokely Carmichael's famous address, "Black Power and the Third World," delivered in Havana in the summer of 1967. According to Carmichael, because "our color has been used as a weapon to oppress us, we must use our color as a weapon of liberation. This is the same as other people using their nationality as a weapon for their liberation." UQAM, Charles Gagnon fonds, 124p–201a. A copy of the speech can also be found in *Stokely Speaks.*

89 See the discussion below on Michèle Lalonde's explosive poem, "Speak White."

90 UQAM, Charles Gagnon fonds, 124p–203/10, Charles Gagnon, "Feu sur l'Amérique," 8.

91 UQAM, Charles Gagnon fonds, 124p–203/10, Charles Gagnon, "Feu sur l'Amérique," 17, 79–81.

92 Vallières, *Les Héritiers de Papineau*, 110.

93 Ibid., 104–5.

94 Pierre Vallières, "Préface (1979). Écrire debout," *Nègres blancs d'Amérique* (Montréal: Typo, 1994), 31.

95 For a selection of these reviews, see ANQ, Éditions Parti Pris fonds, MSS-140, 32

96 Christopher Lehmann-Haupt, "The Making of a Terrorist," *New York Times, Daily Book Review,* (6 April 1971).

97 Regush also stated that *Nègres blancs* "received international attention and Vallières's name became linked with those of Frantz Fanon, Che Guevara, and Eldridge Cleaver. The book has since become a manifesto for the liberty of all oppressed peoples." When he returned to Quebec after his time in New York, he saw the province in a new light: "What I saw was an estranged landscape and a brutalized Quebecois soul." Particularly revealing were Montreal street signs, indicating to him that "Quebec had always been a colony and was one still." Regush, *Pierre Vallières,* 5, 170–4.

98 "En guise de présentation ou d'épilogue à l'édition américaine de 'Nègres blancs d'Amérique'" 9 février 1969, Prison de Montréal. ANQ, Éditions Parti Pris fonds, MSS-140, 32.

99 Seen in Regush, *Pierre Vallières*, 5.

100 Ibid., 6.

101 Gilles Dostaler, "Nègres blancs d'amérique," *Parti Pris* 5, no. 8 (1968): 8.

102 Renaud and Tremblay, "Les nègres blancs d'amérique," 17–25.

103 For details regarding the "Vallières-Gagnon" affair, as well as on the sentences and eventual aquittals, see Fournier, *FLQ*, 156–8.

104 Jacques Thériault, "Les Chansonniers 'noirs' du Québec," *Le Devoir*, 29 mai 1968.

105 Michèle Lalonde, "'Le français' c'est notre couleur noire ...'" *Le Jour*, 1 juin 1974.

106 The poem was published in *Socialisme 68*, see "Speak White," *Socialisme 68*, no. 15 (1968): 19–21.

107 The comparison of the plights of the francophone Quebeckers and American Blacks spread around the world, even finding its way into Eric Williams's history of the Caribbean. See Eric Williams, *From Columbus to Castro*, 506.

108 Bryan Palmer, *Canada's 1960s*, 342–4.

109 Pierre Beaudet, *On a raison de se révolter*, 95.

110 See, for example, "Black Writers Congress: The Organizers Talk…" *The Review* (*McGill Daily Supplement*), 11 October 1968.

111 Vallières, *White Niggers of America*, 21. When Vallières was again making the case for the concept of *nègres blancs* in a documentary film which appeared in the early 1990s, Michaël Jean quickly reminded him that, in Quebec, the "nègres blancs" also had their "nègres noirs." Jean-Daniel Lafond, *La manière nègre*.

112 Dorothy W. Williams, *The Road to Now*, 109.

113 Monique Chénier, "La ségrégation raciale ça existe à Montréal," *Révolution québécoise* 1, no. 8 (1965): 39.

114 Robert [photos by Guy Kosak] Tremblay, "Reportage: les noirs d'ici," *Parti Pris* 5, no. 6 (1968).

115 Ibid., 23.

CHAPTER FOUR

1 By far the most important accounts of Black political organizing in Montreal are those of David Austin in "All Roads Led to Montreal," and Dorothy W. Williams, *The Road to Now*, chapter seven. For a look at the reactions of the French- and English-language media to Black activism, see Marcel Martel, "'S'ils veulent faire la révolution, qu'ils aillent la faire chez eux à leurs risques et périls.'"

2 On the topic of slavery in New France, see Marcel Trudel, *L'esclavage au Canada français*, and (avec la collaboration de Micheline D'Allaire), *Deux siècles d'esclavage au Québec*. Also see Daniel Gay, *Les Noirs du Québec, 1629–1900*, and Sarah-Jane (Saje) Mathieu, "North of the Colour Line." For a discussion of the political organizations of Black women, see Shirley Small and Esmeralda M.A. Thornhill, "HARAMBEC!"

3 Williams, *The Road to Now*, 39. Also see James W. St.G. Walker, *Racial Discrimination in Canada*. For a look at systemic racism in Canada's past, see James W. St.G. Walker, *'Race,' Rights and the Law in the Supreme Court of Canada*.

4 David Austin, "Contemporary Montréal and the 1968 Congress of Black Writers," *Lost Histories* 1998, 59.

5 For an outline of the history and outlook of the NCA, see Richard E. Leslie, "Editorial," *Expression* 1, no. 1 (1965): 5.

6 While divisions existed within the larger community, all groups shared common

experiences of racism in Canadian society. According to James Walker, "When white Canadians express discriminatory tendencies they do so on the basis of colour, making colour a unifying characteristic for West Indians of African descent and giving them a community of experience with other black Canadians. Even the Haitians, who are distinguishable by language, report strikingly similar experiences to those of their anglophone counterparts." James W. St.-G. Walker, *The West Indians in Canada*, 20.

7 Williams, *The Road to Now*, 111, as well as chapter seven.

8 Micheline Labelle, Serge Larose, and Victor Piché, "Politique d'immigration et immigration en provenance de la Caraibe anglophone au Canada et au Québec, 1900–1979," 8–11.

9 Williams, *The Road to Now*, 100.

10 According to David Austin, in "the 1960s and 1970s, the Roberts' apartment on Bedford Street in the Côte-des-Neiges district of Montreal was a political stomping ground where books could be borrowed by friends, Caribbean students, political activists, and aspiring politicians. It was a place where dusk till dawn discussions were held on a wide array of subjects, and where political strategies were mapped out. Alfie and his wife Patricia hosted many sessions in their Montreal home, earning it the name 'The University of Bedford,' and many people, including several future Caribbean prime ministers, came of age politically in their living room." David Austin, "Introduction," in *A View for Freedom*, 20.

11 Alfie Roberts, *A View for Freedom*, 77.

12 Robert Hill, "The Caribbean Island of Montreal: The Caribbean Conference Committee and the Black Radical tradition" at REBELLION, PROTEST, AND CHANGE: *Reflections on the 1960s and the Development of Montreal's Black Community*, 18 February 2006, UNIA Hall, Montreal. Videorecording (available through the Alfie Roberts' Institute, Montreal).

13 Audio recording of George Lamming's address at the 1965 Conference on West Indian Affairs at the Université de Montréal. My thanks to Anne Cools for providing me with this recording.

14 For a vivid description of the conference committee, and a discussion of the political atmosphere in Black Montreal during the 1960s, see Roberts, *A View for Freedom*, 65–73. According to Austin, "It was as a result of the CCWIA activities in Montreal that James was eventually permitted to re-enter the United States for the first time since his expulsion in 1953. James returned to Montreal for the Congress of Black Writers in October 1968 and on several other occasions between 1968 and the early seventies." *A View for Freedom*, editorial note, 72.

15 Jeffrey O.G. Ogbar, *Black Power*, 197. This new outlook is articulated in King's speech against the Vietnam War, "Beyond Vietnam: A Time to Break Silence," delivered at the Riverside Church in New York City on 4 April 1967. Also, in "Black Power Defined," appearing in the *New York Times Magazine*, King argued that

"We must frankly acknowledge that in past years our creativity and imagination were not employed in learning how to develop power." And, he went on, it was now necessary to "take the next major step of examining the levers of power which Negroes must grasp to influence the course of events." Both of these texts are reproduced in Martin Luther King, *I Have a Dream.*

16 For just one example of an author who argues for a re-examination of the divisions between the Civil Rights and Black Power movements, see Timothy B. Tyson, *Radio Free Dixie.*

17 Ogbar, *Black Power*, 156.

18 For a moving account of one person's journey through the Civil Rights movement and its aftermath, see the epilogue to John Howard Griffin, *Black Like Me.* For some of the main arguments of the emerging Black Power movement, see Stokely Carmichael and Charles V. Hamilton, *Black Power.*

19 Clayborne Carson, *In Struggle*, 288.

20 Quoted in Bill Bantey, "Montreal Mourned and Cried with Black and White Together," *The Montreal Gazette*, 8 April 1968, 13.

21 "Editorial," *Expression* 3, no. 1 (1968): 3–5.

22 "Sir George hosts Black conference," *The Georgian*, 1 October 1968, 3. Dennis Forsythe, "The Black Writers Conference: Days to Remember," in *Let the Niggers Burn!*, 58–9, Williams, *The Road to Now*, 118–19.

23 John Shingler, "Panel Discussion," *Expression* 3, no. 3 (1969): 21.

24 McCurdy also spoke of the necessity of forming an alliance with "the Indians," their natural allies. Howard McCurdy, "Problems of Involvement in the Canadian Society with Reference to Black People," *Expression* 3, no. 3 (1969): 13–14, Daniel Hill, "Panel Discussion," *Expression* 3, no. 3 (1969): 18. McCurdy was not alone in his defence of Native Canadians. Montreal economist Barry Mayers spoke of the necessity of confronting discrimination on all fronts, for, "if we can justify discrimination, either by silence or otherwise, of the Indians, of the Eskimos, of the French Canadians, of the English Canadians, then there is no reason why the society can't justify discrimination against Negroes." The problem was largely one of poverty, and the Canadian population "will never get any kind of meaningful involvement unless we change the whole social structure of the Canadian Society and so make it possible to remove from isolation not only the Negro but the Indian, the Eskimo and, in a general sense, the entire population." Barry Myers, "Panel Discussion," *Expression* 3, no. 3 (1969): 25–6.

25 Forsythe, "The Black Writers Conference," 60.

26 Stanley Aleong, "'Dynamique de la libération noire': Congrès des écrivains noirs– McGill, 11–14 octobre," *Le Quartier latin*, 8 Octobre 1968, 12.

27 "Black Power Is Coming," *McGill Daily*, 27 September 1968, 1. The McGill West Indian Society was not pleased, however, by the fact that the *Daily* described the conference as a "Black Power conference" and demanded a retraction, to which the *Daily* consented. "Letter to the Editor," *McGill Daily*, 9 October 1968.

28 Leroy Butcher, "The Sir George Williams Affair and Its Aftermath" "REBELLION, PROTEST, AND CHANGE: *Reflections on the 1960s and the Development of Montreal's Black Community*, 18 February 2006, UNIA Hall, Montreal. Videorecording.

29 UQAM, Gérald Godin fonds, 81p–660:02a/16, Elder Thebaud and Rosie Douglas, "Editorial," Souvenir Program of Congress of Black Writers, held at McGill University 11–14 October 1968.

30 UQAM, Gérald Godin fonds, 81p–660:02a/16, Souvenir Program of Conference on Black Writers, held at McGill University 11–14 October 1968.

31 Austin, "Contemporary Montréal and the 1968 Congress of Black Writers," 58.

32 Forsythe, "The Black Writers Conference," 63.

33 Austin, "All Roads Led to Montreal," 523.

34 Cited in ibid.

35 UQAM, Gérald Godin fonds, 81p–660:02a/16, Letter signed by the Negro Community Centre Inc., Negro Theatre Arts Club, Montreal Negro Alumni Group, The Jamaica Association of Montreal, Canadian Conference Committee (Black Organisations), and the Trinidad and Tobago Association (Montreal).

36 An edited version of Forman's speech can be found in James Forman, "Black Writers Hail Frantz Fanon," *Guardian*, 23 November 1968, 20–1.

37 Mike Boone, "Stokely Preaches Violent Revolution," *McGill Daily*, 15 October 1968, 2.

38 Forsythe, "The Black Writers Conference," 62.

39 Boone, "Stokely preaches violent revolution," 1.

40 See the account of Ekwueme Michael Thelwell in *Ready for Revolution*, 544.

41 Quoted in Austin, "All Roads Led to Montreal," 525.

42 Interview with Stanley Gray, 10 June 2005, Hamilton.

43 Gérald Godin, "La folie bilinguale," *Parti Pris* 3, no. 10 (1966): 56.

44 Austin, "Contemporary Montréal and the 1968 Congress of Black Writers."

45 UQAM, Gérald Godin fonds, 81p–660:02a/16, Souvenir Program of Conference on Black Writers, held at McGill University 11–14 October 1968.

46 UQAM, Gérald Godin fonds, 81p–660:02a/16, untitled memo, Gérald Godin, 16 octobre 1968.

47 Barbara Jones, "A Black Woman Speaks Out," *McGill Reporter*, 4 November 1968.

48 Forsythe, "The Black Writers Conference," 62–6.

49 Ibid., 64.

50 Editors, "Black Militants and Red Guards," *McGill Reporter*, 4 November 1968, 1.

51 Rosie Douglas, Rita Sherman, and Robert Chodos, "No Time for Coalitions," *McGill Daily*, 21 October 1968, 5.

52 The Congress of Black Writers also had important international ramifications. The international nature of the struggle was made clear when Walter Rodney, lecturer at the University of the West Indies in Jamaica, was banned from returning to Jamaica after his appearance at the conference in Montreal. News of the ban quickly spread to Jamaica, where angry crowds took to the streets. Police unleashed

clouds of tear gas, and made generous use of guns and clubs. The riots left down-town Kingston in shambles; fifty buses were burned, and three people were killed in the confrontations. At a mass rally held at Sir George Williams University in sup-port of Rodney, Rodney himself took to the podium. He insisted that the violence was not a mere student uprising, but was a "revolutionary manifestation of social malaise" on the part of the entire population of Kingston. The audience listened intensely as Rodney spoke of his dedication to working with lower class Blacks. These people, he stated, humbled him with their knowledge about heritage and cul-ture, and about the beauty of Black people. The audience, clearly moved, repeat-edly broke into enthusiastic applause, and when Rodney concluded his speech by saying that they will "celebrate victory with black drums," the crowd burst into a standing ovation. Robert Wallace, "Local rally supports Jamaican students," *McGill Daily*, 21 October 1968, 1. It should be noted as well that after the Congress of Black Writers, Bobby Seale of the Black Panthers came to the city for the Hemispheric Conference to End the War in Vietnam at the end of November 1968. "Bobby Seale Makes It …" *McGill Daily*, 2 December 1968, 3.

53 "SGWU Hearing Folds: 200 Students Occupy Computing Center," *McGill Daily*, 30 January 1969, 1.

54 Rosie Douglas received an eighteen-month sentence, and Anne Cools a four-month sentence. Austin, "All Roads Led to Montreal," 531–2.

55 Carl Lumumba, "The West Indies and the Sir George Williams Affair: An Assess-ment," in *Let the Niggers Burn!*, 179.

56 See Ibid., 181, Austin, "Introduction," n12.

57 According to the editors of *UHURU*, "most" of the students arrested were Black, but Blacks comprised only forty-two of the ninety-seven people arrested. See "Edito-rial: Deep Ramifications," *UHURU*, 16 February 1970, 2. The event has received vir-tually no attention in works dealing with the Quiet Revolution.

58 The Sir George Williams Affair had ramifications that spread far beyond the Cana-dian border, initiating a series of political revolts throughout the Caribbean. See *Let the Niggers Burn!*

59 Roberts, *A View for Freedom*, 57–8.

60 Ibid., 73, 81–2.

61 Austin, "Contemporary Montréal and the 1968 Congress of Black Writers," 59. In both the short and medium term aftermath to the incidents of 11 February, many different groups began speaking up against the racist backlash that was occurring. The West Indian Students Association, for example, wrote that "We cannot accept the hysterical cries of 'hoodlums,' 'rioters,' 'dangerous agitators,' 'foreigners,' 'Red Chinese agents,' and 'let the niggers burn.' We reject the overt racism and anti-student sentiment comparable in many ways to the witch-hunt atmosphere of McCarthyism in the early 1950's." WRDA, Anderson Affair Fonds. West Indian Stu-dents Association memo, n.d.

62 Gilroy, *"There Ain't No Black in the Union Jack,"* 27.

63 Ibid., 11, 38.

64 See *The Georgian*, 4 February 1969.

65 For examples of this backlash, see the many articles in the 19 February 1969 edition of *The Georgian*.

66 For an example of a West Indian student speaking about how many West Indian students were opposed to the occupation, see A.R. Ali, "The Price of Courage to Disagree," *The Georgian*, 19 February 1969, 8.

67 "SGWU pulls out of UGEQ," *McGill Daily*, 17 February 1969, 1. Also, see "Fired Georgian Editor to Receive CUP Verdict," *McGill Daily*, 26 February 1969, 3. For the letter from the "radical faculty," see CUA, Dr Marsden Papers, Statements, "An Open Letter to Leftwing Faculty and Students at Sir George Williams University from a Group of Radical Professors," 1969. Also see Eugene Genovese, *In Red and Black*, v–vi.

68 Presse release, "Sir George Williams et le cas de Charles Gagnon: les Deux Masques de la Répression," 21 février 1969. ASCN, CCSNM, publications. On the occasion of a conference held on the twentieth anniversary of the Sir George Affair, on 11 February 1989, Michel Chartrand gave a paper entitled "The Affair and Quebec's National Question." See "The Computer Centre Incident 20 Years Later: Feb. 11, 1969–Feb. 11, 1989," Alfie Roberts Institute, Montreal.

69 Roméo Bouchard, "Vous êtes des nègres," *Le Quartier latin*, 11 février 1969, 2.

70 Kenneth-Charles De Puis, Jacques Michon, and Pierre Larivière, "On soutient toujours son frère et sa soeur," *Le Quartier latin*, 25 février 1969, 12.

71 Jacques Maassen, "Values and the Computer," *McGill Daily*, 14 February 1969, 4.

72 Dorothy Eber, *The Computer Centre Party*, 271, 220.

73 Ibid., 152, 157.

74 Leroy Butcher, "The Sir George Williams Affair and Its Aftermath."

75 Williams, *The Road to Now*, 121.

76 Dennis Forsythe, "By Way of Introduction: 'The Sir George Williams Affair'," in *Let the Niggers Burn!*, 8.

77 "Editorial. Canadian Liberalism: Fact or Fiction," *Expression* 3, no. 3 (1969): 3–6.

78 See Caribbean International Service Bureau, "Black Spark Edition," *McGill Free Press: Black Spark Edition* (1971): 1.

79 Leroy Butcher, "The Sir George Williams Affair and Its Aftermath."

80 Brenda Dash, "Thursday Night Rally Re-Opens," *UHURU*, 12 January 1970, 7.

81 See Austin, "All Roads Led to Montreal: Black Power, the Caribbean, and the Black Radical Tradition in Canada," 535.

82 For an overview of many of these developments, see Williams, *The Road to Now*, chapter seven.

83 Because of its radical tone, *UHURU* did not, of course, speak for all of Montreal's Black community. At the first national meeting of the Canadian Conference Committee in Toronto in October 1969, a major confrontation erupted between Mon-

treal radicals – demanding that the fallout of the Sir George Williams Affair be discussed as a priority – and other Black organizations. Through the pages of the new publication *Umoja*, a frustration with those involved in the Sir George Williams Affair was palpable. According to Clarence S. Bayne, "a black community cannot be built on the basis of people who are continually living in a state of returning to the West Indies, who are not committed to making this country theirs." "Editorial Note: Black Unity," *Umoja* 1, no. 1 (1969): 1, "A Programme of Action for the National Black Coalition," *Umoja* 1, no. 2 (1969): 1, 4. C.S. Bayne, "A Report on the Canadian Conference Committee," *Umoja* 1, no. 1 (1969): 3.

84 "Focus on Uhuru," *UHURU*, 8 December 1969, 4. Omowale, "The Brother on the Corner," *UHURU*, 31 July 1969, 5.

85 The print run of *Parti Pris* in the mid-1960s stood at roughly 4,000. "Lettre au lecteur," *Parti Pris* 2, no. 1 (1964): 18.

86 "Focus on Uhuru," 4.

87 Stokely Carmichael and Miriam Carmichael, "Letter to the Editor," *UHURU*, 2 February 1970, 2.

88 "Focus on Uhuru," 4–5.

89 In an October 1968 publication by members of the Conference Committee meant to coincide with the Congress of Black Writers, several authors spoke of the neo-colonial role that Canadian capital and Canadian companies played in the Caribbean. See, for example, A. Eustace, "On the Economism of the 'Movement ... As the West Indian Society for the Study of Social Issues'," *Caribbean International Opinion: Dynamics of Liberation* 1, no. 1 (1968): 26–31, Feleon, "On Haiti," *Caribbean International Opinion: Dynamics of Liberation* 1, no. 1 (1968): 61–4.

90 Powerful analyses of race and of the connections between Canada and the Caribbean sometimes even made their way into mainstream leftist writing. "SGWU Blacks Get a Taste of Just Society," *The Last Post* 1, no. 3 (1970): 5–7.

91 "Sir George and O'Brien," *UHURU*, 18 August 1969, 1.

92 LeRoi Butcher, "The Anderson Affair," in *Let the Niggers Burn!*, 106.

93 Rosie Douglas, "Solidarity Day against Canadian Racism and Beyond," *UHURU*, 23 March 1970, 4.

94 Frantz Fanon, *Black Skin, White Masks*, trans. Charles Lam Markmann, 190.

95 "The Sixties: Revolution or Evolution?," *UHURU*, 12 January 1970, 4.

96 His title drew explicitly on a chapter from *Black Skin, White Masks*. Maurice Tremblay, "The Facts of Blackness," *UHURU*, 1 June 1970, 6–8.

97 See, for example, Omowale, "The Need for a Black United Front in Montreal," *UHURU*, 18 July 1969, 4.

98 Williams, *The Road to Now*, 109.

99 For Howard McCurdy, "[w]e cannot look at black power as based on numbers in this country." McCurdy, "Problems of Involvement in the Canadian Society with Reference to Black People," 14.

100 Rosie Douglas, "Stokely Carmichael Returns to U.S.," *UHURU*, 13 April 1970, 1.

101 See *UHURU*, 31 July 1969, 5, and 2 September 1969.

102 See *UHURU*, 12 January 1970.

103 Edmund Michael, "'Red Power in Canada'," *UHURU*, 29 September 1969, 3.

104 Ibid.

105 "Check Point: Montreal," *UHURU*, 12 January 1970, 6.

106 Asher, "Red Nationalism on the Rise," *UHURU*, 2 March 1970. The 12 January 1970 edition of the paper also noted the occupation of Alcatraz Island in San Francisco Bay.

107 At a meeting held at Sir George Williams University in November 1968, for example, American Civil Rights activist Floyd McKissick and history professor Arvarh Strickland spoke to a crowd of two hundred students, and were immediately asked whether the plight of Blacks could be related to the struggles of francophone Quebeckers in Canada. McKissick, clearly caught off guard, could only muster a confused reply. According to the *Georgian*, "Mr. McKissick replied that his concern was with the immediate, local racial problems and that he considered racism to differ from region to region, not necessarily along Marxist class lines." "'White Racist System Ain't Healthy for Whites or Blacks'–McKissick," *The Georgian*, 26 November 1968, 6.

108 Rosie Douglas, "Black Writers Congress: The Organizers talk…" *The Review* (*McGill Daily supplement*), 11 October 1968, 2.

109 Elder Thébaud, "Black Writers Congress: The Organizers Talk…," 4–5.

110 Douglas, "Black Writers Congress: The Organizers Talk…" 5.

111 ASCN, CCSNM fonds, Congrès 1969, Fernand Foisy, "Rappord du sécrétaire – décisions du comité exécutif," 19.

112 Sister Obiageli, "Thursday Night Rally Revival!" *UHURU*, 2 March 1970, 6.

113 "C.B.C. Use Innocent Black Children," *UHURU*, 27 April 1970, 1, 8.

114 Charles, "Black Children and Bilingualism," *UHURU*, 13 April 1970, 7.

115 "Editorial," *UHURU*, 27 April 1970, 2.

116 "Editorial," *UHURU*, 11 May 1970, 2. For a more radical position which rejects the PQ, advocating instead the ideas of Quebec decolonization associated with Charles Gagnon and Pierre Vallières, see Rosie Douglas, "The Irrelevance of the Quebec Elections," *UHURU*, 27 April 1970, 6.

117 Dennis Forsythe, "Preface," in *Let the Niggers Burn!*, 3.

118 Forsythe, "By Way of Introduction: 'The Sir George Williams Affair'," 10.

119 Ibid., 14, 12.

120 Bureau, "Black Spark Edition," 1.

121 Butcher, "The Anderson Affair," 77.

122 Winston Franco, "Two Views of the Conference of Black Writers – II," *Expression* 3, no. 3 (1969): 43–4.

123 Omowale, "Respectable Faces Students Twelve Charges," *UHURU*, 18 August 1969, 7.

124 Seen in Eber, *The Computer Centre Party*, 126.

125 "Dear Brother Black," UHURU, 14 October 1969, 6.

126 Quoted in Austin, "Introduction," editorial note, 21.

127 "Dear Brother," UHURU, 22 December 1969, 6.

128 "Letter to the Editor," UHURU, 8 December 1969, 2.

129 "Letter to the Editor," UHURU, 24 November 1969, 2.

130 A Black Sister, "Dear Sister," UHURU, 15 September 1969, 6.

131 "Letter to the Editor," UHURU, 8 December 1969, 2.

132 According to Akua Benjamin, who arrived to Toronto from Trinidad in the middle of Toronto's radical upsurge: "Anne Cools came to one of these meetings, and she blasted the men. She challenged us women in the room as to why we were not talking. In those days, I just sat quietly in the back of the room. I would sit there and sweat. I was afraid to speak, afraid that I would get shut down. Anne cursed the men out, saying, 'fucking' this and 'fucking' that. We had never heard a woman talk like that. She really empowered me. After that I thought, 'I'm going to raise my voice.'" Quoted in Judy Rebick, *Ten Thousand Roses*, 9–10.

CHAPTER FIVE

1 Solange Chalvin, "Le Front commun des Québécoises descendra dans la rue, ce soir," *Le Devoir*, 28 novembre 1969. The Montreal Central Council of the CSN both approved of and collaborated with the protestors. See ACSN, CCSNM fonds, Foisy, "Rapport du sécrétaire," Congrès 1970, 39. At its general assembly held at the beginning of December 1969, the organization unanimously passed a proposal "D'appuyer et de féliciter le Front Commun des Québécoises pour leur manifestation du 28 novembre 1969." ACSN, CCSNM fonds, Procès-Verbaux, Assemblé Général, 2 décembre 1969, 113.

2 Conférence de presse du Front commun des Québécoises, 28 novembre 1969. Cited in Véronique O'Leary and Louise Toupin, *Québécoises deboutte!* vol. 1, [hereafter QDI] 55.

3 Ibid.

4 FLF, "FLFQ: Historique," été 1970. QDI, 65–6.

5 CWMA, Box 31, "Revolution in the Revolution: second manifesto by a collective of women in the Front de liberation des femmes Québecoises," Montreal, September 1971, 1. For a discussion of the interrelated nature of feminism and other movements, see bell hooks, *Feminist Theory: From Margin to Center*.

6 For a brilliant new look at feminism in the United States which explores the contributions of those outside the self-defined women's liberation movement, see Anne Enke, *Finding the Movement*.

7 For a discussion of the changing lives of women in the postwar period, see Clio Collective, *Quebec Women: A History*, as well as Denyse Bailargeon, *Un Québec en mal*

d'enfants. For a discussion of women's activism in Quebec's unions, see Mona-Josée Gagnon, "Women in the Trade-Union Movement in Quebec," in *Quebec since 1945*.

8 For a brief exploration of the history of Black women's activism in Quebec, see Shirley Small and Esmeralda M.A. Thornhill, "HARAMBEC!"

9 See Irène Demczuk and Frank W. Remiggi, eds., *Sortir de l'ombre*, as well as Viviane Namaste, *C'était du spectacle!*

10 For details regarding the organizational histories of these two groups, see O'Leary and Toupin, *QDI*. For a detailed look at the FLF, see Marjolaine Péloquin, *En prison pour la cause des femmes*.

11 Micheline de Sève, "Féminisme et nationalisme au Québec, une alliance inatten-due," 159.

12 Violette Brodeur et al., *Le Mouvement des femmes au Québec*, 27, and Micheline Dumont, "The Origins of the Women's Movement in Québec," in *Challenging Times*, 86.

13 Lucie Piché, "Entre l'accès à l'égalité et la préservation des modèles," 189.

14 Judy Rebick, *Ten Thousand Roses*, 3–4. Quebec Voice of Women members, Brief to the Royal Commission on the Status of Women, May 1968, 1. Also, see Simone Monet-Chartrand, *Les Québécoises et le mouvement pacifiste (1939–1967)*. For Monet-Chartrand's more general reflections on women's activism, see *Pionnières québécoises et regroupements de femmes d'hier à aujourd'hui*.

15 Micheline Dumont, *Le féminisme québécois raconté à Camille*, 109–10.

16 For an interesting look at the conditions which led to the establishment of the Royal Commission, see Monique Bégin, "The Royal Commission on the Status of Women in Canada: Twenty Years Later," in *Challenging Times*, 22–4.

17 See Simone de Beauvoir, *The Second Sex*, trans. H.M. Parshley, and Betty Friedan, *The Feminine Mystique*.

18 See Quebec Voice of Women members, Brief to the Royal Commission on the Status of Women, May 1968, 2; Confederation of National Trade Unions (CNTU), confederation des Syndicats Nationaux (CSN), Brief to the Royal Commission on the Status of Women, June 1968; the Young Men's and Young Women's Hebrew Association and Neighbourhood House Services, Montreal, to the Royal Commission on the Status of Women, 11 April 1968.

19 Brief of the Marriage Counselling Centre of Montreal, Royal Commission on the Status of Women, April 1968.

20 Medical Students' Society, McGill University, Montreal, Brief to the Royal Commission on the Status of Women, May 1968, 1, 13.

21 *Le Centre de Planification familiale*, Montreal, Brief to the Royal Commission on the Status of Women, 14 June 1968, 1–2, 14–15, 21.

22 "How to Play the Game ... of Being a Woman," *The Review* (*McGill Daily supplement*), 1 November 1968.

23 For examples of radical women writing in the *McGill Daily* in 1968, see Myrna Wood and Marsha Taubenhaus, "The Doll House, Revisited: Further Notes on the Condition of Women in Our Society," *The Review* (*McGill Daily supplement*), 22 November 1968, 7, and Martine Eloy, "Woman: Why Is She?" *The Review* (*McGill Daily supplement*), 6 December 1968, 5.

24 See Bryan Palmer, *Canada's 1960s*, 297–304.

25 Myrna Wood and Kathy McAffee, "Her Only Real Fulfillment Is Supposed to Come from Her Role as Girlfriend, Wife or Mother," in *McGill Student Handbook*, 72.

26 Donna Cherniak and Allan Feingold, "Introduction," *Birth Control Handbook* 6th edition, 3.

27 Donna Cherniak and Allan Feingold, "Birth Control Handbook (1971)," in *Women Unite!* 109–10. Susan Brownmiller talks of the handbook being distributed as far away as Austin, Texas. See *In Our Time*, 119.

28 Marie Henretta, "The Oppression of Women in Canada," *Montreal Women's Liberation Newsletter*, March 1970, no. 1.

29 Martine Lanctôt, "La genèse et l'évolution du mouvement de libération des femmes à Montréal, 1969–1979," 52.

30 Ibid., 53.

31 For an important look at the movement in the United States, see Alice Echols, *Daring to be Bad*.

32 Brownmiller, *In Our Time*, 41.

33 Henretta, "The Oppression of Women in Canada."

34 According to Geoff Eley, the "'personal' meant less an individualistic private domain than the contexts of everydayness – the quotidian and the local." This was a form of politics in which old ideas of the "Party" played no role, and in which "[p]lurality and flexibility were the rule." Geoff Eley, *Forging Democracy*, 372.

35 Henretta, "The Oppression of Women in Canada."

36 "Art through Revolution through Art," *Montreal Women's Liberation Newsletter*, June 1970, 5.

37 Henretta, "The Oppression of Women in Canada," 1–2.

38 Cherniak and Feingold, "Introduction," *Birth Control Handbook* 7th edition, 2.

39 Cherniak and Feingold, "Introduction," *Birth Control Handbook* 6th edition, 2–3.

40 Cherniak and Feingold, "Introduction," *Birth Control Handbook* 7th edition, 4. According to Christabelle Sethna, the politicized editorial content of the handbook sparked such a controversy that the "Royal Victoria Hospital, the Montreal General Hospital, the Family Planning Association of Montreal and Dialogue, an interdenominational organization that distributed contraception information, returned a total of 3,000 *Handbooks*. The town of Pembroke, Ontario banned the publication. In the United States, the city of Miami, Florida did the same. Copies were burned in Missoula, Montana." A controversy even broke out at Princeton over

allegations that the handbook was Maoist propaganda. Christabelle Sethna, "The Evolution of the *Birth Control Handbook*," 102.

41 Cherniak and Feingold, "Birth Control Handbook (1971)," 111.

42 Henretta, "The Oppression of Women in Canada," 2.

43 L. Wynn, "The Pill Scare," *Montreal Women's Liberation Newsletter*, March 1970, no. 1, 5.

44 Lanctôt, "La genèse et l'évolution du mouvement de libération des femmes à Montréal, 1969–1979," 58. See also, "F.L.F.Q. Historique," été 1970, QDI, 65.

45 Péloquin, *En prison pour la cause des femmes*, 29.

46 Ibid., 34.

47 Lanctôt, "La genèse et l'évolution du mouvement de libération des femmes à Montréal, 1969–1979," 56.

48 Cherniak and Feingold, "Birth Control Handbook (1971)," 110, Lanctôt, "La genèse et l'évolution du mouvement de libération des femmes à Montréal, 1969–1979," 63. Lanctôt maintains that the centre was opened due to the financial help of Dr Morgentaler. For an important look at the battle for abortion rights in Quebec, see Louise Desmarais, *Mémoires d'une bataille inachevée*.

49 Claude-Lyse Gagnon, "Le Front de libération des femmes prépare l'escalade," *La Patrie*, 7 mars 1971.

50 O'Leary and Toupin, *Québécoises deboutte!*, 81.

51 "Bulletin de liaison FLFQ," no. 1, juillet 1971, QDI, 102, and O'Leary and Toupin *Québécoises deboutte!*, 98.

52 Guy Deshaies, "Un commando féminin prend d'assaut la tribune des jurés," *Le Devoir*, 2 mars 1971, 1–2. See Péloquin, *En prison pour la cause des femmes*.

53 "F.L.F.Q. Fonctionnement" été 1970, QDI, 67.

54 Péloquin, *En prison pour la cause des femmes*, 245.

55 Women have also been involved in the long history of the left in Quebec before the 1960s. See Andrée Lévesque, *Red Travellers*, Thérèse F. Casgrain, *A Woman in a Man's World*, Susan Mann Trofimenkoff, "Thérèse Casgrain and the CCF in Québec," and Simone Monet-Chartrand, *Ma vie comme rivière*.

56 "Art through Revolution through Art," 5.

57 Sara Evans, *Personal Politics*, 220, 214–15.

58 See the many testimonies reproduced in Péloquin, *En prison pour la cause des femmes*.

59 Note de l'éditeur, un groupe de femmes de Montréal, *Manifeste des femmes québécoises*, 7.

60 Un groupe de femmes de Montréal, *Manifeste des femmes québécoises*, 11–23.

61 Ibid., 12.

62 Ibid., 22–4.

63 Ibid., 38–51.

64 "F.L.F.Q. Historique," été 1970, QDI, 65–6.

65 FLF, "Bulletin de Liaison FLFQ – cellule journal," no. 2, août 1971, QDI, 117.

66 "Introduction," *Pour un contrôle des naissances* (2ᵉ édition, Montréal, février 1971), 3.

67 For a look at gender in the work of Vallières, see Katherine Roberts, "'Mère, je vous hais!'"

68 Quoted in "Introduction," *Pour un contrôle des naissances*, 3.

69 Ibid.

70 FLF, "FLFQ: Historique," été 1970, QDI, 66.

71 FLF, "Bulletin de Liaison FLFQ – cellule journal," no. 2, août 1971, QDI, 115.

72 Péloquin, *En prison pour la cause des femmes*, 256.

73 Véronique O'Leary et Louise Toupin, "Nous sommes le produit d'un contexte," QDI 27.

74 Front de libération des femmes du Québec, "Lettre à des féministes américaines," 4 décembre 1970, QDI, 80.

75 FLF, "Bulletin de Liaison FLFQ – cellule journal," no. 2, août 1971, QDI, 117.

76 FLF, "Bulletin de Liaison FLFQ – ex-cellule 'X' et cellule 'O comme dans vulve,'" no. 2, août 1971, QDI, 119.

77 "Bulletin de liaison FLFQ – cellule garderie," no. 2, août 1971, QDI, 118.

78 "Bulletin de liaison FLFQ – ex-cellule 'X' et Cellule 'O come dans vulve,'" no. 2, août 1971, QDI, 120.

79 O'Leary and Toupin, *Québécoises deboutte!*, 74–5.

80 FLF, Press Release 8 mai 1970, Montréal, QDI, 71.

81 Véronique O'Leary et Louise Toupin, "Un bilan de parcours," QDI, 76–7. At this time, the main theoretical influences on the francophone members of the group were Simone de Beauvoir's *The Second Sex*, Betty Friedan's *The Feminine Mystique*, and *The Origin of the Family, Private Property and the State* by Friedrich Engels. It was not until the beginning of 1971 that they received copies of the special issue of the French journal *Partisans* on women's liberation containing French feminist texts. See Péloquin, *En prison pour la cause des femmes*, 32.

82 Véronique O'Leary et Louise Toupin, "Un bilan de parcours," QDI, 76–7. For a slightly different take on the FLF's decision to expel its anglophone members, see Péloquin, *En prison pour la cause des femmes*, 258–60.

83 Heather Jon Maroney, "Contemporary Quebec Feminism," 251.

84 For a summary of the ideological differences within the different groups of the FLF, see "Bulletin de liaison FLFQ," no. 2, août 1971, QDI. Lanctôt, "La genèse et l'évolution du mouvement de libération des femmes à Montréal, 1969–1979," 77–81.

85 Péloquin, *En prison pour la cause des femmes*, 240.

86 "Bulletin de liaison FLFQ – cellule II," no. 2, août 1971, QDI, 111–12.

87 Ibid., 114. Cellule cinéma-animation-formation.

88 "Bulletin de liaison FLFQ – ex-cellule 'X' et cellule 'O comme dans vulve,'" no. 2, août 1971, QDI, 119.

89 Clio Collective, *Quebec Women*, 360. Heather Jon Maroney estimates that a total of roughly two hundred women attended the FLF's meetings. See "Contemporary Quebec Feminism," 249.

90 Péloquin, *En prison pour la cause des femmes*, 238.

91 Louis Fournier, *Louis Laberge*, 202–6.

92 Pierre Vennat, "2,000 Québécois portent Michèle Gautheir en terre," *Le Quotidien Populaire*, 3 novembre 1971, 16.

93 Péloquin, *En prison pour la cause des femmes*, 244–5.

94 Marjolaine Péloquin discusses how some women who had originated in the left before coming to the FLF brought feminists analyses with them when they returned to their old groups. Ibid., 240–7.

95 Dumont, *Le féminisme québécois raconté à Camille*, 137–63.

96 Even the *Birth Control Handbook* maintained silence about homosexuality until 1973. Sethna, "The Evolution of the *Birth Control Handbook*," 104. For a study of lesbianism in Montreal from 1950–72, see Line Chamberland, *Mémoires lesbiennes*, and Irène Demczuk and Frank W. Remiggi, eds., *Sortir de l'ombre*. Marjolaine Péloquin describes FLF members' shock when they encountered the lesbian subculture of jail, and notes their lack of understanding of the discrimination faced by lesbians in society generally. Péloquin, *En prison pour la cause des femmes*, 82.

CHAPTER SIX

1 Pierre Godin refers to the language question of the period as a "poudrière linguistique" in his book of that title.

2 As I hope to demonstrate, in the late 1960s "Language" became a lightning rod that focused debates about cultural and economic power.

3 "Montreal's Diagram for Defence," *Canadian Magazine*, 7 June 1969, 2, Robert Chodos, "Hitting a Sore Spot," *McGill Daily* (*extra*), 2 April 1969, 4, "L'opération McGill coûtera aux contribuables de $50,000 à $100,000," *Le Devoir*, 31 mars 1969, 1, Peter Allnutt and Robert Chodos, "Quebec: Into the Streets," *Radical America* 6, no. 5 (1972): 43, and François Barbeau, Jean-Claude Leclerc, and Normand Lépine, "L'opération McGill," *Le Devoir*, 29 mars 1969, 1–2. For discussions of the McGill français movement, see Marc V. Levine, *The Reconquest of Montreal*, 76–7. The most important treatment so far is found in Jean-Philippe Warren, "L'Opération McGill français. Une page méconnue de l'histoire de la gauche nationaliste." Also see Bédard, "McGill français: un contexte de fébrilité étudiante et nationaliste," Jean-Philippe Warren, *Une douce anarchie*, and Robert Chodos, "A Short History of Student Activism at McGill," in *McGill Student Handbook*.

4 William D. Coleman, "The Class Bases of Language Policy in Quebec, 1949–1975," 97. The origins of the language crisis of the late 1960s, as well as of the decision of the provincial government to begin legislating on language questions, have been the

subject of a great deal of discussion. In his book-length study, *The Independence Movement in Quebec 1945–1980*, Coleman argues that Quebec's language policies were "adjuncts to the policies of economic development and thus … facilitating greater integration of Quebec's francophone community into the North American economy and culture" (184). Also see Richard Jones, "Politics and the Reinforcement of the French Language in Canada and Quebec, 1960–1986," in *Quebec Since 1945*, 223–40; Ramsay Cook, *Watching Quebec*, 30; Karim Larose, "L'émergence du projet d'unilinguisme. Archéologie de la question linguistique québécoise," 181–4; Karim Larose, *La langue de papier*; Guy Bouthillier, "Aux origines de la planification linguistique québécoise," in *L'État et la planification linguistique II*, 7–22. For a new look at language legislation in Canada, see Martin Pâquet and Marcel Martel, eds., *Légiférer en matière linguistique*.

5 Le Mouvement de Libération Populaire et la revue Parti Pris, "Manifeste 1965–1966," *Parti Pris* 3, no. 1–2 (1965): 17.

6 Ibid., 26–7.

7 For a look at the new significance that language played in the 1960s, see Cook, *Watching Quebec*, 30.

8 See Coleman, "The Class Bases of Language Policy in Quebec, 1949–1975," 93–117.

9 For his remarkable study, see Larose, *La langue de papier*. Other works on the question of unilingualism include Larose, "L'émergence du projet d'unilinguisme," and Bouthillier, "Aux origines de la planification linguistique québécoise," 7–22.

10 See two works by Michael D. Behiels, "The Commission des Écoles catholiques de Montréal and the Neo-Canadian Question: 1947–63," 39, and *Quebec and the Question of Immigration*.

11 Paul-André Linteau, "The Italians of Quebec: Key Participants in Contemporary Linguistic and Political Debates," in *Arrangiarsi*, 182–9, Coleman, *The Independence Movement in Quebec 1945–1980*, 202.

12 Linteau, "The Italians of Quebec," 188–90. According to Michael Behiels, "Between 1955–56 and 1962–63 the number of Italian children enrolled in the CECM more than doubled from 7,434 to 16,556. Furthermore, the percentage enrolled in the English sector during this period rose from 61.2% to 74.8%." See "The Commission des Écoles catholiques de Montréal and the Neo-Canadian Question: 1947–63," 55.

13 Linteau, "The Italians of Quebec," 191.

14 For an extremely nuanced discussion, see Miguel Simão Andrade, "La Commission des écoles catholiques de Montréal et l'intégration des immigrants et des minorités ethniques à l'école française de 1947 à 1977," 475–8.

15 Levine, *The Reconquest of Montreal*, 67–8. Coleman, *The Independence Movement in Quebec 1945–1980*, 202.

16 Seen in Levine, *The Reconquest of Montreal*, 69.

17 Ibid., 68–9, 73–4.

18 Warren, *Une douce anarchie*, 34.

19 Ibid., 15.

20 Ibid., 27.

21 Ibid., 102–3, 242.

22 For a vivid portrait of the occupation at the École des Beaux-arts, see Claude Laflamme, "La République des Beaux-arts: la Malédiction de la momie," (Canada: Vent d'Est Films, 1997).

23 Allnutt and Chodos, "Quebec: Into the Streets," 39, Nick Auf der Maur, "'Operation McGill' Viewed from Inside," *McGill Reporter*, 31 March 1969, 2.

24 Robert Chodos, "Désormais," *McGill Daily*, 23 October 1968, 5. For an important look at the student revolts of the fall of 1968, including Opération McGill, see Warren, *Une douce anarchie*. Also see his excellent description of the march in "L'Opération McGill français."

25 "McGill ne déposerait pas de plainte contres ses onze 'occupants' francophones," *Le Devoir*, 5 décembre 1968, 3.

26 For an overview of student activism at McGill throughout the 1960s, see Peggy Sheppard, "The Relationship between Student Activism and Change in the University: With Particular Reference to McGill University in the 1960s." A useful overview of the transformation of student politics at McGill throughout the 1960s can also be found in Chodos, "A Short History of Student Activism at McGill." For an alternative view, see Stanley Brice Frost, *McGill University*, vol. 2, 443–64.

27 Frost, *McGill University*, 449.

28 Chodos, "A Short History of Student Activism at McGill," 88.

29 My thanks to Mark Wilson for this insight.

30 Stan Gray, "For a Critical University," *McGill Daily* (*Review*), 24 October 1968, 4–5.

31 Interview with Stan Gray, June 10, 2005, Hamilton.

32 Chodos, "A Short History of Student Activism at McGill," 87–8, Frost, *McGill University*, 459.

33 Robert Lantos, "The Rise of the Left at McGill," *Together*, 25 February 1970, 5.

34 Ibid.

35 Stan Gray, "Stan Gray: The Greatest Canadian … Shit-Disturber," 12–13. Interview with Stan Gray, June 10, 2005, Hamilton, Ontario.

36 Mark Starowicz, "Why Was This Man Honoured?" *McGill Daily*, 10 October 1968, 5.

37 Kristin Ross, *May '68 and Its Afterlives*, 25.

38 Ibid., 74.

39 Jean-Philippe Warren notes, for example, the joining of students and workers in the protest against Murray Hill in October 1968. Warren, "L'Opération McGill français," 98.

40 Vincent Prince, "Quelques réflexions sur la manifestation de vendredi soir à l'université McGill," *Le Devoir*, 31 mars 1969, 4.

41 Don Mitchell, *The Right to the City*, 6.

42 Chodos, "Hitting a Sore Spot," 4.

43 Pierre Beaudet, *On a raison de se révolter*, 79.

44 Interview with Stan Gray, June 10, 2005, Hamilton. It should be noted that some left-ist groups at McGill refused to participate in the march, as they saw it as not focused enough on issues of class. See Warren, "L'Opération McGill français," 102.

45 Beaudet, *On a raison de se révolter*, 79.

46 Allnutt and Chodos, "Quebec," 42. Also, see Louis Fournier, FLQ, 203. The Central Council voted to support the protest on the 28, denounced McGill and invited all workers to take part in the march on the university. It also pledged $100 to the organization that published *Bienvenue à McGill*. In the protest that took place on the evening of 28 March, many workers of various affiliations took the advice of the Montreal Central Council and attended. ASCN, CCSNM fonds, Congrès 1969, Fernand Foisy, "Rapport du secrétaire – décisions du comité exécutif," 7, 26.

47 Jacques Rouillard, "La CSN et la protection de la langue française (1921–1996)," 12–15.

48 Interview with Stan Gray, 10 June 2005, Hamilton. Also, see Gray, "Stan Gray: The Greatest Canadian ... Shit-Disturber," 14.

49 MUA, Opération McGill, RG2 C401. Flyer for "teach in" at McGill held 26 March 1969, n.d.

50 Marlene Dixon, *Things Which Are Done in Secret*, 50. The *McGill Daily*, of course, immediately rallied to his defense. See, for example, Robert Chodos and Mark Starowicz, "Don't Put Out the Fire – Stop the Fire Alarm," *McGill Daily*, 13 February 1969, 4.

51 MUA, Opération McGill fonds, RG2 C401, Message left by Mrs Roschon for Rocke Robertson, 10 March 1969.

52 "Gray Outlines Defence," *McGill Daily* (*extra*), 2 April 1969, 3.

53 Michel Chartrand, "Chartrand Statement," *McGill Daily*, 3 March 1969, 3.

54 See the many memos and documents held in MUA, Opération McGill fonds, RG2 C401.

55 WRDA, Opération McGill fonds, Organizers of Opération McGill français in Regards to Police Actions, 30 March 1969, 1. Fournier, *FLQ: Histoire d'un mouvement clandestin*, 203.

56 Gray, "Stan Gray: The Greatest Canadian ... Shit-Disturber," 14.

57 Claude Ryan, "Éditorial: McGill et son avenir," *Le Devoir*, 26 mars 1969.

58 WRDA, Opération McGill fonds, Organizers of Opération McGill français in Regards to Police Actions, 30 March 1969, 4.

59 Allnutt and Chodos, "Quebec: Into the Streets," 42.

60 "La SSJB de Montréal se dissocie de la manifestation de vendredi prochain," *Le Devoir*, 26 mars 1969, Cahier 2.

61 Stan Gray, "For a Critical University," 4, and "McGill and the Rape of Quebec – Part I," *McGill Daily*, 10 February 1969, 4–5.

62 Mark Starowicz, "Terrorism in the Press," *McGill Daily*, 2 April 1969, 6.

63 Gray, "McGill and the Rape of Quebec – Part I," 4.

64 Ibid.

65 Stan Gray, "McGill and Quebec, Part II," *McGill Daily*, 12 February 1969. For a similar use of broad generalizations describing the relations of labour and capital in Quebec, see Mark Wilson, "A Short History of McGill," in the *McGill Student Handbook*.

66 Maurice Roy, "La gauche mcgilloise: 'pas une deuxième université de Montréal,'" *Le Quartier latin*, 18 mars 1969, 5.

67 WRDA, Opération McGill fonds, "Who's Who in that Two-Faced McGill?" *Le Sainte-marie: journal des étudiants du collège Sainte-Marie de Montreal*, 24 March 1969, 7.

68 J.-P. Dallaire, "McGill un autre St. Léonard?," *Le Quartier latin*, 18 mars 1969, 2.

69 Ibid.

70 The signatories included the following organizations: Comité Indépendance-Socialisme; Comités d'action des CEGEPs: Ahuntsic (St-Ignace), Bois-de-Boulogne, De Mortagne, Edouard-Montpetit, Maisonneuve, Rosemont, Vieux Montréal (Arts Appliqués, Marie-Victorin, Ste-Marie); Comités Ouvriers: Rosemont, Ste-Marie; Comité d'action de l'U. de M. (Hec. Philosophie, Sciences sociales, Histoire, Lettres); Comité d'action école normale Ville-Marie; Front de libération populaire; Intellectuels ouvriers patriotes du Québec; McGill radical students alliance; Mouvement d'intégration scolaire; Mouvement pour l'unilinguisme français au Québec; Société nationale populaire; Université libre d'art quotidien; Union générale des étudiants du secondaire. The document was republished in various newspapers, but it was not reproduced in exact detail everywhere. In the student newspaper for Montreal's Sainte-Marie's College, for example, the following uncompromising concluding paragraph was added: "Selon Albert Memmi, il y a deux réponses possibles pour le colonisé face à la violence de la situation coloniale: l'identification aux colonialistes ou la recherche d'une identité; donc … soumission ou révolte." WRDA, Opération McGill fonds, "Who's Afraid of a French McGill?," *Le Sainte-marie*, 24 mars 1969, 2–3.

71 See "Une douzaine d'organismes signent un manifeste sur 'l'opération McGill'," *Le Devoir*, 13 mars 1969, 3.

72 WRDA, Opération McGill fonds, "Operation McGill" typed document. Montreal, March 1969, 2–6.

73 The McGill student council, which had originally agreed to provide the funding for the special edition of the paper, revised its decision, believing that the paper raised the possibility of inciting violence. "Des étudiants de McGill publient un journal en français," *Le Devoir*, 19 mars 1969, 16.

74 "Hitting a Sore Spot," 5. "Des étudiants de McGill publient un journal en français," 16. ASCN, CCSNM fonds, Congrès 1969, Fernand Foisy, "Rapport du sécrétaire – décisions du comité exécutif," 7.

75 WRDA, Opération McGill fonds. "Message de solidarité avec la manifestation McGill," *Bienvenue à McGill: Journal publié par des étudiants de l'Université McGill appuyant la manifestation du 28 mars*. n.d.

76 WRDA, Opération McGill fonds. Stan Gray, "McGill: Option Anti-Quebec" *Bienvenue à McGill*, 4–5.

77 Beaudet, *On a raison de se révolter*, 80.

78 My thanks to Mark Wilson for this insight.

79 For a critical assessment of radical student politics at McGill from the incoming president of the McGill students' society, see Julius Grey, "What Is McGill, What Are We Doing Here, and What Ought We To Do?," in *McGill Student Handbook.*

80 For a detailed discussion of these events, see Warren, *Une douce anarchie.*

81 On 16 March 1969, the MIS held a meeting at which it changed its name to the Ligue pour l'intégration scolaire (LIS). The chair of the assembly, Pierre Jobin of Laval University, had difficulty maintaining a quorum in the tumultuous assembly, where amendments, propositions, and counter-propositions were debated simultaneously. François Barbeau, "Le MIS devient la Ligue pour l'intégration scolaire et adopte sa première constitution," *Le Devoir*, 17 mars 1969, 3.

82 Levine, *The Reconquest of Montreal*, 78.

83 Ibid., 79.

84 WRDA, Stanley Gray fonds, Box 1, Stanley Gray, "The Struggle in Quebec – 1969." Speech delivered at the Year of the Barricade conference at Glendon College in Toronto on 25 October 1969, 11.

85 Gilles Provost, "Un Front commun du 'Québec français' organise la résistance contre le bill 63," *Le Devoir*, 27 octobre 1969, 1. For details on the functioning of the FQF, see Denis Turcotte, *La culture politique du Mouvement Québec Français*, 10–12.

86 Provost, "Un Front commun du 'Québec français' organise la résistance contre le bill 63," 1–2.

87 ASCN, CCSNM fonds, Assemblé Général, François-Albert Angers, invité, 18 novembre 1969, 85–6.

88 WRDA, Campaign Against Bill 63 fonds, F.-Albert Angers, "Le Droit des parents" *L'Information nationale.* novembre 1969, 7.

89 Beaudet, *On a raison de se révolter*, 88.

90 Léandre Bergeron, *The History of Quebec*, 226, and Stan Gray, "Le mouvement contre le bill 63," *Mobilisation* 5 (1970): 17–18.

91 Gilles Provost, "Des milliers d'étudiants descendent dans la rue," *Le Devoir*, 29 octobre 1969, 1–2.

92 Ibid., 2.

93 According to Gray, the protest was organized by the FLP and its worker committees, with the collaboration of the Saint Jacques citizens' committee. See "Le mouvement contre le bill 63," 17–18.

94 "Une mer de manifestants déferle rue Craig," *Le Devoir*, 30 octobre 1969, 1–2.

95 Jean-Luc Duguay, "La violence éclate devant le parlement," *Le Devoir*, 1 novembre 1969, 1.

96 WRDA, Campaign Against Bill 63 fonds, "Travailleurs unissons nous contre le bill 63,"

pamphlet put out by the Comité ouvrier de St-Henri, Comité ouvrier de St-Marie, Comité ouvrier Centre-Ville, Comité ouvrier Hochelaga Maisonneuve, Comité de citoyens de Mercier, Comité de citoyens de St-Jacques, n.d.

97 "Notre position," *Québec-Presse*, 2 novembre 1969, 1A.

98 "Le Bill 63," *Québec-Presse*, 2 novembre 1969, 7A.

99 Ibid.

100 WRDA, FRAP fonds, 'Jérôme Proulx' *Le Pouvoir* 2, no. 4. n.d., 2.

101 WRDA, FRAP fonds, Raymond Parent, "La CSN," *Le Pouvoir* 2, no. 4. n.d., 2.

102 WRDA, FRAP fonds, Fernand Daoust, "La FTQ," *Le Pouvoir* 2, no. 4. n.d., 3.

103 Martin Pâquet, "Un nouveau contrat social. Les États généraux du Canada français et l'immigration, novembre 1967."

104 Ibid., 132. For a fuller discussion of these developments, see Martin Pâquet, *Tracer les marges de la cité*.

105 It is, of course, rather ironic that the debate was framed around the integration of immigrants. According to Michael Behiels, throughout most of the twentieth century, neither francophone nor anglophone communities were particularly eager to accommodate immigrants, and neither "wanted the provincial government to alter the dual ethnic and religious constitutional structure." "Their respective unwillingness to come to terms with religious and ethnic pluralism," Behiels argues, "set the pattern for nearly seven decades and contributed in no small measure to the linguistic and cultural crises of the 1970s and 80s." Behiels, *Quebec and the Question of Immigration: From Ethnocentracism to Ethnic Pluralism, 1900–1985*, 5.

106 Kimon Valaskakis, "La crise du bill 63 vue par un Néo-Québécois: L'alliance des nationalistes et des mouvements de gauche débouchera-t-elle sur une monolithisme intolérant?" *Le Devoir*, 12 novembre 1969, 5.

107 Ibid.

108 Rénald Bourque, "L'esprit de Stan Gray n'est pas mort," *Le Quartier latin*, 1 octobre 1969, 10.

109 UQAM Archives, Collection de publications de groupes de gauche et de groupes populaires, 21p 900:04/67, "Faisons le point," Le Bulletin du C.H.A.P. (Comité haitien d'action patriotique – Montréal) 20 mars 1971, 3.

110 In addition to the publications cited in chapter four, see, for example, UQAM, Collection de publications de groupes de gauche et de groupes populaires, 21p 900:04/3, *African Voice, Organ of the African Progressive Study Group* 1, no. 2 (Montreal, 10 June 1972).

111 Interview with Daya Varma, 24 June 2007, Montréal.

112 See "Fascist Attacks Against Ho Chi Minh Book-Store and Its Workers," *National Minority News* 1, no. 1 (1971): 9, and "Fascist Attacks Against Palestinian House," *National Minority News* 1, no. 1 (1971): 10.

113 In the early 1970s, the Afro-Asian Latin American People's Solidarity Committee met for discussion groups in English at McGill University on Thursday, and the paral-

lel Comité de Solidarité des Peuples d'Afrique, d'Asie et d'Amérique Latine met for their French-language discussion groups on Tuesdays at the newly established Université du Québec à Montreal. See "A Brief Review of Some Activities," *Third World Solidarity: Journal of the Afro-Asian Latin American People's Solidarity Committee* 3, no. 1 (1972): 16, and "Third World Centre," *Third World Solidarity* 3, no. 1 (1972): 13.

114 "Solidarity Statement by Movement Progressiste Italo-Quebecois," *National Minority News* 1, no. 1 (1971): 14.

CHAPTER SEVEN

1 Frantz Fanon, *The Wretched of the Earth*, trans. Constance Farrington, 108–9.

2 See, most notably, Herbert Marcuse in *One Dimensional Man*, and *An Essay on Liberation*.

3 Claude Julien, *America's Empire*, trans. Renaud Bruce, 400.

4 Pierre Vallières, "Le nationalisme québecois et la classe ouvrière," *Révolution québécoise* 1, no. 1 (1964): 16.

5 By the early 1970s, the Quebec labour movement was receiving a significant amount of attention in the American press. In the fall of 1972, an entire edition of *Radical America* was devoted to it (September–October 1972).

6 See Nick Auf der Maur, "Lessons on Fighting City Hall: A Study of Montreal's 'Mouvement de libération du taxi'," *The Last Post* 1, no. 3 (1970): 19–25.

7 Black Rose Books Editorial Collective, "The Radicalization of Quebec Trade Unions," *Radical America* 6, no. 2 (1972): 59–62. For a look at the changing ideology of the CSN, see Bernard Solasse, "Les idéologies de la Fédération des travailleurs du Québec et de la Confédération des syndicats nationaux, 1960–1978" in *Idéologies au Canada français, 1940–1976, Tome II*.

8 The essential place to begin for studies on the CSN, as well as on the labour movement in general, is the work of Jacques Rouillard. This includes "Major Changes in the Confédération des travailleurs catholiques du Canada, 1945–1960," in *Quebec Since 1945*, and especially *Histoire du syndicalisme au Québec*, *Histoire de la CSN, 1921–1981*, and *L'expérience syndicale au Québec*.

9 Rouillard, *Histoire du syndicalisme au Québec*, 155.

10 In Pepin's case, authors and intellectuals such as Jacques Dofny and Pierre Vadeboncoeur were directly involved in putting together the reports. Pepin felt that the 1966 report was his most important, laying the foundations for all of his writing to come. He even goes as far to say that his later reports merely re-enforced and deepened ideas that he had already developed in *Une société bâtie pour l'homme*. See Jacques Keable, *Le monde selon Marcel Pepin*, 285.

11 For just one example, see *Socialisme 67*, no. 11 (1967). According to Ralph Peter Güntzel, "Pepin's moral report of 1966 rallied the delegates together almost unan-

imously." The same would not be the case, however, with Pepin's 1968 report, as an opposition to the radicalization of the CSN began to emerge. See "The Confédération des syndicats nationaux, the Idea of Independence, and the Sovereigntist Movement, 1960–1980," 46.

12 Louis Favreau, Pierre L'Heureux, and Michel Paul, *Le projet de société de la CSN de 1966 à aujourd'hui*, 32.

13 Marcel Pepin, "Une société bâtie pour l'homme."

14 Marcel Pepin, "The Second Front: The Report of Marcel Pepin, National President, to the Convention of the CNTU, October 13, 1968," in *Quebec Labour*. At the same convention, the CSN changed its structure to give more representation to regional central councils, which were more attuned to political action, rather than to professional federations. This would have an important impact on the way in which the union's politics would develop in the years to come. Favreau, L'Heureux, and Paul, *Le projet de société de la CSN de 1966 à aujourd'hui*, 35.

15 ASCN. Rapport du directeur général des services, Amédée Daigle, 44 congrès 6–12 décembre 1970, 243,

16 ASCN, Rapport du comité central d'action politique, au 43ième congrès confédéral de la Confédération des syndicats nationaux, octobre 1968, 5–7, 24.

17 Solasse, "Les idéologies de la Fédération des travailleurs du Québec et de la Confédération des syndicats nationaux," 261.

18 ASCN. Rapport du directeur général des services, Amédée Daigle, 44 congrès 6–12 décembre 1970, 242–8

19 Jean-François Cardin, *Comprendre octobre 1970*, 62.

20 Favreau, L'Heureux, and Paul, *Le projet de société de la CSN de 1966 à aujourd'hui*, 33.

21 See ASCN, Rapport du comité central d'action politique, au 43ième congrès confédéral de la Confédération des syndicats nationaux, 9.

22 Solasse, "Les idéologies de la Fédération des travailleurs du Québec et de la Confédération des syndicats nationaux," 264–5.

23 Throughout the sixties, Les Presses sociales was very important to the left, publishing, in addition to collective bargaining agreements, a wide variety of radical writers, poets, political journals like *Our Generation Against Nuclear War*, *Socialisme*, *Le Peuple* (organ of the PSQ), and *Socialisme 64*. Fernand Foisy, *Michel Chartrand, Les voies d'un homme de parole*, 149, 230–1.

24 Foisy, *Michel Chartrand, la colère du juste (1968–2003)*, 26–9.

25 See Stéphanie Poirier, "Le Conseil central des syndicats nationaux de Montréal (CSN) à l'heure de la radicalisation syndicale, 1968–1980."

26 Unions affiliated to the CSN are represented both geographically, in regional central councils, and by trade or profession, in federations. While the federations are responsible for providing unions with services related to negotiations and the application of collective agreements, central councils are responsible for forging sol-

idarity among workers, organizing and defending workers outside of the workplace, and representing workers politically on a regional level. See ibid., 28–9.

27 McGill professor Immanuel Wallerstein attended the meetings of the Central Council as the representative of the faculty union. Interview with Kari Levitt, 9 December 2006, Montreal.

28 In Jean-François Cardin's words, the Montreal Central Council would become the "porte-flambeau" of the "Second Front." Jean-François Cardin, "La CSN et le syndicalisme de combat (1960–1975)," 36.

29 Favreau, L'Heureux, and Paul, *Le projet de société de la CSN de 1966 à aujourd'hui*, 37.

30 ASCN, CCSNM fonds, Fernand Foisy, "Rapport du secrétaire," Congrès 1970, 19, 36. Also see Pierre Vallières, *Les Héritiers de Papineau*, 175. On the question of unilingualism and the CSN, see Jacques Rouillard, "La CSN et la protection de la langue française (1921–1996)," 17, and Poirier, "Le Conseil central des syndicats nationaux de Montréal (CSN) à l'heure de la radicalisation syndicale, 1968–1980."

31 The Central Council formed part of a coalition of groups that helped found a mass circulation weekly newspaper, *Quebec-Presse* (published between 1969 and 1974), which provided an alternative media source and acted as an independent and critical voice. According to Marc Raboy, "Activists of the period considered that *Québec-Presse* belonged to them, and the people involved with the paper felt that way too." At the end of its existence, it had a circulation of nearly 30,000. Marc Raboy, *Movements and Messages*, 60–2. Also see Foisy, *Michel Chartrand, la colère du juste (1968–2003)*, 92–6

32 Interview with Fernand Foisy, 8 December 2006, Montreal.

33 "Solidarité internationale," *Unité ouvrière* 2, édition spéciale (1978): 30–1.

34 UQAM, Collection de publications de groupes de gauche et de groupes populaires, 21p–900:04/155, "Le secretariat Québec-Amérique Latine et sa place a l'intérieur du mouvement ouvrier québécois," Sécrétariat Québec-Amérique Latine, novembre 1975, 5.

35 Foisy, *Michel Chartrand, la colère du juste (1968–2003)*, 239–40. When the American-backed coup deposed the democratically elected government of Salvador Allende in 1973, the Central Council actively promoted solidarity with Chile. See "Manifestation de solidarité au Forum 1er décembre," *Le Travail, édition de Montréal* 1, no. 8 (1973): 1–2.

36 Interview with Daya Varma, 24 June 2007, Montreal. Interview with Fernand Foisy, 8 December 2006, Montreal.

37 ASCN, CCSNM fonds, Fernand Foisy, "Rapport du secrétaire – décisions du comité exécutif," Congrès 1969, 19; ASCN, CCSNM fonds, Presse release, "Sir George Williams et le cas de Charles Gagnon: les deux masques de la répression," 21 février 1969; and ASCN, CCSNM fonds, Foisy, "Rapport du secrétaire," Congrès 1970, 33.

38 Foisy, *Michel Chartrand, la colère du juste (1968–2003)*, 57–9. ASCN, CCSNM fonds, Procès-verbaux, congrès 1969, 1–4 mai 1969, 2.

39 ASCN, CCSNM fonds, Michel Chartrand, "Rappord du président," congrès 1969, 3.

40 Seen in Foisy, *Michel Chartrand, la colère du juste (1968–2003)*, 60–1.

41 ASCN, CCSNM fonds, "Qu'est-ce qu'il peut faire pour nous autres le Conseil Central?" pamphlet, n.d.

42 Foisy, *Michel Chartrand, la colère du juste (1968–2003)*, 102. Throughout the 1970s, the Montreal Central Council also actively worked to fight the deportation of immigrants. "Solidarité internationale," 30.

43 During the occupation, Bergeron was one of the seven signatories of a letter printed in *The Georgian* denouncing the actions of the administration and concluding with a declaration of support for the students. See David Orton et al., "Dissenting Faculty State Position," *The Georgian*, 4 February 1969, 2.

44 These history courses formed part of a larger efflorescence of popular eductation under the auspices of the Montreal Central Council beginning in 1968. See "L'Éducation: Une priorité continue du Conseil Central," *Unité Ouvrière* 2, no. Édition Spéciale (1978): 3–4. For Bergeron's reflections on his early attempts at popular education, see UQAM, Charles Gagnon fonds, 124p–202a/3, Léandre Bergeron, "Expériences de formation politique de ces dernières années."

45 ASCN, CCSNM fonds, Victor Leroux, Jean-Paul Guillemette, Bernard Leclerc, Clermont Bergeron, Léandre Bergeron, Jean-Yves Vézina, "Rapport du Comité d'Éducation," Congrès 1970, 2–3.

46 ASCN, CCSNM fonds, Fernand Foisy, "Rapport du secrétaire" Congrès 1970, 48. ASCN, CCSNM fonds, Victor Leroux, Jean-Paul Guillemette, Bernard Leclerc, Clermont Bergeron, Léandre Bergeron, Jean-Yves Vézina, "Rapport du Comité d'Éducation," Congrès 1970, 2–3.

47 ASCN, CCSNM fonds, Fernand Foisy, "Rapport du secrétaire" Congrès 1970, 48.

48 See "An Open Letter to W.O. Twaits, Chairman of the Board, Imperial Oil" Appendix 3 to Léandre Bergeron, *The History of Quebec*, Updated ed. The figure of 140,000 copies is found on the front cover of this edition. In September 1970, the popular education courses became more popular than ever, being given three times a week to audiences of as many as two hundred. After a while, however, students began to lose interest. Many said that they no longer needed courses now that all of the information was available in the *Petit manuel*. UQAM, Charles Gagnon fonds, 124p–202a/3, Léandre Bergeron, "Expériences de formation politique de ces dernières années."

49 Bergeron even discusses the ways in which French-Canadians missionaries had been involved in perpetuating "White colonialism in China, Basutoland and the land of the Eskimo." Strangely, however, Bergeron almost completely ignores the history of the Black population of Quebec, with the exception of a footnote outlining the presence of Black slaves. Bergeron, *The History of Quebec*, 6–7, 37, 100–5.

50 Ibid., 174, 19, 26, 40f1.

51 Ibid., 44–5, 214–15.

52 See Jacques Godbout and Jean-Pierre Collin, *Les organismes populaires en milieu*

urbain, 51–60, and Hélène Pilotte, "Quand les adultes aussi contestent la société: Les comités de citoyens," *Châtelaine*, octobre 1969, 33.

53 For a discussion on the development of the community clinic in Pointe Saint-Charles, see The CourtePointe Collective, *The Point Is...*, 91–3.

54 For information on the history of the Pointe Saint-Charles clinic into the 1970s and beyond, see ibid., 89–113.

55 Robert Boivin, *Histoire de la Clinique des citoyens de Saint-Jacques (1968–1988)*, 17–18.

56 Ibid., 32, 53. Also see Bonnie Sherr Klein, "Citizens' Medicine," (Canada: NFB, 1970).

57 Boivin, *Histoire de la Clinique des citoyens de Saint-Jacques*, 35–7.

58 Claire Helman, *The Milton-Park Affair*, 17.

59 Ibid., 30.

60 Ibid., 93.

61 *Les gens du Québec 1, St-Henri*, 64–8.

62 For an important look at alternative media in Montreal during the period, see Raboy, *Movements and Messages*.

63 The above paragraph also relies on Boivin, *Histoire de la Clinique des citoyens de Saint-Jacques*, 70–9. UQAM, Fonds d'archives de la clinique des citoyens Saint-Jacques, 79p1/2, "Manifeste 1." Also see Godbout and Collin, *Les organismes populaires en milieu urbain*, 67–8. For a discussion of a similar move away from focusing on the "poor" and onto the "working class" in English Canada, see Bryan Palmer, *Canada's 1960s*, 277.

64 Louis Favreau and Yves Hurtubise, "L'action politique locale: une autre forme d'organisation communautaire,"123–5. Godbout and Collin, *Les organismes populaires en milieu urbain*, 60.

65 FRAP, *Manifeste 70. À Montréal les salariés passent à l'action politique*, 8–12. Also see Favreau and Hurtubise, "L'action politique locale," 123–7. Marc Comby, "L'expérience du FRAP à Montréal (1970–1974): La tentative de créer au Québec un parti d'extrême gauche," in *Contester dans un pays prospère*, Cardin, *Comprendre octobre 1970*, 58–9, Jean-François Cardin, "Le mouvement syndical et les débuts du FRAP."

66 See Le Front d'action politique, *Les salariés au pouvoir!*, 28–30.

67 See Marc Comby, "Mouvements sociaux, syndicats et action politique à Montréal: l'histoire du FRAP (1970–1974)," 1, Marc Comby, "Le Front d'action politique (FRAP) à Montréal: de la naissance aux élection (1969–1970)." ASCN. Rapport du directeur général des services, Amédée Daigle, 44e congrès 6–12 décembre 1970, 256–7. Activists within the CSN did not hesitate to point out that many passages in the FRAP's program were drawn directly from CSN documentation.

68 ASCN. Rapport du directeur général des services, Amédée Daigle, 44 congrès 6–12 décembre 1970, 259.

69 FRAP, *Les salariés au pouvoir!*, 18, 32.

70 Ibid., 20–2.

71 Ibid., 67–72, 58–9.

72 Ibid., 67–72, 91, 104, 107–8.

73 Ibid., 36.

74 Doucet and Favreau, "L'action politique locale," 128.

75 Max Elbaum, *Revolution in the Air*, 25.

76 Louis Fournier, FLQ, 274–7. I have relied on Fournier for many of the details in the following section.

77 Gérard Pelletier, *La crise d'Octobre*, 87–9.

78 See Éric Bédard, "The Intellectual Origins of the October Crisis," in *Creating Postwar Canada*, as well as the many documents in Comeau, Cooper, and Vallières. *FLQ: un projet révolutionnaire*.

79 Fournier, FLQ: *Histoire d'un mouvement clandestin*, 236–7.

80 Foisy, *Michel Chartrand, la colère du juste (1968–2003)*, 137–8. Chartrand maintained a close relationship with many members of the FLQ and supported its objectives. When Pierre Vallières was released in June 1971, he went to the home of Michel and Simone Chartrand and stayed with them for the entire summer. ASCN, CCSNM fonds, Michel Chartrand, "Allocution de Michel Chartrand sur ses quatre mois en prison," Procès-verbaux, Assemblé Général, 2 mars 1971, 142. Vallières, *Les Héritiers de Papineau*, 223.

81 "Le Deuxième Front," *Unité ouvrière* 2, édition spéciale (1978): 11. Also see ASCN, CCSNM fonds, Fernand Foisy, "Rapport du secrétaire," Congrès 1971, 31, 33.

82 Fournier, FLQ, 285–6.

83 Ronald D. Crelinsten, "The Internal Dynamics of the FLQ during the October Crisis," 62.

84 B.R. journaliste, "Une information 'totalitaire prise à son propre piège,'" 179, Crelinsten, "The Internal Dynamics of the FLQ during the October Crisis," 71–2.

85 Raboy, *Movements and Messages*, 64.

86 Fournier, FLQ, 300–6.

87 For one account of some of the internal politics of the FRAP, see ASCN. Rapport du directeur général des services, Amédée Daigle, 44e congrès 6–12 décembre 1970, 258–9. Also see Comby, "Le Front d'action politique (FRAP) à Montréal," and Comby, "L'expérience du FRAP à Montréal (1970–1974)," 166.

88 R.D. Crelinsten notes in regard to telephone calls to radio talk shows, while "most people condemned the FLQ *action*, the kidnapping itself, more than fifty per cent of the callers were in favour of the spirit of the manifesto." See "Power and Meaning" in *Contemporary Research on Terrorism*, 429.

89 A complete copy of the document is reproduced in Fournier, FLQ, 326–7.

90 Fournier, FLQ, 327–8. "Des centaines de personnes répondent à l'invitation," *Le Devoir*, 16 octobre 1970.

91 Crelinsten, "The Internal Dynamics of the FLQ during the October Crisis," 63.

92 Pierre Richard, "Amorce de débrayage," *Québec-Presse*, 16 octobre 1970, 2–3. Also see Jean-Marc Piotte, "Jour après jour," in *Québec occupé*, 21.

93 Richard, "Amorce de débrayage," 2–3. For a fascinating first-person account, see Pierre Beaudet, *On a raison de se révolter*, 98–9.

94 Richard, "Amorce de débrayage."

95 Jean-Pierre Pare, "'Ce soir, le FLQ c'est vous!'" *Montréal-Matin*, 16 octobre 1970, 5.

96 Fournier, FLQ, 335.

97 Boivin, *Histoire de la Clinique des citoyens de Saint-Jacques*, 79.

98 Gérald Godin, "Diary of a Prisoner of War," in *Québec, Canada and the October Crisis*, 90.

99 On the lack of information regarding arrests, see Le comité de rédaction, "Résister à la répression," *Québec-Presse*, 18 octobre 1970, A6.

100 Dominique Clément, *Canada's Rights Revolution*, 74.

101 Pelletier, *La crise d'Octobre*, 164.

102 The statement is reproduced in Fournier, FLQ, 339–40.

103 Cited in ibid., 342.

104 For a look at the complex reaction of Montreal's English-speaking community to the October Crisis, see Robin Spry, "Reaction: A Portrait of a Society in Crisis," (Canada: NFB, 1973).

105 Clément, *Canada's Rights Revolution*, 110. "Réactions contre la répression" unpublished document, UQAM, Charles Gagnon fonds, 1249–630:01/54.

106 See chapter 6 of *Canada's Rights Revolution*.

107 "Réactions contre la répression" unpublished document, UQAM, Charles Gagnon fonds, 1249–630:01/54.

108 Clément, *Canada's Rights Revolution*, 145.

109 See Eric Bédard, *Chronique d'une insurrection appréhendée*.

110 Comité de rédaction, "Résister à la répression," A6.

111 Edouard Smith, "Opération Démocratie," 101–2.

112 Piotte, "Jour après jour," 23–9.

113 Interview with Dimitri Roussopoulos, 16 May 2006.

114 Fournier, FLQ, 346–9.

115 Cited in Beaudet, *On a raison de se révolter*, 100.

116 Fournier, FLQ, 364–9

117 Crelinsten, "The Internal Dynamics of the FLQ during the October Crisis," 60.

118 For a discussion of the efforts of the three police forces to break into the offices of the main defence organization for political prisoners, as well as the Agence de presse libre du Québec, see Fournier, FLQ, 451–2.

119 Ibid., 415, 424.

120 Sheila Rowbotham, "The Women's Movement and Organizing for Socialism," in *Beyond the Fragments*, 68–70. The above description of the revolutionary is also greatly indebted to Rowbotham.

121 Simard, *Talking It Out*, 30, 51.

122 Ibid., 66.

123 Michel Brault, "Les Ordres," (Canada: Production's Prisma, 1974). For a discussion of the film, see André Loiselle, *Cinema as History*, 103–22.

124 Marjolaine Péloquin, *En prison pour la cause des femmes*, 21–2.

125 Cardin, *Comprendre octobre 1970*, 82.

126 Ibid.

CHAPTER EIGHT

1 Rouillard, *Histoire du syndicalisme au Québec*, 141. The statistics below are drawn from Rouillard, 146. For a brief discussion of the way in which the new labour code disproportionately benefited the CSN, see Jean-François Cardin, "La CSN et le syndicalisme de combat (1960–1975)," in *La CSN, 75 ans d'action syndicale et sociale*, 35.

2 It was at its 1966 convention that the province's teachers' union changed its name from the "Corporation des instituteurs et institutrices catholiques de la province de Québec" (CIC) and decided, at the same time, to begin engaging in political action around questions beyond those relating only to the educational system. Beginning in 1971, the union also began representing non-teaching employees of school boards, CEGEPs, and universities. At its 1972 convention, it decided again to change its name, this time to the "Centrale de l'enseignement du Québec," a decision that took effect in 1974. Jacques Rouillard, *Histoire du syndicalisme au Québec*, 165–7. For a look at the CEQ and Quebec nationalism, see Ralph Güntzel, "The Centrale de l'Enseignement du Québec and Quebec Separatist Nationalism, 1960–1980."

3 The FTQ was founded in 1957 as the provincial wing of the Canadian Labour Congress (CLC), and unions affiliated to the CLC joined the FTQ on a voluntary basis. In 1957, the FTQ only represented one third of Quebec union members affiliated to the CLC, but this number kept increasing over the years. Starting in 1967, the organization reinforced its structure and power, and it also became more present on the Quebec political scene. Rouillard, *Histoire du syndicalisme au Québec*, 145–7.

4 For overviews of the ideology of the CSN, the FTQ, and the CEQ, see two articles by Bernard Solasse, "Les idéologies de la Fédération des travailleurs du Québec et de la Confédération des syndicats nationaux," and "L'idéologie de la Centrale des enseignants du Québec et son évolution, 1960–1973," both in *Idéologies au Canada français, 1940–1976, Tome II*.

5 Favreau, L'Heureux, and Paul, *Le projet de société de la CSN de 1966 à aujourd'hui*, 86–7.

6 For a copy of the joint declaration of the three unions of 17 October 1970, see Jean-François Cardin, *La crise d'octobre 1970 et le mouvement syndical québécois*, 288–9.

For a copy of the declaration adopted at the meeting of 21 October, see "Position des trois centrales syndicales devant la loi des mesures de guerre," *Le Travail*, octobre 1970.

7 "Position des trois centrales syndicales devant la loi des mesures de guerre," *Le Travail*, octobre 1970.

8 Jean-François Cardin, *Comprendre octobre 1970*, 112.

9 For information regarding both dissent and support for the positions taken by union leaders, see ibid., 116–24.

10 Interview with Jean-Marc Piotte, 30 October 2006, Montréal.

11 For information on earlier moments of the unions coming together in common cause, as well as the novelty of the common front of 1970, see Cardin, *Comprendre octobre 1970*, 138–140. My argument above regarding the importance of the October Crisis for the labour movement is indebted to Cardin's analyses.

12 Ibid., 181.

13 It should be noted that the radicalization of workers in Quebec coincided with the grassroots activism and worker control movements in other industrialized countries. See, for example, Dan Georgakas and Marvin Surkin, *Detroit* and George Katsiaficas, *The Subversion of Politics*.

14 In the tumultuous fall of 1969, when protesters were taking to the streets over Bill 63, the FTQ leadership decided to abstain from the language question, and Laberge stated that "Pour les travailleurs, la question linguistique n'est pas une préoccupation prioritaire. On ne peut pas dire que ça intéresse la masse des travailleurs." At a special session of the FTQ leadership, however, the nationalist wing prepared a resolution opposing Bill 63 and declaring its support for the principle that French be the language of work and schooling for immigrant children. At its convention a few days later, the resolution was not only adopted by the delegates (although only by a slight majority), but it was also made more radical. Laberge was openly attacked for his timid approach to the language question, and Fernand Daoust, a well-known left nationalist, was elected as the secretary general of the FTQ. See Louis Fournier, *Histoire de la FTQ, 1965–1992*, 49–52.

15 Jacques Rouillard notes the raised expectations (followed by disappointment) engendered by the Quiet Revolution, and he cites the importance of larger social and political movements. Rouillard, *Histoire du syndicalisme au Québec*, 140–5. For the interrelationship of the Quebec labour movement and the state, see Carla Lipsig-Mummé's essays, "The Web of Dependence: Quebec Unions in Politics before 1976," in *Quebec: State and Society*, "Future Conditional: Wars of Position in the Quebec Labour Movement," and "Quebec Unions and the State: Conflict and Dependence."

16 Nick Auf der Maur, "A Bleu Collar October." *Radical America* 6, no. 5 (1972): 75.

17 For an analysis of these transformations, see Nicole Laurin, "Genèse de la sociologie marxiste au Québec."

18 For the Marxist-inspired pan-Africanists of Montreal's Black community, the events at Sir George Williams University – a university that had a board of directors composed of people directly involved in corporations that did business in the Caribbean – served to highlight the workings of Canadian imperialism. According to *UHURU*, the Sir George Williams Affair, far more than being of mere local importance, "blew the myth of friendly Canada and this resulted in an exposure of the military-imperialistic ambitions of Canada in the West-Indies." "Editorial: Deep Ramifications," *UHURU*, 16 February 1970, 2.

19 Pierre Vallières, *Choose!*, trans. Penelope Williams, viii.

20 UQAM, Collection de publications de groupes de gauche et de groupes populaires, 21p–900:04/155, "Le secretariat Québec-Amérique Latine et sa place a l'intérieur du mouvement ouvrier québécois" Montreal, novembre 1975, 16.

21 For a discussion of the turn to dependency theory by many English-Canadian leftists, see Bryan Palmer, *Canada's 1960s*, 289–97.

22 See *Canadian Dimension* 4, 2 (January–February, 1967), 3. For a fascinating look at some of the consequences of the New Left's turn to left nationalism in Canada, and of the results of the American New Left's very different trajectory, see Steven High, *Industrial Sunset: The Making of North America's Rust Belt, 1969–1984*.

23 See Kari Polanyi Levitt, "Confluences," in *Reclaiming Democracy*.

24 Interview with Kari Levitt, 9 December 2006, Montreal. Also see Kari Levitt, *Silent Surrender*, xix.

25 Interview with Kari Levitt, 9 December 2006, Montreal. For information about the different facets of Levitt's intellectual and political work, see Levitt, "Confluences."

26 Levitt, *Silent Surrender*, xix–xx.

27 See Mel Watkins, Preface to *Silent Surrender*, xvii.

28 The success of *Silent Surrender* spread far beyond Canada's borders. The prime minister of Guyana distributed copies of the book to all of the members of his cabinet, and called Levitt hoping that she would travel to his country to advise on economic development. The prime minister of Trinidad and Tobago, Eric Williams, also read the book closely. Interview with Kari Levitt, December 9, 2006.

29 Levitt, *Silent Surrender*, xix.

30 Ibid., 23–4.

31 *Silent Surrender* would be quoted directly in two of the three major labour manifestos of 1971. CSN, "It's Up to Us," in *Quebec – Only the Beginning*, 35, FTQ, "The State Is Our Exploiter: F.T.Q. Manifesto (1971)," in *Quebec – Only the Beginning*, 201.

32 Kari Levitt, *La capitulation tranquille*, trans. André d'Allemagne, xxiv, xxix. The new postscript, entitled "Post-scriptum à l'édition québécoise. Vers la décolonisation: Canada et Québec," is dated 15 December 1971. Also see Levitt, "Confluences." Interview with Kari Levitt, 9 December 2006, Montreal.

33 Interview with Kari Levitt, 9 December 2006, Montreal. In her dedication to the French-language edition, Levitt states that "Cette édition québécoise de *La capit-*

ulisation tranquille est dédiée à la mémoire de mon père, Karl Polanyi, qui m'a ouvert la perspective d'un socialisme humain. Nous partagions les racines du vieux monde, une existence dans le noveau monde d'Amérique, et les espoirs de libération humaine qui caratérisent le meilleur du Tiers-Monde." Levitt and her mother even decided, in 1970, to donate the last of the funds from a journal that had been run by Karl Polanyi to Chartrand's defence fund. Interview with Kari Levitt, 30 January 2007, Montreal.

34 For detail, see Nick Auf der Maur, "The Trigger Was the 'La Presse' Affair," *The Last Post* 2, no. 3 (1971–72): 8–18.

35 For reflections by one of the most important theoreticians of the labour movement in the 1970s, see Jean-Marc Piotte, *Un certain espoir*, 88–9. For some of the documents that were produced by Piotte and circulated throughout the labour movement, see Jean-Marc Piotte, *Du combat au partenariat*.

36 For a discussion of the plant shutdowns in Quebec, see William D. Coleman, *The Independence Movement in Quebec 1945–1980*, 118, 223. For reactions from inside the labour movement, see Rapport des services, 25 congrès de la CSN, 11 au 17 juin 1972, Québec. Layoffs and plant closures, especially in the metallurgy sector, led to the CSN's adoption of the document *Il n'y a plus d'avenir dans le système économique actuel*.

37 Louis Fournier, *Louis Laberge*, 200–1.

38 Ibid., 202–6. For moving testimony, see Marjolaine Péloquin, *En prison pour la cause des femmes*, 241–5.

39 Fernand Foisy, *Michel Chartrand, la colère du juste (1968–2003)*, 209–12. For vivid images of the event, see Gilles Groulx, *24 heures ou plus* (Montréal: ONF–NFB, 1971). ACSN, CCSNM fonds, procès-verbaux, Assemblé Général, 2 novembre 1971.

40 Nick Auf der Maur, "A Bleu Collar October," 74.

41 Louis Laberge, *A One and Only Front*, 5–6, 27, 44, 30. The radicalization of the FTQ did not emerge out of nowhere. Already in 1967, Laberge spoke about the need to forge a common front between unionists and *groupes populaires* in order to form "un programme de réforme de toute la société." Like Pepin, he worried that "Notre syndicalisme est rapidement en train de devenir, si ce n'est déjà fait, l'expression d'un égoïsme institutionnel et le point de convergences de l'égoïsme individuel d'un trop grand nombre de syndiqués." And, he continued, "Nous sommes en train de créer un syndicalisme de classe moyenne, plus près de la classe possédante que de la masse des 'maudits de la terre.'" Laberge feared that there would be "une révolte des pauvres, non seulement contre nos adversaire traditionnels à nous, employeurs et gouvernants bourgeois, mais aussi contre nos propres syndicats et contre les syndiqués eux-mêmes." Seen in Fournier, *Histoire de la FTQ*, 34–5.

42 Laberge, *A One and Only Front*, 92–4.

43 Fournier, *Histoire de la FTQ*, 72–4.

44 FTQ, "The State Is Our Exploiter: F.T.Q. Manifesto (1971)," 151–60.

45 See Michel Pelletier and Yves Vaillancourt, *Du chômage à la libération*, 5. The manifesto is reprinted at the end of this work. The manifesto goes on to argue that "Nos efforts ne doivent donc pas porter uniquement sur l'obtention d'adoucissements à notre condition d'exploités. Nous devons frapper au coeur de cette bête à profit" (99–110). For the impressions of a young activist at the time, see Pierre Beaudet, *On a raison de se révolter*, 137–8.

46 Rapport du Conseil d'Administration (CEQ), 21 congrès de la C.E.Q., juin 1971, 89–91.

47 CEQ, "Phase One: CEQ Manifesto (1971)," in *Quebec – Only the Beginning*, 99.

48 Ibid., 99–119, 126–7, 134–7.

49 Rétrospective 71–2: *Rapport du Conseil d'Administration*. XXII Congrès de la C.E.Q. Juin 1972, 23–4.

50 Jacques Keable, *Le monde selon Marcel Pepin*, 209.

51 Favreau, L'Heureux, and Paul, *Le projet de société de la CSN de 1966 à aujourd'hui*, 79.

52 It should be remembered that *Ne comptons* was not an official CSN policy document, but rather an official CSN "working document." Marcel Pepin, "Preface," in *Quebec Labour*, 10.

53 Keable, *Le monde selon Marcel Pepin*, 210.

54 "L'origine et le statut des documents," *Le Travail*, (48, 1) janvier 1972.

55 *Ne comptons que sur nos propre moyens* (Service de l'information de la CSN 1971), 44, 68. For an English translation of the document, see CSN, "It's Up to Us."

56 "Le comité des douze et les instruments de vulgarisation," *Le Travail*, (48, 1) janvier 1972. For distribution figures of many of the major CSN documents of the period, see "Évaluation de la réflexion collective sur le document Ne comptons que sur nos propres moyens," (CSN, 1973), 59.

57 "Le comité des douze et les instruments de vulgarisation."

58 Some dissent followed the publication of the document, which built upon tensions that had existed inside the union since Marcel Pepin had first become president. For a discussion of some of these divisions, see Ralph Peter Güntzel, "The Confédération des Syndicats Nationaux, the Idea of Independence, and the Sovereigntist Movement, 1960–1980."

59 Fernand Foisy, "Montréal," *Le Travail*, (48, 1) janvier 1972.

60 "Des documents de travail qui ne moisiront pas sur les tablettes," *Le Travail*, (48, 1) janvier 1972. In the same edition, one can read about the vast consultation taking place over the documents.

61 For a detailed look at the stages of negotiation during the period leading up to the strike, and for an analysis of the political meaning of the strike itself, see Diane Ethier, Jean-Marc Piotte, and Jean Reynolds, *Les travailleurs contre l'État bourgeois, avril et mai 1972*.

62 *Rétrospective 71–72: Rapport du Conseil d'Administration.* XXII Congrès de la C.E.Q. juin 1972, 39–41.

63 Marcel Pepin, "Marcel Pepin, à l'ouverture du conseil confédéral le 14 mars," *Le Travail*, (48, 3) mars 1972.

64 "De nouvelles solidarité," *Le Travail*, (48, 3) mars 1972.

65 "La bataille est la même," *Le Travail*, (48, 3) mars 1972.

66 See *Le Travail*, (48, 3) mars 1972.

67 "Les documents d'étude font leur chemin," *Le Travail*, (48, 3) mars 1972.

68 Quoted in ibid.

69 "Les travailleurs du commerce," *Le Travail*, (48, 4) avril 1972, "Pour une société plus juste: le socialisme coopératif (Le document d'orientation de la Fédération du Commerce)," *Le Travail*, (48, 4) avril 1972.

70 For important information on some of the discussions, see "Évaluation de la réflexion collective sur le document Ne comptons que sur nos propres moyens."

71 Jacques Côté, "Désobeissance à la loi," *Le Piochon*, 9 mai 1972, 13, "Délégation de Sept-Iles," *Le Piochon*, 21 avril 1972, 5.

72 Gérald LeBlanc, "La grève générale paraît reléguée aux oubliettes," *Le Devoir*, 8 mai 1972, 1.

73 UQAM, FTQ fonds, 100p–630:01/7, Communiqué. No. 2, "La FTQ appuie tous les débrayages et les actions de protestations," 10 mai 1972.

74 UQAM, FTQ fonds, 100p–630:01/92. These communiqués give a detailed list of who was on strike and when.

75 "Les débrayages de vendredi," *Quebec-Presse*, 14 mai 1972, 2.

76 Beaudet, *On a raison de se révolter*, 142–4.

77 "Grève à Québec-Presse," *Québec-Presse*, 14 mai 1972, 2.

78 "La maison du quartier," *Le Va vite: Journal des citoyens du Centre-Sud*, 17 mai 1972. It should be noted that *Le Va vite* also complained that other grassroots organizations of the neighbourhood were not reacting in light of the crisis. Comité de rédaction, "C.D.Q.," *Le Va vite: Journal des citoyens du Centre-Sud*, 17 mai 1972.

79 Comité de rédaction, "éditorial – Faut pas lâcher …" *Le Va vite: Journal des citoyens du Centre-Sud*, 17 mai 1972.

80 UQAM, FTQ fonds, 100p–630:01/7, Communiqué. No. 3, "Les viols d'injonction salués par la FTQ," 10 mai 1972.

81 Gérald LeBlanc, "Les dirigeants de la CEQ demandent à être incarcérés avec Yvon Charbonneau," *Le Devoir*, 10 mai 1972, 6.

82 UQAM, FTQ fonds, 100p–630:01/92, Communiqué, "Le Front Commun du secteur public CSN-FTQ-CEQ," and "À tous les membres du front commun secteur public et parapublic – spécialement aux coordonnateurs régionaux," 16 mai 1972.

83 "Woodstock syndical autour d'Orsainville," *Le Devoir*, 15 mai 1972, 1.

84 The Montreal Editorial Group, "Nous: May 1972 Quebec's General Strike," *Our Generation* 8, no. 3 (1972): 32.

85 Emilio Maspero of the Centrale Latina Américaine des travailleurs sent a message of support, saying that he would ask workers from all Latin American countries to support the liberation of workers in Canada. Kjose Lasso of the federation of rural Latin American workers sent a similar message, as did the Confédération française démocratique du travail and the Vancouver Seamen. Other messages of solidarity came from labour organizations from as far away as Venezuela and Luxembourg. UQAM, FTQ fonds, 100p–630:01/92, message to CSN from Emilio Maspero secrétaire générale CLAT, 16 mai 1972. Message of Support from Kjose Lasso Sec. Gen. adjoint "La fédération Latino-Américaine des paysans," 16 mai 1972. Message of Support from La fédération Latino Américaine des travailleurs du bois et du Batiment," 16 mai 1972. Communiqué – May 8 72 Teamsters Local Union 879 Hamilton Ontario. Laurent Lucas, "Paris, 12 mai," *Le Travail*, (48, 5) mai 1972.

86 Jacques Côté, "Réunion de dimanche," *Le Piochon*, 18 avril 1972, 3. Richard Théorêt, "The Struggle of the Common Front," *Radical America* 6, no. 5 (1972): 100. For a look at the social and economic conditions of Sept Iles, and details about the way the strike evolved, see Jean-Marc Piotte's analysis in Ethier, Piotte, and Reynolds, *Les travailleurs contre l'État bourgeois*.

87 The quotation from the radio station comes from "Liberating the Media," *Radical America* 6, no. 5 (1972): 113.

88 Michèle Juneau et al., "Mai 72: une lutte à finir entre le pouvoir et les travailleurs," *Québec-Presse*, 14 mai 1972, 15.

89 In total, twenty-three radio stations were occupied during the May strike, "Liberating the Media," 112-15.

90 Le Comité de rédaction, "Il s'agit de vaincre," *Québec-Presse*, 14 mai 1972, 2.

91 Le comité de rédaction, "Le goût de la véritable démocratie (éditorial)," *Québec-Presse*, 14 mai 1972, 4.

92 UQAM, FTQ fonds, 100p–630:01/92, Joint message by FTQ, CSN, and CEQ, 17 mai 1972.

93 UQAM, FTQ fonds, 100p–630:01/92, "État de la situation chez les enseignants de la CEQ," 16 mai 1972.

94 UQAM, FTQ fonds, 100p–630:01/92, "La situation est loin d'être rose et rassurante dans le secteur de l'éducation au Québec." 17 mai 1972.

95 "La colère des travailleurs," *Le Travail*, (48, 6) mai 1972.

96 See, for example, "Ils n'arrêteront pas la démocracie des travailleurs," *Le Travail*, (48, 7) juin 1972.

97 "La pire vague de terrorisme contre les travailleurs," *Le Travail*, (48, 6) mai 1972.

98 *Le Travail* wrote sarcastically of the government's refusal to yield to the demands of labour. "La pire vague de terrorisme contre les travailleurs," *Le Travail*, (48, 6) mai 1972.

99 See *Québec-Presse*, 14 mai 1972, 5.

100 "Sorel, 11 mai," *Le Travail*, (48, 6) mai 1972.

101 Valmore Tremblay, *Le Piochon*, 28 mars 1972, 11.

102 UQAM, FTQ fonds 100p-630:01/101, CCSNM 14e congrès 1972.

103 Michèle Desfonds, "Le front commun et les femmes," *Le Piochon*, 28 mars 1972, 8.

104 Martine Vaillancourt, "A travail égal, salaire suppose … égal," *Le Piochon*, 12 avril 1972, 4.

105 Carol Leblond, "Yvon-t-y en manger une maudite!" *Le Piochon*, 28 mars 1972, 1.

106 Réjean Langlois, "Solidarité," *Le Piochon*, 28 mars 1972, 10.

107 Fernand Tardif, "On est jamais mieux servi que par soi-même," *Le Piochon*, 28 mars 1972, 3.

108 Martin Poirier, "Les pouvoirs réels," *Le Piochon*, 18 avril 1972, 16.

109 Fabien Mignault, "Camarades grèvistes," *Le Piochon*, 14 avril 1972, 3-5.

110 Côté, "Réunion de dimanche," 5.

111 Serge Tremblay, "Soyons réalistes!" *Le Piochon*, 18 avril 1972, 12.

112 Viateur Beaupré, "Rôle du jardinier," *Le Piochon*, 18 avril 1972, 8.

113 J. Pierre Dallaire, "La peur ou le réalisme," *Le Piochon*, 9 mai 1972, 3.

114 Viateur Beaupré, "Les Anthropophages et leur loi," *Le Piochon*, 9 mai 1972, 6-7, Viateur Beaupré, "Adieu! Adieu!" *Le Piochon*, 9 mai 1972, 12-3, Jacques Côté, "Les jeunesses," *Le Piochon*, 9 mai 1972, 14-15.

115 Valmore Tremblay, "Il faut accentuer la lutte," *Le Piochon*, 9 mai 1972, 10.

116 Suzanne Cormier, "La nouvelle mentalité crée par le front commun," *Le Piochon*, 9 mai 1972, 10.

CONCLUSION

1 Jules LeBlanc, "La marche du premier mai dépasse tous les espoirs des organisateurs," *La Presse*, 2 mai 1973, 1, 6. Louis Fournier, "Un 1er mai pétant de santé!" *Québec-Presse*, 6 mai 1973, 10-11. François Trepanier et Jean-Paul Charbonneau, "Les 'gars' du Gaz métropolitain ont assuré le calme de la marche," *La Presse*, 2 mai 1973, C1. UQAM, Fonds d'archives de l'association pour la défense des droits sociaux du Montréal métropolitain, UQAM 66p1/2, "L'ADDS une organisation politique des non-salariés exploités."

2 Confédération des syndicats nationaux and Centrale de l'enseignement du Québec, *The History of the Labour Movement in Québec*, 218-19.

3 Special supplement to *Québec-Presse* 29 avril 1973, 12.

4 "Nous l'avons vécue dans la rue le 1er mai," *Le Travail (édition de Montréal)*, mai 1973, 1-2.

5 See the messages many union locals printed in the May Day supplement, *Québec-Presse*, 29 avril 1973.

6 For reflections on the meaning of the May 1972 general strike for young Montreal activists, see Pierre Beaudet, *On a raison de se révolter*, 142-3. Also, see Diane Ethier,

Jean-Marc Piotte, and Jean Reynolds, *Les travailleurs contre l'État bourgeois, avril et mai 1972.*

7 Louis Laberge, *En prison pour nous.*

8 Howard Adams, *Prison of Grass*, 181.

9 Louis Fournier, *Histoire de la FTQ, 1965–1992*, 83–92.

10 Laberge, *En prison pour nous.*

11 Yvon Charbonneau, "Cadre générale," *Prospective*, xxii congrès, CEQ juin 1972. Also see Yvon Charbonneau, "Introduction 1972–73: uni intermède agité" *Rétrospective: Rapport des activités de la CEQ pour 1972–73*, XXIII Congrès, juillet 1973, 3. For the continuing importance of class politics in the CEQ in the 1970s, see Bernard Solasse, "L'idéologie de la Centrale des enseignants du Québec et son évolution, 1960–1973," in *Idéologies au Canada français, 1940–1976, Tome II.*

12 Mona-Josée Gagnon, "Women in the Trade-Union Movement in Quebec," in *Quebec since 1945*, 165.

13 Marcel Pepin, *Pour Vaincre*, Rapport moral du Président général de la CSN au 45iéme Congrès, Québec, le 11 juin 1972, 9–11.

14 Louis Favreau, Pierre L'Heureux, avec la collaboration de Michel Paul, *Le projet de société de la CSN de 1966 à aujourd'hui*, 81–97. Also see Jacques Rouillard, *Histoire du syndicalisme au Québec*, 155–7, and William D. Coleman, *The Independence Movement in Quebec 1945–1980*, 119. For a look at the ideology of the Centrale des syndicats démocratiques, made up of unions that broke with the CSN, see Bernard Solasse, "Note sur l'idéologie de la Centrale des syndicats démocratiques, 1972–1979," in *Idéologies au Canada français, 1940–1976, Tome II.*

15 Fournier, *Histoire de la FTQ*, 105–13.

16 Interview with Robert Comeau, 27 September 2006, Montreal. Jean-Marc Piotte's courses on Marxism at UQAM attracted hundreds of students in the early 1970s.

17 For an excellent memoir of one such activist, which conveys much of the excitement, energy, and contradiction of the political organizing in the early 1970s, see Beaudet, *On a raison de se révolter.*

18 Ibid, 135–6.

19 See Charles Gagnon, "Il était une fois … Conte à l'adresse de la jeunesse de mon pays."

20 Max Elbaum writes that, at its height, the American New Communist Movement counted roughly 10,000 core activists. In Quebec, at least 3,000 activists gravitated to the city's three major Maoist organizations (around 1,050 of whom were core members). Elbaum, *Revolution in the Air*, 4, Jacques Benoît, *L'extrême gauche*, 90. See especially Jean-Philippe Warren, *Ils voulaient changer le monde.*

21 For the appeal of China and its Cultural Revolution, see Beaudet, *On a raison de se révolter*, 107–9.

22 Warren, *Ils voulaient changer le monde*, 67.

23 Benoît, *L'extrême gauche*, 82.

24 Warren, *Ils voulaient changer le monde*, 90, 102. The average print run for *En lutte!* in 1979 was 7,000.

25 Ibid., 46, Benoît, *L'extrême gauche*, 11.

26 See "Créons l'organisation marxiste-léniniste de lutte pour le Parti," *EN LUTTE!*, 12 décembre 1974, 9. Mouvement révolutionnaire des étudiants du Québec, *En avant pour la création de l'organisation marxiste-léniniste*, 25–32.

27 Quoted in Nick Auf der Maur, "The Trigger Was the 'La Presse' Affair," *The Last Post* 2, no. 3 (1971–1972): 13.

28 Some people were reported to have been chanting "PQ, travailleurs, solidarité" when leaving an assembly later that evening. "Le PQ esquisse un mouvement vers les travailleurs," *La Presse*, 2 mai 1973, C1.

29 An important document reflecting the party's left wing is André Larocque, *Défis au Parti Québécois*. After the internal controversy over the PQ's decision not to march during the *La Presse* strike in the fall of 1971, the party issued a new manifesto. "Conduire à la victoire un parti populaire," *Le Devoir*, 29 novembre 1971, 5. And on the Montreal Central Council of the CSN's adoption of a highly critical stance towards the PQ in 1973, see Ralph Peter Güntzel, "The Confédération des Syndicats Nationaux, the Idea of Independence, and the Sovereigntist Movement, 1960–1980," 113–15.

30 Charles Gagnon, "Le Parti Québécois et la révolution," *Socialisme 69*, no. 17 (1969): 131.

31 John Huot notes that "much of the FLP base among students and young workers was eroded by the PQ campaign in April 1970," as well as by their involvement in the labour movement and in the FRAP. See "The Development of Socialist Ideology and Organization," *Radical America* 6, no. 5 (1972): 66. According to CSN militant Jacques Bourdouxe, "Quand le PQ a commencé à prendre figure, nos résolutions se sont retrouvées intégralement soumises au congrès du PQ. Sur le plancher, les militants syndicaux disaient qu'ils avaient déjà voté ça au congrès de la CSN." In Favreau, L'Heureux, and Paul, *Le projet de société de la CSN de 1966 à aujourd'hui*, 102.

32 Jean-Philippe Warren, *Une douce anarchie*, 227.

33 Coleman, *The Independence Movement in Quebec 1945–1980*, 221.

34 Pierre Vallières, *Les Héritiers de Papineau*, 244–5.

35 Ibid., 236–7. Pierre Richard, "Pierre Vallières à Mont-Laurier: L'espoir de la population ne saurait être déçu sans risque de violence," *Le Devoir*, 15 mai 1972, 16.

36 See, for example, Marjolaine Péloquin, *En prison pour la cause des femmes*, 242. Also see Sylvain Rivière, *Léandre Bergeron, né en exil*.

37 Jean-Marc Piotte, *La communauté perdue*, 99–113.

38 Pierre Vallières, *Choose!*, trans. Penelope Williams, 130. Publications like *Our Generation*, *Québec-Presse*, and *UHURU* began featuring articles on women's libera-

tion. The FLP even argued that because women were exploited not only by capitalism and colonialism but also by men, "elles constituent au sein du Québec notre 'Tier Monde.'" See WRDA, FLP fonds, "Press statements, Les femmes," n.d., 9.

39 Vallières, *Choose!*, 96.

40 Ibid., 53.

41 Gérald Godin's papers include draft manuscripts of a NFB film in which he would attempt to capture the voices of Aboriginal people. UQAM, Gérald Godin fonds, 81p–660:02/15, draft manuscript. Also see the footage of Aboriginals in Gilles Groulx, *24 heures ou plus* (Montréal: ONF–NFB, 1971).

42 See, for example, Marthe Therrien, "Avec 'leur' loi, les blancs briment les Indiens et les Esquimaux!" *Québec-Presse*, 14 décembre 1969, 10A.

43 *Le Nouveau-Québec, ou comment des colonisés traitent leur colonie…* Mémoire adressé au ministre de l'Education et à l'Assemblée nationale du Québec (Québec: Corporation des enseignants du Québec, 1973), 1–2.

44 *Le Nouveau-Québec, ou comment des colonisés traitent leur colonie…* Annexe B– "Lettre de la C.E.Q. aux membres de l'Assembée nationale du Québec" Sainte-Foy, le 20 décembre 1972, Michel Agnaieff to members of the National Assembly, 42.

45 CEQ, *Rétrospective 71–72: Rapport du Conseil d'Administration*. (XXII Congrès de la C.E.Q. Juin 1972), 25.

46 See "L'Inuit et 'notre' système d'éducation," *Action Pédagogique* 24 (1972): 43.

47 *Le Nouveau-Québec, ou comment des colonisés traitent leur colonie*, 1, 36.

48 Pierre Vallières, "Memmi, le Québec, le Tiers-Monde et la sexualité," in *Paroles d'un nègre blanc*, 173.

49 Details of this episode can be found in Paul Dejean, *Les Haïtiens au Québec*. Also see Martin Pâquet and Érick Duchesne, "Étude de la complexité d'un événement. Les responsables politiques québécois et les immigrants illégaux haïtiens, 1972–1974."

50 See Beaudet, *On a raison de se révolter*, 194, 171.

51 Jean Ménard, a Catholic priest who had been involved with the development of liberation theology while a missionary in Latin America, became an important figure in Quebec-Chile solidarity. See his testimony from the April 2006 edition of *Mission*, cited in Pierre Beaudet, *Qui aide qui?*, 61–2. In April 1972, a group from Quebec attended a meeting of Latin American Christians for Socialism conference in Santiago, Chile. The national report submitted by the Quebec delegation noted that "beyond Mexico, there are the Chicanos, the Blacks, the Puerto-Ricans and also there is Quebec, a society that is searching for its liberating path and that has to confront the same enemy as yours: US and Canadian Imperialism that, to attain its own development needs to under-develop all of the rest of us." Although Quebeckers had come to Latin America as missionaries, thanks to the liberation struggles taking place, they "learned more by their experiences in Latin America than they brought from Quebec." Burke Library Archives, Union Theological

Seminary, New York, MRL9, "Records of Primer Encuentro Latinoamericano de Cristianos por el Socialismo (PELCS), Santiago, Chile, 1972." Translation from the Spanish by Catherine LeGrand.

52 For a brief overview of the gay liberation movement in the United States, see Van Gosse, *Rethinking the New Left: An Interpretive History*, 171–85.

53 Carl Wittman, "Manifeste du Front de Libération homosexuelle," *Mainmise*, no. 2 (1970). Also, see Conrad Rény and Mark Wilson, "Il me semble qu'on s'est déjà vu quelque part ... Les québécois homosexuels trouvent leurs voix. Est-ce une part du gâteau qu'on veut, ou un nouveau gâteau?" *Le Temps Fou* 1, no. 2 (1978): 29–30. Conrad and Wilson note, in this important account of the early gay liberation movement, that in the version of the "Gay Manifesto" that is reproduced, entire sections of the original document are suppressed, including more explicitly political passages and a discussion of the importance of the women's liberation movement to the struggle for gay rights.

54 Rény and Wilson, "Il me semble qu'on s'est déjà vu quelque part," 30.

55 For important insights, see Andrea Hildebran, "Genèse d'une communauté lesbienne: un récit des années 1970," in *Sortir de l'ombre*.

56 Details on the mass arrests and resistance to them can be found in Rény and Wilson, "Il me semble qu'on s'est déjà vu quelque part ..." and Roger Noël, "Libération homosexuelle ou révolution socialiste?" in *Sortir de l'ombre*.

57 Greg Grandin, *The Last Colonial Massacre*, 196.

58 See, for example, The CourtePointe Collective, *The Point Is ... Grassroots Organizing Works*.

59 UQAM, Fonds d'archives de l'association pour la défense des droits sociaux de Montréal métropolitain, UQAM 66p1/2, "L'ADDS une organisation politique des non-salariés exploités."

60 Catherine LeGrand, "L'axe missionaire catholique entre le Québec et l'Amérique Latine. Une exploration préliminaire." Unpublished manuscript. Carolyn Sharp, "To Build a Just Society: The Catholic Left in Quebec," in *Reclaiming Democracy*.

61 For an eloquent discussion, see David Scott, *Conscripts of Modernity*.

BIBLIOGRAPHY

ARCHIVAL AND LIBRARY COLLECTIONS

BURKE LIBRARY ARCHIVES, UNION THEOLOGICAL SEMINARY (New York)
MRL9 – Records of Primer Encuentro Latinoamericano de Cristianos por el Socialismo (PELCS), Santiago, Chile, 1972.
CANADIAN WOMEN'S MOVEMENT ARCHIVES (Ottawa)
Box 31. Front de libération des femmes québécoises (Montréal, QC): manifeste et bilan, 1971.
CONCORDIA UNIVERSITY ARCHIVES (Montreal)
Ready Reference File, "The Computer Riot, Sir George Williams: 1969"
ARCHIVES, CONFÉDÉRATION DES SYNDICATS NATIONAUX (Montreal)
Fonds d'archives, Conseil des syndicats nationaux
rapports, comité central d'action politique, 1968–72
Fonds d'archives, Conseil central des syndicats nationaux de Montréal
rapports de congrès, 1968–74
procès-verbaux, assemblées générales, 1968–74
publications
MCGILL UNIVERSITY ARCHIVES (Montreal)
RG2 C401. Opération McGill fonds
BIBLIOTHÈQUE ET ARCHIVES NATIONALES DU QUÉBEC (Montreal)
MSS140. Fonds Éditions Parti Pris
MSS410. Fonds Gaston Miron
ARCHIVES, UNIVERSITÉ DU QUÉBEC À MONTRÉAL
21P.   Collection de publications de groupes de gauche et de groupes populaires
66P.   Fonds d'archives de l'Association pour la défense des droits sociaux du Montréal métropolitain.

79p   Fonds de la Clinique des citoyens de Saint-Jacques

81p.   Fonds d'archives Gérald Godin

100p.   Fonds d'archives de la Fédération des travailleurs et travailleuses du Québec

124p.   Fonds d'archives Charles-Gagnon

THE WILLIAM READY DIVISION OF ARCHIVES AND RESEARCH COLLECTIONS, MCMASTER UNIVERSITY (Hamilton)

Quebec social and political organizations

Quebec – Anderson Affair at Sir George Williams University

Quebec – Campaign against Bill 63 collection

Quebec – Comité québécois provisoire de solidarité avec le peuple palestinien

Quebec – Confédération des syndicats nationaux

Quebec – Corporation des enseignants du Québec

Quebec – Fédération des travailleurs du Québec

Quebec – Front de libération populaire

Quebec – Front de libération du Québec and Comité d'aide au groupe "Vallières-Gagnon"

Quebec – Front d'action politique

Quebec – Mouvement syndical populaire

Quebec – Opération McGill

Quebec – Parti québécois

Quebec – Union générale des étudiants du Québec fonds

Stanley Gray fonds

POLITICAL JOURNALS (VARIOUS DATES)

Action Pédagogique

Caribbean International Opinion: Dynamics of Liberation (Montreal)

La Cognée (Montreal)

Expression (Montreal)

Femmes du Québec: organne officiel de la ligue des femmes progressistes du Québec (Montreal)

The Last Post (*Montreal*)

Liberation: an independent monthly

Liberté (Montreal)

McGill Student Handbook (Montreal)

Le Militant (Montreal)

Mobilisation (Montreal)

Montreal Women's Liberation Newsletter (Montreal)

National Minority News: organ of the Committee for the Defense of

National Minority People's Rights (Montreal)

Noir et rouge (Montreal)

Our Generation (Montreal)

Our Generation Against Nuclear War (Montreal)

Parti Pris (Montreal)

Québécoises deboutte! (Montreal)

Québec libre (Montreal)

Radical America (Madison)

Révolution québécoise (Montreal)

La Revue socialiste (Montreal)

Socialisme 64… (Montreal)

Socialisme québécois (Montreal)

Third World Solidarity: Journal of the Afro-Asian Latin American People's Solidarity Committee (Montreal)

NEWSPAPERS AND MAGAZINES (VARIOUS DATES)

Canadian Magazine
Châtelaine
Le Devoir
EN LUTTE!
Le Figaro
France Observateur
The Georgian
The Guardian
Le Jour
The McGill Daily
The McGill Free Press: Black Spark
   Edition
The McGill Reporter
The Montreal Gazette
La Patrie

Le Piochon
Le Pouvoir
La Presse
Quartier latin
Québec-Presse
Le Quotidien populaire
The Review (McGill Daily supplement)
Le sainte-marie: journal des
   étudiants du collège Sainte-Marie
   de Montréal
Le Travail
Le Travail, édition de Montréal
UHURU
Umoja
Unité Ouvrière

ROYAL COMMISSIONS

Briefs to the Royal Commission on the Status of Women

INTERVIEWS

Robert Comeau
Fernand Foisy
Stanley Gray

Kari Levitt
Carman Miller
Jean-Marc Piotte

Dimitri Roussopoulos
Daya Varma
Mark Wilson

FILMS

Arcand, Denys. *On est au coton*. Montréal: ONF-NFB, 1970.

Brault, Michel. *Les Ordres*. Canada: Les Productions Prisma, 1974.

Groulx, Gilles. *24 heures ou plus*. Montréal: ONF-NFB, 1971.

Klein, Bonnie Sherr. *Citizens' Medicine*. Montréal: ONF-NFB, 1970.

Labrecque, Jean-Claude. *Le R.I.N.* Canada: Les Productions Virage, 2002.

Laflamme, Claude. *La République des Beaux-arts: la Malédiction de la momie*. Canada: Vent d'Est Films, 1997.

Lafond, Jean-Daniel. *La Manière Nègre ou Aimé Césaire, chemin faisant*. Canada-France co-production: ACPAV (Québec) and RFO (Martinique), 1991.

Labrecque, Jean-Claude and Jean-Pierre Masse. *La Nuit de la poésie 27 mars 1970*. Montréal: ONF-NFB, 1970.

Palcy, Euzhan. *Aimé Césaire: A Voice for History, part II*. United States: California Newsreel, 1994.

FILMS, *continued*

Rebellion, Protest, and Change: *Reflections on the 1960s and the Development of Montreal's Black Community,* February 18, 2006, UNIA Hall, Montreal. video-recording (available through the Alfie Roberts' Institute, Montreal).

Spry, Robin. *Reaction: A Portrait of a Society in Crisis.* Montréal: ONF-NFB, 1973.

BOOKS, THESES, AND ARTICLES

Adams, Howard. *Prison of Grass: Canada from a Native Point of View.* Calgary: Fifth House Publishers, 1989 [1975].

Ali, Tariq. *Street Fighting Years: An Autobiography of the Sixties.* London: Verso, 2005 [1987].

Anctil, Pierre, Ira Robinson, and Gérard Bouchard, eds. *Juifs et Canadiens français dans la société québécoise.* Sillery: Septentrion, 2000.

Anderson, Benedict. *Imagined Communities: Reflections on the Origin and Spread of Nationalism.* London: Verso, 1991 [1983].

Andrade, Miguel Simão. "La Commission des écoles catholiques de Montréal et l'intégration des immigrants et des minorités ethniques à l'école française de 1947 à 1977." *Revue d'histoire de l'Amérique française* 60, no. 4 (2007): 455–86.

Angers, Stéphanie, and Gérard Fabre. *Échanges intellectuels entre la France et le Québec 1930–2000. Les réseaux de la revue Esprit avec La Relève, Cité libre, Parti pris et Possibles.* Paris: Harmattan, 2004.

Appadurai, Arjun. *Modernity at Large: Cultural Dimensions of Globalization.* Minneapolis: University of Minnesota Press, 1996.

Austin, David. "All Roads Led to Montreal: Black Power, the Caribbean, and the Black Radical Tradition in Canada." *Journal of African American History* 92, no. 4 (2007): 516–39.

– "Contemporary Montréal and the 1968 Congress of Black Writers." *Lost Histories* 24, no. 1 (1998): 56–60.

– "Introduction." In *A View for Freedom: Alfie Roberts Speaks on the Caribbean, Cricket, Montreal, and C.L.R. James.* Montreal: Alfie Roberts Institute, 2005, 11–25.

Baillargeon, Constantin. *Pierre Vallières vu par son professeur de philosophie.* Montréal: Médiaspaul, 2002.

Baillargeon, Denyse. *Un Québec en mal d'enfants. La médicalisation de la maternité, 1910–1970.* Montréal: Remue-ménage, 2004.

Beaucage, André. *Syndicats, salaires et conjoncture économique: l'expérience des fronts communs du secteur public québécois de 1971 à 1983.* Sillery: Presses de l'Université du Québec, 1989.

Beaudet, Pierre. *On a raison de se révolter. Chronique des années 70.* Montréal: Les Éditions Écosociété, 2008.

– *Qui aide qui? Une brève histoire de la solidarité internationale au Québec.* Montréal: Boréal, 2009.

Bédard, Éric. *Chronique d'une insurrection appréhendée.* Sillery: Septentrion, 1998.

– "McGill français: un contexte de fébrilité étudiante et nationaliste." *Bulletin d'histoire politique* 9, no. 1 (2000): 148–52.

– "The Intellectual Origins of the October Crisis." In *Creating Postwar Canada: Community, Diversity, and Dissent, 1945–1975,* Magda Fahrni and Robert Rutherdale, eds. Vancouver: UBC Press, 2008, 45–60.

Bégin, Monique. "The Royal Commission on the Status of Women in Canada: Twenty Years Later." In *Challenging Times: The Women's Movement in Canada and the United States,* Constance Backhouse and David H. Flaherty, eds. Montreal: McGill-Queen's University Press, 1992, 21–38.

Behiels, Michael D. *Prelude to Quebec's Quiet Revolution: Liberalism versus Neo-nationalism, 1945–1960.* Montreal: McGill-Queen's University Press, 1985.

– *Quebec and the Question of Immigration: From Ethnocentrism to Ethnic Pluralism, 1900–1985.* Ottawa: Canadian Historical Association, 1991.

– "The Commission des Écoles catholiques de Montréal and the Neo-Canadian Question: 1947–63." *Canadian Ethnic Studies / Études ethniques au Canada* 18, no. 2 (1986): 38–64.

Bélanger, André J. *Ruptures et constantes: quatre idéologies du Québec en éclatement: la Relève, la JEC, Cité libre, Parti pris.* Montréal: Hurtubise HMH, 1977.

Bélander, Yves, Robert Comeau et Céline Métivier, eds. *La révolution tranquille: 40 ans plus tard: un bilan.* Montréal: VLB Éditeur, 2000.

Benoît, Jacques. *L'extrême gauche.* Montréal: La Presse, 1977.

Bergeron, Léandre. *The History of Quebec: A Patriot's Handbook.* Updated ed. Toronto: NC Press, 1971.

– *Petit manuel d'histoire du Québec.* Montréal: Éditions québécoises, 1971.

Berque, Jacques. *Dépossession du monde.* Paris: Éditions du seuil, 1964.

– Preface to *Les québécois.* Paris: François Maspero, 1967.

Bettelheim, Charles. *Planification et croissance accélérée.* Paris: François Maspero, 1964.

"Beyond What? An Introduction." In *Postcolonial Studies and Beyond,* Ania Loomba, Suvir Kaul, Matti Bunzl, Antoinette Burton and Jed Esty, eds. Durham: Duke University Press, 2005, 1–38

Boivin, Robert. *Histoire de la Clinique des citoyens de Saint-Jacques (1968–1988). Des comités de citoyens au CLSC du plateau Mont-Royal.* Montréal: VLB éditeur, 1988.

Bouchard-Saint-Amant, Pierrette. "L'idéologie de la revue *Parti Pris*: le nationalisme socialiste." In *Idéologies au Canada français 1940–1960,* Fernand Dumont, Jean Hamelin and Jean-Paul Montminy, eds. Québec: Les Presses de l'Université Laval, 1981, 315–53

Bourbeau, Amélie. "La réorganisation de l'assistance chez les catholiques Montréalais: La Fédération des Oeuvres de charité canadiennes-françaises et la Federation of Catholic Charities, 1930–1972." PhD, UQAM, 2009.

Boehmer, Elleke, and Bart Moore-Gilbert. "Postcolonial Studies and Transnational Resistance." *Interventions* 4, no. 1 (2002): 7–21.

Bourque, Gilles, Jules Duchastel, and Jacques Beauchemin. *La société libérale duplessiste, 1944–1960.* Montréal: Les Presses de l'Université de Montréal, 1994.

Bouthillier, Guy. "Aux origines de la planification linguistique québécoise." In *L'État et la planification linguistique II. Études de cas particuliers*, ed. André Martin. Québec: Éditeur officiel du Québec, 1981, 7–22.

Brodeur, Violette, Suzanne G. Chartrand, Louise Corriveau, and Béatrice Valay. *Le Mouvement des femmes au Québec: étude des groupes montréalais et nationaux*. Montréal: Centre de formation populaire, 1982.

Brownmiller, Susan. *In Our Time: Memoir of a Revolution*. New York: Dial Press, 1999.

Butcher, LeRoi. "The Anderson Affair." In *Let the Niggers Burn! The Sir George Williams University Affair and Its Caribbean Aftermath*, ed. Dennis Forsythe. Montreal: Black Rose Books/Our Generation Press, 1971, 76–109.

Cardin, Jean-François. *Comprendre octobre 1970. Le FLQ, la crise et le syndicalisme*. Montréal: Éditions du Méridien, 1990.

– *La crise d'octobre 1970 et le mouvement syndical québécois*. Montréal: Collection RCHTQ, Études et documents, 1988.

– "La CSN et le syndicalisme de combat (1960–1975)." In *La CSN, 75 ans d'action syndicale et sociale*, Yves Bélanger and Robert Comeau, eds. Sainte-Foy: Les Presses de l'Université du Québec, 1998, 33–8.

– "Le mouvement syndical et les débuts du FRAP." *Cahiers d'histoire* 3, no. 1 (1987): 3–16.

Carel, Ivan. "*Feu sur l'Amérique. Proposition pour la révolution nord-américaine*, de Charles Gagnon: analyse et mise en perspective." *Bulletin d'histoire politique* 15, no. 1 (2006): 149–61.

Carmichael, Stokely. *Stokely Speaks: Black Power Back to Pan-Africanism*. New York: Random House, 1971.

– and Charles V. Hamilton. *Black Power: The Politics of Liberation in America*. New York: Vintage Books, 1967.

– and Ekwueme Michael Thelwell. *Ready for Revolution: The Life and Struggles of Stokely Carmichael [Kwame Ture]*. New York: Scribner, 2003.

Carson, Clayborne. *In Struggle: SNCC and the Black Awakening of the 1960s*. Cambridge: Harvard University Press, 1981.

Casgrain, Thérèse F. *A Woman in a Man's World*, trans. Joyce Marshall. Toronto: McClelland and Stewart, 1972.

Castro, Fidel. *History Will Absolve Me*. New York: L. Stuart, 1961.

CEQ. "Phase One: CEQ Manifesto (1971)," trans. John Chambers. In *Quebec – Only the Beginning: The Manifestoes of the Common Front*, ed. Daniel Drache. Toronto: New Press, 1972, 99–148.

– *Prospective*, XXIIᵉ congrès, CEQ juin 1972.

– *Le Nouveau-Québec, ou comment des colonisés traitent leur colonie ...* Mémoire adressé au ministre de l'Education et à l'Assemblée nationale du Québec. Québec: Corporation des enseigants du Québec, 1973.

– *Rapport du Conseil d'Administration* (CEQ). XXIᵉ congrèes de la C.E.Q., Juin 1971.

– *Rétrospective 71–72: Rapport du Conseil d'Administration*. XXIIᵉ Congrès de la CEQ, Juin 1972.

- *Rétrospective: Rapport des activités de la* CEQ *pour 1972–73*, XXIIIè Congrès, juillet 1973.

Césaire, Aimé. *Discourse on Colonialism*, trans. Joan Pinkham. New York: Monthly Review Press, 2000 [1955].

- "Le discours sur la négritude, prononcé le jeudi 26 février 1987." In *Discours sur le colonialisme*. Paris: Présence Africaine, 2004, 78–92.

- "Notebook of a Return to the Native Land." In *Aimé Césaire, the Collected Poetry*. Berkeley: University of California Press, 1983, 32–85.

Chamberland, Line. *Mémoires lesbiennes: le lesbianisme à Montréal entre 1950 et 1970*. Montréal: Remue-ménage, 1996.

Chaput, Marcel. *Pourquoi je suis séparatiste*. Montréal: Les Éditions du Jour, 1961.

Charters, David A. "The Amateur Revolutionaries: A Reassessment of the FLQ." *Terrorism and Political Violence* 9, no. 1 (1997): 133–69.

Chartrand, Michel, Vernel Olson, and John Riddell. *The Real Cuba as Three Canadians Saw it*. Toronto: Fair Play for Cuba Committee, 1964.

Cherniak, Donna, and Allan Feingold. "Birth Control Handbook (1971)." In *Women Unite! An Anthology of the Canadian Women's Movement*. Toronto: Canadian Women's Educational Press, 1972, 109–13.

- "Introduction." *Birth Control Handbook* 6th and 7th editions, Montreal, 1971.

Chodos, Robert, and Nick Auf der Maur, eds. *Quebec: A Chronicle 1968–1972*. Toronto: James Lewis and Samuel, 1972.

- "A Short History of Student Activism at McGill." In *McGill Student Handbook*, Robert Chodos, Allan Feingold and Tom Sorell, eds. Montreal: Students' Society of McGill University, 1969, 86–92.

- *The Caribbean Connection*. Toronto: James Lorimer, 1977.

Clément, Dominique. *Canada's Rights Revolution: Social Movements and Social Change, 1937–1982*. Vancouver: UBC Press, 2008.

The Clio Collective. *Quebec Women: A History*, trans. Roger Gagnon and Rosalind Gill. Toronto: Women's Press, 1987.

Cloutier, Yvan. "Sartre en quête d'un éditeur francophone en Amérique." *The French Review* 66, no. 5 (1993): 752–9.

Coates, Ken. *Global History of Indigenous Peoples: Struggle and Survival*. New York: Palgrave Macmillan, 2004.

Coleman, William D. *The Independence Movement in Quebec 1945–1980*. Toronto: University of Toronto Press, 1984.

- "The Class Bases of Language Policy in Quebec, 1949–1975." *Studies in Political Economy*, no. 3 (1980): 93–117.

Collectif Clio. *L'histoire des femmes au Québec depuis quatre siècles*. 2è ed. Montréal: Le Jour, 1992.

Comby, Marc. "L'expérience du FRAP à Montréal (1970–1974): La tentative de créer au Québec un parti d'extrême gauche." In *Contester dans un pays prospère. L'extrême gauche en Belgique et au Canada*, Anne Morelli and José Gotovitch, eds. Bruxelles: P.I.E. Peter Lang, 2007, 153–75.

- "Le Front d'action politique (FRAP) à Montréal: de la naissance aux élection (1969–1970)," *Bulletin du* RCHTQ 27, no. 3 (2001): 3–22.

- "Mouvements sociaux, syndicats et action politique à Montréal: l'histoire du FRAP (1970–1974)." MA, Université de Montréal, 2005.

Comeau, Robert, D. Cooper, and Pierre Vallières. FLQ : un projet révolutionnaire: lettres et écrits felquistes (1963–1982). Outremont: VLB éditeur, 1990.

Comeau, Robert, and Bernard Dionne. Le droit de se taire: histoire des communistes au Québec, de la Première Guerre mondiale à la Révolution tranquille. Outremont: VLB éditeur, 1989.

Confédération des syndicats nationaux, and Centrale de l'enseignement du Québec. The History of the Labour Movement in Québec. Montreal: Black Rose Books, 1987.

Cook, Ramsay. Watching Quebec: Selected Essays. Montreal: McGill-Queen's University Press, 2005.

Cooper, Frederick. Colonialism in Question: Theory, Knowledge, History. Berkeley and Los Angeles: University of California Press, 2005.

The CourtePointe Collective. The Point Is… Grassroots Organizing Works: Women from Point St. Charles Sharing Stories of Solidarity. Montreal: Remue-ménage, 2006.

Crelinsten, Ronald D. "The Internal Dynamics of the FLQ during the October Crisis of 1970." Journal of Strategic Studies 10, no. 4 (1987): 59–89.

- "Power and Meaning: Terrorism as a Struggle over Access to the Communication Structure." In Contemporary Research on Terrorism, Paul Wilkinson and Alasdair M. Stewart, eds. Aberdeen: Aberdeen University Press, 1987, 419–50.

Croteau, Martin. "L'implication sociale et politique de Jacques Couture à Montréal de 1963 à 1976." MA, UQAM, 2008.

CSN. "It's Up to Us." In Drache, Quebec – Only the Beginning, trans. Penelope Williams, 1–95.

- "Évaluation de la réflexion collective sur le document Ne comptons que sur nos propres moyens." CSN, 1973.

d'Allemagne, André. Le Colonialisme au Québec. Montréal: Édition R-B, 1966.

- Le R.I.N. de 1960 à 1963: étude d'un groupe de pression au Québec. Montréal: Éditions l'Étincelle, 1974.

Davenport, T.R.H. "Nationalism and Conciliation: The Bourassa-Hertzog Posture." Canadian Historical Review 44, no. 3 (1963): 193–212.

David, Hélène, and Louis Maheu. "Problèmes sociaux, contradictions structurelles et politiques gouvernementales." In Québec occupé. Montréal: Éditions Parti Pris, 1971, 87–91.

de Beauvoir, Simone. Force of Circumstance. Middlesex: Penguin Books, 1968 [1963].

- The Second Sex, trans. H.M. Parshley. New York: Vintage Books, 1989 [1953].

de lpola, Emilio. "Le FRAP devant la crise." In Québec occupé. Montréal: Éditions Parti Pris, 1971, 141–56.

Dejean, Paul. Les Haïtiens au Québec. Montréal: Les presses de l'Université du Québec, 1978.

Deleuze, Magali. L'une et l'autre indépendance 1954–1964: Les médias au Québec et la guerre d'Algérie. Outremont: Les Éditions Point de fuite, 2001.

Desmarais, Louise. *Mémoires d'une bataille inachevée. La lutte pour l'avortement au Québec, 1970–1992.* Montréal: Éditions Trait d'union, 1999.

Demczuk, Irène, and Frank W. Remiggi, eds. *Sortir de l'ombre: histoires des communautés lesbienne et gaie de Montréal.* Montréal: VLB éditeur, 1998.

Denis, Roch. "Le terrorisme dans la révolution au Québec." In *Québec occupé.* Montréal: Éditions Parti Pris, 1971, 157–78.

Desbiens, Jean-Paul. *Les insolences du Frère Untel.* Montréal: Éditions de l'homme, 1960.

de Sève, Micheline. "Féminisme et nationalisme au Québec, une alliance inattendue." *Revue internationale d'études canadiennes,* no. 17 (1998): 157–75.

Desroches, Vincent. "Uprooting and Uprootedness: Haitian Poetry in Quebec (1960–2002)." In *Textualizing the Immigrant Experience in Contemporary Quebec,* Susan Ireland and Patrice J. Proulx, eds. Westport: Praeger, 2004, 203–16.

de Vault, Carole, with William Johnson. *The Informer: Confessions of an Ex-Terrorist.* Toronto: Fleet Books, 1982.

Dion, Léon. *La révolution déroutée, 1960–1976.* Montréal: Boréal, 1998.

– *Québec: The Unfinished Revolution.* Montreal: McGill-Queen's University Press, 1976.

Dirlik, Arif. "Rethinking Colonialism: Globalization, Postcolonialism, and the Nation." *Interventions* 4, no. 3 (2002): 428–48.

Dixon, Marlene. *Things Which Are Done in Secret.* Montreal: Black Rose Books, 1976.

Dofny, Jacques, and Marcel Rioux. "Les classes sociales au Canada français." *Revue française de Sociologie* III (1962): 290–300.

Dolment, Marcelle, and Marcel Barthe. *La femme au Québec.* Ottawa: Les Presses Libres, 1973.

Dorsinville, Max. *Caliban without Prospero: Essay on Quebec and Black Literature.* Erin: Press Porcépic, 1974.

Drache, Daniel. *Quebec – Only the Beginning.* Toronto, New Press, 1972.

Dubinsky, Karen, Catherine Krull, Susan Lord, Sean Mills, and Scott Rutherford, eds. *New World Coming: The Sixties and the Shaping of Global Consciousness.* Toronto: Between the Lines Press, 2009.

Dumont, Fernand. *The Vigil of Quebec.* Toronto: University of Toronto Press, 1974.

Dumont, Micheline. *Le féminisme québécois raconté à Camille.* Montréal: Remue-ménage, 2008.

– "The Origins of the Women's Movement in Québec." In *Challenging Times: The Women's Movement in Canada and the United States,* 72–89.

Eber, Dorothy. *The Computer Centre Party: Canada Meets Black Power.* Montreal: Tundra Books, 1969.

Echols, Alice. *Daring to Be Bad: Radical Feminism in America 1967–1975.* Minneapolis: University of Minnesota Press, 1989.

Elbaum, Max. *Revolution in the Air: Sixties Radicals Turn to Lenin, Mao and Che.* London: Verso, 2006 [2002].

Eley, Geoff. *Forging Democracy: The History of the Left in Europe, 1850–2000.* Oxford: Oxford University Press, 2002.

Enke, Anne. *Finding the Movement: Sexuality, Contested Space, and Feminist Activism*. Durham and London: Duke University Press, 2007.

Ethier, Diane, Jean-Marc Piotte, and Jean Reynolds. *Les travailleurs contre l'État bourgeois, avril et mai 1972*. Montréal: L'Aurore, 1975.

Evans, Sara. *Personal Politics: The Roots of Women's Liberation in the Civil Rights Movement and the New Left*. New York: Vintage Books, 1979.

Fanon, Frantz. *Black Skin, White Masks*, trans. Charles Lam Markmann. New York: Grove Press, 1967 [1952].

– *A Dying Colonialism*. New York: Grove Press, 1965 [1959].

– *The Wretched of the Earth*, trans. Constance Farrington. New York: Grove Press, 1963 [1961].

Farber, Jerry. *The Student as Nigger: Essays and Stories*. North Hollywood: Contact Books, 1969.

Favreau, Louis, Pierre L'Heureux, avec la collaboration de Michel Paul. *Le projet de société de la CSN de 1966 à aujourd'hui: crise et avenir du syndicalisme au Québec*. Montréal: Centre de formation populaire, 1984.

Favreau, Louis and Yves Hurtubise. "L'action politique locale: une autre forme d'organisation communautaire." In *Théorie et pratiques en organisation communautaire*, Laval Doucet and Louis Favreau, eds. Sillery: Les Presses de l'Université du Québec, 1991, 119–46.

Foisy, Fernand. *Michel Chartrand: les voies d'un homme de parole (1916–1967)*. Outremont: Lanctôt Éditeur, 1999.

– *Michel Chartrand: la colère du juste (1968–2003)*. Outremont: Lanctôt Éditeur, 2003.

Forsythe, Dennis, ed. *Let the Niggers Burn!* 1971.

Fournier, Louis. *FLQ: Histoire d'un mouvement clandestin*. Outremont: Lanctôt Éditeur, 1998.

– *Histoire de la FTQ, 1965–1992. La plus grande centrale syndicale au Québec*. Montréal: Éditions Québec/Amérique, 1994.

– *Louis Laberge: le syndicalisme c'est ma vie*. Montréal: Éditions Québec/Amérique, 1992.

Friedan, Betty. *The Feminine Mystique*. New York: W.W. Norton, 2001 [1963].

Le Front d'action politique. *Les salariés au pouvoir!* Montréal: Presses libres, 1970.

Frost, Stanley Brice. *McGill University: For the Advancement of Learning*. Vol. II. Montreal: McGill-Queen's University Press, 1984.

FTQ. "The State Is Our Exploiter: F.T.Q. Manifesto (1971)." Trans. Claude Hénault. In *Quebec – Only the Beginning*, 150–272.

Gagnon, Charles. "Hommage à Pierre Vallières." *Bulletin d'histoire politique* 7, no. 3 (1999): 9–18.

– "Il était une fois … Conte à l'adresse de la jeunesse de mon pays." *Bulletin d'histoire politique* 13, no. 1 (2004): 43–56.

– *Feu sur l'Amérique : écrits politiques (1966–72), textes réunis par Charles Gagnon; présentés par Robert Comeau, Ivan Carel et Manon Leroux*. Montreal: Lux Éditeur, 2006.

– *Le Référendum: un syndrome québécois: essai*. Lachine: La Pleine Lune, 1995.

– *Pour le parti prolétarien*. Montréal: Equipe du Journal, 1972.

Gagnon, Henri. *Les militants socialistes du Québec: d'une époque à l'autre*. Saint-Lambert: Héritage, 1985.

Gagnon, Mona-Josée. "Women in the Trade-Union Movement in Quebec." In *Quebec since 1945: Selected Readings*, Michael D. Behiels, ed. Toronto: Copp Clark Pitman, 1987.

Gandhi, Leela. *Affective Communities: Anticolonial Thought, Fin-de-Siècle Radicalism, and the Politics of Friendship*. Durham: Duke University Press, 2006.

Gauthier, Yves. *Monsieur Livre: Henri Tranquille*. Sillery: Septentrion, 2005.

Gauvreau, Michael. *The Catholic Origins of Quebec's Quiet Revolution, 1931–1970*. Montreal: McGill-Queen's University Press, 2005.

– "From Rechristianization to Contestation: Catholic Values and Quebec Society, 1931–1970." *Church History* 69, no. 4 (2000): 803–33.

Gay, Daniel. *Les élites québécoises et l'Amérique latine*. Montréal: Éditions Nouvelle Optique, 1983.

– *Les Noirs du Québec, 1629–1900*. Sillery: Septentrion, 2004.

Gélinas, Claude. *Les Autochtones dans le Québec post-confédéral, 1867–1960*. Sillery: Septentrion, 2007.

Gélinas, Xavier. *La droite intellectuelle québécoise et la Révolution tranquille*. Québec: Les Presses de l'Université Laval, 2007.

Gendron, Robin S. *Towards a Francophone Community: Canada's Relations with France and French Africa, 1945–1961*. Montreal: McGill-Queen's University Press, 2006.

Genovese, Eugene. *In Red and Black; Marxian Explorations in Southern Afro-American History*. New York: Pantheon Books, 1971.

Georgakas, Dan, and Marvin Surkin. *Detroit: I Do Mind Dying*. Cambridge: South End Press, 1998.

Gibson, Nigel C. *Fanon: The Postcolonial Imagination*. Cambridge: Polity Press, 2003.

Gilmore, John. *Swinging in Paradise: The Story of Jazz in Montréal*. Montreal: Véhicule Press, 1988.

Gilroy, Paul. *"There Ain't No Black in the Union Jack": The Cultural Politics of Race and Nation*. Chicago: University of Chicago Press, 1991.

Gitlin, Todd. *The Whole World Is Watching: Mass Media in the Making and Unmaking of the New Left*. Berkeley: University of California Press, 2003.

Godbout, Jacques, and Jean-Pierre Collin. *Les organismes populaires en milieu urbain: contre-pouvoir ou nouvelle pratique professionnelle?* Montréal: I.N.R.S.-Urbanisation, 1977.

Godin, Gérald. "Diary of a Prisoner of War." In *Québec, Canada and the October Crisis*, ed. Dan Daniels. Montreal: Black Rose Books, 1973, 87–93.

Godin, Pierre. *La poudrière linguistique*. Montréal: Boréal, 1990.

Gordon, Alan. *Making Public Pasts: The Contested Terrain of Montréal's Public Memories, 1891–1930*. Montreal: McGill-Queen's Press, 2001.

Gosse, Van. *Rethinking the New Left: An Interpretive History*. New York: Palgrave MacMillan, 2005.

– *Where the Boys Are: Cuba, Cold War America and the Making of a New Left.* London: Verso, 1993.

Gott, Richard. *Cuba: A New History.* New Haven: Yale Nota Bene, 2005 [2004].

Grandin, Greg. *The Last Colonial Massacre: Latin America in the Cold War.* Chicago: University of Chicago Press, 2004.

Gray, Stanley. "Stan Gray: The Greatest Canadian … Shit-Disturber." *Canadian Dimension* 38, no. 6 (2004): 12–21.

Grey, Julius. "What is McGill, what are we doing here, and what ought we to do?" In *McGill Student Handbook*, 93–4.

Griffin, John Howard. *Black Like Me.* New York: Signet, 1976 [1960].

Guevara, Ernesto. *Che Guevara Speaks: Selected Speeches and Writings.* New York: Merit Publishers, 1967.

Güntzel, Ralph Peter. "The Confédération des Syndicats Nationaux, the Idea of Independence, and the Sovereigntist Movement, 1960–1980." MA, McGill University, 1991.

– "The Centrale de l'Enseignement du Québec and Quebec Separatist Nationalism, 1960–1980." *Canadian Historical Review* 80, no. 1 (1991): 61–82.

– "'Rapprocher les lieux du pouvoir': The Québec Labour Movement and Québec Sovereigntism, 1960–2000." *Labour/Le Travail,* Fall 2000, 369–95.

Hamilton, Roberta. "Pro-natalism, Feminism, and Nationalism." In *Gender and Politics in Contemporary Canada*, ed. François Pierre Gingras. Toronto: Oxford University Press, 1995, 135–52.

Handler, Richard. *Nationalism and the Politics of Culture in Quebec.* Madison: University of Wisconsin Press, 1988.

Helman, Claire. *The Milton-Park Affair: Canada's Largest Citizen-Developer Confrontation.* Montreal: Véhicule Press, 1987.

High, Steven. *Industrial Sunset: The Making of North America's Rust Belt, 1969–1984.* Toronto: University of Toronto Press, 2003.

Hildebran, Andrea. "Genèse d'une communauté lesbienne: un récit des années 1970." In *Sortir de l'ombre. Histoires des communautés lesbienne et gaie de Montréal,* edited by Irène Demczuk and Frank W. Remiggi. Montréal: VLB Éditeur, 1988, 207–33.

Hobsbawm, Eric. *Interesting Times: A Twentieth-Century Life.* London: Allen Lane, 2002.

– *Uncommon People: Resistance, Rebellion, and Jazz.* New York: The New Press, 1988.

hooks, bell. *Feminist Theory: From Margin to Center.* Cambridge: South End Press, 2000 [1984].

Iacovetta, Franca. *Gatekeepers: Reshaping Immigrant Lives in Cold War Canada.* Toronto: Between the Lines, 2006.

Ignatiev, Noel. *How the Irish Became White.* New York: Routledge, 1995.

Jameson, Fredric. "Periodizing the 60s." In *The Ideologies of Theory: Essays 1971–1986, Vol. 2, Syntax of History.* Minneapolis: University of Minnesota Press, 1988, 178–208.

Jenson, Jane, and Martin Papillon. "Challenging the Citizenship Regime: The James Bay Cree and Transnational Action." *Politics and Society* 28, no. 2 (2000): 245–64.

Jones, Richard. "L'Idéologie du Parti Québécois." In *Idéologies au Canada français, 1940–1976*, 235–66.

– "Politics and the Reinforcement of the French Language in Canada and Quebec, 1960–1986." In *Quebec Since 1945*, ed. Michael D. Behiels. Toronto: Copp Clark Pitman, 1987, 223–40.

Jourdain, Jacques. "De Cité Libre à L'urgence de choisir: Pierre Vallières et les palinodies de la gauche québécoise." MA, QUAM, 1995.

journaliste, B.R. "Une information 'totalitaire prise à son propre piège'." In *Québec occupé*. Montréal: Éditions Parti Pris, 1971, 179–216.

Julien, Claude. *America's Empire*, trans. Renaud Bruce. New York: Pantheon Books, 1971 [1968].

Katsiaficas, George. *The Subversion of Politics: European Autonomous Social Movements and the Decolonization of Everyday Life*. New Jersey: Humanities Press International, 1997.

Keable, Jacques. *Le monde selon Marcel Pepin*. Outremont: Lanctôt Éditeur, 1998.

Kelley, Robin D.G. *Freedom Dreams: The Black Radical Imagination*. Boston: Beacon Press, 2002.

– "A Poetics of Anticolonialism." In *Discourse on Colonialism*. New York: Monthly Review Press, 2000, 7–28.

Kessler-Harris, Alice. *Gendering Labor History*. Urbana and Chicago: University of Illinois Press, 2007.

Kicksee, Richard Gordon. "'Scaled Down to Size': Contested Liberal Commonsense and the Negotiation of 'Indian participation' in the Canadian Centennial Celebrations and Expo '67, 1963–1967." MA, Queen's University, 1995.

King, Martin Luther. *I Have a Dream: Writing and Speeches that Changed the World*. San Francisco: HarperSanFrancisco, 1992.

Kostash, Myrna. *Long Way From Home: The Story of the Sixties Generation in Canada*. Toronto: Lorimer, 1980.

Labelle, Micheline, Serge Larose, and Victor Piché. "Politique d'immigration et immigration en provenance de la Caraibe anglophone au Canada et au Québec, 1900–1979." *Canadian Ethnic Studies / Études ethniques au Canada* 15, no. 2 (1983): 1–24.

Laberge, Louis. *En prison pour nous. Historique du front commun*. Montréal: Fédération des travailleurs du Québec, 1973.

– *A One and Only Front: Opening Address by Louis Laberge to the 12th Convention of the Quebec Federation of Labour*. Montreal: Quebec Federation of Labour, 1971.

Lachaîne, Alexis. "Black and Blue: French Canadian Writers, Decolonization and Revolutionary Nationalism in Quebec, 1960–1969." PhD, York University, 2007.

Lacroix, Michel, and Stéphanie Rousseau. "Introduction. 'La terre promise de la coopération.' Les relations internationales du Québec à la lumière du missionnariat, de l'économie sociale et de l'éducation." *Globe: revue internationale d'études québécoises* 12, no. 1 (2009): 11–16.

Lafond, Jean-Daniel. *La manière nègre. Aimé Césaire, chemin faisant*. Montreal: l'Hexagone, 1993.

Laliberté, Louis. *Culture politique de la* CEQ. Québec: Laboratoire de sciences administratives et politiques, Université Laval, 1975.

Lamarre, Jean. *Le devenir de la nation québécoise: selon Maurice Séguin, Guy Frégault et Michel Brunet, 1944–1969*. Sillery: Septentrion, 1993.

– "'Au service des étudiants et de la nation': L'internationalisation de l'Union générale des étudiants du Québec (1964–1969)." *Bulletin d'histoire politique* 16, no. 2 (2008): 53–73.

Lamonde, Yvan. *Histoire sociale des idées au Québec*. Montréal: Fides, 2000.

Lamoureux, André. *Le* NDP *et le Québec, 1958–1985*. Montréal: Éditions du Parc, 1985.

Lamoureux, Diane. *Fragments et collages: essai sur le féminisme québécois des années 70*. Montréal: Remue-ménage, 1986.

– "La lutte pour le droit à l'avortement (1969–1981)." *Revue d'histoire de l'Amérique française* 37, no. 1 (1983): 81–90.

– "Nationalisme et féminisme: impasse ou coïncidences." *Possibles* 8, no. 1 (1983): 43–59.

Lanctôt, Martine. "La genèse et l'évolution du mouvement de libération des femmes à Montréal, 1969–1979." MA, UQAM, 1980.

Lanthier, Stéphanie. "L'impossible réciprocité des rapports politiques et idéologiques entre le nationalisme radical et le féminisme radical au Québec 1961–1972." MA, Université de Sherbrooke, 1998.

Lantos, Robert. "The Rise of the Left at McGill." *Together*, 25 February 1970, 4–5.

Lapointe, Mathieu. "Nationalisme et socialisme dans la pensée de Raoul Roy, 1935–1965." MA, Université de Montréal, 2002.

Larivière, Claude. *Albert Saint-Martin: militant d'avant-garde (1865–1947)*. Laval: Éditions coopératives Albert Saint-Martin, 1979.

Larocque, André. *Défis au Parti québécois*. Montréal: Éditions du Jour, 1971.

Larose, Karim. *La langue de papier. Spéculation linguistiques au Québec*. Montréal: Les Presses de l'Université de Montréal, 2004.

– "L'émergence du projet d'unilinguisme. Archéologie de la question linguistique québécoise." *Globe. Revue internationale d'études québécoises* 7, no. 2 (2004): 177–94.

Laurendeau, Marc. *Les Québécois violents: la violence politique, 1962–1972*. Montréal: Boréal, 1990.

Laurin, Nicole. "Genèse de la sociologie marxiste au Québec." *Sociologie et sociétés* 37, no. 2 (2005): 183–207.

Lavigne, Mathieu. "L'idée de décolonisation québécoise. Le discours tiers-mondiste au Québec et sa quête identitaire (1963–1968)." MA, Université de Montréal, 2007.

LeGrand, Catherine. "L'axe missionaire catholique entre le Québec et l'Amérique Latine. Une exploration préliminaire." Unpublished manuscript.

Lemelin, Maurice. *Les négociations collectives dans les secteurs public et parapublic: expérience québécoise et regard sur l'extérieur*. Montréal: Les Éditions Agence d'ARC, 1984.

Lerner, Gerda. *The Creation of Feminist Consciousness: From the Middle Ages to Eighteen-Seventy.* Oxford: Oxford University Press, 1993.

Les gens du Québec 1, St-Henri. Montréal: Éditions québécoises, 1972.

Les gens du Québec 2, Petite Bourgogne. Montréal: Éditions québécoises, 1973.

Létourneau, Jocelyn. "La grève de l'amiante entre ses mémoires et l'histoire." *Journal of the Canadian Oral History Association* 11 (1991): 8–16.

– "La mise en intrigue. Configuration historico-linguistique d'une grève célébrée: Asbestos, P.Q., 1949." *Recherches sémiotiques, Semiotic Inquiry* 12, no. 1–2 (1992): 53–71.

– "Le 'Québec moderne': un chapitre du grand récit collectif des Québécois." *Discours social/Social Discourse* 4, no. 1–2 (1992): 63–88.

– "Québec d'après guerre et mémoire collective de la technocratie." *Cahiers internationaux de Sociologie* 90 (1991): 67–87.

Létourneau, Jocelyn, and Sabrina Moisan. "Mémoire et récit de l'aventure historique du Québec chez les jeunes québécois d'héritage canadien-français: coup de sonde, amorce d'analyse des résultats, questionnements." *Canadian Historical Review* 85, no. 2 (2004): 325–56.

Lévesque, Andrée. *Red Travellers: Jeanne Cobin and Her Comrades,* trans. Yvonne M. Klein. Montreal: McGill-Queen's University Press, 2006.

– *Virage à gauche interdit: les communistes, les socialistes et leurs ennemis au Québec, 1929–1939.* Montréal: Boréal Express, 1984.

Lévesque, René. *Memoirs,* trans. Philip Stratford. Toronto: McClelland and Stewart, 1986.

– *An Option for Quebec.* Toronto: McClelland and Stewart, 1968.

Levine, Marc V. *The Reconquest of Montreal: Language Policy and Social Change in a Bilingual City.* Philadelphia: Temple University Press, 1990.

Levitt, Kari. *La capitulation tranquille: la mainmise américaine sur le Canada,* trans. André d'Allemagne. Montreal: Réédition-Québec, 1972.

– "Confluences." In *Reclaiming Democracy: The Social Justice and Political Economy of Gregory Baum and Kari Polanyi Levitt,* ed. Marguerite Mendell. Montreal: McGill-Queen's University Press, 2005, 141–66.

– *Silent Surrender: the Multinational Corporation in Canada.* Toronto: Macmillan, 1970.

Linteau, Paul-André. *Histoire de Montréal depuis la Confédération.* 2ᵉ ed. Montréal: Boréal, 2000.

– "Un débat historiographique: l'entrée du Québec dans la modernité et la signification de la Révolution tranquille." *Francofonia. Studi e ricerche sulle letterature di lingua francese* XIX, no. 37 (1999): 73–87.

– "The Italians of Quebec: Key Participants in Contemporary Linguistic and Political Debates." In *Arrangiarsi: The Italian Immigration Experience in Canada,* Roberto Perin and Franc Sturino, eds. Montreal: Guernica, 1989, 179–207.

Linteau, Paul-André, René Durocher, Jean-Claude Robert, and François Ricard. *Histoire du Québec contemporain. Le Québec depuis 1930, tome II.* Montréal: Boréal, 1989.

Lipsig-Mummé, Carla. "Future Conditional: Wars of Position in the Quebec Labour Movement," *Studies in Political Economy* 36 (1991), 73–107.

– "Quebec Unions and the State: Conflict and Dependence," *Studies in Political Economy* 3 (1980): 119–46.

– "The Web of Dependence: Quebec Unions in Politics before 1976," in *Quebec: State and Society*, ed. Alain G. Gagnon. Toronto: Methuen, 1984: 286–313.

Loiselle, André. *Cinema as History: Michel Brault and Modern Quebec.* Toronto: The Toronto International Film Festival Inc., 2007.

Lortie, André, ed. *The 60s: Montreal Thinks Big.* Montreal: Canadian Centre for Architecture, 2004.

Macey, David. *Frantz Fanon: A Life.* London: Granta Books, 2000.

Maclure, Jocelyn. "Narratives and Counter-Narratives of Identity in Québec." In *Québec: State and Society*, ed. Alain-G. Gagnon. Peterborough: Broadview Press, 2004, 33–50.

Maheu, Pierre. *Un parti pris révolutionnaire.* Montréal: Parti Pris, 1983.

Mailer, Norman. *The White Negro.* San Francisco: City Lights Books, 1957.

Manifeste des femmes québécoises. Montreal: l'étincelle, 1971.

Marcuse, Herbert. *An Essay on Liberation.* Boston: Beacon Press, 1969.

– *One Dimensional Man: Studies in the Ideology of Advanced Industrial Society.* Boston: Beacon Press, 1991 [1964].

Maroney, Heather Jon. "Contemporary Quebec Feminism: The Interrelation of Political and Ideological Development in Women's Organizations, Trade Unions, Political Parties and State Policy, 1960–1980." PhD, McMaster University, 1988.

– "'Who Has the Baby?' Nationalism, Pronatalism and the Construction of a 'Demographic Crisis' in Quebec, 1960–1988." *Studies in Political Economy* 39 (1992): 7–36.

Marsolais, Gilles. "L'équipe française de l'ONF (1958–1962): l'expérimentation dans le court métrage." In *Michel Brault, oeuvres 1958–1974. Textes et témoignages.* Montreal: National Film Board, 2006, 11–14.

Martel, Marcel. "'S'ils veulent faire la révolution, qu'ils aillent la faire chez eux à leurs risques et périls. Nos anarchistes maisons sont suffisants': occupation et répression à Sir George-Williams." *Bulletin d'histoire politique* 15, no. 1 (2006): 163–78.

Mathieu, Sarah-Jane (Saje). "North of the Colour Line: Sleeping Car Porters and the Battle against Jim Crow on Canadian Rails, 1880–1920." *Labour / Le Travail*, no. 47 (2001): 9–41.

McGraw, Donald. *Le développement des groupes populaires à Montréal, 1963–1973.* Montréal: Editions coopératives A. Saint-Martin, 1978.

McLoughlin, Michael. *Last Stop, Paris: The Assassination of Mario Bachand and the Death of the FLQ.* Toronto: Viking, 1998.

McRoberts, Kenneth. *Quebec: Social Change and Political Crisis*, 3rd edition. Don Mills: Oxford University Press, 1993.

Memmi, Albert. *The Colonizer and the Colonized*, trans. Howard Greenfeld. Boston: Beacon Press, 1967.

– *Portrait du colonisé. Précédé du Portrait du colonisateur, et d'une préf. de Jean-*

Paul Sartre. Suivi de Les Canadiens français sont-ils des colonisés? Éd. rev. et corr. par l'auteur. Montréal: L'Étincelle, 1972.

Ménard, Yves. "Le lock-out de *La Presse* et l'émeute du 29 octobre 1971: un conflit d'envergure nationale." *Bulletin du RCHTQ* 28, no. 2 (2002): 5–35.

Meren, David. "Strange Allies: Canada-Quebec-France Triangular Relations, 1944–1970." PhD, McGill, 2007.

Meunier, E.-Martin, and Jean-Philippe Warren. *Sortir de la 'Grande noirceur.' L'horizon 'personnaliste' de la Révolution tranquille.* Sillery: Septentrion, 2002.

Mills, C. Wright. *Listen, Yankee: The Revolution in Cuba.* New York: Ballantine Books, 1960.

Mills, Sean. "La gauche montréalaise, le nationalisme, et les années soixante." In *Contester dans un pays prospère*, Morelli and José Gotovitch, eds. Bruxelles: P.I.E. Peter Lang, 2007, 115–33.

‒ "When Democratic Socialists Discovered Democracy: The League for Social Reconstruction Confronts the 'Quebec Problem.'" *Canadian Historical Review* 86, no. 1 (2005): 53–81.

Milner, Henry, and Sheilagh Hodgins Milner. *The Decolonization of Quebec: An Analysis of Left-Wing Nationalism.* Toronto: McClelland and Stewart, 1973.

Mitchell, Don. *The Right to the City: Social Justice and the Fight for Public Space.* New York: The Guilford Press, 2003.

Monet-Chartrand, Simone. *Ma vie comme rivière*: récit autobiographique. Montréal: Remue-ménage, 1981–1992. 4 vols.

‒ *Les Québécoises et le mouvement pacifiste (1939–1967).* Montréal: Les Éditions Écosociété, 1993.

‒ *Pionnières québécoises et regroupements de femmes d'hier à aujourd'hui.* Montréal: Remue-ménage, 1990.

Mouvement révolutionnaire des étudiants du Québec. *En avant pour la création de l'organisation marxiste-léniniste.* Montréal, 1974.

Mullen, Bill V. *Afro-Orientalism.* Minneapolis: University of Minnesota Press, 2004.

Nadeau, Jean-François. *Bourgault.* Montréal: Lux Éditeur, 2007.

Namaste, Viviane. *C'était du spectacle! L'histoire des artistes transsexuelles à Montréal, 1955–1985.* Montreal: McGill-Queen's University Press, 2005.

‒ "La réglementation des journaux jaunes à Montréal, 1955–1975. Le cadre juridique et la mise en application des lois." *Revue d'histoire de l'Amérique française* 61 (2007): 67–84.

Noël, Roger. "Libération homosexuelle ou révolution socialiste? L'expérience du GHAP." In *Sortir de l'ombre: Histoires des communautés lesbienne et gaie de Montréal*, Irène Demczuk and Frank W. Remiggi, eds. Montréal: VLB éditeur, 1998, 187–206.

Ogbar, Jeffrey O.G. *Black Power: Radical Politics and African American Identity.* Baltimore and London: The Johns Hopkins University Press, 2004.

O'Leary, Véronique, and Louise Toupin. *Québécoises deboutte! Une anthologie de textes du Front de libération des femmes (1969–1971) et du Centre des femmes (1972–1975).* Vol. 1 and 2. Montréal: Remue-ménage, 1982.

Owram, Doug. *Born at the Right Time: A History of the Baby-Boom Generation*. Toronto: University of Toronto Press, 1996.

Page, Carole. "Décolonisation et question nationale québécoise." MA, UQAM, 1978.

Palmer, Bryan. *Canada's 1960s: The Ironies of Identity in a Rebellious Era*. Toronto: University of Toronto Press, 2009.

– *Cultures of Darkness: Night Travels in the Histories of Transgression*. New York: Monthly Review Press, 2000.

– *Working-Class Experience: Rethinking the History of Canadian Labour, 1800–1891*. Toronto: McClelland and Stewart, 1992.

Pâquet, Martin. *Tracer les marges de la cité: Étranger, Immigrant et État au Québec, 1627–1981*. Montréal: Boréal, 2005.

– "Un nouveau contrat social. Les États généraux du Canada français et l'immigration, novembre 1967." *Bulletin d'histoire politique* 10, no. 2 (2002): 123–34.

Pâquet, Martin, and Marcel Martel, eds. *Légiférer en matière linguistique*. Québec: Les Presses de l'Université Laval, 2008.

Pâquet, Martin and Érick Duchesne, "Étude de la complexité d'un événement. Les responsables politiques québécois et les immigrants illégaux haïtiens, 1972–1974," *Revue d'histoire de l'Amérique française* 50, no. 2 (1996): 173–200.

Parry, Benita. "Liberation Theory: Variations on Themes of Marxism and Modernity." In *Marxism, Modernity, and Postcolonial Studies*, Crystal Bartolovich and Neil Lazarus, eds. Cambridge: Cambridge University Press, 2002, 125–49.

Pelletier, Gérard. *La crise d'Octobre*. Montréal: Éditions du Jour, 1971.

Pelletier, Michel and Yves Vaillancourt, *Du chômage à la libération*. Montréal: Éditions Québécoises, 1972.

Péloquin, Marjolaine. *En prison pour la cause des femmes: la conquête du banc des jurés*. Montréal: Remue-ménage, 2007.

Pepin, Marcel. *Pour Vaincre*, Rapport moral du Président général de la CSN au 45ᵉ Congrès, Québec, le 11 juin 1972.

– "Preface." In *Quebec Labour: The Confederation of National Trade Unions Yesterday and Today*, Black Rose Books Editorial Collective. Montreal: Black Rose Books, 1972, 9–11.

– "The Second Front: The Report of Marcel Pepin, National President, to the Convention of the CNTU, October 13, 1968." In *Quebec Labour: The Confederation of National Trade Unions Yesterday and Today*, 47–99.

– "Une société bâtie pour l'homme." In *Procès-verbal. Quarante-deuxième session du Congrès de la C.S.N.* Montreal, 1966, 7–37.

Piché, Lucie. "Entre l'accès à l'égalité et la préservation des modèles: Ambivalence du discours et des revendications du Comité Féminin de la CTCC-CSN, 1952–1966." *Labour/Le Travail* 29 (1992): 187–209

Pierre, Samuel, ed. *Ces Québécois venus d'Haïti – Contribution de la communauté haïtienne à l'édification du Québec moderne*. Montréal: Presses internationales Polytechnique, 2007.

Piotte, Jean-Marc. *La communauté perdue: petite histoire des militantismes*. Montréal: VLB éditeur, 1987.

– *Du combat au partenariat. Interventions critiques sur le syndicalisme québécois.* Montréal: Les Éditions Nota Bene, 1998.

– "Jour après jour." In *Québec occupé.* Montréal: Éditions Parti Pris, 1971, 13–68.

– "Charles Gagnon, *Feu sur l'Amérique* (Écrits politiques, vol. I, 1966–1972)." *Bulletin d'histoire politique* 15, no. 3 (2007): 311–18.

– "Présentation." In *Québec occupé.* Montréal: Éditions Parti Pris, 1971, 7–12.

– *Un certain espoir.* Montréal: Les Éditions Logiques, 2008.

– *Un parti pris politique.* Montréal: VLB éditeur, 1979.

Pleau, Jean-Christian. *La révolution québécoise: Hubert Aquin et Gaston Miron au tournant des années soixante.* Saint-Laurent: Fides, 2002.

Poirier, Stéphanie. "Le Conseil central des syndicats nationaux de Montréal (CSN) à l'heure de la radicalisation syndicale, 1968–1980." MA, Université de Montréal, 2005.

Pour un contrôle des naissances, 2ᵉ édition. Rédacteurs-en-chef: Donna Cherniak et Allan Feingold. Ed. française: rédacteur-en-chef [et traductrice]: Lisette Girouard. Montréal, février 1971.

Prashad, Vijay. *The Darker Nations: A People's History of the Third World.* New York: The New Press, 2007.

Provost, Francis. "Étude sur les dissensions entre la 'droite' et la 'gauche' au sein du Rassemblement pour l'indépendance nationale entre 1966 et 1968." *Bulletin d'histoire politique* 12, no. 2 (2004): 204–13.

Pulido, Laura. *Black, Brown, Yellow and Left: Radical Activism in Los Angeles.* Berkeley: University of California Press, 2006.

Raboy, Marc. *Movements and Messages: Media and Radical Politics in Quebec,* trans. David Homel. Toronto: Between the Lines Press, 1984.

Rebick, Judy. *Ten Thousand Roses: The Making of a Feminist Revolution.* Toronto: Penguin, 2005.

Regush, Nicholas M. *Pierre Vallières: The Revolutionary Process in Quebec.* New York: The Dial Press, 1973.

Reid, Malcolm. *The Shouting Signpainters: A Literary and Political Account of Quebec Revolutionary Nationalism.* Toronto: McClelland and Stewart, 1972.

Rény, Conrad, and Mark Wilson. "Il me semble qu'on s'est déjà vu quelque part… Les québécois homosexuels trouvent leurs voix. Est-ce une part du gâteau qu'on veut, ou un nouveau gâteau?" *Le Temps Fou* 1, no. 2 (1978): 25–31, 34–5.

Retamar, Roberto Fernández. *Caliban and Other Essays,* trans. Edward Baker. Minneapolis: University of Minnesota Press, 1989.

Ricard, François. *La génération lyrique: essai sur la vie et l'oeuvre des premiers-nés du baby-boom.* Montréal: Boréal, 1992.

Rice-Maximin, Micheline. "Frantz Fanon and Black American Ideologists in the 1960s." *Contemporary French Civilization* 5, no. 3 (1981): 369–79.

Rivière, Sylvain. *Léandre Bergeron, né en exil.* Trois-Pistoles: Éditions Trois-Pistoles, 2007.

Roberts, Alfie. *A View for Freedom: Alfie Roberts Speaks on the Caribbean, Cricket, Montreal, and C.L.R. James.* Montreal: Alfie Roberts Institute, 2005.

Roberts, Katherine. "'Mère, je vous hais!': Quebec Nationalism and the Legacy of the Family Paradigm in Pierre Vallières' *Nègres blancs d'Amérique*." *British Journal of Canadian Studies* 20, no. 2 (2007): 289–304.

Roediger, David R. *The Wages of Whiteness: Race and the Making of the American Working Class*. London: Verso, 1991.

Ross, Kristin. *Fast Cars, Clean Bodies: Decolonization and the Reordering of French Culture*. Cambridge: M.I.T. Press, 1995.

– *May '68 and Its Afterlives*. Chicago: University of Chicago Press, 2002.

Rouillard, Jacques. *Histoire de la CSN, 1921–1981*. Montréal: Boréal Express, 1981.

– "La Révolution tranquille: rupture ou tournant?" *Journal of Canadian Studies/ Revue d'études canadiennes* 32, no. 4 (1998): 23–51.

– *Le syndicalisme québécois. Deux siècles d'histoire*. Montréal: Boréal, 2004.

– "La grève de l'amiante de 1949 et le projet de réforme de l'entreprise. Comment le patronat a défendu son droit de gérance." *Labour/Le Travail*, no. 46 (2000): 307–42.

– *L'expérience syndicale au Québec: ses rapports à l'État, à la nation et à l'opinion publique*. Montréal: VLB éditeur, 2009.

– "La CSN et la protection de la langue française (1921–1996)." In *La CSN, 75 ans d'action syndicale et sociale*, Yves Bélanger and Robert Comeau, eds. Sainte-Foy: Presses de l'Université du Québec, 1998, 12–25.

– "Major Changes in the Confédération des travailleurs catholiques du Canada, 1940–1960." In *Quebec Since 1945: Selected Readings*, ed. Michael D. Behiels. Toronto: Copp Clark Pitman, 1987, 111–32.

Rowbotham, Sheila, Lynne Segal, and Hilary Wainwright. *Beyond the Fragments*. London: Merlin Press, 1979.

Rowbotham, Sheila. "The Women's Movement and Organizing for Socialism," in *Beyond the Fragments*, 21–155.

Rudin, Ronald. *Making History in Twentieth-Century Quebec*. Toronto: University of Toronto Press, 1997.

Rutherdale, Myra, and Jim Miller. "'It's Our Country': First Nations' Participation in the Indian Pavilion at Expo 67." *Online Journal of the Canadian Historical Association* 17, no. 2 (2006): 148–73.

Said, Edward W. *Culture and Imperialism*. New York: Vintage Books, 1994.

– *Humanism and Democratic Criticism*. New York: Columbia University Press, 2004.

– "Travelling Theory Reconsidered." In *Reflections on Exile and Other Essays*, ed. Edward W. Said. Cambridge: Harvard University Press, 2000, 436–52.

Salkey, Andrew. *Havana Journal*. Baltimore: Penguin, 1971.

Sartre, Jean-Paul. *Being and Nothingness*, trans. Hazel E. Barnes. New York: Washington Square Press, 1966.

– *Colonialism and Neocolonialism*, trans. Azzedine Haddour, Steve Brewer and Terry McWilliams. London: Routledge, 2001.

– *Critique of Dialectical Reason*, trans. Alan Sheridan-Smith. London: Verso, 2004.

– *Nausea*, trans. Lloyd Alexander. New York: New Directions, 1964.

– *Sartre on Cuba*. Westport: Greenwood Press, 1974 [1961].

– *Sartre visita a Cuba: idelogía y revolución, una entrevista con los escritores cubanos, huracán sobre el azúcar*. Habana: Ediciones R, 1961.

Scott, David. *Conscripts of Modernity: The Tragedy of Colonial Enlightenment*. Durham: Duke University Press, 2004.

Sekyi-Otu, Ato. *Fanon's Dialectic of Experience*. Cambridge: Harvard University Press, 1996.

Sethna, Christabelle. "The Evolution of the *Birth Control Handbook*: From Student Peer-Education Manual to Feminist Self-empowerment Text, 1968–1975." *Canadian Bulletin of Medical History* 23, no. 1 (2006): 89–118.

Sewell, William H. *Logics of History: Social Theory and Social Transformation*. Chicago: University of Chicago Press, 2005.

Sharp, Carolyn. "To Build a Just Society: The Catholic Left in Quebec." In *Reclaiming Democracy: The Social Justice and Political Economy of Gregory Baum and Kari Polanyi Levitt*, Marguerite Mendell, ed. Montreal: McGill-Queen's University Press, 2005, 43–55.

Sheppard, Peggy. "The Relationship Between Student Activism and Change in the University: With Particular Reference to McGill University in the 1960s." MA, McGill University, 1989.

Sherwood, David H. "The N.D.P. and French Canada, 1961–1965." MA, McGill University, 1966.

Simard, Francis. *Talking It Out: The October Crisis from the Inside*, trans. David Homel. Montreal: Guernica Editions, 1987.

Simon, Sherry. *Translating Montreal: Episodes in the Life of a Divided City*. Montreal: McGill-Queen's University Press, 2006.

Small, Shirley, and Esmeralda M.A. Thornhill. "HARAMBEC! Quebec Black Women Pulling Together." *Journal of Black Studies* 38, no. 3 (2008): 427–42.

Smith, Edouard. "Operation Democratie." In *Québec, Canada and the October Crisis*, 98–103.

Solasse, Bernard. "L'idéologie de la Centrale des enseignants du Québec et son évolution, 1960–1973." In *Idéologies au Canada français*, 325–41.

– "Les idéologies de la Fédération des travailleurs du Québec et de la Confédération des syndicats nationaux, 1960–1978." In *Idéologies au Canada français*, 219–94.

– "Note sur l'idéologie de la Centrale des syndicats démocratiques, 1972–1979." In *Idéologies au Canada français*, 381–6.

Tremblay, Michèle. *De Cuba le FLQ parle*. Montreal: Les Éditions Intel, 1975.

Trofimenkoff, Susan Mann. *The Dream of Nation: A Social and Intellectual History of Quebec*. Toronto: Gage, 1983.

– "Thérèse Casgrain and the CCF in Québec." *Canadian Historical Review* 66, no. 2 (1985): 125–53.

Trudeau, Pierre. *La grève de l'amiante*. Montréal: Les éditions Cité libre, 1956.

Trudel, Marcel (avec la collaboration de Micheline D'Allaire). *Deux siècles d'esclavage au Québec*. Montréal: Hurtubise HMH, 2004.

– *L'esclavage au Canada français: histoire et conditions de l'esclavage.* Québec: Presses universitaires de l'Université Laval, 1960.

Turcotte, Denis. *La culture politique du Mouvement Québec français.* Québec: Centre international de recherche sur le bilinguisme, 1976.

Tyner, James. *The Geography of Malcolm X: Black Radicalism and the Remaking of American Space.* New York: Routledge, 2006.

Tyson, Timothy B. *Radio Free Dixie: Robert F. Williams and the Roots of Black Power.* Chapel Hill: University of North Carolina Press, 1999.

Vaillancour, Yves, and Michel Pelletier. *Du chômage à la libération. Suivi du manifeste de la FTQ.* Montréal: Édition québécoise, 1972.

Vallières, Pierre. *Choose!* trans. Penelope Williams. Toronto: New Press, 1972 [1971].

– *Paroles d'un nègre blanc, Anthologie préparée par Jacques Jourdain et Mélanie Mailhot.* Montréal: VLB éditeur, 2002.

– *Les Héritiers de Papineau. Itinéraire politique d'un "nègre blanc" (1960–1985).* Montréal: Québec/Amérique, 1986.

– *White Niggers of America,* trans. Joan Pinkham. Toronto: McClelland and Stewart, 1971 [1968].

Varon, Jeremy. *Bringing the War Home: The Weather Underground, the Red Army Faction, and Revolutionary Violence in the Sixties and Seventies.* Berkeley: University of California Press, 2004.

Villeneuve, Paquerette. *Une Canadienne dans les rues de Paris pendant la révolte étudiante.* Montréal: Éditions du jour, 1968.

Von Eschen, Penny M. *Race Against Empire: Black Americans and Anticolonialism, 1937–1957.* Ithaca: Cornell University Press, 1997.

Walker, James W. St.G. *"Race" Rights and the Law in the Supreme Court of Canada: Historical Case Studies.* Toronto: The Osgoode Society for Canadian Legal History and Wilfrid Laurier University Press, 1997.

– *Racial Discrimination in Canada: The Black Experience.* Ottawa: Canadian Historical Assocation, 1985.

– *The West Indians in Canada.* Ottawa: Canadian Historical Association, 1984.

Warren, Jean-Philippe. *Ils voulaient changer le monde. Le militantisme Marxiste-Leniniste au Québec.* Montréal: VLB éditeur, 2007.

– *"L'Opération McGill français. Une page méconnue de l'histoire de la gauche nationaliste." Bulletin d'histoire politique* 16, no. 2 (2008): 97–115.

– *Une douce anarchie: les années 68 au Québec.* Montréal: Boréal, 2008.

Weintraub, William. *City Unique: Montreal Days and Nights in the 1940s and '50s.* Toronto: McClelland and Stewart, 1996.

Wilkins, Fanon Che. "'In the Belly of the Beast': Black Power, Anti-Imperialism, and the African Liberation Solidarity Movement 1968–1975." PhD, New York University, 2001.

Williams, Dorothy W. *The Road to Now: A History of Blacks in Montreal.* Montreal: Véhicule Press, 1997.

Williams, Eric. *From Columbus to Castro: The History of the Caribbean.* New York: Vintage Books, 1984 [1970].

Wilson, Mark. "A Short History of McGill." In *McGill Student Handbook*, 79–85.

Wood, Myrna, and Kathy McAffee. "Her Only Real Fulfilment Is Supposed To Come from Her Role as Girlfriend, Wife or Mother." In *McGill Student Handbook*, 69–73.

Wright, Robert. *Three Nights in Havana: Pierre Trudeau, Fidel Castro and the Cold War*. Toronto: HarperCollins, 2007.

X, Malcolm. *Malcolm X Speaks: Selected Speeches and Statements Edited with Prefatory Notes by George Breitman*. New York: Grove Weidenfeld, 1966 [1965].

Young, Cynthia. "Havana Up in Harlem: LeRoi Jones, Harold Cruse and the Making of a Cultural Revolution." *Science and Society* 65, no. 1 (2001): 12–38.

Young, Cynthia Ann. *Soul Power: Culture, Radicalism, and the Making of a U.S. Third World Left*. Durham: Duke University Press, 2006.

Young, Robert. *Postcolonialism: An Historical Introduction*. Oxford: Blackwell Publishing, 2001.

– *White Mythologies: Writing History and the West*. London: Routledge, 1990.

– "Fanon and the Turn to Armed Struggle in Africa." *Wasafiri* 20, no. 44 (2005): 33–41.

INDEX